OUT OF THE DARKNESS

ALSO BY IAN O'CONNOR

Coach K: The Rise and Reign of Mike Krzyzewski

Belichick: The Making of the Greatest Football Coach of All Time

The Captain: The Journey of Derek Jeter

Arnie & Jack: Palmer, Nicklaus, and Golf's Greatest Rivalry

*The Jump: Sebastian Telfair and the
High-Stakes Business of High School Ball*

PRAISE FOR *OUT OF THE DARKNESS*

"I appreciate the kind of research that Ian O'Connor did. . . . I commend him. He was trying to do a really good job and get the entire picture." —Aaron Rodgers

"Ian O'Connor's *Out of the Darkness* is a Shakespearean tale of a prince and his prodigal son that answers the question 'What if Macbeth could throw like Montana?' Many themes are not so subtly buried within the text, including obsessiveness, abandonment, wealth, friendship, and vengeance." —Kyle Brandt, *Good Morning Football*

"Sports biographer extraordinaire Ian O'Connor . . . uses his keen reporting eye and attention to detail to explore who Rodgers is beneath his championship arm and controversial brain. Already a *New York Times* bestseller, the fifth of O'Connor's career along with those about Bill Belichick, Derek Jeter, and Mike Krzyzewski, it's a great read for any football fan." —*Boston Globe*

"Rigorously reported. . . . There's a lot to root for in the Aaron Rodgers story, because nothing came easy. O'Connor delivers a clear sense of his evolution as a person as well as a passer. It's a remarkable journey." —*Washington Post*

"I knew—I just *knew*—that Ian O'Connor would paint a masterwork on Aaron Rodgers. This book perfectly details the roots of the enigmatic Rodgers, starting with the World War II fighter-pilot grandfather with no fear, the quasi-rebellious father who refused to do what his domineering dad said just because. Wonder about Rodgers's unflagging confidence? You won't after you see the kid who reported for his first day at junior college, determined to shred the best cover guy on the team. O'Connor answers every question, deftly and deeply, that we've had about the most controversial person in America's biggest game." —Peter King

"One of the greatest writers I have ever seen. Ian O'Connor is a spectacular talent as a writer. . . . If you want somebody to write something on you, you want it to be Ian O'Connor. Go get the book just because of him." —Stephen A. Smith, *The Stephen A. Smith Show*

"Aaron Rodgers is one of the most uniquely complex superstar athletes of my lifetime and Ian O' Connor peels back dozens of layers, maybe hundreds. The depth of reporting is relentless. Ian goes a mile deep and keeps on digging. Every story, better than the next. . . . I've wanted this book to be written and Ian delivers a masterclass in storytelling." —Colin Cowherd

"Ian O'Connor has done it once again with *Out of the Darkness*, which is everything you would expect from a gifted reporter and storyteller, and sheds as much light on the enigma that is Rodgers as could ever possibly be shed. Just a terrific read."

—Mike Vaccaro, *New York Post*

"America's premier sports biographer has done it again. With exquisite detail and energetic prose, Ian O'Connor pulls back the curtain on this country's most enigmatic athlete, telling the real Aaron Rodgers story with all of its polarizing complexities. Many sports fans look at Rodgers and ask, 'What's with this guy?' O'Connor goes deep in addressing that question, and the answers will amaze."

—Bill Plaschke, *Los Angeles Times* sports columnist and panelist on ESPN's *Around the Horn*

"An important resource for historians of the sport for decades to come."

—Neil Best, *Newsday*

"O'Connor is a terrific writer who . . . makes you feel like you were present for the humiliating 2005 NFL draft when Rodgers fell way below the top five picks he had been promised he'd be among."   —Chris Hewitt, *Minnesota Star Tribune*

"Ian O'Connor's biographies are always a must-read and whether you like or loathe Rodgers he's undeniably a fascinating sportsman. It's very good."

—Brendan Crowley, Sports Book Reviews

"A well-crafted portrait of perhaps the most talented QB of all time."   —*Kirkus Reviews*

"Fascinating."   —*The New Yorker*

"I loved this book. I'm not a big football fan, but I was so fascinated by Aaron Rodgers's story."   —Harvey Levin, *TMZ on TV*

"It's so freakin' good. The detail and the layers and the different people he talked to, seriously, it's so good. Much respect to Ian. This is a great football book. Highly recommend."   —Jeff Pearlman, author of *Gunslinger: The Remarkable, Improbable, Iconic Life of Brett Favre*

OUT OF THE DARKNESS

THE MYSTERY OF AARON RODGERS

IAN O'CONNOR

MARINER BOOKS
New York   Boston

Without limiting the exclusive rights of any author, contributor or the publisher of this publication, any unauthorized use of this publication to train generative artificial intelligence (AI) technologies is expressly prohibited. HarperCollins also exercise their rights under Article 4(3) of the Digital Single Market Directive 2019/790 and expressly reserve this publication from the text and data mining exception.

OUT OF THE DARKNESS. Copyright © 2024 by Ian O'Connor. Afterword copyright © 2025 by Ian O'Connor. All rights reserved. Printed in the United States of America. No part of this book may be used or reproduced in any manner whatsoever without written permission except in the case of brief quotations embodied in critical articles and reviews. For information, address HarperCollins Publishers, 195 Broadway, New York, NY 10007. In Europe, HarperCollins Publishers, Macken House, 39/40 Mayor Street Upper, Dublin 1, D01 C9W8, Ireland.

HarperCollins books may be purchased for educational, business, or sales promotional use. For information, please email the Special Markets Department at SPsales@harpercollins.com.

hc.com

The Mariner flag design is a registered trademark of HarperCollins Publishers LLC.

A hardcover edition of this book was published in 2024 by Mariner Books.

FIRST MARINER BOOKS PAPERBACK EDITION PUBLISHED 2025.

Designed by Emily Snyder

Library of Congress Cataloging-in-Publication Data has been applied for.

ISBN 978-0-06-329785-2

25 26 27 28 29 LBC 5 4 3 2 1

*For Jack Orbine, the late, great Mr. O.
Thanks for teaching me how to be a dad.*

*For the memory of Cherry Starr, a Green Bay
legend. Thanks for your kindness and trust.*

CONTENTS

INTRODUCTION: MALIBU MAN ... 1

1: AMERICAN HERO ... 7
2: THE PRODIGY ... 21
3: PLEASANT VALLEY ... 33
4: RIGSBEE ... 52
5: BERKELEY ... 72
6: THE PLUNGE ... 98
7: BRETT ... 123
8: A STAR IS BORN ... 149
9: PAIN ... 177
10: THE ISLAND ... 201
11: NO LOVE LOST ... 227
12: DIVORCE ... 251
13: HEARTBREAK ... 276
14: THE COMEBACK ... 304

AFTERWORD ... 327
ACKNOWLEDGMENTS ... 341
SOURCES ... 345
INDEX ... 355

OUT OF THE DARKNESS

INTRODUCTION: MALIBU MAN

"Nice backyard," I told Aaron Rodgers.

"It doesn't suck," the quarterback replied.

We were staring out at the Pacific Ocean, which appeared close enough for Rodgers to reach with one of his back-foot throws. It was a sunny afternoon in Malibu in February 2024, a chamber-of-commerce day in a season of relentless rain, flooding, rockslides, and mudslides that forced road closures near Rodgers's place.

His home had the look of an updated Venetian palazzo. At one time a long-shot kid from upstate Chico, Rodgers landed this four-bedroom, four-bathroom spread (and guesthouse) for $28 million in 2019, when it was reported that he bought it with then-girlfriend Danica Patrick, the race car driver.

"I didn't buy it with anybody," he told me, correcting those reports.

It was all his, all 4,636 square feet of wide-open California cool, with no walls or windows separating his indoor living area from his resort-style deck overlooking the blue sea. Rodgers's former teammate with the Green Bay Packers, David Bakhtiari, ribbed him about hanging out with Leonardo DiCaprio and other West Coast elites on a yacht. But it was hard to mock this self-made man about anything while standing in the middle of his charmed life on a beachside bluff.

He was wearing shorts and a tank top carrying the name of the pizza shop, Homecourt, that sponsored the sixth-grade AAU basketball team he led to an Oregon state title. Having added muscle definition to his upper chest and shoulders, Rodgers projected the physicality of a strong safety in his prime, not that of a forty-year-old quarterback coming off a devastating Achilles tear.

We sat across from each other outside, with Rodgers facing the sun and the ocean, working on his tan while I fact-checked anecdotes and claims from the 250 interviews I conducted for this unauthorized book. I had endured a bomb scare on my United flight from Newark to Los Angeles, forcing a seven-hour diversion to Chicago, where law enforcement found no explosives on board despite the reported written threat found in a plane bathroom. I later took that same plane from O'Hare to LAX and drove my Ford Edge rental through the winding mountain roads still littered with debris from the rocks and mud to get to Malibu to meet the world-famous quarterback of the New York Jets.

Rodgers was widely regarded to be among the two or three most talented players ever at the most glamorous position in American team sports. He was a Super Bowl MVP who had won the NFL's regular-season MVP award four times, more than Tom Brady (three times) or any other player in league history not named Peyton Manning (five). By the metric that used completion percentage and yards, touchdowns, and interceptions per attempt to measure performance, Rodgers was the best NFL passer of all time, a hair better than Patrick Mahomes.

I had parked in the street and pressed an intercom button at the villa entrance before the gate swung wide. As I walked down to the main house on the other side of the pool, Rodgers opened the front door and thanked me for moving up our meeting ninety minutes on short notice. I handed him a gift that I bought on Amazon for $15.99—a set of bamboo wood coasters memorializing his favorite TV show, *The Office*.

One coaster was graced by an illustration of the boss, Michael Scott, alongside his go-to line, "That's what she said." Rodgers seemed to get a kick out of it.

We were meeting at the site of his five-hour summit with Jets officials nearly a year earlier, which led to the April trade that compelled me to abandon (at least for now) my plans to write a LeBron James biography for one on a more mysterious sports superstar who had been dealt into my market. Rodgers hosted Woody and Christopher Johnson, chairman and vice chairman, along with general manager Joe Douglas, team president Hymie Elhai, head coach Robert Saleh, and offensive coordinator Nathaniel Hackett, a Rodgers favorite from their days in Green Bay.

Woody, the former U.S. ambassador to the United Kingdom, presented Rodgers with an interesting gift during the recruiting visit.

"He gave me some honey from the queen's garden," the quarterback said.

Honey from Queen Elizabeth's garden?

"It is a cool gift," Rodgers said.

I told him that Woody's gift was better than my $15.99 coasters.

"Well," he said, "you weren't ambassador to England."

We talked about everything from the makeshift radio device that his eighth-grade coach installed in his helmet to his Jimmy Kimmel/Jeffrey Epstein controversy to the heroic feats of his paternal grandfather as a World War II combat pilot in the European theater. While meeting with war-crimes investigators, Edward Rodgers provided details of the maltreatment he endured as a prisoner of war that he never shared with his family. I gave his grandson a heads-up about those details and later mailed him a copy of the war-crimes interview so he wouldn't first hear about them from this book.

We discussed Mike McCarthy's coaching, and Matt LaFleur's too. We discussed the one mistake Rodgers admitted making about his COVID-19 vaccination status, and the one regret Rodgers had about the way he handled rumors surrounding his sexuality.

We talked about the quarterback's desire to become a father, and about why he did not throw the ball on the opening-night play against the Buffalo Bills in September 2023 that left him with a ruptured Achilles tendon and a broken heart and left the Jets rudderless during a 7-10 season.

We talked about his family and agreed that no credible Aaron Rodgers bio could be written without covering his estrangement from his parents, his two brothers, and other relatives. He had virtually no communication with them for close to a decade.

Virtually.

Before arriving at his first Jets training camp, Rodgers made his annual trip to Lake Tahoe to compete in the celebrity golf tournament sponsored by American Century, which was won by Steph Curry on a walk-off eagle. Aaron finished fifth, just ahead of Annika Sorenstam (not bad!!), after a wild and crazy weekend on the packed course that saw him interact with Jets and Packers fans and even sign a pregnant woman's belly.

People who were close to Rodgers, or who had been close to Rodgers, all noticed the same things about him throughout the summer of 2023.

He seemed happier, lighter, and more approachable. He looked downright unburdened.

"Like the old Aaron," said one family member.

Amid the golf tournament chaos, Rodgers spotted his first coach in the crowd. His father, Ed Rodgers, a Chico chiropractor, had gotten a ticket to this Saturday round from a patient of his. Getting that particular ticket was critical, Ed thought, because Sunday's final round was sure to be more crowded, more hectic, and less likely to present an opportunity for visual contact with his middle child.

Aaron's father was trying to position himself for an acknowledgment or exchange of some sort. "I'm just going to keep praying," his wife, Darla, had told him from home.

Sure enough, Aaron had seen his old man in the gallery while playing the front nine of the Edgewood Tahoe course. He was walking down the ninth fairway when he realized he needed to take a bathroom break. He figured his father might be standing nearby on his way out of the john, so he reviewed his options.

Should I skip the bathroom? Should I keep walking without acknowledging him? Should I act like I'm talking on my phone?

"I could do a lot of things," Rodgers said. "But I just thought, 'What's best in this moment, and what kind of gift could I give him?' Because I do love him. I don't have animosity toward him, even with all the stuff that's been said and done."

Ed Rodgers had temporarily lost track of his son. He was looking back toward the tee box from the gallery ropes before turning around and seeing his boy, in the flesh, not even twenty feet away, looking right at him.

Amazingly enough, they found themselves alone in a clearing. The crowd had parted. It was just the two of them, a grown-up child with a golden arm locking eyes with a dad who had taught him how to throw the ball.

"It had been so long since we even looked at each other," Ed said. "I just kind of froze."

Aaron broke the ice. "Hi Pops," he said as he walked toward his dad.

Father and son embraced.

"I love you," Aaron Rodgers said.

"I love you too," Ed Rodgers responded.

It was the first time they had spoken in nearly nine years. "It was amazing," Ed said. He had dreamed of this moment for so long, imagining how it would feel to hug his son one more time. Tears filled his eyes. Nothing more needed to be said between these men, and Ed's boy had a tournament round to finish anyway.

"That was a special moment," Aaron said.

In his car after the round, Rodgers and his caddie and longtime friend, Jordan Russell, had a brief exchange about that moment.

"Dude, that was beautiful," Russell said.

"Yeah man," Rodgers replied. "I think that was what needed to happen."

I spent hours with Ed and Darla Rodgers to find out why so much time had passed without any contact with their son, and why there was no follow-up after this brief encounter at Lake Tahoe. I drove them to and from Aaron's fateful opening night as a Jet on the 9/11 anniversary in the hope of getting to know them better, and to find out why they still felt compelled to attend their son's games.

The answers were like everything else about Aaron and his family—complicated. And yet there were words spoken on both sides of the divide that suggested a reconciliation was possible.

Back in Malibu in February, my conversation with the quarterback was briefly interrupted by the sounds of a low-flying helicopter and workers who milled about the property with their machines buzzing. But the soundtrack for the interview was the soothing, rhythmic roll of the ocean, which could take the edge off any question.

Early on, Rodgers put his immense hands over my recording devices and asked if I wanted them moved to avoid the sun. I told him later to let me know if he wanted my phone and tape recorder turned off at any point during our discussion. He never asked for that to happen.

I told Rodgers that there would not be a lot of opinion in this book, but that I was criticizing his brothers for some social media daggers fired his way, and that I was criticizing him for bailing late on a buddy's wedding—as a groomsman—because that former college roommate had also invited the Rodgers family. Aaron called that opinion "fair" but added, "I don't think you're educated enough to understand the complexity of the whole situation."

The interview was a healthy and respectful give-and-take, with a couple of tense exchanges. This was still weeks before the news that independent presidential candidate Robert F. Kennedy Jr. was considering Rodgers as his running mate (RFK Jr. later picked attorney and entrepreneur Nicole

Shanahan), which CNN followed with a report that Rodgers had shared loathsome conspiracy theories about the 2012 Sandy Hook Elementary School shooting with one of its journalists during a private conversation at a Kentucky Derby party in 2013.

Rodgers wrote on X the following day that he had already been on record stating "what happened in Sandy Hook was an absolute tragedy," and that he had "never been of the opinion that the events did not take place." He was a one-man, never-ending news cycle.

As our February meeting at his house was ending, Rodgers walked me back inside and introduced his personal chef, Jason Pabst, who was joined by the quarterback's friend of fifteen years, Ryan West. Rodgers asked if a book cover had been selected, and I showed him the image on my laptop.

"Interesting," he said, before asking where the photo came from. Rodgers promised to email me about any and all mistakes made in this book in one breath, then said in the next breath, "Listen man, you've done a lot of research. A lot of stuff I don't care about, honestly."

Rodgers escorted me through the front door, toward the pool where he had done early rehab work. We shook hands, and soon enough I was on the Pacific Coast Highway thinking about what past subjects had accomplished in the seasons that my books were published.

Derek Jeter became the first Yankee ever to reach three thousand hits on a home run in the middle of a 5-for-5 day. Bill Belichick won his sixth and final Super Bowl title as head coach of the Patriots. Mike Krzyzewski preannounced his retirement at Duke and then broke the record he shared with John Wooden with his thirteenth Final Four appearance before saying goodbye.

Coming off major surgery and facing a forty-first birthday before the start of the playoffs, Aaron Rodgers did not figure to lead the Jets to their first Super Bowl appearance since they won it all in January 1969. But if he pulled it off, that would likely stand as the biggest story of my four decades covering sports in New York.

Either way, if healthy, Rodgers would enter the 2024 season as the most talked-about person in the NFL. It did not matter that Mahomes was playing for a three-peat with the Kansas City Chiefs. Rodgers was the most compelling and polarizing figure in professional football, hands down, and he had been for years.

I wrote this book to explain why.

1
AMERICAN HERO

You can start the Aaron Rodgers origin story in a hundred different places, but there is no more compelling place than the skies above Nazi-controlled Europe on July 7, 1944. There, Rodgers's grandfather was fighting for control of a B-24 bomber that was on fire and destined to crash.

Edward Wesley Rodgers was a twenty-six-year-old pilot who had done more than his share of damage to Adolf Hitler's war machine. He had flown forty-three prior missions over enemy territory, at a time when the average mission lifespan for a combat pilot was much shorter than that.

As a member of the 737th Bomb Squadron of the 454th Bombardment Group of the Fifteenth Air Force, Rodgers had navigated his B-24 Liberator through waves of enemy fighter jets and antiaircraft fire, or flak, and attacked oil refineries, marshaling yards, airfields, manufacturing plants, and armament factories. He had earned many medals and honors for his acts of heroism, along with a promotion from second lieutenant to first lieutenant.

Born in Chicago on November 7, 1917, Rodgers grew up in Decatur, Illinois, where he delivered the *Herald & Review* newspaper. He joined the Boy Scouts of America and, after moving with his family to Dallas, became a car hop at Crater's Pig'n Whistle restaurant to help pay for college.

Rodgers started out wanting to be a lawyer and studied at the University of Texas. He quickly realized he couldn't stand law and quit in his second year to focus on becoming a civil engineer.

During his time at UT, Rodgers was a member of the men's glee club and the staff of the *Daily Texan* school paper while also working summers as a refrigerator salesman and a road construction laborer. In 1940, as a copywriter at the *Austin American-Statesman*, Rodgers was making an annual salary of $960, or $240 less than his father, Alexander, was making as a salesman.

On October 20 of that same year, before an altar made up of palms and ferns and a Smilax-covered platform, Rev. William T. Morris married Rodgers and a fellow former UT student and private secretary named Kathryn Odell in the garden of her Hillsboro home. Edward had impressed her with his ability to work a dance floor and the musical instrument of his choice.

Four days before his wedding Rodgers had registered for the draft in Austin, describing himself as 5 feet 10 1/2 inches tall and 145 pounds, with blue eyes, brown hair, and a light complexion. He enlisted on May 5, 1942, five months after the Japanese bombed Pearl Harbor, and joined the U.S. Army Air Corps in September, leaving his job as an advertising manager for the *Bonham Daily Favorite* newspaper.

Rodgers was an aviation cadet who learned the trade at airfields in Arkansas and Alabama before graduating from pilot training school at George Field in eastern Illinois on June 30, 1943. He was stationed at several U.S. air bases before making stops in British Guiana, Brazil, and French Morocco on the way to a twenty-five-day training period in Tunisia in January 1944. Rodgers then flew to the San Giovanni airfield, five miles west of the southern Italian town of Cerignola.

On February 8, 1944, Rodgers embarked on his first combat mission. He took off at 9:30 a.m. with nine other planes in his squadron and thirty other aircraft from the group to attack the enemy airfield and installations of Orvieto, Italy.

Every bomb hit its target, and no American aircraft was struck by flak. The military's declassified assessment read this way: "The 'perfect mission' was a tremendous stimulus to the morale of the squadron. Ground personnel took great pride in their part in making the mission possible and airmen were elated over the successful outcome. The squadron got a flying head start on an excellent combat record with this first mission."

Despite their value to the war effort, the airmen were housed in tents and were effectively served different dishes of Spam for breakfast, lunch, and dinner. A fellow B-24 pilot who would join the 737th at San Giovanni that summer at the astonishing age of nineteen, Tom Faulkner, said the food was so terrible that "we finally got to a point where we didn't even go to eat.

"The conditions weren't great. We knew the Eighth Air Force was doing the same thing we were doing in the Fifteenth Air Force, and yet they were living in English towns near the big cities, near London, and going out with the English girls and drinking and having a good time while we were living in tents in Italy. When we went into town there were no women to be seen."

The only women in sight were depicted in provocative, scantily clad poses on the fuselages of B-24s. Ed Rodgers named his Liberator in honor of his wife, a beauty queen in Texas: the words "Sassy Lassy" were painted in white below the Liberator's cockpit next to an oversize portrait of a curvaceous young woman.

The Liberator was a massive bird with a 110-foot wingspan powered by four Pratt & Whitney engines. The heavy bomber was armed with ten .50-caliber machine guns, and it could carry a maximum bomb load of eight thousand pounds and travel up to three hundred miles per hour. The B-24 had an almost rectangular fuselage that inspired the nickname "Flying Boxcar." No, it didn't quite have the same ring to it as the B-17's "Flying Fortress."

Pilots were known to joke that the B-24s were the crates that the B-17s were shipped in. The Liberators had a longer range, a higher top speed, and a bigger bomb load than the B-17s, but they were harder to fly. One historian reported that "you could ID a B-24 pilot by his overdeveloped left bicep, flying with his right hand on the throttles."

Ed Rodgers was flying a workhorse of a weapon that was deployed in the European and Pacific theaters and was particularly effective in destroying the German U-boats that hunted Allied ships in the Atlantic. And yet the B-17 later romanticized by Hollywood (*Twelve O'Clock High* and *Memphis Belle*) was considered the safer aircraft because it could fly higher, avoiding flak, and because its broader wings could withstand more damage. German fighters preferred targeting the B-24, inspiring B-17 airmen to joke that, by drawing most of the enemy fire, the Liberators made for the best possible escorts.

The German air force, or Luftwaffe, was hardly the Allied pilots' only formidable opponent in the sky. At twenty-eight thousand feet in the winter months, the men flying the Liberators could confront temperatures of sixty degrees below zero, which overmatched the electrically heated suits they wore beneath their sheepskin jackets and their wool and fleece clothing. Frostbite was a common occupational hazard.

For Rodgers and his fellow airmen in the 454th Bombardment Group, the missions were grueling, life-and-death propositions. They started a typical day by waking up around 03:00 hours for a briefing and breakfast, and often heard a mission prayer read by a chaplain.

On St. Patrick's Day, 1944, Rodgers was among thirty-two B-24 pilots who were bombing an industrial area of Vienna from completely overcast skies when his plane was hit by enemy fire on the left side. As Rodgers swerved the Sassy Lassy away from the target, the plane took three direct hits.

Flames engulfed the No. 2 engine on the left side, and the wing was riddled with flak holes. The nose gunner, Sgt. John Baran, said the ship "began to shudder like some giant hand was shaking us violently." Baran was knocked off his feet. The ball turret gunner, staff sergeant Richard Bell, hit his head and blanked out momentarily.

The tail gunner, Staff Sgt. Thomas Whelan, described the heavens as "filled with all types of fighters and the Krauts, firing rockets, [making] the whole scene look like the Fourth of July back home." Whelan said that two German twenty-millimeter cannon shells exploded in the tail turret, that he was showered with glass fragments, and that there were eight bullet holes "about eight inches above my head."

Rodgers was struggling to maintain control of the aircraft. "Almost all of our instruments failed," he said. "All we had left was a magnetic compass, an artificial horizon, and lots of pea soup outside the window."

The rest of his formation pulled away and disappeared into the clouds. Meanwhile, Rodgers recalled, "we sank lower off to one side, all alone over Germany. It was the loneliest feeling in the world."

His wife, Kathryn, and two-and-a-half-month-old daughter, Linda, were staying with Kathryn's parents in Hillsboro. Rodgers was planning to finally see them when taking leave in August.

The Sassy Lassy was alone from the time it left the Vienna target until it reached the Adriatic Sea. On the journey back Rodgers thought it might be time to abandon ship, and his copilot, second lieutenant Karl Renz Jr., ordered the crew to strap on parachutes and prepare to jump. The crew members responded that they thought the ship could get them back to Italy, and Rodgers listened to his men.

Staff sergeants Grover Dunn and Walter C. Mauser performed a miracle fix of the damaged engine while other crew members threw overboard a half ton of ammunition, guns, and cargo to lighten the load. The plane stabilized at three thousand feet.

After deploying his emergency red flares, Rodgers landed his B-24 at a base in Italy. Whelan, an Irish boy from St. Louis, said that he prayed to St. Patrick as the Liberator limped home and made Rodgers "tie a bit of the green onto his flying suit." Truth was, the outcome had little to do with luck, and everything to do with courage and poise.

Rodgers, a second lieutenant, was among those granted a rare R&R break on May 27—ten days before the Allied invasion of Normandy—at the rest camp on Capri, where servicemen stayed in villas (not tents). He returned to combat and was promoted to first lieutenant. A few weeks later, on July 7, 1944, he climbed into the cockpit of a different plane.

His beloved Sassy Lassy had been shot down in May, leaving Rodgers and ten fellow airmen to fly in a plane named the "Powder Room" that some called "Sassy Lassy II." Rodgers took off at 06:30 hours and headed for the Odertal synthetic oil and coking plant in Germany with more than a hundred other B-24s.

The lone Texan aboard, Rodgers had quite an eclectic crew with him, including young men from Illinois, Georgia, New Jersey, New York City, Massachusetts, Alabama, Pennsylvania, Kentucky, and Missouri. They included a copilot, a navigator, a nose gunner, a bombardier, a radio operator, a flight engineer, a waist gunner, a top turret gunner, a ball turret gunner, and a tail gunner. The weather on the route from San Giovanni up the Adriatic Sea and on to Odertal was clear except for the altocumulus clouds above the mountains and a light ground haze at the target area.

While facing intense and accurate flak, the Liberators above Odertal dropped more than two hundred tons of bombs on the target at 11:30 from a range of nineteen thousand to twenty-two thousand feet. One report from the Mediterranean Allied Strategic Air Force stated that there were five direct hits on the vulnerable section of the plant, and direct hits on fuel storage and chemical facilities caused three violent explosions. However, another report from the 304th Bomb Wing headquarters stated that the specific bombs from the 454th "struck to the north of the objective."

Rodgers and the other American pilots steered their heavy bombers toward what was called a target of opportunity, the Dubnica Armament Works in Czechoslovakia. Once there, the Liberators were confronted by two dozen enemy aircraft—Focke-Wulf 190s and Messerschmitt 109s, which formed the single-seat, single-engine heart and soul of the Luftwaffe. The pilots of the 454th had better luck at Dubnica, where, the Mediterranean Allied Strategic Air Force reported, one wave of bombs "cut across the center of [the] plant with numerous hits on underground workshops."

Rodgers and other pilots were attacked by enemy fighters as they made their way south toward Hungary's Lake Balaton, the largest lake in Central Europe. Flak from antiaircraft guns exploded around them in black clouds, sending jagged shrapnel tearing through their planes.

Rodgers had survived these perilous encounters before, even though he could barely see anything from the cockpit amid the chaos. The enemy fighters were coming from all angles at two, three, six, and nine o'clock. After a half-hour engagement, two Me-109s with white noses, yellow and green stripes, and bluish fuselages came out of the sun at about eleven o'clock and went undetected, drawing no Allied fire.

"Several bursts of twenty-mm burst around us," said Air Corps captain Jack L. Graham, "and as the enemy aircraft broke away, Lt. Rodgers's ship was reported to be burning. Lt. Rodgers was flying on my right wing and by looking across the cockpit I could see a large fire burning under his #1 engine."

His outer left engine was in flames twenty-two thousand feet over Hungary. Mauser, a radio operator from New York City, said the pilot tried to put out the fire with the automatic CO_2 extinguisher but found it empty. Rodgers moved his crippled B-24 a half mile away from his squadron. "The pilot pulled us away," Mauser said, "in case we blew up, so that we would not endanger the other ships."

Rodgers was under extreme duress with a heavy bomber that had been called a widow-maker, a death trap, and a flying coffin. Safely removed from the forty-plane formation at around 13:15 hours, the pilot told his ten crewmen to strap on their parachutes and prepare to bail out. Minutes later, Rodgers ordered his crew out of the plane.

Airmen in other B-24s saw ten of eleven parachutes open at about twenty-one thousand feet; Rodgers was the last man to exit the ship. The pilot jumped, said Charles Stanley, second lieutenant of the Air Corps, "just as the plane started to nose into a dive."

The Liberator crashed in the village of Hajmasker, just north of Lake Balaton. The airmen who jumped hit the ground at around 13:40 hours. Everyone survived the ordeal except for the navigator from Atlanta, John Simmons, whose body was found on the ground with his unopened chute. At least one crew member believed Simmons had hit his head exiting the plane and was knocked unconscious.

Rodgers touched down about a hundred yards north of Kadarta, near the lake. Airmen could encounter any number of scenarios upon landing, including friendly locals, hostile locals, or enemy airmen who might treat them with more respect than they might afford Allied infantrymen. Nobody wanted to be captured by the SS, Hitler's brutal paramilitary organization.

As soon as Rodgers hit the ground, he was met by a group of at least thirty civilians, at least ten Hungarian soldiers, and several Hungarian policemen. These locals gathered around the fallen pilot and began to beat him.

"I was kicked with hobnail boots, beaten with gun butts, and one Hungarian policeman, who seemed to be the ringleader of this group of people, hit me a severe blow and blackened my eye," Rodgers later recalled.

One of the civilians spoke English and acted as an interpreter for Rodgers and the angry mob. "Apparently the reason for the treatment which I received at the hands of this group of people was the fact that the Germans had put out considerable propaganda in the neighborhood which attributed the loss of civilian life and property . . . to bombings by American airmen," Rodgers said.

He had suffered two shrapnel cuts—one on his shin and another on his forehead—before absorbing this beating. The pilot asked the group's ringleader for medical attention. "But he refused to allow anything to be done," Rodgers said.

Hungarian police jailed him for thirty-six hours before he was transferred to a penitentiary in Budapest, where he remained for a week. Rodgers watched as one of his injured crew members, Grover Dunn, was forced to carry all their flight equipment and paraphernalia—without ever being allowed to set down the load—for the entire train ride and march to the penitentiary. Rodgers and others made repeated requests for Dunn to receive medical care for the extreme pain he was feeling from an apparent ruptured appendix suffered while landing, but those requests were ignored.

Rodgers and three fellow survivors were sent to Stalag Luft III in the Nazi-occupied Polish town of Sagan, arriving on July 19, 1944. In March, this prisoner-of-war camp for Allied airmen had been the scene of what came to be known as the Great Escape. Seventy-six prisoners had crawled through a tunnel to their freedom, only for seventy-three to be recaptured. Hitler personally ordered the execution of fifty of them.

The Nazis were clearly losing the war at this point, leaving their POWs uncertain of how their captors' desperation might impact conditions in the camps. With the Soviet Red Army closing fast from the east, the Third Reich evacuated Stalag Luft III on January 27, 1945, when Rodgers was forced to join a southwest march of two thousand POWs from Sagan to Nuremberg, a journey of more than three hundred miles as part of what were called the Death Marches.

Rodgers and his fellow prisoners started walking at eleven o'clock at night and didn't stop until they reached the town of Freiwaldau at ten or eleven the following morning. "During this period the temperature was twenty or thirty degrees below zero," Rodgers said. "During the march the German guard promised us we would have closed quarters when we got to Freiwaldau, but when we got there, they only had room for about two hundred; there were some two thousand in our group."

The following day the POWs marched between twenty-five and thirty-one miles through the night in the snow and bitter cold, suffering from frostbite, untreated wounds, and sheer exhaustion. The men in his group, Rodgers said, "fell out of ranks like flies.

"I had running sores on my feet, and even during the rest periods we had to keep moving to keep from freezing."

Eventually the POWs reached Spremberg, where they were loaded onto a train—fifty men for every forty-man boxcar—and transported to Nuremberg. On arrival, Rodgers recalled, "we had to stand out in the bitter cold for another hour or so while the Germans were trying to find a place to quarter us."

While at the Nuremberg-Langwasser camp, Rodgers said, "the Germans made no attempt to delouse us. There was no fuel, straw ticks, not nearly enough blankets, and no medical attention. One loaf of black bread was furnished daily. . . . Any soup which we had had worms in it, and one day they brought us cheese which had been exposed to bombing and was covered with ammonium hydroxide. The German guards commented that this cheese was not fit for human consumption. Occasionally we would get a very small piece of meat in our soup, and sometimes we would have two small, spoiled potatoes."

Years later, Rodgers wasn't in the habit of telling family members many stories about his treatment in the camps. The tales he did tell often focused on relatively positive interactions and events. Rodgers, for instance, wrote plays that the POWs performed, hoping to earn extra rations if they entertained the German guards.

But in the end, the airman's experience was a nearly ten-month nightmare. In early April 1945, just before American forces liberated Nuremberg-Langwasser, Rodgers was moved to the Moosburg camp in the south, about thirty-five miles northeast of Munich. He was among the more than a hundred thousand Allied prisoners of war who had been packed into barracks built for ten thousand men—and subjected to subhuman sanitary conditions.

On April 29, Sherman tanks rolled across the emerald Bavarian hills near Rodgers's camp and barreled through the overwhelmed SS positions. An American flag was raised to the top of a church steeple in town. The tanks of the Fourteenth Armored Division of the United States Army crashed through the POW camp's double ten-foot wire fences and were immediately swarmed by delirious men who represented every nation that had fought the Nazis.

The following afternoon, Hitler shot himself to death in his Berlin bunker. Seven days later, Germany surrendered, and the Allied fighters who won the war in Europe began making plans to go home.

• • •

EDWARD RODGERS DESPERATELY wanted a son. He had reconciled with his wife after a separation, and they were a day or two away from adopting a boy when Kathryn surprised everyone—including the doctor who told her she couldn't have any more children—by sharing the news that she was pregnant. Ed Jr. was born in 1955 in Texas but attended a Catholic elementary school in Spain, where his father was serving in the Sixteenth Air Force and where his two younger sisters were born.

After the family returned to the States, Rodgers eventually settled into a career as a lieutenant colonel and chief civil engineer at Vandenberg Air Force Base in Southern California. Fifteen minutes from the base, his growing teenager, Ed Jr., had become a football star at Lompoc High School with hopes of playing big-time Division I ball on the road to the NFL.

The bomber pilot with the Purple Heart and the Air Medal wanted no part of his boy's vision.

Ed Sr. wanted Ed Jr. to attend the Air Force Academy. Ed Jr. had a rebellious streak that often compelled him to do the opposite of whatever his father wanted him to do.

Ed Sr. also had potential interest in steering his boy to Texas A&M, where he had taught in the ROTC program and, by his account, had once lunched with the great Bear Bryant. "He was kind of overpowering," Ed Jr. said, "and it didn't sit well with my personality."

And yet Ed Jr.'s older sister Linda assured him that he was forever the apple of their old man's eye. "I always felt loved by him," Ed Jr. said. Father and son went fishing and camping together. The boy was oblivious to the trauma that the combat and the POW camps had surely inflicted on his dad.

Ed Sr. was fond of his alcohol, sometimes too much so, but he was never mean to his spouse or his four kids when he drank. The pilot's wife, on the other hand, had a different approach. The way Ed Jr. told it, his mother was a cold and detached homemaker who rarely expressed her love for her children. Ed Jr. said he was surprised his parents had four children; he rarely, if ever, saw them hug and kiss.

In Kathryn's later years, her only son recalled, she softened up and became affectionate and told him that she loved him. "But I never heard it growing up," Ed Jr. said.

When it was time to make his college choice in 1973, Ed Jr. had precious little guidance. As soon as his father realized that his boy was not going to follow his military academy plan, Ed Jr. was on his own.

That was how a Division I talent ended up at a Division II school. Ed Jr. was a tall, quick, 235-pound offensive lineman who had drawn varying degrees of interest from the likes of Stanford, Rice, Nebraska, and UCLA, along with his father's preferred choices of Air Force, Army, Navy, and Texas A&M.

UCLA wanted Rodgers to visit along with his Lompoc teammate Mike Tatum, who accepted the Bruins' scholarship offer the following year. "I don't know why I didn't go," Ed Jr. said. "I didn't have that kind of mentorship from my dad. As good a dad as he was in a lot of respects, it all fell by the wayside."

Ed Jr. needed a plan, and fast. As it turned out, his high school coach had played ball with Pete Riehlman, the head coach at Chico State, a school originally built on a small cherry orchard that was ninety miles north of Sacramento. As a Division II program, Chico wasn't offering a scholarship. It offered something else that caught Ed Jr.'s eye.

Girls.

"A lot of girls," Ed Jr. said. "It was a big party school, so I'll go."

Years later *Playboy* magazine ranked Chico State as the No. 1 party school in America, and for good reason. Thousands of visitors poured into the rural college town of Chico every year for the seemingly endless celebration of uninhibited drinking known as Pioneer Week. At the end of every football season, said Chico State tight end Gary Eckley, the players gathered at a club known as the Oasis determined to plow through more kegs of beer than the previous year's team had emptied. One star player said the police would not arrest a team member "unless you deserved it. They would help you before they'd arrest you."

Ed Rodgers Jr. did his share of partying in this climate, yet that didn't stop him from starting on the offensive line as a freshman for a coach who never started freshmen. Teammates took to calling Rodgers "Fast Eddie" because he could explode out of a stance and pull outside quicker than any guard around. Eckley said his friend knew how to engage a defensive lineman or linebacker and almost subtly turn him away from where the hole was designed to be.

The kid was a natural, that was clear. Riehlman, a card-carrying hardass, sat him down one day and told him, "If you didn't screw around so much and worked harder, you could do anything you want. You could be one of the best linemen that ever came through here."

Chico State wasn't exactly USC or Michigan or Notre Dame. Rodgers was studying physical education and exercise science and having his fun off the field, and he wasn't quite as serious as his coach was about competing in front of crowds ranging from 2,500 to 7,500.

Riehlman went 7-3 in the 1973 season before leaving to coach pro ball with the Hawaiians of the World Football League. His assistant Dick Trimmer took over and, for the next three years, failed to push the Wildcats past the .500 mark.

But Rodgers made the all-conference team for him all three years. "He was an outstanding offensive guard," Trimmer said. "He was big, he was tough, he was smart, and he very rarely missed an assignment."

Star fullback Dino Visinoni, who ran behind Rodgers as much as possible, called him one of the smartest players he ever met. After failing to make the final cuts in a couple of Canadian Football League tryouts, Rodgers found a semiprofessional home in the California Football League with the Twin Cities Cougars of Marysville, an hour's drive from Chico.

The Cougars practiced two or three times a week and played their home games at Marysville Memorial Stadium on Saturday nights. Rodgers carpooled with a couple of Cougars teammates and Chico State players from Wingate High School in Brooklyn, Curtis Holder and Kenzie Gray.

"We were best buddies," Rodgers said. "The stories they told growing up in Brooklyn, and here was this white boy from some little Podunk farming town. It was eye opening."

Out of the Howard Houses projects in Brownsville, among the toughest neighborhoods in New York, Holder got to see a whole different world in Chico too, and not merely because of its agriculture. He first visited the campus during the Pioneer Week party-fest. "It was crazy," he said. "I couldn't believe it. Nobody was going to class."

As a linebacker, Holder went helmet to helmet with Rodgers nearly every practice. "I used to beat the crap out of him," he said through a laugh. "Let's just say we got each other ready for games."

The Cougars represented Marysville and Yuba City, and Holder described them as a collection of misfits and characters who mimicked the defiant playing style of the Oakland Raiders. As a weekend-warrior team fortified by former major-college talents and veterans cut from NFL teams, the Cougars were a handful too.

They won four consecutive California Football League titles from 1979 to 1982, beating their bitter rivals, the San Jose Tigers, along the way, and Rodgers was part of their two national semipro championship triumphs in '80 and '81. The first was a 37–20 victory over the Delavan (Wisconsin) Red Devils—before a standing-room-only crowd of 6,000 in Marysville—that was sanctioned by the Minor Professional Football Association. The second was a 61–7 rout of the Pittsburgh Colts before 4,500 in Marysville that lacked the MPFA's blessing because of a dispute over postseason travel expenses.

"It was some of the most fun football I've ever played," said Rodgers, who gave up the game after three years.

The good times could not last forever, not with Rodgers preparing to start a family with a woman who was a football fan long before they had met at Chico State.

• • •

DARLA PITTMAN WAS the daughter of a frozen food distribution business owner in Ukiah who was a member of the First Presbyterian Church and a passionate fan of the San Francisco 49ers. Chuck Pittman worked six days a week serving Mendocino and Lake Counties, with Sundays reserved for family time.

Chuck and his wife, Barbara, a dedicated Camp Fire Girls leader, had three daughters and a son. The kids were not allowed to watch TV after school. When they were done with their homework, they could entertain themselves in the backyard pool.

Chuck played pinochle with his wife and taught his children how to stay upright on skis and took his family on long vacations across the country, putting thousands of miles on his cherished Mercury. The Pittman kids worked in their father's business, starting out as janitors cleaning the bathrooms and working their way up. They had a blast joining their parents on Sunday afternoon trips to watch the 49ers play.

"It was a huge part of our lives," Darla said. John Brodie, All-Pro, was her kind of quarterback.

Chuck Pittman got his Saturday chores done early just to make sure he could watch ABC's *Wide World of Sports* with his youngest daughter. Darla was a cheerleader and a member of the dance team, or song-leading team, at Ukiah High School. She joined her sister at Sacramento State because she was an avid skier who wanted to attend school relatively close to the Lake Tahoe resorts. Darla transferred to Chico State as a junior for its gerontology program and ended up in a community service class with an athlete named Bernie Kelley, who wanted to introduce this natural beauty to his best friend.

"I've got a guy for you," Bernie assured her.

Darla already had a boyfriend and assured her classmate that she didn't need his matchmaking help. Bernie had been something of an irritant, forever roping Darla into helping him with class projects.

So, when he waved her over one day on campus, Darla headed in his direction only to decline whatever request he was going to make. "Instead, he introduces me to Ed," she said.

Darla had no time or patience for this. She had gone to Chico State specifically for her major, and she had promised her father that she'd remain focused on her grades.

But before her was this strapping stranger in a blue jacket. "Ed was just ripped and he was really tall," Darla said. She thought he was quite a sight in that blue jacket.

Meanwhile, Ed couldn't believe his eyes—or his luck. Later, he said to Bernie, "Dang, is this who you've been telling me about?" Ed fell hard for Darla on the spot.

The following weekend Ed asked her out on a date. San Francisco was their favorite place to go for day trips. In 1979, they celebrated their engagement with the sixty-one-year-old war hero, Edward Wesley Rodgers Sr., and the rest of their families at a formal dinner party in the wine cellar of the city's Blue Fox restaurant. They were married on April 5, 1980, at the United Presbyterian Church in Ukiah, the church Darla grew up in. Bernie Kelley was the groom's best man.

Ed and Darla were blessed with three children over the following eight years, all boys, including one who would show a special talent for the game of football. And unlike his old man, the combat pilot, Ed Rodgers Jr. was not about to put any obstacles between his son and wherever that talent might take him.

2
THE PRODIGY

AARON RODGERS WATCHED the 1986 season about as closely as any dedicated NFL fan could.

He was two years old at the time.

"I've never seen another kid do that and not get distracted," his father Ed said.

Aaron was studying and understanding the formations of his favorite team, the San Francisco 49ers, before his fifth birthday. His father had made him a little football field out of plywood, and with six-year-old brother Luke in school and baby brother Jordan in his mother's arms, Aaron spent his entire mornings moving his Starting Lineup figurines up and down the board.

"He developed little play cards, little plays, his own plays," his father said. "He learned math by looking at stats and players' heights and weights.... He did that for hours."

Luke was wired differently. He always wanted to go outside and play with a friend while his younger brother was glued to the TV set and the image of his hero, Joe Montana. Aaron knew the year Montana was drafted out of Notre Dame. He knew Joe Cool's stats in this season and that one.

As a young boy Aaron had an even, room-temperature disposition, and never gave his parents more than a few minutes of trouble. So, with Aaron in kindergarten at Pines Elementary in Magalia, Darla was excited to go to the first parent-teacher conference arranged to discuss her middle son.

But the teacher, Bette Lawler, surprised Darla with a less-than-glowing report. Mrs. Lawler told Mrs. Rodgers that her son was too busy drawing up Xs and Os and organizing football games during his class's free time.

Darla was confused. "You said this is free time," she responded. "I don't see what's wrong with that."

"Well," Mrs. Lawler said, "he's always the quarterback."

"And the kids are OK with that," Darla shot back. "He's kind of a natural leader."

Darla was not about to let the kindergarten teacher spin a positive into a negative. She was determined to be her children's most fervent advocate, and to be the kind of stay-at-home mother that Barbara Pittman was for her.

Ed had earned his Chico State master's degree in exercise physiology and was thinking of becoming a doctor. As it turned out, the births of Luke in 1982 and Aaron in 1983 sent their father's big-picture ambitions off course.

Ed planned to apply for physical therapy school. But as Darla put it, "Our children kept messing the whole thing up. Not in a bad way."

Though Ed and Darla had hoped to stay in Chico, the old combat pilot, Ed Sr., asked them to move into his retirement community in the nearby foothills, Forest Ranch, where he owned property that he planned on giving them. Neither husband nor wife wanted to stay in a retirement place with their young boys for long.

So, they bounced from Forest Ranch to Lakeport to Magalia to Darla's hometown of Ukiah, where Ed worked in a health club and did some coaching and teaching at Mendocino College. By age nine, their second son was already featured in the local newspaper.

Aaron Rodgers made the front page of the January 3, 1993, edition of the *Ukiah Daily Journal* by sinking enough free throws in the annual Hoop Shoot contest to become the Elks Lodge's first district winner since the 1970s.

Aaron also made a name for himself in the classroom at Oak Manor Elementary, where he finished inside the top 3 percent on a state test that earned him a spot in a weekly gifted-and-talented education class taught by Jan Steliga. The GATE subjects ranged from meteorology and oceanography to the humanities, and the class focused on problem solving, science experiments, and interactive studies of topics such as the Middle Ages and Greek mythology.

"No doubt Aaron was one of the higher-level thinkers there," Steliga said. She took her GATE students on field trips and recalled a visit to the airport weather station and a question about the wind that veteran Mendocino meteorologist Bob Wallen posed to her class.

"Aaron raised his hand and gave the correct answer," Steliga recalled, "and Bob got all excited about it."

Aaron's mother recalled that Steliga once gave her GATE students a test to determine how gifted students process information, asking the children how they would get from Point A to Point B. Steliga wanted to know if they looked at the journey from above, seeing everything, or if they saw it from the ground view as a street-sign-to-street-sign process.

At a parent-teacher conference, Steliga told Aaron's mother, "He knows at all times what's going on. He's up above seeing everything." That observation stayed with Darla and Ed from youth team to youth team, season to season, year to year, victory to victory.

"We'd have multiple coaches in his travel soccer and in basketball say, 'Aaron has an uncanny ability to know where everybody is and what everybody is doing simultaneously, and their assignments, almost as if he was above it,'" Darla said. "[Steliga] was actually onto something that ended up gifting Aaron in his athletics."

As parents who described themselves as very traditional, Darla and Ed were in complete agreement that she should remain a stay-at-home mom for as long as possible. This was a top priority for both.

"We just knew that God would honor our decision for me to be the primary caregiver of our children," Darla said, "instead of farming them out."

That decision put Ed and Darla at a significant financial disadvantage, a truth they were willing to accept. "We agreed we would live ten years behind our peers financially," Darla said. "The peers that were two-income families were going on a different trajectory, and we were OK with that. And I wouldn't change it for anything, being the one that was home with my babies."

Over time Ed realized that his rise through the Mendocino College ranks was not unfolding as quickly as he had hoped. He told his wife that he had no interest in remaining at the school for ten years, without a certain promotion in sight, and that the family needed to make yet another move.

In his late thirties, Ed was still searching for what, exactly, he wanted to be. His time in the fitness industry had him thinking he might run health clubs. He also enjoyed coaching and teaching, yet he was fairly certain he did not want to work for someone else.

Ed ultimately decided to become a chiropractor. To earn acceptance into Western States Chiropractic College in Portland, he needed to pass one organic chemistry course at Portland State, a class from hell.

Ed called this decision and this move "a wild risk," because the family had no income that summer and he was cramming a brutal one-year course into eight frantic weeks. Ed and Darla got by on savings and on the generosity of Ed's older sister Linda and her husband, Nelson Leonard. They opened their Eagle Point, Oregon, home to Darla, Aaron, and Jordan, with Ed attending school five hours away and Luke playing all-star baseball back in California.

Linda and Nelson lived on a llama farm, and Darla saw it as a chance for her boys to enjoy a summer adventure while getting to see their father on weekends. Uncle Nelson was an archaeologist who did not have any children, so Darla made sure Aaron and little Jordan earned their keep.

Uncle Nelson and Aunt Linda had about fifty llamas on the farm, and Darla and the boys raked their pens and cleaned their poop. They worked around the farm and around the house to earn their video game time. Meanwhile, Ed earned a B-plus in that organic chemistry class. He enrolled in Western States, then moved with his wife and sons to Beaverton (the home of Nike), where Aaron started in fifth grade. With Jordan heading into all-day school, Darla returned to work as a preschool teacher.

Though Aaron did not fully appreciate the sacrifice at the time, he watched his father retreat to the family garage for quiet time to study for four hours at a clip. The man was taking exams on little or no sleep. Aaron would say years later, "He was doing it all for us."

Ed was a fan of boxing, the Showtime Lakers, and just about any competitive event on TV. He wanted his boys to remain active in sports, to play a different one every season to stay occupied and out of trouble. Darla felt the same way, and yet tackle football was not an option in the boys' middle school years.

Though Ed had loved the game when he played it, he had seen too many youth coaches who acted like they were competing for a spot in the NFC Championship Game, and who did not appear overly concerned with player safety. He did not want his sons subjected to an unnecessary series of blows to their developing bodies and brains.

Outside their home, Ed did teach his boys a thing or three about the sport during a family game they called "Pass Patterns," with the father in the role of quarterback (sometimes Jordan snapped him the ball), and Luke and Aaron in alternating roles as receiver and defensive back. The wideout ran designed routes against the sibling covering him, Ed fired away, and then all hell broke loose as the brothers battled for the ball in the air.

As the older, bigger boy, Luke did not mind imposing his physicality and will on Aaron. The brothers were fiercely competitive in everything from basketball to Wiffle ball to soccer to roller hockey to a preferred car seat to who would get the biggest chicken breast at dinner.

The front yard, the backyard, and the street were their usual arenas of engagement. Their games often included physical altercations that Luke almost always won. When Aaron finally blocked one of Luke's shots in a one-on-one basketball game, it was an occasion worthy of celebrating. When the boys took their rough-and-tumble competitions too far, their mother half-jokingly wished she'd had a daughter.

Aaron thought that his mom was worthy of sainthood. "The stuff that she dealt with is amazing," he said.

Darla and Ed allowed their boys to play Sega Genesis games for an hour on weeknights if their homework was completed, and for two hours on Saturdays (Sundays were off-limits). Sometimes on Saturday mornings, Aaron and Luke woke up extra early, at 6 a.m., to get some unsanctioned time in while their parents slept, before playing again during their sanctioned 8–10 a.m. slot.

When Jordan thought he was old enough to play with the big boys, Aaron, a pro-wrestling fan, wasn't above hurting his kid brother with a WWF move. If Jordan wailed for his mother, Aaron faked an injury to intentionally enrage Jordan and redirect his attention away from summoning Darla, who was always close enough to the action to intercede.

The boys talked about someday being star players in the NFL and the NBA, and Darla and Ed never tried to temper their sons' ambitions. Luke was more naturally athletic than his younger brothers. "He was super fast, he could throw a ball like crazy, and he could jump like crazy," his father said. "But his personality wasn't one to work on stuff. . . . As much talent as he had, he just didn't like the work. He liked to play."

Aaron, on the other hand, had the talent and the desire to maximize it. Darla recalled driving around Aaron and his friends and hearing them in the back of the car talking about Bo Jackson and trying to decide what two sports they would play professionally.

Aaron loved the San Francisco Giants (especially when Kevin Mitchell was in the lineup) and the NBA of the 1990s. He was a Chicago Bulls and Michael Jordan fan, along with a Chicago Cubs and Harry Caray fan (on good nights his TV antenna picked up WGN telecasts). He was a real player in both sports.

As a young point guard in basketball, Aaron could dribble behind his back, shoot with both hands, shoot the three, and blow by perimeter defenders. He executed one crossover dribble so effectively that he toppled one middle-school rival in Oregon, Scott Dougherty, a future Division I player who had a scar on his knee for years after that fall.

"Aaron was also further along mentally than the rest of us in youth sports," Dougherty said.

He described Aaron's jump-shooting form as perfect, and likened his burgeoning game to those of John Stockton and Steve Nash. And yet Ed Rodgers was certain his eleven-year-old son was a better prospect on the baseball diamond, in the Raleigh Hills Little League.

Ed thought his boy was destined to become a major leaguer. "He'd hit home runs like crazy and nobody could touch him as a pitcher," Ed recalled.

Aaron played for the Nickel Ads team coached by Dr. Joe Kaempf, who saw him at tryouts and figured he would never get a chance to draft him with the second overall pick. The doctor lucked out when the guy holding the first pick drafted a friend's son, Grant Zimmerman, so the two men could coach together.

Kaempf was a believer in visualizing success before taking the field or the court, so he told Aaron and his teammates that they should close their eyes and picture themselves throwing a strike, or hitting a double into the gap, or sinking the game-clinching foul shots. Aaron practiced that technique for the rest of his competitive life.

Kaempf's team won the Little League title two straight years with Aaron, the pitcher and shortstop with a cannon for a right arm. "Every Little League has a star kid who usually matured early, has underarm hair when he's eleven and a mustache when he's twelve, with an August birthday," said Kaempf's son Joey, Aaron's teammate and friend. "Aaron was that good but he was really small, a late bloomer."

Joey recalled that their team was a dominant force in their second year together, and that his father removed Aaron from the mound in the last inning of the championship game with Nickel Ads holding a 22–0 lead. Dr. Kaempf assigned the final outs to Joey's ten-year-old brother, Abraham, who gave up a run. At the pizza party afterward, Aaron approached Joey with a dour look on his face.

"I'm really pissed at your father now," Aaron told him. "I can't believe he took me out. He owed it to me to get that complete-game shutout."

Aaron played on the thirteen-year-old Beaverton team that reached the Babe Ruth regional final. He also starred on a sixth-grade AAU basketball team with Kaempf, sponsored by Homecourt Pizza, which won a state title. But deep down, Aaron always thought he was a football player first. A quarterback first. That sentiment was handed down by the same man who had installed a temporary ban on the ultimate full-contact sport.

"My dad gave me my passion for football," Aaron said.

While attending Vose Elementary in Beaverton, Aaron brought a Nerf ball to class and diagrammed plays that he used to pick apart opposing fifth graders at recess. Life was good for the middle child, except when he was forced to spend ninety minutes in the after-school program before his mother could pick him up. Aaron was miserable until a kindly teacher named Mary Mayer sensed his unhappiness and pulled him out of the program so he could throw around the football while cleaning a few bulletin boards.

The Rodgers family adored the Beaverton experience, aside from the rain, but Ed finished four years of schooling at Western States in three years and turned down an enticing local job offer to head back to Chico. And so, in 1997, the family returned to the college town of more than fifty thousand residents that sat in the Sacramento Valley between the snowcapped Sierra Nevada mountain range to the east and the Sacramento River to the west.

Chico was known for its surrounding almond trees and rice fields, for the Sierra Nevada Brewing plant, for summer temperatures that could soar past 110 degrees in the shade, and for the state university with the *Animal House* reputation. Some faculty members were embarrassed enough by Chico State's party-school rep that they sometimes conveniently forgot to wear their identification badges at academic conferences. "It was a terrible blight and very painful to all of us who were serious people," said one such longtime faculty member.

In truth, of course, there were far worse places to earn a degree. Ed Rodgers was proud of his alma mater; he and Darla loved their friends in Chico and loved their church there too.

"We didn't do anything without turning it into a prayer project," Darla said. "We just really felt like God was telling us to return to Chico.

"Everyone was on board with that except Aaron. Aaron was very unhappy to return."

He did not want to leave his Whitford Middle School friends or his winning teams. It was a dizzying series of moves for a thirteen-year-old who called his maternal grandparents' home on West Mill Street in Ukiah "the Forever House" because it was the one constant in his childhood, owned by Chuck and Barbara Pittman since 1954.

Darla explained to Aaron and his brothers, "God would not have this be the will of your father's life without it also being the will of your life. We're supposed to return to California."

In one profound respect, Ed and Darla were returning to a different Chico than the one they had left. Ed's father had died just after Christmas in 1996, at age seventy-nine. The old combat pilot had heart issues that led to surgery before he succumbed to congestive heart failure. Ed Sr. had retired in 1985 after twenty years as chief civil engineer at Vandenberg Air Force Base. His heroism in World War II earned him a burial in Arlington National Cemetery.

A few months before Ed Sr.'s death, Ed Jr.'s mother gave him a treasure chest of his father's combat and service medals, along with reassuring postcards from his dad's days as a prisoner of war. Ed Jr. regretted that as a kid he did not realize he was living with such a distinguished American hero. Ed Sr. was older than the fathers of Ed Jr.'s friends, and the distance between them conspired against the son's appreciation of the father's feats.

Ed Jr. remembered a B-24 being part of a Chico air show and getting in the plane and feeling awed by what his father and his crew accomplished with such a modest-looking machine. Ed Sr. did not talk much about his combat service, with one exception: the St. Patrick's Day mission. His B-24 was shot up and on fire over Nazi Germany, and Edward Wesley Rodgers felt like the loneliest man in the sky, and still he found a way to get that plane back to Italy and to get his men back on Allied ground.

"My father was most proud about that," Ed Jr. said. "He had to be a pretty amazing pilot."

Ed Jr. cherished the picture he had of himself and his son Luke in front of Ed Sr.'s headstone at Arlington National, Section 60, Grave No. 2951. Aaron recalled how much he appreciated the Swiss Army knife that his grandfather had given him for his tenth birthday, and how much Ed Sr. cherished the train set he brought home from Germany.

In his own way, even after disregarding his only son's pursuit of a football scholarship at a nonmilitary school, Ed Sr. was proud of his boy's athletic career. He attended some of his Chico State and semipro games. Despite their differences, Ed Jr. understood that his father loved him. He also knew that he wanted to deploy a different approach in parenting his own boys.

"Ed and I were huge about launching our sons," Darla said. "Ed felt like he was never launched, being from a military dad who always wanted to be in control. We purposefully decided we would equip our sons as best we could, through eighteen years under our roof, and there would be rules."

Those rules included no tattoos and no long hair, at least until the Rodgers boys were on their own. Of greater significance, a commitment to Christianity was at the very least an expectation, if not an outright mandate.

Darla was raised Presbyterian and Ed was raised Roman Catholic, though he said his family included a number of atheists. Together they decided to express and celebrate their faith through the Neighborhood Church of Chico, part of the evangelical Christian and Missionary Alliance. They were introduced to the Neighborhood Church by their best friends, Larry and Diane Ruby, while Ed and Darla were having problems in their first year or two of marriage.

Darla said her husband, who started his Catholic education as a schoolboy in Spain, "didn't have a clear understanding of a personal relationship with Jesus Christ. It felt like the priests were the ones who talked to Jesus, so that was a revelation, and actually Larry Ruby brought that all to fruition and helping in his friendship with Eddie to understand, 'Hey, I'm not saying it's going to fix everything in your marriage, but if you have the opportunity to put Jesus in the center of your marriage, you guys would at least have a fighting chance.'"

Darla and Ed signed up for couples' Bible studies and made the church the underpinning of just about everything they did. Without that foundation, Ed said, "we probably wouldn't be here."

Ed was eternally grateful that the church helped grant him the opportunity to raise three boys. "He would have given his right arm for a brother," Darla said, "so the fact that he got to have one son, let alone three, and they could have that brother camaraderie, he was just in heaven."

On the family's return to Chico, Ed started essentially going door-to-door to treat his chiropractor patients, with Jordan tagging along and carrying his father's table. Meanwhile, Ed and Darla found a junior high for Aaron, who was entering eighth grade. Given that Aaron had left Oregon kicking and screaming, his parents decided that he needed a supportive environment at his next school, leading them to Champion Christian.

Ed knew fathers who had sent their kids there. He set up an interview with the school's principal, who asked young Aaron what he planned on contributing to the Champion Christian culture.

"I'm going to improve your sports programs," he replied.

Ed and Darla thought Aaron's response got the family off to a bad start with the school. Even when Aaron was young, Darla thought his confidence was mistaken for something it was not.

"They've always said he was arrogant, which he's not, but that's the first label they'll put on it," she said. "There's a little disconnect right there, so it becomes 'arrogant young man' instead of 'a confident young man.'

"Aaron knows he's going to a small private school. He's just coming off a regional [final] in baseball, a state championship in basketball. I think he figures he can probably raise their level . . . and he said it confidently. And he did. The tiny private school with half a dozen boys ended up beating the big juggernaut junior highs in basketball."

Aaron was a small point guard even by eighth-grade standards, in the five-foot-two range, and yet he made big-boy plays all over the floor. His shooting, playmaking, and court vision had people talking as Champion Christian won nearly every game it played. He was honoring the promise he had made to the school's principal.

Thomas Wilson, a fast and athletic player at the Notre Dame School in

Chico, recalled one eighth-grade meeting with Champion Christian that was dominated by Rodgers.

"My coach told me I've got to guard this kid, and he hit three or four three-pointers in a row on me," Wilson said. "My coach then tells me, 'Step out in front of the three-point line; he's not going to shoot it from back there.'

"Aaron looked at my coach and then looked at me and smiled. He pulled up from back there and made it, and I looked at my coach and said, 'What do you want me to do now?'"

Aaron averaged about twenty points a game for Champion Christian, and in the spring he starred for his Chico Rice team in American Legion baseball. But the kid wanted more. He wanted football, and he wanted it now. He kept pushing his old man to relent, to give him just one season of full pads and full contact before he attended high school.

When Ed Rodgers found out that his good friend and former semipro teammate with the Twin Cities Cougars, Curtis Holder, was coaching the team that Aaron would play for, he finally did something his own father rarely did—he compromised. Ed and Darla said they wanted to launch their kids, after all, and it was time to let Aaron choose his path.

Holder told Ed that he already had a quarterback in place, but that he would give young Mr. Rodgers a fair-and-square look. Holder knew Aaron was an accomplished junior high point guard, and right away in practice the coach recognized the kid's ability to see everything that was unfolding around him.

"Aaron could stand in the pocket and throw the football," Holder said. "I told him, 'If you throw interceptions or incomplete passes, we're not throwing anymore. We'll just run the football.' That was my threat I put over him."

Ed remembered that his son needed a few weeks to supplant the Jaguars' incumbent, and then immediately lit up the opposition. Holder recalled that Aaron ascended to first string sooner than that, in part because he could compensate for the offensive line's deficiencies.

"He had to run for his life sometimes, but he could run," Holder said. "He got away from people."

As much as he hated shotgun formation, and the increased possibilities of a bad snap and a live ball on the ground, Holder sometimes put Aaron in the shotgun to buy him extra time against the pass rush. Though the kid did not yell at receivers back then, he did give them stern warnings.

"You'd better catch it," Aaron told them, "or I won't be able to throw passes anymore."

To ensure that Aaron wasn't seeing something defensively that wasn't there, Holder had one of his assistants install a radio device in Aaron's helmet so the staff could relay calls to him. Aaron described the device as "rinky-dink" and said it was "taped on my neck, in my ear." Despite that supplemental mode of communication, Aaron threw too many passes to kids wearing the colors of the opposition. "I think we lost 30–0 and I threw four picks," the quarterback recalled.

And that was OK. This was Aaron Rodgers's first year as a football player, after all, his first year as a quarterback. All that mattered was that he avoided the hits his father was concerned about and gleaned something useful from the failure.

He took away the realization that he could never again be so careless with the football if he wanted to keep throwing it.

3
PLEASANT VALLEY

As a teenager, Ron Souza was a four-sport athlete who was a good enough baseball player to become a sixth-round draft pick of the New York Mets. As a veteran high school coach nearly two decades later, he knew what a prospect looked like.

And Aaron Rodgers, freshman, did not look anything like a prospect.

"He was a tiny little puke," Souza said.

Upon arrival at Pleasant Valley High, Rodgers was five foot four in thick-soled shoes and maybe 110 pounds. He was a sleepy-eyed kid who had nothing to him, other than his considerable ears, his enormous hands, and his outsized feet.

One Pleasant Valley coach and faculty member, Tony Tallerico, thought Aaron's big head made him look like a bobblehead doll. One of PV's freshman receivers, Zack Steel, thought Rodgers looked like a puppy dog. "Sometimes he had to jump over the linemen to pass," Steel recalled.

Worse yet, Aaron's eighth-grade mobility did not seem to carry over to the ninth grade. Kyle Lewis, a five-nine, 145-pound defensive end and weakside linebacker, never had trouble tracking down his much smaller teammate when the first-string offense matched up with the first-string defense in practice. "He was so slow," Lewis said.

But what young Rodgers lacked in physical stature and foot speed, he made up for with luck.

Another quarterback his age from Chico, Marc Guillon, had moved out of town to play at a more competitive high school level in the Bay Area. Guillon was a bigger kid who looked the part of a starting quarterback.

He was everything that Rodgers was not, and he ended up landing his first major-college scholarship offer before he even played varsity ball.

Guillon's move presented an opportunity for Rodgers, though he needed to fend off a challenge from another big, strapping kid, Glen Wood, a rising pitcher in Souza's baseball program. Wood was a sophomore, and Rodgers a freshman, when he decided to give football a shot.

One day they were taking turns running plays under the nose of Souza, the junior varsity's offensive coordinator. Wood and Souza were standing in the backfield, reading the linebackers, when the freshman walked to the line of scrimmage with his brand-new white cleats.

"And the first two snaps Aaron took, he came out from underneath the center and tripped over his big feet and went down twice in a row," Wood recalled. "I looked over at Ron like, 'What the heck is going on here?'"

As the freshman pulled himself from the grass, Wood surveyed him from head to toe. This felt like a moment for the kid quarterback. The older boys wondered if he even belonged out there.

Undeterred, Rodgers brushed himself off and got right back in the huddle, and then right back under center. He took the snap cleanly, kept his feet while dropping back, and let it rip.

"Once he finally got the ball off," Wood said, "I mean, I'd never heard a ball like that. You could hear the ball come off his fingers. He threw such a great ball and a great spiral. I looked over at Ron again like, 'OK, now I see it.' And Ron looked at me over his glasses, with his eyebrows up, and points to him and says, 'He is going to be very good.'"

Wood decided to stick with baseball, and Rodgers decided he was never giving up the starting job in his quest to become the Vikings' varsity quarterback. His first PV head coach was Ric Pitsker, a former Marine who volunteered for a tour in Vietnam and who carried his military ethos to the football field. He stood six foot two, with a blacksmith's shoulders, and he demanded that his young men play a disciplined brand of ball at all times.

"If you don't follow the rules," Pitsker told them, "you're gone."

Coach Pit had a soft spot for respectful, goal-oriented kids who had the requisite work ethic to achieve. Kids like Aaron Rodgers. The local junior college coach at Butte jokingly called Pitsker "the cockroach" because he always went into hiding when the lights came on and pushed his players forward.

Pitsker gave Aaron the ball and control of the team. In his first official

PV game, as a freshman wearing jersey No. 5, Rodgers completed 6 of 9 attempts for 65 yards in a 6–0 victory over Oroville. He helped beat Anderson in his second game by completing 5 of 7 attempts for 75 yards before spraining his ankle early in the second half. Rodgers recovered in time the following week to throw his first Pleasant Valley touchdown, a 12-yarder to Peter Grap in a victory over Enterprise.

In Week 4, Rodgers threw a 20-yard scoring pass to Zack Steel and completed 12 of 20 attempts for 150 yards in a loss to Corning. In Week 7, Rodgers threw for 2 touchdowns, including a 50-yarder to David Jackson, in a victory over Paradise.

He was something to see in his white helmet, dark blue jersey, white pants, and floppy white shoes. Under center, barking out signals, Rodgers was just as assertive as the grown-up Viking mascot with the cape, bushy beard, and a gold helmet with horns who stood on the bench and blew his makeshift Gjallarhorn.

Rodgers had gained confidence by throwing after school with a PV junior named Dan Mehan, who took the freshman under his wing. Michael Huyck, Aaron's geometry teacher, watched the end result from the stands. Huyck had a brother and cousin who had played football with Aaron's father, Ed, at Lompoc High, but that wasn't the reason he attended the games.

Aaron's talent put him in those seats. A former high school player himself, Huyck made a habit of staying clear of freshman football. "It tends to be run, run, run," he explained. "Freshman football is usually 32 Dive, 32 Dive, 36 Dive."

But with Rodgers at quarterback, the Vikings did not need to be so one-dimensional. Aaron's passing, Huyck said, "was incredibly accurate for a freshman. And if the opposing team was up playing the run, he'd eat them alive."

The one game the Vikings couldn't lose was the meeting with their rival, Chico High. Pleasant Valley–Chico was the town's answer to Army-Navy and Michigan–Ohio State, and the schools' annual clash was called the Almond Bowl, in a nod to Chico's top crop. At the freshman level, the game was known as the Peanut Bowl, and PV won it, 6–0, on the strength of its defense and its tailback, Jackson, who covered for the quarterback's rare bad day—Rodgers was intercepted three times.

The Vikings were blown out by Shasta High and finished the season with a 5-4 record, but they walked away with the belief that they had found a difference maker in the program. The PV coaches were not terribly concerned about Aaron's size, not after they surveyed the size of his parents and his older brother, Luke.

With a relatively successful football season behind him, Aaron made a seamless transition to the basketball court, where he could already palm a ball. His freshman coach, John Shepherd, first saw Rodgers in a summer camp dribbling with his head up the entire time. He recalled that Rodgers's poise at the point calmed down all of his nervous teammates.

"Aaron would wait for kids to get in the right spot to get them the ball," Shepherd said. "At five-four with size-thirteen feet he wasn't going to outrun anybody, but he outthought everybody all the time."

Rodgers helped lead the Vikings to a league championship, but it was how he carried himself away from the gym that most impressed Shepherd, a future Pleasant Valley principal. "Aaron is someone who gets the disenfranchised kids, the people who are not athletes and who haven't been to football games," Shepherd said.

"Aaron met people where their feet were. He took them for who they were, not for what they were perceived to be. If you've got a graduating class at PV of five hundred students, with two hundred and fifty boys, I'd say one or two of those kids can connect with all groups. Aaron was one of those one or two."

Though he played the most coveted position in American high school sports—quarterback—Aaron did not think he was cool enough to be a certified member of PV's popular kids, nor did he think he was nerdy enough to be a certified nerd. He was a boy without a clique, a unifier without a self-serving cause.

"Aaron was smack-dab in the middle," said classmate Thomas Wilson. "He was kind of a dork, but in a very good way. He wasn't trying to fit in, but he fit in fine."

Rodgers was hardly the only student in the class of 2002 who matched that description. Offensive tackle Tim Bushard said many of the PV football players their age were "a little more brainy and the quote-unquote good kids," while the class one year ahead of them was more interested in having fun.

And having fun at Rodgers's expense. Some players in the class of 2001 took to calling the younger quarterback "Martha"—the name of the boy character (Matthew) in the Rodney Dangerfield film *Ladybugs* who secretly dressed up as a girl (Martha) to help Dangerfield's struggling girls soccer team win the league title.

Louis Yiskis, one of the players who delighted in calling Rodgers "Martha," said the quarterback laughed about it and took it in stride. A part-time center, Yiskis recalled that Aaron was "athletic but goofy" and that "if you saw him, you wouldn't think he played football."

Classmates and teammates called Rodgers by the nickname "Feet." Huyck, the freshman geometry teacher, once asked that Rodgers "move his water skis out of the aisle so I don't step on them." They had some fun with it, teacher and student, because they bonded over the way Aaron applied himself in class.

"I'm not sure I taught him anything," Huyck said. "He could teach himself as well as I could teach him. Geometry isn't an easy class; it was certainly easy for him."

Rodgers was a distinguished student who had received only one final grade lower than an A from first through tenth grade. The PV teachers generally adored him, and for good reason. One day his Spanish teacher, Janet Topete-Tallerico, was feeling ill in class and suddenly found herself struggling to speak. Topete-Tallerico, who had been on medication, recalled that Aaron rose from his seat, approached her, and gently took the teacher's lesson book from her hands.

"He sat down right next to her, and the kids thought they had set it up as a teaching thing for the day," said Janet's husband Tony.

"They took me to the nurse," Topete-Tallerico recalled, "and Aaron continued on with the lesson. He was a shy kid, not the kind of kid to do that at all. The next day he told me he had continued on after I left, and that was the coolest thing. . . . Teenagers don't do that."

After his freshman year, Aaron dropped basketball to focus solely on football. Tom Melton, an economics and U.S. history teacher who had a classroom next to the PV practice field, saw Rodgers out there nearly every day in the offseason working out with his receivers.

"He was the most diligent athlete I saw in the football program come through the school," Melton said.

Rodgers played another year under Pitsker as a sophomore starter on the junior varsity team, with Ron Souza as his offensive coordinator. Aaron called Souza a genius. He was a creative mind who challenged Rodgers about ball security and, like Curtis Holder before him, warned the quarterback that if he turned the ball over, he would be sitting on the pine.

Aaron emerged in his second year as something of a dominant force. He was a little bigger as a sophomore, and a lot stronger with his delivery. "I was pass blocking one day as a tight end on the JV," said Casey Helmick, "and a rocket blew past us. It was like, 'Who threw that?' I looked behind me and it was Aaron."

Rodgers powered the Pleasant Valley junior varsity to a perfect season in 1999, ten opponents up and ten opponents put down. Early that year, Aaron delivered a monster game against Enterprise, throwing for 221 yards and 2 touchdowns, including the winning fourth-quarter post pass to close friend Ryan Gulbrandsen, his Ping-Pong, poker, and film partner who made a pact with the quarterback to spend their high school years as serious ballers who stayed clear of the party scene.

By the time Rodgers was throwing two more touchdown passes to beat Red Bluff in a one-point game, Souza was giving his quarterback the freedom to call the game the way he saw it, giving him a package of options to choose from on the fly.

Rodgers hooked up with Gulbrandsen for a 30-yard touchdown in a victory over Paradise, then led Pleasant Valley into its rivalry game with the Chico Panthers. In the middle of the fourth quarter, the Vikings were down 18–13 before an engaged crowd at Chico State's University Stadium, a big-time setting for a JV game.

The ball was spotted on their own 10-yard line. "We have done this before," Rodgers told his teammates in the huddle. "We have to go ninety yards.... We're going to go all the way down and score a touchdown."

Helmick was struck by Rodgers's calm and confident tone despite the fact that he had completed only one throw all evening before that drive—a 31-yard scoring pass to Gulbrandsen. Sure enough, Aaron drove his team down the field, completing a series of midrange passes, including one on fourth-and-11 from the Chico 22 that was good enough for a first down. With 1:36 to play, the Vikings finally broke the Panthers' defense and scored the winning touchdown.

Of course, the Vikings were helped by the fact that they had twelve men on the field. From the sideline, with no time-outs to burn, a horrified Souza realized that his two-receiver, two-tight end, one-back set had somehow become a two-receiver, two-tight end, two-back set, and he gestured in a minipanic toward his quarterback.

"And Aaron calmly looked back at me," Souza said, "and put his hand up as if to say, 'I got this.' . . . We punch it in, and we're trying to get the PAT done as fast as we can while Aaron is running off the field. In the commotion of our kids jumping up and down, Aaron ran off so the refs could not count and see that we had twelve men out there.

"That's how smart he was. He's a JV player and he knows we've got twelve men on the field and no time-outs and still figures it out. That was a college move. Some guys in the NFL probably can't do that."

The Chico coach, Curtis Colwes, saw the infraction on the film afterward and was swearing years later to his friend Souza that PV intentionally cheated. Souza tried to convince Colwes that it was accidental, at least up until Rodgers realized that, in his coach's words, PV "had more hamburgers than they had buns," and then did what he had to do to win.

The following week, Rodgers made a more profound statement on the road by beating Grant Union of Sacramento, 9–6, on his touchdown pass to Travis Ortiz. (The PV varsity lost to Grant, 51–0.) It meant something for a Butte County school that attracted no major-college recruiters to travel south to the state capital to beat a public-school team that produced Division I prospects.

"That's where I started thinking Aaron had a chance to do something beyond high school," said his father, Ed.

Aaron had complete command of Souza's complex playbook, and his ability to survey and solve a defensive scheme at the line separated him from the vast majority of high school quarterbacks. Aaron already understood triangle reads and the tenets of the West Coast offense. Souza said Rodgers was also watching how defenses played the 49ers, how they disguised blitzes and coverages, and then applying those lessons at PV.

Aaron's immediate football future looked especially bright, in part because the varsity had just endured a 1-9 season and was banking on the JV powerhouse to restock and rejuvenate the team. Meanwhile, Aaron turned sixteen that December. After growing up in the Neighborhood Church with his family, he was feeling a pull away from his religious beliefs and the church's stated core purpose, which was to "experience and share the life to the fullest that Jesus came to give us."

Aaron had described his faith-based upbringing in a home built around a trust in God as the most important aspect of his childhood. He said the family leaned on God during difficult financial times "for resources and guidance on where to live, where to go to school, and how to get through those times."

But Aaron made it clear he was seeking a personal relationship with God, not one experienced exclusively through his parents' faith. He did not connect with the Neighborhood Church the way he connected with the Christian ministry group known as Young Life. Aaron loved Young Life, he said, "because for the first time I saw how much fun Christians could have. I went from going to church on Sundays, knowing how important that was to my parents, to a desire to grow deeper in the Lord."

Aaron called Matt Hock, the area director of Young Life, "the coolest Christian I know" and said he appreciated the fact that the group's organizers and members did not care about "what you look like or wear, or if you're in the cool group. It's just, 'We want you to come and have a good time.' And the Gospel was presented in a way that's not over your head, with analogies and demonstrations that make you think, 'Jesus is someone I could really hang out with.'"

Aaron savored the two trips he made to Mexico with fellow Young Life members during his sophomore and junior spring break weeks to build homes for the underprivileged. On one of the trips Aaron and his girlfriend Micala Drews, a PV volleyball star, joined other students in a white passenger van driven by Hock for a journey to the Rosarito area that felt like it lasted twenty hours.

Aaron had bought a Conway Twitty cassette tape at a travel center and then played it nonstop across the border into Mexico. Many years later, Drews said she was still haunted by the Twitty song with Loretta Lynn that seemed to be on a continuous loop, "Louisiana Woman, Mississippi Man." Aaron called the Mexico experience one of the greatest of his life.

The following summer, Rodgers passed on a chance to spend a week at Young Life's Malibu Club camp about a hundred miles north of Vancouver, British Columbia. He wanted to go, badly, at least until his Pleasant Valley coach told him he could not afford to miss the practice time if he planned on entering training camp as the No. 1 varsity quarterback.

Rodgers had a choice, football or faith, and he did not hesitate. He buckled up his chinstrap and headed for the field.

• • •

IN EARLY JANUARY 2000, after his sophomore season, Aaron Rodgers was playing pickup basketball at Neal Dow Elementary School when he chased down a bad pass on the fast break. He turned, planted, and passed the ball back toward the rim.

He should have just let the damn thing bounce out of bounds.

Rodgers felt pain in his left knee. He saw a doctor, and the diagnosis was grim. Torn ACL. It was not a complete tear, but the damage was significant enough for one doctor to advise him to give up football, which, of course, was not happening.

If Rodgers's football journey would be shaped by defiance, this would be his first defiant act. "I think it was the beginning of people telling me I couldn't do stuff," he said. "I said, 'All right, we'll see about that.'"

Aaron avoided major surgery by strengthening his leg through weight training, working his hamstring, quad muscles, and calf. He agreed to have arthroscopic surgery in the spring to stabilize the ACL (but not fully repair it) and fix cartilage damage, and then took the field with a brace on the knee. Rodgers was not eager to share the news of his injury. He did not want to put any unnecessary hurdles on his dream path to a major-college scholarship.

At the start of PV football season that fall, Mike Vought was teaching his advanced placement U.S. history class when a girl sitting in the back of the room blurted out, "Mr. Vought, our football team is going to stink this year."

Taken aback, the teacher simply responded, "Why?"

The girl, Melissa Sinclair, pointed to the boy sitting next to her, Aaron Rodgers. "Because he's our quarterback," she said.

Vought recalled laughing along with Melissa and the rest of the students. "I remember Aaron was even smiling his way through that," the teacher said. "He wasn't offended in the least. He dealt with it by having a good sense of humor, which is pretty representative of how I remember him."

Of course, anyone familiar with Aaron's raging competitive fire might have guessed that he could never forget who made that comment, or when it was made, or how it felt inside when he heard it made.

But even Aaron could not hold a serious grudge against a kindred spirit such as Melissa Sinclair, who was also caught somewhere between the cool kids and the nerds. She thought Aaron did not give himself enough credit at PV, that he was clearly one of the cool kids, but that was what she liked about him.

"He was always very kind, and that unfortunately isn't always the case in high school," Melissa said. "He had a beautiful humility about him."

She also thought Aaron was wickedly witty and quite smart and, well, worthy of an invitation to a Sadie Hawkins dance. Melissa asked him right in front of his football teammates, while offering up a huge Mrs. Fields cookie as an inducement, and Aaron, in her words, "was too kind to turn me down."

The dance was held at a skating rink under the rules of TWIRP—The Woman Is Required to Pay. Aaron was voted TWIRP's king, the dance's version of a homecoming king.

He showed up wearing a dark long-sleeved shirt and tie, a boutonniere, suspenders, and a Marine buzz cut, while Melissa arrived wearing a stunning red dress and white corsage. They posed for a picture against a backdrop image of the Eiffel Tower above the caption "Nuit D'Amour." Night of love.

"I got to be on his arm as his date," Melissa said. "That was the most exciting thing."

But there was something about that picture, with her right hand on his left shoulder and his right hand around her waist, that still struck Melissa Sinclair many years later.

"We were shockingly almost the same size," she said. "I was five-seven, one hundred pounds soaking wet, and Aaron was not standing much taller than that."

He was the first-string varsity quarterback regardless, even though he did not carry himself that way. (How many starting varsity quarterbacks in America would list *The Princess Bride* as their favorite all-time movie?) Mike Vought saw Rodgers as an agreeable kid who interacted particularly well with adults. He found it refreshing that a student—and an accomplished athlete to boot—could spend as much time as Aaron did asking about others rather than talking about himself.

"His confidence was a quiet confidence," said Vought, who was PV's boys soccer coach. "He was never the type to say, 'Hey, come out to the game, we're playing this team.' It never felt like it was about him. He fit in super easily because he just had that big smile, and that's an icebreaker that can really take you places. Aaron belonged to a lot of different tribes."

Rodgers had been a strong student for basically his entire schooling life, and he would score 1310 on his SATs. As much as he appreciated Aaron's strengths, Vought did not see that level of aptitude in his classroom.

"Let's say the time and the effort he might've put into academics he was putting into athletics," the teacher said. "I remember quite vividly his junior year, at one point going around the room and wandering back to where Aaron's at. He's drawing up football plays. As opposed to being defensive, he does what he always does. He smiles and puts it away and says, 'I'm sorry, I was preoccupied.' I don't think he ever did that to excuse himself from what everybody else needed to do. He did it because, 'I know I'm not supposed to do it, but this is what I love to do.'"

Unbeaten on the field as a sophomore, and packing a 2-0 career record against Chico High, Rodgers was no longer playing for Ric Pitsker and Ron Souza, though Souza kept a reduced varsity role as what he called a distant assistant. Rodgers was now playing for Sterling Jackson, a former Chico State running back in his early thirties who grew up twenty miles east of Los Angeles.

Jackson had the look of a former Division II tailback. He was a short, powerfully built man who embraced a direct and intense style of leadership. Including playoff games, Jackson calculated that he was making about ten cents an hour to coach the Pleasant Valley Vikings. At that rate you'd better bring passion to the office every day.

Jackson was a rare figure at Pleasant Valley—a Black leader in a white community where only 2 percent of the population was African American. "I was the first African American head coach at PV in any sport," Jackson said. "I was the head girls soccer coach, the head track coach, and the head football coach. At one time I was head coach in all three."

He had planned to get his degree from Chico State and then to immediately head back to Southern California. But he never left Chico. Jackson said the community and the school had been fair to him and neighborly to his family. He was hoping to open a pipeline of Black head coaches at PV.

The job of fielding a sectional championship contender there was not an easy one, even if PV had made it look easy by reaching six sectional finals in the seven years preceding its disastrous '99 season. The former Pleasant Valley coach, Jim Barrett, had told Jackson that the PV kids who played varsity football were generally five foot ten or five foot eleven, 165 to 175 pounds.

"People would come in and walk the campus and say, 'Where are your football players?'" Jackson said. "You can't just walk on campus and say, 'There's an athlete. There's an athlete. There's an athlete.' You've got to make them here."

Jackson agreed that a principal part of his job was to toughen up the suburban kids. Of course, a great quarterback can compensate for almost any weakness.

In the season opener, Aaron Rodgers threw for 3 touchdowns in a 33–14 defeat of Oroville under the Friday night lights at PV's Asgard Yard field, inspiring Luke Reid of the *Chico Enterprise-Record* to write that the quarterback "showed uncommon poise, accuracy, and awareness" in his first career start.

Rodgers passed for 2 more touchdowns, including an 87-yarder to Ben Olberg on the first play of the second half, in the Vikings' 1-point victory over Anderson, before falling to Enterprise (on a failed Rodgers fourth-and-goal sneak from the 1-yard line) and then to unbeaten Corning, which intercepted Aaron twice and returned one of the picks for a score.

After starting out 2-2, Pleasant Valley suddenly became a different team. The Vikings would not lose another regular-season game, in large part because their quarterback came of age.

"Rodgers Passes PV Past LP," read the *Enterprise-Record* headline after he lit up Las Plumas for 171 first-half yards, 3 touchdowns, and 42 points, to launch a seven-game winning streak.

Rodgers had to leave a homecoming victory over Shasta early after getting poked in the eye—classmates mocked him over his bloodshot eye that Monday, because of course they did—but returned for the second half. Three weeks later, Rodgers shredded Red Bluff with 251 passing yards to improve PV's record to 7-2 and 4-0 in the Eastern Athletic League, then credited Sterling Jackson's game plan, the receivers, the offensive line, and the defense—everyone except himself.

"It means a lot to the seniors who won just one game last year," he said. Aaron was even looking out for the guys who called him "Martha."

One of those guys, Louis Yiskis, cited the quarterback's knowledge of every position's responsibility on each play and praised his arm strength and accuracy.

"His long ball was something of beauty," Yiskis said. "It was just perfect every time."

Truth was, Rodgers wanted to throw the ball more. Jackson had believed in Aaron from the first day he saw him in a skills camp as a freshman, showing off his advanced mechanics.

But Jackson was a former running back who wanted to pound the rock, and he admitted that he preferred his team to run the ball 65 percent of the time and throw it 35 percent of the time. That was why his featured back, Matt Shelton, was given 32 carries against Corning, 30 carries against Shasta, and a whopping 40 carries (for 255 yards) against Paradise.

Sometimes Aaron returned home after practice and complained to his father that he only threw the ball about a dozen times that day. Other days he showed his frustration with teammates who might not have shared his advanced knowledge of football by throwing up his hands in disgust or by barking over a missed assignment or an imprecise route.

One player who was called up to the varsity as a sophomore—electric running back Keola Pang—felt the full force of the quarterback's exasperation. "They moved me out to the slot to get me outside, and Aaron had zero patience with me learning a new position," Pang said.

"We're young, I just got moved up, and I've already got this dude yelling at me, 'You've got to cut your break at 3.5 or 4 yards. You can't run a slant like that. You can't round off your break.' He had that mentality.... I told him, 'You'd better work on that if you want to be a coach someday.' The players are going to be like, 'Fuck this guy.'"

Though Rodgers did address his frustrations with teammates in private conversations with Souza, the coach who had developed the closest relationship with him, he did not bring his grievances to his head coach's desk.

"Aaron was very team oriented and really got along with everybody," Jackson said. "He wasn't a prima donna at all. He never said, 'I need to do this, or I need to do that, to go on and play at the next level.' He definitely understood what we were trying to accomplish."

Success at Pleasant Valley meant beating Chico High, the rival school found three miles away. Chico High sits on the Esplanade, the city's main north–south thoroughfare, defined by its well-appointed homes hidden by the tall, majestic trees planted to provide sanctuary from the heat.

City residents could choose their preferred public school, but Pleasant Valley attracted more students who pulled up to the building in luxury cars. One PV coach likened the school to a country club.

"There was a stereotype that we were the rich white kids," said Pleasant Valley tight end Casey Helmick.

Chico High was winless entering the thirtieth edition of the Almond Bowl, but then again, so was the previous year's PV team before it beat the Panthers. Nothing was guaranteed in this matchup, other than the loser's lasting pain.

Into this cauldron stepped Aaron Rodgers, No. 12 in the Pleasant Valley program. And on a memorable Friday night, the quarterback wearing the school's signature Vikings horns on each side of his white helmet beat Chico like no PV quarterback ever had.

"Historic Roasting in Almond Bowl" announced the front-page *Enterprise-Record* headline. The Vikings won Almond Bowl XXX by a 43–7 count, the largest margin of victory in the event's history, to move to 8-2 overall and to win the Eastern Athletic League with a 5-0 record.

With his extended family in the stands, Rodgers threw the long ball and went 11 for 15 for 235 yards and 2 touchdowns. "We knew we could exploit them on the corners," he said afterward. One writer on the scene, Greg Ball of the *Enterprise-Record*, noted that the Vikings "seemed shockingly reluctant to feature their standout quarterback and core of receivers."

In other words, Rodgers could have dropped 55–60 points on Chico if he had been completely cut loose. The extra touchdowns weren't necessary, nor would they have reflected the true spirit of the rivalry. Either way, this was a night for the Vikings' quarterback to hold on to, a truth that became painfully clear after Rodgers and PV blew out Red Bluff in the sectional playoff opener, only to fall to Enterprise, 40–21, in the semis.

Aaron had protected the ball all year before getting picked off four times against Enterprise. He finished the year with 2,101 passing yards and 15 touchdowns, good enough to be named second team all-section. It was a hell of a year for a first-time varsity starter.

And yet in the locker room afterward, star receiver Charles Coleman, a senior, approached his quarterback to remind him that he still had one more year to win a sectional crown.

"Aaron was not content. He was pissed," Coleman recalled. "He said, 'I wanted to win it this year.' He was a little different, and that's when I knew he would come back his senior year as a different player."

• • •

AS A BASKETBALL enthusiast, Aaron Rodgers's girlfriend, Micala Drews, grew up doing Pete Maravich drills to work on her ballhandling. She had watched the movie *The Pistol: The Birth of a Legend*, and later decided that the film provided a window on Aaron's youth.

"A funny yet slightly awkward kid," she said. "However, he was a natural-born leader, but not so much in words as he led by action and humble confidence."

Micala saw similarities in how Press Maravich raised his boy Pete to become a devastating scoring machine and in how Ed Rodgers was so invested in his son's development. Aaron loved it when his old man kept a running account of his passing numbers while sitting in the crowd.

"Aaron and his dad had such a close relationship," Micala said, "and Aaron had that with his brothers and mom as well. But Ed took so much time, and on any Friday night Ed would be in the stands taking copious stats for Aaron. [Pete Maravich] . . . just outworked everybody, and Aaron was similar. He's not exceptionally tall or muscular, but he worked really hard."

During Aaron's senior year of high school, he shared an early morning sports conditioning and weightlifting session with Drews. She was the only girl in that 6:45 a.m. group, overseen by Sterling Jackson, and she remembered Aaron as the only boy who showed up before the session had even started to do footwork drills with a speed ladder.

Micala recalled Aaron as a playful soul who got down on his knees to let her nine-year-old brother Chase tackle him in games of living-room football. She also recalled him as a competitor far more interested in improving on the field than he was in celebrating any touchdown pass he threw.

Aaron and his brothers had heard from their father that they shouldn't waste their talents and opportunities by drinking or smoking pot with their friends. Ed Rodgers did not go to a single party while a student at Lompoc High School. He couldn't say the same about his time at Chico State.

"We used to go on campouts with the boys and I was always straight with my kids," Ed said. "It was like, 'You know what, I did this. I experimented with this. I wished I wouldn't have. . . . Keep your nose clean and it will pay off for you.'"

Aaron listened to his father. That was why Micala rode along to games with Ed and Darla Rodgers having no expectation of hanging out with their son afterward. "When most guys were going out to have fun with friends, Aaron went home and watched the VHS of the game he had just played with his father," she said. "He took notes on himself, he criticized himself, and he looked at his strong points and his weak points. He was a student of the game even then. That's what his Friday night was like after the Friday night lights went out."

Before his final high school season, Rodgers did what he could to make his physical stature appealing to college coaches. He had grown to about six feet, 180 pounds. He finally looked more like a young man and less like a boy.

Rodgers helped himself as a senior by working with strength and conditioning coach Steve Henderson, displaying the passion he did not show the year before.

"I said to my assistant, 'You take that Rodgers kid. He's not going to go anywhere. He's goofing around,'" Henderson said, referring to Aaron's junior year. "If you weren't trying to get Aaron through a workout, you would just stand back and giggle at him. I got a little frustrated at times.

"But Aaron flipped the switch as a senior. His personality was the same, but he was on task a lot better . . . He wanted to play college football, and he needed to get stronger, faster, and more powerful. At that age, my philosophy was to make him as athletic as we possibly could, and along the way develop hip and leg power."

Rodgers saw Henderson two or three times a week for workouts ranging from an hour to ninety minutes, and his enhanced athleticism showed at PV in his pocket movements, on his designed rollouts and bootlegs, and on his unscripted scrambles. Aaron had sculpted calf muscles, and Ed and Darla agreed that his leg strength and mobility came from his mother, the former dance team member who could dust her husband on cycling trips in the hills.

"Whenever he got away from somebody and threw downfield, he loved calling people out at practice," said PV's kicker, Garth Archibald. "He ran a 4.7 forty and was elated. He wrote it on the board and circled it."

Archibald and Rodgers turned everything into a one-on-one competition, the kicker said, even comparing the number of college recruiting letters each received on a particular day.

"One day I'd have a couple more than him," Archibald said. "Some were handwritten from lower-division schools, but we still appreciated them because any recruitment was great."

Especially when there was no recruitment from Division I schools, and when one of the Division III schools interested in Rodgers, Occidental, planned for him to sit out his first year. Rodgers wanted to play for Florida State icon Bobby Bowden, but Bowden did not want Rodgers to play for him. Aaron had tapes and letters sent to the likes of Purdue, Colorado State, and Illinois. Purdue sent Rodgers his first official rejection letter and told him, "Good luck with your attempt at a college football career." San Diego State showed a little interest until it fired head coach Ted Tollner.

The first ominous recruiting sign came over the summer, at a football camp at the University of Illinois. Sterling Jackson had hired the nephew of Illinois head coach Ron Turner, Ron O'Dell, to serve as quarterbacks coach for his senior season, and so Rodgers joined a group of teammates that included Archibald, Nick Rosemann, Derek Lawrence, and Keola Pang on a trip to Champaign, where Aaron was, by all accounts, the best quarterback in camp.

And yet Illinois offered a scholarship to another quarterback. Jackson said that Rodgers was "head and shoulders above the competition" in the camp, which included Illinois recruits and other prospects who were traveling the Big Ten summer circuit. The PV coach said he took his case to Turner, who told him that California players don't often thrive in the Champaign weather.

"This is going to be a big mistake," Jackson responded.

Aaron Rodgers was proving to be a tough sell. One day his father, Ed, happened to be sitting on a plane next to an Arizona State assistant who recruited California and tried to persuade the man to make an unscheduled stop in Chico to scout his son. The assistant never showed up at PV.

Aaron simply was not a known and trusted commodity, in part because of his size, in part because of Pleasant Valley's location and lack of high-level competition, and in part because his coaches didn't have the networking connections that others had in the Bay Area and in Southern California. When Aaron checked Rivals.com or other sites on the PV library computer, looking for his name among the nation's top prospects, it was nowhere to be found.

He thought to himself, *It doesn't matter, because those guys are out there, and they think they got it made. . . . I'm going to wake up every morning before school and work out. I'm going to stay after school and work out. I'm going to throw three times a week with my buddies and when those guys are enjoying the top of the list, I'm going to be out there outworking them and know at some point it's going to catch up.*

At the same time, Ed Rodgers was wondering if the Vikings' relatively conservative offense had worked against his son. "If we'd have thrown thirty to forty times a game, we would've killed everybody in this area," he said.

Entering the season, Jackson had entrusted Aaron to pick a check-with-me call at the line of scrimmage from a package of two, three, or four options. Rodgers identified vulnerabilities in a defense like few teenagers could, and his accuracy stunned even those who witnessed it every day in practice.

"He didn't need arm strength because he could put it right over your shoulder," tight end Derek Lawrence said. "It was easy, effortless. I never had to sell out for a ball when I was open. He just floated the ball where it was supposed to be."

The season played out as expected, with Rodgers performing at a higher level than his team did, keeping the flawed Vikings in playoff contention. They won six of their first eight games before suffering a stunning shutout loss to Red Bluff. Then Rodgers beat Chico High for a fourth straight year with a touchdown run and a 75-yard scoring pass to Thomas Wilson, clinching the sixth and final postseason seed.

Now he wanted that sectional title as his PV exclamation point. Every teenage boy who strapped on the pads held firmly to that hope—a victory in that last prep game, a championship trophy, maybe even a celebratory kiss with the prettiest girl in school.

In the first round of the playoffs, Rodgers set a new single-season school record for passing yards by finishing the ten-point victory over Red Bluff with 2,252, avenging the shutout loss to the Spartans during the regular season. He was awarded the game ball and another shot at the opponent who had eliminated the Vikings in 2000.

PV had beaten Enterprise in September. Rodgers was at his best against the Hornets, throwing for 298 yards and hitting Wilson for 3 touchdowns in a 37–32 shootout victory.

"They're an explosive team," Enterprise coach Clay Erro said before the sectional semifinal rematch. Recent rain had left the Enterprise field a muddy mess and dramatically reduced the chances of Pleasant Valley scoring another 37 points on the Hornets, who, in fairness, were the more physical and opportunistic team.

As it turned out, Rodgers was dreadful in what would be his farewell Pleasant Valley game. He completed only 4 of 18 passes for 66 yards and failed on two quarterback sneaks near the goal line. He was also intercepted twice by the opposing coach's son, Ryan Erro, who made his father proud.

"He had two picks against the best tonight," Clay Erro said.

The best. Aaron Rodgers. A high school star who went out on a 17–7 loss in a mud pit.

"The conditions were tough," Rodgers said, "but that was no excuse."

Keola Pang, who had been limited to 54 yards after thrashing Enterprise in September for 136, recalled that after the game the Vikings were "all huddled around and pretty much on a knee, and just sobbing, but also just telling everyone how much we meant to each other."

Derek Lawrence recalled feeling that Enterprise hit harder than other opponents, and that he got very emotional in the last two minutes when it was clear Pleasant Valley was done. Tackle Tim Bushard remembered the seniors sharing in a somber moment, "knowing that for ninety-nine percent of us, that was the last game we were ever going to play."

As a first-team all-section choice who set school records while playing through a torn ACL, Aaron Rodgers was one Viking who still had some football left in him—perhaps.

That summer, while Aaron was hanging out at Micala Drews's house for a postgraduation swim, Micala decided the time was right to quiz the boy she called "Airs" about his future plans.

"So, Airs, what are you going to do when you grow up?" she asked as they sat next to the pool.

Without a second of hesitation, and with that quiet inner confidence that Micala always admired, Aaron answered in a serious tone that belied his smile.

"I'm going to play in the NFL," he said.

She could tell Aaron was not joking.

"You have a great name for it," Micala replied. "Someday people will refer to your home stadium as 'Mister Rodgers' Neighborhood.'"

4
RIGSBEE

Opening day of preseason football at a junior college can be a madhouse, and that is how JJ Stallings remembered it in the summer of 2002. The Butte College Roadrunners had gathered in the gym for the first time, and players were filing in from every conceivable walk of life.

Stallings, the team's top cover man, recalled that the cornerbacks and safeties had just completed their drills and were manning a section of the bleachers with their fellow defensive players when a stranger wandered over from the offensive side of the gym.

"Who is JJ Stallings?" the stranger asked as he eyed the group.

Taken aback by the question and wondering how this freshman knew his name, Stallings, a sophomore, sized him up from head to toe.

"This skinny white kid is coming in," Stallings said, "and I'm looking around and I actually thought he wanted to fight."

Stallings paused for a few seconds before announcing to this skinny white kid, "I'm JJ Stallings," in a tone that screamed, *And who wants to know?*

As it turned out, Aaron Rodgers was the inquiring mind standing before him.

"I just wanted to meet the guy who I'm going to be torching every day in one-on-ones," the quarterback said.

Stallings was shocked by the kid's unmitigated gall. He looked at his brother Roderick, a safety, and thought to himself, *Who the hell is this guy?*

That was what a lot of players at the community college in Oroville, just outside of Chico, were asking about the eighteen-year-old quarterback who looked two or three years younger than that.

Who the hell is this guy? And how the hell did he get here?

As a Pleasant Valley High School senior who had completed his final football season, Rodgers often sat in Ron Souza's office, demoralized over the fact that no big-time college had recruited him. Aaron still had that knee injury that he had never fully fixed. He was thinking about quitting football for good. He was pondering a career in the military, or life as a lawyer, when on one wintertime day Souza asked him to join his baseball team.

Rodgers had not played the game since the eighth grade, but PV's head baseball coach wanted to get his mind off football and off the scholarship that wasn't to be. "If Aaron sat there and dwelled on it," Souza said, "it would have eaten him alive."

So, Rodgers took him up on it and threw with the Vikings' pitchers and catchers on the blacktop, in the soupy fog, with temperatures in the low thirties. His velocity improved by the week. Of greater consequence, Rodgers rediscovered his competitive fire on the mound. During the season he regularly threw his fastball in the high eighties, occasionally topping out in the low nineties.

"He could have eventually been a Division I baseball player and then the Milwaukee Brewers' closer," Souza said.

Rodgers's successful one-and-done season as a high school pitcher did not inspire him to trade his football ambitions for baseball ambitions. Deep down he was a quarterback, a fact that was notarized on an August night at Shasta College, where Rodgers threw for a couple of touchdowns and raced 30 yards for another in a 1-point loss in the Lions Northern California All-Star game.

That game and that run were so meaningful to Rodgers because he was playing without a knee brace for the first time in two years; his leg exercises had stabilized his torn ACL, and he figured the brace might scare off Division I recruiters. Throwing and running and thriving in that game convinced Rodgers that he deserved a higher-profile destination than the local juco that was a fifteen-minute drive from his Chico home.

Butte College was not exactly Aaron's dream school, Florida State, and the man who showed up at his front door was not exactly his dream coach,

Bobby Bowden. But as folksy and neighborly and likable as Bowden could be on recruiting visits, Craig Rigsbee was his equal. He was a grizzly bear of a man with a mop of dark hair atop a big, friendly face, and in a phone call he persuaded Aaron's father, Ed, to grant him the courtesy of an in-person chat.

Rigsbee had just moved into his new home on New Foster Place, the only finished house on the cul-de-sac. He had no idea that the Rodgers family was living right behind him at 1 Alyssum Way.

Out his front door, Rigsbee turned left and walked through a series of empty lots and arrived at Aaron's doorstep a few minutes later. Darla Rodgers answered the knock.

She was not in a welcoming mood. Darla's middle child had a 1310 SAT score.

"No son of mine is going to a junior college," she told Rigsbee.

The juco coach was going to need all of his considerable charm as a recruiter to navigate his way through this visit.

"The guy could sell a ketchup Popsicle to a woman in white gloves," said one of Rigsbee's players, Taylor Catrett.

Rigsbee also had a more open-minded participant in the house in Ed Rodgers. Ed had reminded his wife of the advice given Aaron by one of his personal coaches, former NFL and Canadian Football League quarterback Greg Barton, who told him there was nothing wrong with starting at a junior college if pro ball was the ultimate goal.

Ed took an instant liking to Rigsbee, while Darla was having a tougher time with the pitch. She kept thinking about Aaron's SAT score and his advanced placement classes and his consistently high grades. What was the point of all that study time and hard work if the payoff was a two-year school just down the road?

Rigsbee pressed on. He had wanted Rodgers ever since he saw him at Butte's high school passing league in 2000, making plays all over the field despite that brace on his knee. Rigsbee was impressed by Aaron's accuracy, quick release, and intelligent decisions, so he kept tabs on him.

Now he had to close the deal. Rigsbee told Darla that her son could take virtually the same classes at Butte that he might take at a distinguished four-year school, and that the credits were all transferable. He pointed out that a degree from a major university did not come with an asterisk if the student spent the first two years at a community college.

Aaron was on the couch listening carefully, while his thirteen-year-old brother, Jordan, was bouncing around the room. Maybe if he had gone to the right Nike camp for the necessary exposure, or maybe if his PV coaches knew how to play the Division I recruiting game, Aaron would not have been in this position.

But there he was, locked in on the guest who could talk and talk without ever coming up for air. Rigsbee told Aaron that he would throw the ball at Butte more than he did at Pleasant Valley. He rattled off the players he helped send to major-college programs, and he brought up Larry Allen, the massive offensive guard who had played at Butte and was now in the middle of a Hall of Fame career with the Dallas Cowboys.

A little more than a half hour into his visit, Rigsbee knew he was on a roll. He promised Aaron that he would deliver him to the national stage necessary to get drafted into the pros. As the sit-down morphed into a mutual lovefest, Darla brought out a plate of cookies.

"I'm in," Rigsbee said to himself.

He started talking about his returning quarterbacks and the competition that needed to be conquered when Aaron cut him off.

"I really don't care who you have coming back," he said. "I just need to ask you two questions. Will I be given a legitimate shot to win the starting job? And can I leave early if I have a big year in my first season?"

Rigsbee was jolted by Aaron's abrupt approach. He thought to himself, *Slow down a little bit. You're not even being recruited by anybody and you're already talking about leaving after one year?*

The coach promised the quarterback that he would get a fair crack at being The Guy at Butte. "And if you can go to a great school after one year," Rigsbee told him, "I'll promote the hell out of you."

Aaron was sold, and his parents stood no chance against this force of human nature. Rigsbee wore them all down and made the short walk back to New Foster Place knowing that Aaron was going to be his quarterback.

Even after Rodgers committed to Butte, Rigsbee kept showing up at his Pleasant Valley baseball games. He was afraid to let Aaron out of his sight, afraid to give an opening to other junior college recruiters. He attended enough games, home and away, that people assumed he was the Butte baseball coach.

"You don't have to come to all these games," Aaron told him. "I'm coming to Butte regardless. I guarantee you I'll be there."

Rigsbee let that sweet assurance marinate for a moment before responding, "OK, great. I'll see you at the Enterprise game next week."

Aaron laughed. It felt good to have a college coach believe in him and chase him like this. Now it was time to honor that faith.

Rodgers came into his own athletically that summer. He worked out with fellow incoming freshman Jesse Hejny, a linebacker, at a sports club in Chico. While Hejny was lifting weights, Rodgers was usually found throwing a football or playing hoops.

"He'd walk onto the basketball court, touch his ankles, stand underneath the hoop, and spring up and dunk it with two hands," Hejny said. "He was freaky athletic and super springy. . . . His legs, for a freshman, were pretty developed. From his knees down to his calves he was rocked up."

Upon arrival at Butte, Rodgers was about six foot one, 190 pounds, with a right arm powerful enough to make any throw required of a high-major-college quarterback. His former teammate at Pleasant Valley, Derek Lawrence, recalled that the difference in Aaron's arm strength from his PV days "was night and day. I remember standing in the [Butte] end zone and he was warming up; it was the first time I'd seen him since high school. He tossed me a ball and I was like, 'Jeez.' I didn't show it, but after six or seven passes I was like, 'All right, I've got to leave now and go practice with the receivers.'"

Butte players said that more than 150 hopefuls showed up for the start of camp. One of them, offensive lineman Heath Prichard, grew up in Linden, California, where a man named Wayne Judge coached him in basketball while Judge's young son, Aaron, ran around the athletic complex and softball fields years before he became a record-setting slugger for the New York Yankees.

Prichard walked up to Butte orientation with Aaron Rodgers and got on the end of a long line before Rigsbee grabbed both and moved them to the front. "They told us they were going to keep only eighty players," Prichard said. "But Rigsbee said, 'I never cut anybody.'"

He didn't have to. To hear the Butte players tell it, Rigsbee's camp amounted to a couple of weeks of pure misery, a latter-day version of Bear Bryant's infamous Junction Boys camp at Texas A&M in 1954.

The oppressive heat was a given, with temperatures soaring well above one hundred degrees, turning the players' black jerseys into sauna suits and costing them 5 percent of their body weight. That's preseason football in the summer. Most of the college boys could handle that.

On a 928-acre campus that doubled as an official wildlife refuge, the mosquitoes were a different story. "They were unbearable," said Joaquin Echauri, offensive lineman.

"Those mosquitoes were almost unexplainable, they were so fuckin' bad," said safety Roderick Stallings, among the many Roadrunners who blamed the infestation on a nearby creek.

Some players coated their jerseys in bug spray; others said they held off because pesticides were off-limits in the wildlife refuge. "It was a legit home-field advantage," said offensive tackle Mark Parrish. "You'd see visiting teams on the sidelines, swatting at swarms of mosquitoes that would chase them back to the locker room. With our team, with all the city boys who had never been around deer or snakes, God forbid a snake got on the field, guys would lose their minds screaming."

William Shoulders, running back, said it wasn't a rare occurrence for a deer to stroll into a classroom. This is what Aaron Rodgers had signed up for, paying $11 a unit to share a campus of woodlands, grasslands, and wetlands with coyotes, river otters, bobcats, and the occasional mountain lion. He was a juco kid playing at a school that 99 percent of college football fans around the country had never heard of, and playing on a field that didn't even have lights. He was the opposite of a blue-chip freshman at UCLA or USC.

"You dream about playing on Saturdays on ABC and Keith Jackson calling your games," Rodgers said. "You're not thinking about playing at Cowan Stadium in Oroville, California, in front of five hundred people."

Aaron was a teenager playing with men as old as their midtwenties (one player privately confessed he was twenty-seven), including some who had been in the military, in prison, in the Canadian junior football league, or in Division I programs in the United States that had booted them for bad grades, bad behavior, and/or bad performance. Guys who had gotten a second chance were competing for roster spots with guys who had gotten a third.

Rigsbee made them all earn their helmets and pads. Charles Coleman, Rodgers's former Pleasant Valley teammate, recalled that on the first two days of practice the head coach "lined us up and just ran us until people quit.... It looked like a battlefield after practice, with trainers running around the field, and cramps everywhere."

Prichard argued that the dust around Butte's practice field was worse than the mosquito swarm as the Roadrunners raced from station to station in full pads, trying to survive double-session days and the fury of the Oklahoma drill. "I've seen twenty-five-year-olds in the best shape of their lives go into the bathroom and never come out," Prichard said.

A six-foot-five, 290-pound former offensive lineman at Utah State, Rigsbee adored his players—especially those who played tackle, guard, and center—and took them out to Mountain Mike's for all-you-can-eat pizza.

But at practice Rigsbee took shit from no man, American or Canadian, Black or white, teenager or grown-up, Division I prospect or hopeless walk-on. "He used to wear these tiny little shorts," Echauri said, "and every time he was yelling and screaming those little shorts would ride up on him."

When the Roadrunners whined about all the running they were doing in camp, Rigsbee had a good comeback. "I used to tell them, 'You've got the sun and the sand and the women of Chico. This is Miami Beach.' The players got all pissed off at that."

Through it all Aaron Rodgers was throwing passes in camp that had teammates and coaches looking at each other, as if to say, *We might have something here with this kid.*

"Everyone speaks of Aaron's chip on his shoulder," said Roadrunners assistant coach Scott Bootman. "When he got to Butte, he had the whole block on his shoulder."

The starting QB in 2001, Matt Ray, had put up record numbers at Butte before signing with Troy State, and most people around Rigsbee assumed that his opening-day nod in 2002 would go to Bryan Botts, a physical specimen who had already been in the program for three years. Botts was the guy who looked awfully good getting off the bus.

He had Division I talent, that was clear. But Rob Christie, twenty-five-year-old center from British Columbia, observed a clear difference in what the two quarterbacks were seeing, or not seeing, at the line of scrimmage in practice. Christie thought Botts was too committed to the original play call to identify and react to the audible opportunities in front of him, while the freshman was more flexible.

On the fourth day of practice, Rodgers made a play that separated him from Botts for keeps. Rigsbee was standing behind the offense when his freshman quarterback sprinted to his right, planted, and fired a tight 50-yard spiral to his left, hitting his receiver in the chest for a touchdown.

"Did you just see that shit?" Rigsbee asked one of his assistants.

"Yeah," the assistant responded. "He's been doing that for three days."

"He's going to be pretty damn good," Rigsbee said.

The head coach walked up to Rodgers. "You're getting bigger, aren't you?" he asked.

"I'm almost six-two now, 195 pounds," Aaron answered proudly.

Rigsbee had seen enough. *The quarterback competition is over*, he told himself. He thought Rodgers already knew the offense better than Botts did, and soon enough he'd share his decision with his staff.

The coaches sat down on the Sunday before the season opener against West Hills to come to an official decision on Butte's QB1. And every assistant coach in the room said the Roadrunners should start Botts because he had been waiting so long for the opportunity and didn't deserve to lose out to a freshman.

"It's his turn," those assistants said.

"Nope," the head coach responded. "It's not his turn. I hate to do it, but the other guy is already better, and pretty soon he's going to be ten times better. He's the guy we've got to go with."

At the time he made that decision, Rigsbee had a career record of 102-24-2 in his twelve years at Butte. He had been named the NorCal Conference Coach of the Year eight times and had earned six conference titles. He had the bona fides to overrule his entire staff and make this difficult call.

It was a decision that set up the most important season of football that Aaron Rodgers would play—ever—and leave Rigsbee as the man most responsible for changing the trajectory of his career. And given where the coach came from, that might have been the biggest upset of all.

• • •

AS PRODUCTS OF a broken home, bounced from town to town in California and enrolled in at least fifteen different elementary and middle schools, Craig Rigsbee and his older brother, Glen, essentially raised themselves from age eleven on up. They engaged in twenty-seven fistfights (by their count), most handled and won by the bigger Craig, and they took the junior college route to Division I football scholarships at Utah State.

"It was us against the world," Glen said.

Craig was a teacher, a bartender, a juvenile counselor, and an assistant coach in the 1980s before he took over at Butte. He recruited prospects from Texas, Florida, and the Pacific Northwest, and kept a pipeline running into Canada. Out-of-state players expecting gorgeous beaches and L.A. glamor were stunned by the northbound drive from the Sacramento airport to Butte, and all the almond and walnut orchards and rice fields off California State Road 99 en route to the middle-of-nowhere prairielands around the school.

Rigsbee relished providing support to juco kids from broken families and tough socioeconomic backgrounds. From his own personal experience, Rigsbee could tell those kids that they could rise above any adversity.

"Every kid that struggled," he said, "I saw myself in."

Rigsbee also enjoyed placing bets on underdogs like Aaron Rodgers. The quarterback came from a stable home and a family financial situation that, while once challenging, didn't compare to what some of his Butte teammates had endured.

But at Pleasant Valley, nobody believed in Rodgers like Rigsbee did. "I remember Craig going to Aaron's house many times and convincing him, showing him, and painting the dream and vision that he had painted for himself in our room early in life," Glen Rigsbee said.

Rodgers wanted to wear No. 12 at Butte, his PV number, but it was already taken. He was a fan of Green Bay Packers quarterback Brett Favre, so he opted to wear No. 4.

On a sunny Saturday in Oroville, Rodgers began his college career on the grass inside a bowl-shaped stadium that was more like a glorified high school field, with bleachers wedged into the hillside behind both benches. A giant American flag stood above the visitors' hill, and a small press box stood above the home team's hill.

On his very first series, Rodgers threw an interception on a play called "14 H Corner"—he sprinted left and fired and got beaten to a corner route by a defensive back. One of the Butte assistants emerged from the booth to deliver a message to the head coach.

"I told you he wasn't ready," the assistant said of Rodgers.

"Hey, I don't want to hear it," Rigsbee replied.

Rodgers then answered West Hills's first touchdown with a unique one of his own, off a play called "Utah." Wearing his black uniform and a gold helmet with white "BC" lettering, along with a dangling white towel and white shoes, Rodgers waited for a man in right-to-left motion to clear through the backfield before taking the snap and completing a screen pass to his left.

The visiting Falcons likely didn't know that the receiver was actually the backup quarterback, or that the screen was actually a lateral pass. Bryan Botts then threw the ball back across the field to a wide-open Rodgers, who ran untouched for a 12-yard score before raising his closed left fist in the end zone.

Down 9–6 at the half, the Roadrunners ran a fast break in the third quarter, scoring 35 points to secure a 44–22 victory. Rodgers finished with two touchdown passes—a 30-yarder to Shaun Bodiford off a play-action fake, and a 26-yard fade to Garrett Cross, formerly of Chico High—and completed 15 of 21 attempts for 253 yards. The freshman praised the receivers and offensive linemen afterward, and everyone on the home side went home happy.

Well, not everyone. Playing behind Rodgers, Botts had also thrown for two scores and had completed all five of his passes, without an interception. "And his mother runs over and rips my ass after the game," Rigsbee said. She told the coach that her boy would have outperformed Rodgers had he been given the same amount of playing time.

By using both quarterbacks, Rigsbee had tried and failed to please everyone. "I'll never do that again the rest of my life," he told himself.

So, he didn't. Even though his team was trailing 42–14 the following Saturday night in Fresno, Rigsbee declined to bench Rodgers. "Botts left us at halftime of that Fresno game," he said. "He packed his stuff up and left at halftime with his mom."

Rodgers stayed behind and put on a show. That the Roadrunners lost, 55–42, to a Fresno City College team ranked fourth in the nation was beside the point. Rodgers finished with 4 touchdowns, two throwing and two running. He arrived that night as a star.

One of the Fresno coaches ran across the field after the game and told Aaron's father, Ed Rodgers, "Your son is going to be a special player."

The stats backed up the projection, even if the numbers were all over the place. One report had Rodgers passing for 330 yards and running for 80, while a later account put his total yardage for the night at 440, a school record. Over time, as Rodgers's reputation grew, the numbers against Fresno grew with it, all the way up to 465 passing yards and 165 rushing yards.

This was life a million miles from the big time. Junior college football often mirrored the high school experience, complete with fundraisers required to pay for equipment, uniforms, and bus fuel. (Rigsbee needed that annual Crab Feed fundraiser to come through in a big way.)

But on this night, with future Division I players all over the field, Rodgers made a distinct big-time impression on a loaded opponent with his athleticism and arm.

"We could not tackle him or stop him in the second half," said Fresno coach Tony Caviglia. "We had underestimated his ability to run with the football and scramble and make plays. We had control, but we ended up trying to shorten the game a little to keep the ball out of his hands."

Said Fresno City's highly rated quarterback Mark Hetherington: "Aaron wasn't very big; I remember his sleeves hanging down past his elbows. But nobody on defense could get their hands on him. He was elusive and fast and he could throw it on the run, and the ball just came out differently. He just had lightning in his arm.

"It just came out with the flick of his wrist too. It didn't matter what position his body was in; the ball didn't lose any velocity. He was just different than anything else we'd seen. If he had a pedometer, he would've covered a few miles that night. He ran for his life, but he was never out of control."

As angered as they were about their defensive breakdowns against Fresno, Butte coaches and players now knew exactly what they had at quarterback. By the time he was done playing his second college game, Aaron did not look like such a precocious eighteen-year-old anymore.

"Aaron Rodgers got his scholarship out of that game," Tony Caviglia said.

All because another Fresno guy was smart enough to offer it to him.

• • •

IN THE MIDDLE of his first season as a head coach, Jeff Tedford had already returned the California Golden Bears to a level of competence and relevance after they went 1-10 the previous year under a different man.

The former quarterback and offensive coordinator at Division I Fresno State had the Bears on the way to a 7-5 season when he found himself in his office looking at Butte College film. He was interested in the Roadrunners' tight end, Garrett Cross, but it was the freshman who was throwing Cross the ball that commanded his attention.

Aaron Rodgers had been busy tilting scoreboards all over Northern California. He threw for 286 yards and 2 touchdowns, and ran for a score, in a 48–0 rout of Yuba. He threw for 285 yards and 4 touchdowns in a 45–6 rout of College of the Siskiyous. As the state's top-rated quarterback, Rodgers shredded Shasta with 6 touchdown passes—*six*—including three to Cross, in a 48–21 victory.

When he wasn't finding his athletic tight end, Rodgers was going deep to Mark Onibokun and hitting another reliable receiver, Bobby Bernal, on intermediate routes. He had thrown only 2 interceptions, and his offense was averaging more than 500 yards per game.

Rigsbee and his offensive coordinator, Jeff Jordan, had themselves a perfect point guard to run a Showtime offense. Rodgers told his head coach that he preferred the speed and air-it-out nature of the college game to what he had experienced at PV. No kidding.

So, while watching Rodgers tear it up on the Butte tape, Tedford summoned to his office Bob Foster, the Cal linebackers coach who was responsible for recruiting the Butte area. It was going to take a village to make this happen.

Cross had already sent tapes of himself to another Cal coach and recruiter, Dave Ungerer, with one twist: To help out his fellow Chico native, the tight end included video of games that showcased Rodgers's talent more than his own. The gesture spoke to Cross's selflessness and to Aaron's ability to inspire his teammates.

"Hey, your quarterback. How old is he?" Ungerer asked the tight end.

"Yeah, he's a freshman," Cross responded, "but he's not going to be around for a second season."

Foster said that he had a discussion with Rigsbee about Rodgers, and that he had other tape on the quarterback he would watch with Tedford. "What was phenomenal to me was how quick his release was, how fast he went from his ear to delivering the ball," Foster said.

"As a defensive coach, you always teach linebackers to anticipate the quarterback's throw by his body position and arm action. But with Aaron Rodgers, you couldn't anticipate it because he got rid of the ball so quickly."

What was Tedford's reaction to the first films he watched of Rodgers?

"He just said, 'Oh man, this guy is good,'" Foster recalled. "He said, 'I'd love to get this guy. How do we get this guy?'"

Yet another Cal assistant, Jim Michalczik, called Craig Rigsbee, who told him that Rodgers was an academic qualifier. In other words, the kid could leave Butte for a Division I school without completing his second year of junior college. Foster believed that few, if any, major schools realized that Rodgers was eligible to play after one Butte season.

Tedford called Rigsbee, who told him that no other major college was recruiting Rodgers. "Can I come to practice tomorrow?" Tedford asked. He didn't have to ask twice. Cal's quarterback, Kyle Boller, was a departing senior heading into the first round of the NFL draft, and his coach needed an elite replacement.

On Monday, October 28, Tedford traveled north on a fateful 154-mile drive to Oroville to see his prospect in the flesh. Rodgers had just struggled a bit in a 36–20 victory over Foothill, throwing two picks, and Tedford could not have cared less.

Rigsbee usually kept it light on Mondays, asking his players to watch film, stretch, jog, and lift. On this Monday, the Butte coach confused his team by running intense seven-on-seven passing drills for up to forty-five minutes.

"Oh shit," Rodgers said, "somebody must be here."

The quarterback found out soon enough.

"It's funny now because I'm taller than [Tedford]," Rodgers recalled years later. "But it felt like he was about six-eight. He had these glasses on, and everybody was on edge that day. 'Hey, we got a college coach here today.' It was Monday, we usually don't do anything. I heard whispers on campus that he was coming. I was nervous."

To Butte's VIP guest, Rodgers did not appear to be a nervous quarterback that afternoon. "I remember standing on the sideline with Coach Rigsbee and just seeing Aaron's physical ability and leadership qualities and just how everyone on the team gravitated toward him," said Tedford, a former Canadian Football League quarterback. "The head coach is talking to me, and Aaron is running the show and it's pretty impressive."

Tedford asked Rigsbee if he was OK with the prospect of Cal taking Rodgers away from Butte after one season.

"Does he have a chance to start?" Rigsbee responded.

"Yeah, he definitely does," Tedford said. "We're losing Boller and it's going to be an open competition."

Rigsbee recalled that after practice, his guest wanted to watch tape of Butte's most recent game against Foothill. "He watched one slant route," Rigsbee said, "and we turned off the tape and Tedford goes, 'Yeah, this kid is special. That's the best junior college quarterback I've ever seen. That kid is going to play in the NFL.'

"And I said, 'You think so?' And he said, 'I know so.'"

On the ride back to Berkeley, Tedford decided he could not wait even a day to offer Rodgers a scholarship. He was struck by everything about the kid, especially his release and velocity.

"I actually heard from Tedford before I saw Aaron," said Darla Rodgers. "He called and said, 'I want to offer your son. I just saw him in person.' I remember being the one on the phone call, getting off and going, 'Who's Coach Tedford?'"

Coach Tedford got on the phone with Aaron and gave him the news. Rodgers had played only a handful of junior college games and already a coach considered one of the best quarterback teachers in the nation (Boller would be the fifth first-round pick whom Tedford helped develop at that position) believed he was worthy of a full Division I ride.

Rodgers spoke with Rigsbee, the man who had walked into his home and promised to let him leave Butte after one year if a big school came calling. Aaron loved playing for Rigsbee, and appreciated the risk the coach took when he handed over his team to a freshman instead of going with the safer veteran, Botts.

But this was the dream all along. One of Butte's offensive tackles, the massive Mark Parrish, recalled Rodgers's voicemail greeting as indicative of how focused the quarterback was on realizing that dream.

"He had his statistics on his answering machine," Parrish said. "Anybody who called him . . . it was, 'Hey, this is Aaron Rodgers. I'm six feet tall, I have a laser rocket arm, I have 12 touchdowns this year,' and that was his answering machine through juco. He was always just selling himself, trying to get to the next step."

Asked if Rodgers's voicemail message was strictly humorous, or a serious advertisement for any Division I recruiter who might call, Parrish said: "I think it was both. It was like, 'Dude, if anyone calls me, they need to hear this.' I gave him shit about it all the time, and it didn't matter. Aaron is Aaron. He is who he is regardless."

And Rodgers always thought of himself as one of the best quarterbacks in the country. Not only was Rodgers now being given a chance to play in the big time, he was being given a chance to do it three hours from Chico.

Every home game would be a family reunion. The epic Almond Bowl rivalry between PV and Chico High would merely be upgraded to the epic Big Game rivalry between Cal and Stanford.

Rodgers had no choice but to accept Tedford's offer. "I feel bad for you guys," he told Rigsbee.

"Don't feel bad for us," the Butte coach responded.

"All right, I want to go," Rodgers said.

"Good," Rigsbee said. "Go."

Before he could go anywhere, Rodgers had to keep driving the Roadrunners toward a state championship and he had to keep attending class. Over that 2002–03 academic year, his favorite course might have been the Introduction to a Career in Coaching class taught by Russ Critchfield, a former basketball star at UC Berkeley who played on the Oakland Oaks team with Rick Barry, Larry Brown, and Doug Moe that won the 1969 American Basketball Association championship.

Critchfield recalled Rodgers taking the exact same seat for every session. "The last seat in the middle row in the back, every time," the teacher said. "It was like everyone in front of him was on the offensive line. That's where he always wanted the vision of everything, like he was behind the line of scrimmage."

Critchfield described Rodgers as an A student who was intellectually curious and "really reflective before he spoke. . . . He had charisma. You felt as an educator, here's a student who knows himself pretty well and will probably be successful at whatever he decides to do. He's empowering when he talks and people listen to him. When we talked about leadership, he just projected all of those qualities."

Years later Rodgers credited this class for teaching him that leadership is not a one-style-fits-all proposition, and that different methods were needed to motivate different people.

Rodgers had plenty of on-the-job training on the Butte football field. On game day, as he stood before his ten offensive teammates, Rodgers preferred to stick with his stoic approach.

"His play spoke for itself," said guard Scott Lee. "When you have that type of ability and walk the walk, the rest of us went along with it."

Except for this one time, when running back William Shoulders was trying to fire up his teammates in the huddle, and the play clock was bleeding out, and Rodgers was too stressed to keep his cool.

"Shut the fuck up," he screamed at Shoulders.

"Using the f-word really surprised us," Lee said. "Aaron was a very quiet, humble, churchy kid. We all looked at each other like, 'What?' . . . That to me was when he took over."

Aaron's preparation fueled his confidence, and his confidence fueled his low-volume leadership. Defensive players spoke of how much they believed in him and his ability to sustain long drives that kept them off their feet and fresh.

"It was his calmness," said cornerback JJ Stallings. "He had the perfect confidence where he wasn't cocky, but he was always so calm. There was a tight game where I remember him being like, 'Relax, we're going to go down here and we're going to score.' And you just believed it."

Rodgers scored a lot of points with teammates by never treating them as lesser lights, according to defensive tackle Brett Bischofberger, and by always talking up his offensive line and receivers after lighting up opponents. The *Enterprise-Record* reporter who regularly covered the Roadrunners, Dave Davies, confirmed that his postgame interviews with Rodgers were always shaped by the quarterback's effort to deflect praise to others.

For all of his selflessness, Rodgers had established himself as one of the finest junior college players in America. And he did that by knowing the responsibilities of every offensive player on the field, and by reading the opposing defenses at the line of scrimmage and calling plays based on their formations.

"The amount of freedom Aaron was given as a freshman with the check-with-me series was parallel to that of a college senior," said Rob Christie. "He was given that freedom because he was so smart. The guy never made a mistake, and when I say 'never' I mean it."

Christie cited a long and late touchdown drive against Foothill—after the Owls had turned a 23–0 deficit into a 23–20 free-for-all—as the most conspicuous example of Rodgers relaxing his team with his even temperament, and with his advanced ability to diagnose whatever problem a defensive scheme presented.

Craig Rigsbee thought of his quarterback as an assistant coach, and as someone who, at age eighteen, probably knew the Butte offense better than he did. Though Rigsbee was a hulking, intimidating presence on game day, dropping f-bombs and spiking clipboards up and down the sideline, Rodgers was not afraid to take control and to take chances. Teammates thought of the quarterback as the de facto offensive coordinator, even though they respected the man who held the actual title, Jeff Jordan.

"When Aaron needed to produce," Prichard said, "he always had that smirk on his face.... Aaron would do stuff in the game that we wouldn't know if it came from him or from Coach or somebody on the sideline, and that was the beauty of him. You didn't need to know. You were confident because he was confident, and that was part of his charisma and swagger."

Rodgers made executive decisions on the fly, all the time. Mark Parrish remembered one particularly perilous game situation that left Butte's backup left tackle trying and failing to block a tall, fierce, long-armed pass rusher. Without getting clearance from the coaches, Rodgers told the six-foot-six, 330-pound Parrish to trade places with the backup and move from right tackle to left.

"Aaron's maybe 180 pounds and he's telling me what to do," Parrish said. "He made it happen. He forced it to happen. We were yelling at the new guy to block him, and Aaron said, 'If you think you can do a better job, you go over there and block him.' And it worked. He dropped back and threw a dime over the middle to Garrett [Cross]."

The coaches did not question it because Rodgers could do things with the football that nobody else could. As physically underwhelming as the quarterback was, Parrish believed Rodgers had one physical trait that elevated him above the competition.

"His hands were the same size as mine on his little, tiny body," Parrish said. "He wore the same size gloves as me. I was like, 'How are you the same hand size of the right tackle towering over you?' I wore Double X gloves."

One other secret weapon that worked in Rodgers's favor: his restraint. He did not party like his old man did at Chico State. He listened to his father's warning about staying clear of booze and drugs—"Keep your nose clean and it will pay off for you"—and, well, it paid off for him.

Not that it was easy to play the role of the serious-minded, churchgoing student-athlete in Chico. "It was the Wild West," Scott Lee said. "MTV was over there, *Playboy* was over there, and we could've gotten into so much trouble."

There were certainly ways for a star teenage quarterback to beat the drinking age of twenty-one if he wanted to. Chico State no longer had a football program, making the Butte Roadrunners the only game in town. If the underaged among them wanted to work their way into a local bar, they wouldn't have been met with great resistance.

If Rodgers did not want to risk getting caught in a bar, all he needed to do was head over to the apartment complex known as The Zoo, where the code of conduct was best described as anything goes, every night of the week, including the night before a game.

"The Zoo was literally a zoo," Echauri said. "I'm convinced they called it The Zoo because all the apartments were inside a fenced area. Everybody was having parties—upstairs, downstairs, across the way. It was crazy."

And yet the Butte players all said that Rodgers was a hopelessly committed homebody. Many said they did not see him out even once during the season.

Parrish said he went out with his quarterback a few times because they were both passionate 49ers fans and had mutual friends through Aaron's church. The way defensive lineman Joshua Check remembered it, Rodgers did actually show up to a team party or two.

"But he would make an appearance and disappear," Check said. "My impression at least was he was only doing it out of a sense of team spirit and camaraderie."

• • •

BEFORE AARON RODGERS left Chico for Berkeley and a new life as an independent student at a world-renowned institution, he had one last football game to claim. The 9-1 Roadrunners had won eight straight and were coming off one of the biggest Saturdays of Craig Rigsbee's career—a 35–10 victory over three-time defending state champ City College of San Francisco before an overflow home crowd of three thousand—and still they were denied a spot in the Northern California title game, which served as a semifinal for the state championship.

Butte players and coaches thought the snub was political. "We got screwed out of going . . . because no one liked us up in Butte," Rodgers said, "because we beat everybody's asses."

San Francisco coach George Rush saw it the same way, believing that Rigsbee and his players had every right to be enraged. Rush had jokingly called the Butte coach after Rodgers had committed to Cal to tell him how happy he was that the quarterback would not be returning for his sophomore year.

Rigsbee had hit a walk-off home run with the recruitment of Rodgers, and with the choice to start him over Bryan Botts, and his thanks came in the form of a letter from Botts's mother, who roasted him for making the wrong call.

As Rigsbee recalled it, the letter included lines like these: "You don't know shit about quarterbacks, you played left tackle.... You don't know talent.... The Rodgers kid is never going to do anything."

The Rodgers kid had already been named conference MVP and had already set Butte single-season records for touchdown passes (26) and passing yards (2,156) for a team that averaged 40 points a game. He threw only 4 interceptions all year, and his consolation prize for missing out on the playoffs was a matchup with another 9-1 team, San Joaquin Delta, in the Tri Counties Bank Holiday Bowl at Butte's Cowan Stadium.

It would be the last time the locals saw Aaron Rodgers line up in Butte's shotgun formation, his right foot slightly forward. It would be the last time his teammates watched him throw on the same frayed shirt that he wore underneath his shoulder pads.

"He wore a fuckin' Joe Montana old-school shirt that had holes in it," Heath Prichard said. "It had Joe Montana cartoon-head drawings on it.... When I tell you it had holes in it, this shirt had holes in it like Swiss cheese."

This was the last time Rodgers would get a chance to run the play known as "86 Y Shake" and hit Bobby Bernal, who was fighting through the lingering effects of a broken arm. This was the last time Rodgers would get a chance to hit Mark Onibokun behind the secondary, on a grass field looking as choppy as Wimbledon's baselines after two weeks of tennis.

But in the early stages of the game, the Roadrunners still seemed deflated by their perceived snub. San Joaquin Delta ripped off an 88-yard touchdown run to take a 13–0 lead.

"Hey man, we thought we were too good for this game," Rigsbee told his team. "Well, it doesn't look like it."

No, the Roadrunners could not go out like this. Rigsbee turned over the cause to his quarterback. He had met every Friday with Rodgers before Saturday games to ask him what plays he wanted to run that week.

"If you give kids a little bit of power," the coach said, "nobody will want to make that play better than the kid who called it."

And nobody was better than Rodgers was at calling check-with-me plays at the line. That was a principal reason the Roadrunners had so much faith in him.

"You never felt like you were going to lose a game with him in there," JJ Stallings said.

As William Shoulders was cutting through and around the San Joaquin defense, making it a 20–13 game on a couple of scoring runs, Rodgers was starting to find his rhythm. When he hit Bernal on a 42-yard touchdown pass in the middle of the second quarter, allowing the home team to make it a tied game at the half, the Roadrunners had a good feeling about the end result. After all, Rodgers would call every play at the line in the second half.

Shoulders scored his third touchdown of the day before his quarterback sealed the victory early in the fourth quarter on the twenty-eighth and final touchdown pass he threw for Butte College, on a play known as "44 Drop Pass." Rodgers had a receiver run a deep cross, another run a shallow cross, and Onibokun run a post pattern. Just before he got hit, Rodgers threw a strike down the field to Onibokun, who took it in for a 61-yard score.

The quarterback ran off the field and toward his head coach. "We jumped and hip-bumped," Rigsbee recalled.

The coach stopped his quarterback to ask him a curious question.

"Hey," Rigsbee said, "are you going to get me tickets?"

"Tickets for what?" Rodgers replied.

"Tickets for when you're playing in the NFL," the coach said.

The most important season of Rodgers's career ended with a 37–20 victory over a public community college team from Stockton, California, and an MVP award in a bowl game that didn't quite rank with the Rose Bowl.

But Craig Rigsbee had made good on his pledge to find the quarterback a pathway to the biggest stage in college football. It was all on Aaron Rodgers to take it from there.

5
BERKELEY

Richard Schwartz, backup quarterback at Cal, paid a visit to his head coach, Jeff Tedford, in the summer of 2003. Schwartz had been recruited by the previous coach and wanted an update on his status.

More to the point, Schwartz wanted intel on one of Tedford's new recruits, a junior college quarterback named Aaron Rodgers. Was Rodgers going to leapfrog Schwartz and projected starter Reggie Robertson?

Tedford did not give Schwartz a direct answer. The coach reminded him that the Golden Bears had not even played a game yet and gave him a coach-speak song and dance that left Schwartz with a sinking feeling.

"I could tell right away that Aaron was Jeff's guy no matter what," he said.

At six foot four and 215 pounds, Schwartz was another quarterback who was bigger and stronger than Rodgers. But as they got better acquainted during preseason camp, Schwartz recognized in his competition what Tedford saw at Butte.

"When everybody else was eating dinner after practice," Schwartz recalled, "we'd try to throw a ball thirty yards into a trash can. And when Aaron religiously put it in the trash can, I knew he was really good."

Later on, Rodgers and Schwartz altered their one-on-one accuracy contests.

"We would hit the crossbar from the 20-yard line, and then from the 30-yard line, I kid you not," Schwartz said. "One night we were at the 40, and Aaron hit the crossbar seven times in a row. The best I ever did was two in a row. These were 50-yard throws because the crossbar is ten yards deep.

"If I would've done it all over again, I would've transferred out. I would've said, 'Hey Coach, I know this is your guy. Let me go to a junior college.'"

Truth was, Schwartz's Cal career had all but ended the previous December, when Rodgers and Butte teammate Garrett Cross officially announced their commitment to the Bears in a Chico bar and restaurant known (fittingly enough) as The Bear.

Berkeley was three hours and fifteen minutes from Butte, but it was worlds away as an institution. Cal was one of the nation's best research universities, and while it competed against USC and other revenue sports heavyweights in the Pac-10 Conference, it was not a place where academia catered to the jocks.

Quite the opposite, in fact. Berkeley was home to Nobel laureates and Pulitzer winners, not Heisman winners. Cal professors seemed to relish the chance to remind the jocks that they did not deserve any special treatment.

The message, according to Cal punter and kicker Tyler Fredrickson, was delivered with force every day: "This is an academic school first and foremost and don't you forget it."

Fredrickson said he was the first Cal player to meet Rodgers on his first campus trip—in the weight room during an offseason visit. The kicker was not terribly eager to bond with Rodgers, not when he already had a strong relationship with Aaron's main competition for the starting job, Robertson, who also doubled as Fredrickson's holder.

"But Aaron didn't have a place to stay," the kicker said. "Aaron slept on our couch for a week. We were all Christian athletes, all members of Athletes in Action. Aaron had expressed some Christian beliefs, and we were all excited to walk in faith with another one of our football brothers."

The kicker noticed that the quarterback immediately learned every teammate's name. "I quickly started to see how gifted of a leader he was," Fredrickson said. "I saw how his connectiveness really stood apart. Aaron really had no airs about him, and he was willing to connect with everybody because it was his job as a leader to win them over as quickly as possible so . . . there would be an unspoken communication that would play out on the field."

And yet there was skepticism at first, just like there had been at Butte. "Aaron comes in," said receiver Geoff McArthur, "and he doesn't look like Kyle Boller." Another receiver, former walk-on Vinny Strang, described Rodgers as "the skinny little juco transfer." (The five-foot-eight Strang was barely 150 pounds himself.) It was hard not to compare Aaron to his predecessor.

Rated the best high school quarterback in America, and compared to California prep legend John Elway, Boller had salvaged three fairly dreadful seasons under his first Cal coach, Tom Holmoe, by throwing for 28 touchdowns in leading the Golden Bears to a 7-5 record in Tedford's first year.

He could run the 40-yard dash in 4.59 seconds and he could throw the deep ball. At the direction of his trainer, Thomas Weatherspoon, Boller famously ended his Pro Day workout before the 2003 draft by dropping to a knee at the 50-yard line and launching a football straight through the goalposts—just as he had claimed he could do at the scouting combine. One teammate compared his looks to Leonardo DiCaprio's, so yes, he was a tough act to follow.

Before Rodgers spent the summer at Berkeley in a dingy frat house, Cal's offensive coordinator, George Cortez, recalled that the quarterback spent time with the team during his second semester at Butte, calling it the transfer's spring break week. And during that week, said offensive tackle Andrew Cameron, Rodgers opened his bid to be the starting quarterback behind closed doors.

"He was in Tedford's office ten hours a day watching film," Cameron said. "It was nuts to think about what he did. He took on a pro-style offense with one of the best coaches in the game and learned it."

During the spring, McArthur recalled, Tedford was already setting up Rodgers to be the one to take control of the team. "Aaron hadn't been here," the receiver said, "and we're watching this guy leading the stretch lines already. I barely knew his last name."

Everyone knew Aaron's last name by the end of the summer.

"Tedford said it usually takes five to seven months to fully learn his offense," Schwartz said. "Aaron knew it in sixty days."

Tedford had signaled as far back as April, after watching Robertson and Schwartz play effectively in Cal's Blue-Gold scrimmage, that the Butte transfer would be a factor when the coach made his decision on a starter after preseason camp. "Rodgers has it all," Tedford said then.

In the days before his August decision, the coach praised all three quarterbacks, though he acknowledged that the former juco player was still adjusting to the speed of the Division I game. Rodgers sounded prepared for the likelihood that Tedford would go with the six-foot-two, 190-pound redshirt junior, Robertson, on account of his experience.

"If Reggie starts," Aaron said, "I'll be his biggest fan."

On August 18, Tedford made it official that he was starting the veteran. To a man, the Bears liked, respected, and believed in Robertson.

Tedford also made it easier for Rodgers to support Robertson by installing him as the No. 2 quarterback, ahead of Schwartz, and by making it clear he would give Aaron his share of playing time. The Cal coach called the transfer's performance in preseason camp "tremendous" and his grasp of the offense "unbelievable." Disappointed and a bit frustrated on decision day, Rodgers again pledged his full support for Robertson—Aaron's hotel roommate for road games. And yet he promised reporters, "This won't be the last you guys hear from me."

When the Golden Bears traveled to Kansas City to play one of the nation's finest teams, Kansas State, in the Black Coaches Association Classic, they had every reason to believe they were closing the gap on the major-college powers. Finally.

Holmoe had gone 16-39 in his five years at Berkeley, and 1-10 in his final season, leaving behind a broken team, and an NCAA probation and one-year postseason ban. Defensive tackle Tom Sverchek said Tedford, former offensive coordinator at Oregon, restored the players' confidence with his positivity. Those 2002 Golden Bears responded by dropping 70 points on Baylor in the season opener. By the end of the day, the home crowd inside Memorial Stadium was chanting, "We love Tedford." Not a bad way to launch a new era.

"And then walks in the junior college transfer," Fredrickson recalled.

Rodgers watched as Robertson took the Arrowhead Stadium field to lead the Bears against Kansas State in the 2003 nationally televised opener. Cal had lost a procession of starters from its '02 team, so this had the makings of a rout.

With 8:35 left in the third quarter, it was trending that way. The Wildcats held a 35–14 lead, with quarterback Ell Roberson and running back Darren Sproles gashing the Cal defense. The deficit afforded Tedford the opportunity to get Rodgers on the field.

Out trotted Cal's No. 8, wearing his white jersey, blue helmet, thick chinstrap, and a play card wrapped around his left forearm. "A new quarterback coming into the lineup, Aaron Rodgers," ESPN's play-by-play announcer Ron Franklin said on the broadcast.

Rodgers organized the Bears, got under center, and on his first major-college snap handed off to J. J. Arrington, who was stopped for no gain. On his second snap, Rodgers dropped back, felt the pressure, and scrambled for 2 yards.

Franklin's ESPN partner, Mike Gottfried, correctly said that Rodgers was "thinking right now they're a little faster than they were at Butte Junior College." It was a hot, steamy night inside the Kansas City Chiefs' stadium—the on-field temperature was reported to be 106 degrees. Rodgers walked into the huddle, relayed the play, and got back under center to face his first third-and-long situation. He dropped back, looked downfield, and never saw the blitzing defensive back to his right racing around end. Jesse Tetuan sacked him for a 5-yard loss. Three and out.

On the opening play of his second possession, Rodgers completed his first Cal pass by firing a strike to McArthur on the right sideline for a 14-yard gain. "You could see the arm strength of Aaron Rodgers on that play right there," Franklin said on the broadcast.

Rodgers then showed his inexperience again by making two bad throws, by wasting a time-out, and by taking another third-down sack. He burned yet another time-out on his third series, clearly annoying Tedford, before bouncing back on a third-and-10 with a 31-yard completion to McArthur. On the next play, Rodgers beat the pressure by hitting Arrington on a short middle screen for a 22-yard touchdown.

The quarterback charged toward the end zone pumping his raised right fist. The Bears had cut Kansas State's lead to 35–21 with 12:34 to go, and suddenly they had an outside shot to pull off the upset.

But the Wildcats were not about to collapse on this night. For Cal, the most alarming development of this 42–28 defeat unfolded with 6:10 left, when Rodgers rolled right and, after releasing what would be a completed pass, took a brutal hit to the midsection from six-foot-four, 265-pound defensive end Andrew Shull.

Rodgers was down on his left knee; he rose as the official near him called time-out. He looked at the Cal sideline, waved for help, then doubled over. He had the wind knocked out of him, at the very least. Rodgers ended up flat on his back as two trainers tended to him before pulling him to his feet. The quarterback jogged off under his own power as the crowd cheered for him.

Robertson returned to the field and finished that drive with his third touchdown pass, sealing a Week 2 start against Southern Mississippi in Berkeley. Diagnosed with a bruised chest, Rodgers planned to be available to play in seven days. He had done a lot of good things in this debut, confirmed by a box score that had him completing 9 of 13 attempts for 121 yards and that touchdown.

Fans seeing the Cal quarterback for the first time noticed something peculiar about his style—the position of the ball on his dropbacks. Tedford wanted the ball up high above his right shoulder, near his earhole, like a waiter carrying a serving tray through a crowded bar. "We like it to be what's called 'on the shelf,'" he said. The top shelf. It made for a faster release.

"Aaron's was unusually high mainly because his back arm was high," Tedford said. "I worked primarily on footwork, the dropback, shoulder profile. He was higher than the rest of our guys. But I didn't mess with it because he was phenomenal."

Rodgers threw only four passes off the bench in a blowout victory over Southern Miss in the home opener at Memorial Stadium, and then did not play at all the following week in a home loss to Colorado State. Robertson had thrown for 5 touchdowns against 2 interceptions in those games and had played smart, efficient football. He had not done anything to lose his job.

Was Tedford about to abandon the idea of keeping the Butte transfer part of a quarterback rotation? Rodgers's father was concerned enough about that possibility to approach Butte coach Craig Rigsbee after the Colorado State game.

"I wonder if we made a mistake coming to Cal," Ed Rodgers told him. "Maybe we should leave and go somewhere else."

"No, don't worry," Rigsbee replied. "They needed a game manager the first few games, and Tedford is just biding his time with Aaron. He'll be the guy soon."

"Soon" arrived five nights later on September 11, the second anniversary of the terrorist attacks, when the Golden Bears played Utah in Salt Lake City. Rodgers and his teammates were wearing "9-11" stickers on the backs of their helmets in a Thursday-night matchup that felt significant—it was the only game on the national TV schedule. Mike Tirico, Kirk Herbstreit, and Lee Corso were in the ESPN booth, and after three Cal possessions went nowhere, Aaron Rodgers was in the game with 4:05 left in the first quarter and Utah already holding a 14–0 lead.

An injury to the Utes' starter compelled them to start sophomore Alex Smith for the first time, a move that would loom larger in Rodgers's life down the road. For now, the Cal quarterback sought to honor the faith his coach had placed in him. Tedford was clearly trying to install him as the Bears' permanent quarterback, or else he wouldn't have made the in-game change so quickly.

Reggie Robertson saw it coming, and no, he did not think Tedford was being fair to him. He felt that his performance over the first three games had earned him a greater benefit of the doubt. He did not think the play calling early against Utah matched up with his strengths, and he said teammates mentioned that to him when he got to the sideline.

"I said, 'I can't do this. I'm not calling these plays,'" Robertson recalled. "It was frustrating. All in all, I could have done more. In the end Tedford saw stuff in [Rodgers] that he was looking for, something he could work with, which was unfortunate for me."

In that first quarter, after Tedford told him that he was about to replace Robertson, Rodgers walked up to backup tackle Andrew Cameron and said, "Hey, Coach is putting me in. Give me a pep talk."

A pep talk?

"I'm like, 'Who am I? I'm a backup left tackle,'" Cameron said. "I told him, 'You do it every day in practice and you know exactly what you're doing. You got it.'"

Like the rest of the Bears, Cameron was astonished by Rodgers's ability to throw the ball as if he were throwing a dart, and to repeatedly place it right over the outstretched hands of defenders. He was one of many offensive linemen who thought the typical Rodgers pass made a distinct sound as it sailed by his helmet.

"It's hard to describe," Cameron said. "It's a rush of air that's clean and fresh and efficient sounding. You can sense it, feel it, hear it, and it was every time. It wasn't that sometimes he threw the ball well and sometimes he didn't. He could repeat his mechanics over and over and over."

With Cal trailing by two scores, Rodgers led the Bears on a drive early in the second quarter that featured a scramble to his right and a 24-yard laser to receiver Burl Toler that had Herbstreit and Corso oohing and aahing in the booth. "I heard it," shrieked Corso. "I mean, I heard it hit his pads." Added Herbstreit: "Toler got in the way of that one. There's a Nike implant, I think, right on his chest."

On the next play, Rodgers followed up his four-seam fastball with a changeup over the top of a Utah defender and into the arms of McArthur in the left side of the end zone for a 21-yard touchdown. This quarterback could beat you with power and with finesse.

In the closing seconds of the first half, after Utah had regained a 2-touchdown lead, Rodgers had the ball on the Utes' 35 when he revealed his fearless side. He motioned McArthur to move from his initial backfield spot to the outside receiver position on his left, and then tried to find him inside the 10-yard line.

Problem was, McArthur decided to run a post-corner route toward the sideline, while Rodgers wanted to be more aggressive and hit him in stride toward the end zone behind Utah freshman Shaun Harper.

"My mentality at the time was, I don't think we should go for a big chunk play now," McArthur said. "It's a low-percentage throw. If I can break this thing off in front of a Cover 3 back, we can keep the drive going and I can get out of bounds. So, I snapped it off.... When I looked back, I was pissed. [Rodgers] was doing all these hand signals, yelling at me from 30 yards away. He was telling me, 'No, you've got to go high angle, that's what we're coached to do.'

"From that moment on, I listened to him every time. I'm like, 'Shit, he's got the gun. I don't.' I was playing scared, and he was playing confidently. He wanted a touchdown and I was being a bit conservative."

The disconnect between receiver and quarterback didn't last long. Rodgers found McArthur for another 21-yard touchdown that gave the Bears the lead with twenty-eight seconds left in the third quarter. Tedford decided to attempt a two-point conversion, and on the play a pressured Rodgers stepped up in the pocket, veered to his right, and, after forcing the defense to react to the possibility that he would run it in, dumped the ball over the top to Vinny Strang.

"Aaron had to improvise on the fly . . . and he broke contain," Strang said. "That's the first time you saw Aaron extend a play."

In the end it wasn't good enough. Utah tied it on a field goal and took the lead on Brandon Warfield's 14-yard run with 1:06 to play. On the final possession, Rodgers fumbled away Cal's long-shot bid to force overtime, and that was that.

He completed 15 of 25 attempts for 224 yards and those 2 touchdowns. His counterpart, Alex Smith, passed for only 136 yards (with no touchdowns), but hurt Cal by running for 71 yards and a score.

"I never doubted myself," Rodgers said about his first-quarter entrance. "I felt comfortable. I didn't even need to warm up."

During the game, Craig Rigsbee had left a message on his former quarterback's phone that went like this:

"Aaron, this is Rigs. You're playing the game right now, but this is your team. Right now. You're going to be the starter now. This is exactly what Tedford wanted to do. Now you're the man. Relax, kick ass, and let's go."

Rodgers was named the first-string quarterback for Cal's fifth game, a meeting with Illinois and the same coaching staff that refused to give him a scholarship after he lit up its football camp the summer before his senior year at Pleasant Valley. What were the odds that young Aaron would return to the Champaign campus a little more than two years later as a taller, bigger, better version of his high school self, ready to make an impression in his first Division I start?

Making the situation a bit more surreal, Aaron's quarterbacks coach at Pleasant Valley, Ron O'Dell, was now working on the Illinois staff with his brother Dan and their uncle, Ron Turner.

On game day, Rodgers no longer looked like that undersized Illinois camper whose tight spirals were all but ignored. He had grown into a six-foot-two, 200-pound young man who could impose his will on a Division I team that he was supposedly not good enough to join.

Rodgers completed 17 passes for 236 yards and 1 touchdown in the first half alone as Cal took a 21–7 halftime lead. The coaches on the home side no longer thought Rodgers looked like a non-scholarship player. The visitors carried a 31–14 lead into the middle of the fourth quarter before the Illini staged a furious rally, recovering an onside kick late and nearly tying the game.

Rodgers's coach at Pleasant Valley High School, Sterling Jackson, had told the Illinois coach that he was making a big mistake by not offering his quarterback a scholarship, and that prediction had become prophecy.

Rodgers now prepared to face third-ranked USC in a season that would end in a bowl game. Ron Turner, meanwhile, began the brutal Big Ten stretch of an Illinois season that would end with a 1-11 record.

• • •

JEFF TEDFORD'S STAFF supplied the players each week with video of the upcoming opponent. The Golden Bears were always one computer click away from, say, viewing all of USC's first-down tendencies.

"They gave us the computer on Sunday night," said third-string quarterback Richard Schwartz. "I wouldn't know it until Wednesday or Thursday. Aaron would know all of the opponent's tendencies by Monday afternoon."

And that was why on the night after Christmas, inside Bank One Ballpark in Phoenix, Rodgers was standing on his 35-yard line with a chance to give Cal its first bowl victory in ten years, and only its fourth since 1938.

The Bears and Virginia Tech were locked inside a wonderfully wild and crazy 49–49 game, after Tech's DeAngelo Hall had taken a 52-yard punt return for a touchdown that turned the Insight Bowl upside down. The Hokies sent the ensuing kickoff on a wayward journey out of bounds to give Cal the ball on its 35 with 3:11 to play.

Rodgers had accounted for 4 touchdowns, two on the ground and two through the air. He had secured his fifth game of at least 300 passing yards in his last seven starts, and now he had an opportunity to enhance his standing as a rising major-college star by leading the Bears to a winning score.

He did not take the smoothest road to get to this point. After his triumph over Illinois, Rodgers was replaced by Reggie Robertson in the middle of a classic triple-overtime home victory over third-ranked USC, the Bears' first defeat of an opponent ranked that highly in more than half a century. Rodgers had thrown two scoring passes and run for another in the first half before he began to unravel—he threw his first interception after nearly going 100 passes without a pick, he fumbled away the ball, and he threw a pick-six in the middle of the third quarter.

Robertson was brilliant in the 34–31 victory sealed by a field goal from Tyler Fredrickson, who had two earlier kicks blocked. Fans stormed the Memorial Stadium field. Afterward, Tedford said Rodgers had reported to him that he was "really banged up" with knee and ankle injuries and agreed that he should take off a couple of series. "He was limping around," the coach said. "I think he felt he couldn't perform to his ability. When you play USC, you get knocked around pretty good."

Fredrickson saw something different in his teammate and friend. He was not only a kicker and punter; he was a storyteller who received Tedford's permission to bring a camera into the locker room and into hotel rooms to interview players for a documentary on the 2003 team. Rodgers told the kicker that on game days he liked to listen to music from John Mayer and Bebo Norman, a contemporary Christian musician.

Fredrickson had tremendous respect for Rodgers's intellect and talent. But as someone who studied his Cal teammates as closely as anyone did, Fredrickson thought he identified something rare in Rodgers's eyes— doubt. "I think Tedford looked in his eyes at halftime," the kicker said, "and saw he was shaken. . . . I think Aaron was a bit of a deer in the headlights in that game."

Either way, Tedford kept him in there the following week against Oregon State, which turned out to be the worst game of Rodgers's career. Under heavy blitz pressure, he misfired on 25 of 34 passes while throwing for no scores and finishing with a lousy 52 yards in the 35–21 defeat. Tedford blamed himself for devising a flawed game plan, but Rodgers accepted his share of responsibility. "I feel bad because I feel that I embarrassed him and the coaching staff," he said. Rodgers added that he thought he had "embarrassed my family, myself, and my team."

This was fixable. Tedford knew how to reach Rodgers and get the best out of him. After one particularly rough practice, the coach sat down the quarterback in his office and told him to take a breath, relax, and remember that he was going to be a great player at Cal and a longtime player in the NFL. Rodgers needed to hear that. He needed to be reminded that Tedford believed in him.

The Bears had a bye week before facing UCLA at the Rose Bowl. Rodgers grew up dreaming of playing on Saturdays on ABC with Keith Jackson on the call, and here he was playing on Saturday on ABC with Keith Jackson on the call, making up for the mess he made against Oregon State.

Down 20–12 with eighteen seconds left, facing a fourth-and-10 on the UCLA 35, Rodgers fired a strike on the move to Burl Toler that Jackson's broadcast partner, Hall of Famer Dan Fouts, called "the throw of the century." Tedford had wanted a play designed for McArthur or Strang before

Rodgers successfully lobbied for a Toler seam route. His two-point conversion pass to star running back Adimchinobe Echemandu sent the game to overtime before the Bruins won on a field goal.

Rodgers had to win four of his last five regular-season games to land Cal a bowl bid. He ended the Bears' 28-year home losing streak to Washington by accounting for 4 touchdowns and helping set a school record with 729 total yards in a 54–7 shredding of the Huskies. Then he punctuated the run with a 28–16 victory at Stanford in one of the sport's enduring rivalries.

Rodgers overcame an early interception and a couple of fumbles to throw for 3 touchdowns and a career-high 359 yards, the most for a Cal quarterback over 106 editions of the Big Game. He connected with McArthur a school-record sixteen times for 245 of those yards. He predicted in the huddle that he would find Strang for a touchdown on a play called "Right Tom R Spin 437 Stretch Boot R Slide," and sure enough he honored that prediction.

"He was Joe Cool," Strang said.

After he proved to be the biggest player in the Big Game, Rodgers said, "I'd like to be in the Rose Bowl. Is that possible?"

No, with a 7-6 record, the Insight Bowl would have to do. Before he made the trip to the desert, Rodgers returned to Butte as something of a homecoming hero to watch his former junior college team face Feather River College in the Tri Counties Bank Holiday Bowl. During pregame warmups, while making small talk with old teammates, Rodgers picked up a ball and took a knee at the 50-yard line. He then let rip two straight 60-yard throws that hit his target in the back of the end zone.

"He did it once and I said, 'Did he just hit the crossbar?'" offensive lineman Heath Prichard recalled. "I was doing my thing with my headphones warming up, and then he hit the crossbar again. I laughed and shook my head like, 'Holy shit.'"

While a Cal Bear, Rodgers also met up with his former high school receiver Thomas Wilson here and there at Pleasant Valley to get in extra work. "We'd go to PV to go throw, and I had gloves on," Wilson remembered. "They changed his mechanics a bit at Cal, and Aaron came back slinging those things so hard, even with gloves on, that he tore some of the skin between my fingers."

Rodgers was known to dislocate a receiver's finger here or there. During the opening practice for the Insight Bowl, McArthur ran a post pattern and had to lower his body on the run to reach for the ball.

"Aaron had so much velocity on the ball, it took my forearm into my knee and I broke my arm," the receiver said. "Nobody touched me. The velocity of his ball and my knee pushing out, that's what snapped my arm."

McArthur's absence was expected to compromise Cal's odds of beating Virginia Tech. On the other hand, McArthur himself said of Rodgers's accuracy, "My great-grandmother could've caught his passes."

Later in Rodgers's first year in the big time, everything about him was getting stronger, quicker, and more explosive by the week. His confidence was growing at the same rate. One Cal defensive back, James Bethea, recalled that Rodgers—a Garth Brooks–loving guitar player—was so comfortable with who he was in team settings that he sometimes performed strange dance moves to what Bethea called "inappropriate rap music" in the locker room. He said Rodgers often came across as "a goofball who didn't really have a care in the world.

"I know he cares, but he does have a nonchalant attitude to him . . . I think a part of who he is that makes him great is that mentality of being able to slow things down and still go one hundred percent and throw at a high accuracy. Rodgers is never moving a thousand miles an hour. He has this relaxed gunslinger mentality, and that's why he's a beast."

Without McArthur in the Insight Bowl, Rodgers turned to receiver Chase Lyman, a burner who worked his way through a bad ankle and averaged 30 yards on his 5 receptions to give the Bears a shot to win the shootout. On the first play of that final possession, Rodgers was sacked and stripped of the ball. Cal tackle Chris Murphy fell on it, leaving his team facing a second-and-16 with the Hokies riding a wave of momentum. Rodgers responded with an 11-yard swing pass to J. J. Arrington, and then with an 18-yard throw over the middle to Brandon Hall for a first down at the Virginia Tech 42.

On the next play, with just more than a minute to go, Rodgers moved up against the rush and hit Toler for 22 yards. The Bears ran down the clock to two seconds and asked Fredrickson to nail a 35-yard field goal to avoid overtime and end the season with a trophy.

After that drive, Strang said of his quarterback, "you knew this guy was going to play on Sundays."

Fredrickson had made all 54 of his extra-point kicks but had missed

15 of 29 field-goal attempts, including his previous five. As Rodgers left the field pumping his right fist, he stopped to pat Fredrickson on the ass and to offer words of encouragement. The quarterback then looked up and pointed his index fingers skyward. He had finished 6 yards shy of the 400-yard passing mark.

Virginia Tech coach Frank Beemer called time-out to ice Fredrickson, but the delay did nothing to fracture his focus. His final college kick was high and true, and the Bears came racing onto the field to celebrate.

"They didn't respect us before the game," Rodgers, the bowl's offensive MVP, said of the Hokies. "But after we put up fifty-two points on them, I think they know what we're about."

While his teammates partied deep into the desert night, Rodgers went out to dinner with his family and Craig Rigsbee. In the restaurant the quarterback pointed to his modest-sized MVP award.

"He said, 'My trophy at Butte was ten times better than this little shit-ass trophy,'" Rigsbee recalled. "And we all laughed like hell."

• • •

JEFF TEDFORD HAD never been so nervous. It was Saturday afternoon, October 9, 2004, inside the iconic Los Angeles Memorial Coliseum. The 4-0 USC Trojans were the No. 1 team in America, and the 3-0 Cal Golden Bears were ranked No. 7.

One of Cal's freshman linemen, Jeff Fritch, the son of a USC grad who grew up in awe of this building, looked from the visitors' sideline into the hazy sunshine and the crowd of more than ninety thousand, and said, "It felt like that stadium went on forever."

This was the first time in more than fifty years that the Trojans and the Golden Bears were meeting as top-ten teams. Tedford was feeling every ounce of the burden on his shoulders. He had inherited another man's 1-10 team and built it into a credible national contender, meaning his was no longer a cute long-shot story. The Bears had the talent, potentially, to go unbeaten. Now they faced an elite program with two all-everything players in quarterback Matt Leinart and running back Reggie Bush.

Tedford's job was to make sure that his student-athletes were cool, calm, and collected in the hour before kickoff, but he was too busy pacing to perform the task. Aaron Rodgers filled the void.

"There was so much tension and pressure, and the way he handled that was something I'd never really seen before," Tedford said. "He was oblivious to what was going on. He was slapping them on the butt, saying, 'Here we go,' just a jovial attitude. It wasn't a light attitude, but just an air of confidence that put everyone at ease."

Including the head coach.

Much like Craig Rigsbee, Tedford overcame a hardscrabble childhood that was short on parental supervision to become a Division I athlete and, ultimately, a college coach. He made a good life out of developing quarterbacks, just none as gifted as Rodgers. In their early days together they played checkers, with Tedford moving the black defensive pieces and asking Rodgers to react with his red offensive pieces.

Tedford gave his quarterback freedom at the line of scrimmage via check-with-me packages of four plays and run-pass options and helped him with unbalanced slot formations. Mistakes were sometimes made, but Rodgers described his coach as a reassuring mentor, and as a voice who kept the perfectionist inside of him level-headed and positive.

Meanwhile, Tedford honored the not-so-grand coaching tradition of sleeping overnight in his office on an air mattress. He lived about twenty-five minutes from campus, slept only three or four hours a night, and didn't want to spend one of those hours driving.

It was a grind for sure, but he was the head coach, offensive coordinator, and play caller. The way Tedford saw it, he had little choice but to sleep in the office from Sunday night through Wednesday night, and to spend Friday night with his team, leaving him only two nights at home.

Cal athletic director Steve Gladstone, the celebrated rowing coach who had hired Tedford, realized that these absurd hours could lead to burnout. But as a member of the profession himself, Gladstone did not believe in micromanaging the men and women in charge of his programs.

"Jeff knew what got him to where he was," the AD said, "and he was not going to let go of that drive.... Prior to my hiring Jeff, people would say, 'You can't win big-time football at Cal.' They had a whole bunch of reasons why it can't be done, and of course they were all bogus. If you get the right coach, the team will be successful."

The right coach who signs the right quarterback, anyway.

Cal offensive coordinator George Cortez knew early on that Rodgers might become the best quarterback in school history. He explained that there was a pass play the Bears ran in the 2003 season that required a receiver to run a post pattern and a tight end to run a wheel route behind it. Rodgers was supposed to peek at the post pattern and then to throw to the tight end heading upfield.

"We'd never thrown it to the guy running the post," Cortez said. "We always threw the ball to the tight end, even in practice. So, in the game the guy running the post didn't look and Aaron's ball hit him in the head forty yards downfield."

To make certain that never happened again, Cal's receivers coach, Eric Kiesau, decided his group needed to follow specific Rodgers rules, or what were called 8-route rules, as a nod to the quarterback's jersey number. The rules could be reduced to one simple instruction.

"If 8 is in the game," Cortez said, "you'd better look."

In the Coliseum that day against USC, Rodgers, who had bulked up to 220 pounds, played as big as just about any college quarterback ever has, starting on the very first snap of the game—a short pass to Chris Manderino off a play-action fake that gained 14 yards. The quarterback pumped his right fist forcefully for punctuation.

And then Rodgers went on a tear that lasted into the fourth quarter, slicing up a defense shaped by NFL talent. Eight yards here, twelve yards there. One intermediate pass after another that the Trojans were powerless to defend. He did not throw a single incomplete in his first ten attempts, fifteen attempts, twenty attempts.

Somehow USC prevented the big play and held the lead throughout the game, fueling the massive crowd. "We couldn't hear anything," said Cal left tackle Andrew Cameron. "Aaron is screaming audibles and I'm looking at his mouth and I can't hear anything, and behind his head I see the Goodyear blimp in the background. It was a very surreal experience, but Aaron owned it."

As the game barreled toward its climax, Cameron kept telling himself, "Don't be the guy to screw it up." He was the player most responsible for protecting Rodgers, for walling off his blind side, and he did his job. The Cal linemen gave their quarterback a chance to do something special.

Rodgers tied an NCAA record set by Tennessee's Tee Martin in 1998 by completing twenty-three consecutive passes and established a new NCAA record by completing twenty-six straight over two games. In fact, with nine minutes to play, Rodgers's first incomplete was not even a legitimate attempt—he intentionally sailed the ball out of bounds to beat the heavy pressure and avoid the inevitable sack. As Keith Jackson said on the air, Rodgers threw it in the cheap seats. And that was just fine.

"Aaron played against one of the best defensive minds in the game," Cameron said, "and he ate up Pete Carroll. I remember us marching down the field and the USC defensive linemen and linebackers looking at Carroll with shrugs and their hands out like, 'Are we doing anything?' And Pete looks at them and shrugs with his hands out like, 'I don't know. What do you want from me?'"

Trailing 23–17 in the closing minutes, ball at the Cal 35-yard line, Rodgers stepped into his huddle, locked eyes with his teammates, and announced, "We're going to go 65 yards here and get the win."

Rodgers used his athleticism to escape the pocket and run to the left side for 14 yards. He had finally undergone surgery on his bum left knee in January after living with it for four seasons and after aggravating it against USC, making him a healthier player with a cleaner gait.

Five plays later, Rodgers put the Golden Bears on the Trojans' 9-yard line with a 17-yard dart to a covered McArthur on the right sideline. It was his 29th completion in 31 attempts for 267 yards and a touchdown.

Now Cal had options. It could lean on J. J. Arrington, who would rush for more than 2,000 yards in this 2004 season, including 112 against USC, or on emerging freshman running back Marshawn Lynch. Or it could ask the quarterback who was wearing the Joe Montana shirt under his pads to make like his hero and settle the game with his right arm.

Rodgers was nine yards away from a shot at winning his school's first Heisman Trophy, and a shot at leading Cal to the Rose Bowl for the first time since the 1958 season.

On first and goal with 1:47 to go, Rodgers rolled right and unleashed a fastball into the end zone to Noah Smith, who couldn't bring it in. On second and goal, Rodgers scrambled right to evade the rush but was sacked from behind by Manuel Wright.

Tedford called time-out. The Coliseum was all but shaking, as the situation for Cal had grown dire. But as Tedford was reminded before kickoff, Rodgers's presence always had a calming effect on his coaches and teammates. With the Cal defense on the field late in a different tense and tight game, Cameron recalled approaching the quarterback and asking if a minute and a half represented enough time for him to take the team the length of the field.

Rodgers laughed at him. "I only need twenty to thirty seconds," he said.

So, when the Golden Bears left Tedford on the sideline and headed back to the field, they believed they were about to defeat the finest college football team in the land. They believed because Aaron Rodgers believed.

It was third-and-goal from the 14, 1:27 left, when Rodgers took the snap and started backpedaling, holding the ball up near his earhole as always. He felt pressure again and this time took off to his left before throwing on the run, against his body, to McArthur, who was covered in the end zone by USC's Eric Wright. When the cornerback made his move to break up the play, he whiffed on the ball. It was a remarkable throw that hit McArthur in the hands but fell to the painted grass.

"I never saw the ball," the receiver said. "It just appeared, and I tried to do a late reaction."

Fourth and goal, 1:21 to play. Chase Lyman had been lost earlier in the day to a season-ending knee injury, eliminating one of Cal's most dangerous playmakers. But Rodgers had completed passes to nine different receivers in this game, including seven to McArthur. He had enough options to cover the 14 yards separating Cal from paydirt.

Rodgers walked up to the line of scrimmage, surveyed the USC defense, and then turned to an official and signaled for the Bears' final time-out.

The quarterback and Tedford talked, weighed the possibilities, and made their decision. Rodgers returned to his huddle, and the roaring crowd rose in anticipation.

"An enormous moment for both these teams is at hand," Keith Jackson said. The legendary announcer reminded his audience that Cal had never, ever beaten a No. 1–ranked team.

Back at the line, Rodgers pulled out from under center and faced the two receivers to his left, slapping his hands together as a signal. And then he took the snap, dropped back to the 20-yard line, and let it rip toward a spot in the USC end zone between the gold *U* and *S*, out of the reach of third-year receiver Jonathan Makonnen.

At first glance, it was a rare Rodgers misfire at the worst possible time. But replays showed that Makonnen slipped coming out of his break, that he would have had his defender beaten, and that he likely would have caught the go-ahead touchdown pass had he kept his balance.

Pete Carroll, world's oldest teenager, bounced around the USC sideline with his arms in the air, relieved that his outright national title hopes were still intact. As the Trojans bled the final seconds off the clock, a distraught Rodgers walked the visitors' sideline rubbing the back of his head with a white Gatorade towel. After the last snap, Carroll and Matt Leinart ran to each other and the coach jumped into the eventual Heisman winner's arms. They did not beat Aaron Rodgers as much as they survived him.

"It was a really fantastic, incredible showing by their quarterback," Carroll said. "That guy was frickin' lights out."

The box score was not in agreement with the Coliseum scoreboard. The Golden Bears had more than doubled the Trojans' total yardage, compelling their free safety, Ryan Gutierrez, to say that they would beat USC nine times out of ten. Cal arguably would have toppled any other team in America with its quarterback playing at such a historic level.

"It's pretty frustrating," Rodgers said, "because we dominated the game. We couldn't get the job done. I couldn't get the job done." He would later call this defeat "one of the greatest failures" of his college career.

Even if it felt otherwise, the consequences were not fatal. The Bears could still achieve their primary goal. Rodgers had seven more games to become the first quarterback to lead Cal to the Rose Bowl in forty-six years.

• • •

JUST LIKE AT Butte, Aaron Rodgers was not one to show up at on- or off-campus parties. He was not one to use his celebrity status and/or a fake ID to work his way into a bar before his twenty-first birthday on December 2, 2004.

He was one to savor his regular poker games with teammates and friends. "It was the only thing I ever saw Aaron do for fun," said Andrew Cameron.

He was good at poker too. Over his three semesters at Cal, Rodgers played weekly with six or seven other guys, often at Vinny Strang's apartment. One of the regulars, Tom Schneider, the starting kicker during Rodgers's junior year, said the buy-in for the cash games ran between a hundred and three hundred bucks, with the pot growing up to a thousand.

"Aaron hated to lose," said Chris Manderino, his fullback. "There was a subtle cockiness to him, so it was always good to take him down when maybe he was bluffing, or just to get the best of him."

That subtle (or not-so-subtle) cockiness was a topic of conversation among the Golden Bears. One writer who interviewed Rodgers at Cal called him the cockiest person he had ever met. Before the start of the 2004 season, Rodgers had admitted to another writer, Dave Newhouse, that he had extreme self-confidence. "I probably think I'm a lot better than I really am," Rodgers said. "But that attitude is contagious. The team feeds off of it."

Cameron said he noticed a shift in the quarterback's personality after his historic performance in the USC loss. The left tackle thought Rodgers became a bit quieter, a bit more reserved, and he wasn't alone. Cameron recalled that an assistant coach privately asked players if they had noticed it too, and if they needed to adjust to the quarterback's new temperament.

"It was the type of thing, 'Does he think he's better than everybody and have a sense of superiority now?'" Cameron recalled. "Maybe it was a sense of separation, like, 'If anything bad happens now, it's certainly not Aaron's fault. He's perfect.'"

Asked about this perception years later, Rodgers said he did not intend to create distance between himself and his team. He expressed his affection for Cameron, called him "a warrior," and said he appreciated the feedback.

"I'm sorry he felt like that," Rodgers said for this book, "but there was no conscious decision that I made that, 'I'm the fuckin' man now.'"

Only this much was clear: late in the season, when injuries put younger receivers on the field, Rodgers had little patience for their lack of playbook command. Offensive coordinator George Cortez said the freshmen did not always look for the ball on time when running their routes.

"So, he just hit them with the ball," Cortez said. "That was cute the first day, but they're going to play in the game. . . . Aaron said, 'They're on scholarship too.'"

But the vast majority of the stories teammates and coaches told about Rodgers painted him as the same inclusive leader he was in junior college. McArthur said his quarterback never projected a "you should bow down to me" vibe and never did anything with teammates "that came from a place of ego."

To emphasize that point, Jeff Fritch recalled showing up to Cal as a walk-on offensive lineman who missed preseason camp with a back injury. He felt overwhelmed, out of place.

"I felt I was the lowest man on the totem pole," he said.

About a week into practice, Fritch ended up at the team's training table for dinner. He grabbed a plate, filled it, then searched for a place to sit.

The tables were all taken by upperclassmen on scholarship, leaving Fritch to look around the dining hall at a bunch of relative strangers who were ignoring him.

"Aaron was just sitting down, and he turns to me and says, 'Hey man, do you want to sit and eat dinner with me?'" Fritch recalled. "It was just the two of us at his table, and then it filled in from there. Aaron made me feel like I was part of the team."

Marvin Philip, one of the nation's best centers, recalled returning to Cal in 2003 from a two-year mission for the Church of Jesus Christ of Latter-day Saints and fielding an introduction from the new quarterback, who immediately made it clear that he had read up on him. Rodgers asked the young man who would snap him the ball about his South Dakota mission and about his availability to be his roommate (Philip was already committed).

"Aaron got along with everybody," Philip said. "Our team was unique in that we had guys from all different kinds of backgrounds. Marshawn Lynch was from Oakland, and you had guys from the suburbs playing with him. Aaron did a great job of bringing everyone together. You'd see him with Marshawn joking around, and other guys he would joke with, and that was the basis of the respect he got from the team.

"He was not a guy who thought he was better than anyone else. Some quarterbacks can't relate to guys like he could."

Rodgers lived in Cal's Clark Kerr dorms his sophomore year with a fellow juco transfer and good friend, Francis Blay-Miezah. Then he moved off campus his junior year and lived with his best friend and former Pleasant Valley classmate Jordan Russell, a burgeoning chef. They had virtually no money and lived in what Rodgers called a rough area near the Ashby BART station, where the nighttime sound of gunfire was not uncommon. They used the living room as a second bedroom in their six-hundred-square-foot apartment, and Rodgers drove his scooter to and from campus.

Russell was a great cook; Rodgers particularly loved the pastries that his roommate made at culinary school. The quarterback once went on a hunt with former Cal quarterback Mike Pawlawski, who shot three teals that day. Rodgers, a terrible shot, brought home Pawlawski's ducks, and Russell prepared them for dinner.

In the unlikely event that football didn't work out, Rodgers thought briefly of becoming a broadcaster. He bailed on his communications major when he realized it wasn't focused on getting him an NFL analyst job in a network booth and switched to his preferred history courses in American studies. Along the way he ended up in a food appreciation class with a professor who had no appreciation for the way his study group cited sources in a paper. She gave everyone a grade of F, and, by Rodgers's account, did not grant him the same opportunity to rewrite the paper that she had granted others.

The quarterback decided he needed to show up late to a 2 p.m. practice so he could confront the professor during her office hours.

"I went in there and she was ready for me," he said. "She ripped me apart and said athletes always want stuff given to them, I wasn't going to be able to rewrite my paper, and on and on and on, this tirade that she went on about athletes and entitlement. She basically picked on the wrong person in class because I was probably the best student out of the eleven football players in there."

When the professor asked the student what he wanted to do with himself, Rodgers told her that he planned to play in the NFL.

"No way in hell," she said through a laugh, according to the quarterback. "You won't make it. You'll get hurt. . . . What I've seen from you is, you won't amount to anything."

Rodgers met that withering scouting report with this two-word response:

"Watch me."

• • •

MARSHAWN LYNCH TOOK the handoff with 3:42 left in the third quarter against Stanford, and Cal leading by a 13–3 count. It appeared to be a garden-variety run to the right side for a short gain, at least until Lynch broke a tackle at his own 45-yard line, then cut left and headed for daylight. As he raced downhill into the Stanford secondary, a blur in blue came flying past him on the inside.

Aaron Rodgers. He was about to throw the critical block that freed Lynch on his 55-yard touchdown run. In fact, the quarterback did not just make initial contact with Stanford safety Oshiomogho Atogwe, an NFL talent, at the Cardinal 35. Rodgers finished him off with a second hit at the 26, landing Atogwe flat on his back to give Lynch the cutback lane to his right that he needed to go the distance.

Given the circumstances, and what is and is not expected of a quarterback, this might have been the best play Rodgers ever made as a Cal Golden Bear.

"Aaron was willing to put his body and his career on the line," Geoff McArthur said, "and that's how touchdowns happen."

The quarterback had earned so much of his teammates' trust through his effort and execution that his center, Marvin Philip, likened Rodgers's dominance of opposing defenses to that of a star athlete playing backyard basketball against a much younger, much smaller cousin. One uncontested layup after another.

Rodgers's last game at Memorial Stadium had to be the Big Game against the Cardinal, with the winner earning yearlong possession of the Stanford Axe—the head of an axe mounted on a wooden plaque. He did not have to throw much in this 41–6 victory, as J. J. Arrington and Lynch dominated on the ground.

But this was a day when Rodgers stood as tall as Cal's famed clock and bell tower known as the Campanile. This stadium, built on the Hayward Fault at the base of the Berkeley Hills and at the mouth of Strawberry Canyon, was the quarterback's house for the final time. Inside one of the sport's most scenic arenas, with the bridges and the bay in the distance, the sellout crowd of 72,981 moved to thank Rodgers for delivering the first unbeaten home season since 1950.

Thousands of fans poured onto the field after time expired, and a fair number of them went looking for their quarterback. Rodgers had been one throw against USC away from an 11-0 record and a crack at the national title. The fans thanked him by lifting them on their shoulders and giving him a forever ride while he spread his arms wide and held a red rose in his right hand.

Rodgers already knew that he was leaving school for the NFL Draft, and that he might have a chance to be the No. 1 overall pick. Though he would fall to a ninth-place finish in the Heisman Trophy voting, 259 first-place votes behind the winner, USC's Matt Leinart, Rodgers had become a favorite of NFL scouts and draft analysts.

None of that mattered in this moment as he was carried by the fans with the Bears' ultimate goal still in front of him. First played as "the Tournament East-West Football Game" on New Year's Day in 1902, the Rose Bowl was nicknamed "the Granddaddy of Them All" by Keith Jackson. It meant everything to the Pac-10 and Big Ten schools vying to meet there.

USC was booked for the Orange Bowl, the designated site of the national title game in the Bowl Championship Series, opening a Rose Bowl slot for members of the various major conferences opposite the Big Ten champ, Michigan.

The Bears had protected their No. 4 national ranking in the polls, and it seemed everyone agreed that they would clinch that Rose Bowl berth by beating Southern Mississippi on the road in a hurricane-delayed finale to be played in two weeks.

Until everyone got a lesson in how the game is really played.

• • •

SOME PLAYERS CRIED. Some shouted. Some seethed. Some stared in disbelief.

Some headed out into the Memorial Stadium stands to be alone with their thoughts.

"It was just a sickening feeling," Chris Manderino said.

The Golden Bears had beaten Southern Miss to go 11-1, and they had outplayed the top-ranked USC Trojans in their building. They deserved to keep their No. 4 ranking in the Bowl Championship Series standings and their coveted trip to the Rose Bowl. The last time the Bears advanced to Pasadena, Alaska and Hawaii were still on the verge of statehood. It had been a long time.

But the head coach at the University of Texas, Mack Brown, had been in the business for three decades and had been running Division I programs for two of them. He knew how to work the system. He knew how to campaign for votes.

Before facing Southern Miss, Cal had been ahead of Texas in the convoluted BCS standings by .0013 points. After Cal beat Southern Miss, 26–16, in a game that was undecided deep into the fourth quarter, the idle Longhorns hurdled the Bears and finished .0129 points ahead of them to seize the Rose Bowl berth opposite Michigan and to send Aaron Rodgers and friends to a Holiday Bowl meeting with Texas Tech.

Jeff Tedford met with his players in what became a grief-counseling session. "The kids were just devastated," he said. "A lot of tears. I'll never forget walking back and some guys were spread out through the stadium and hollering, they were so frustrated. There was a lot of pain that day."

Some people at Cal, Tedford said, would rather go to the Rose Bowl than win the national championship.

The nation's only team ranked in the top six in scoring offense and scoring defense, Cal had everything but the blowout victory over Southern Miss that the voters apparently needed, and the political know-how to debate the Longhorns' Brown as he went from national interview to national interview pushing his Big 12 Conference cause.

"I called for an investigation," Tedford said. "I'd like to see who changed their votes and find out why they changed their votes."

As it turned out, nine media members moved the Longhorns ahead of Cal in the Associated Press poll, including three from Texas. In the USA Today/ESPN poll, six coaches dropped the Bears out of the top six while two elevated Texas to No. 3.

Tedford had Rodgers take a knee at the end of the Southern Miss game rather than attempt to add points to the final score. "Would Bob Stoops [of Oklahoma] and Mack Brown have gone for the score there?" Rodgers said. "Yes. But Coach Tedford is a classy guy. He isn't going to beg for votes, ever."

The Cal quarterback called Brown "a little classless" for talking down the Bears the way he did. Rodgers said he woke up that morning thinking he was Rose Bowl–bound, then started to get a sinking feeling after checking the online polls.

Now Rodgers had to close out his college career on an unworthy stage, with a team that had no particular interest in winning the Holiday Bowl in San Diego.

"Did anybody want to play in the Holiday Bowl? No," said Cal defensive back Donnie McCleskey.

The Golden Bears were $11\frac{1}{2}$-point favorites, and yet they were down 10 points at halftime, and 21 points after three quarters. They lost, 45–31, because a former Texas Tech walk-on named Sonny Cumbie threw for 520 yards and 3 touchdowns, and Rodgers threw for 246 yards and one. On his last play as an amateur athlete, Rodgers scored on a 1-yard sneak. He then headed to the sideline and motioned to the crowd with both hands extended, his bittersweet wave goodbye.

All anyone could talk about was how the BCS and Mack Brown were proven right. "This Is No Way for Rodgers to End His Career at Cal," read the headline above Neil Hayes's column in the *Contra Costa Times*.

"I'm going to think about it for a couple of days and talk to my family and make a decision," said Rodgers, who finished his Cal career with 43 touchdown passes against 13 interceptions.

Four days later, he made it official that he was turning pro. Rodgers said he consulted with family and friends, coaches and pastors, before making his decision. He said that the opportunity was too good to pass up, and that it made sense to "pursue something I've been wanting to do since I was a child."

The day before, the San Francisco 49ers had clinched the first overall pick in the draft by finishing 2-14. Rodgers had been watching the Niners since he was two years old. He called them "my first love."

Now he had three and a half months to compel them to love him back.

6

THE PLUNGE

THOMAS WEATHERSPOON HAD a specific goal when working with college football players hoping to get drafted. Of course, the trainer wanted his clients to become stars in the National Football League.

But Weatherspoon was not in the business of molding these college kids into highly productive pros. "My job is to make these guys look real pretty so the NFL would ask them to the prom," he said.

The 1983 national collegiate champion in the long jump and triple jump at the University of Wisconsin–Stevens Point, Weatherspoon knew what pro football teams wanted. "The NFL buys speed because they know they can build bodies," he said. "I sell speed."

For a fee of $6,500, Weatherspoon trained prospects who knew that quicker, more explosive movements could be the difference between fame and fortune and a permanent career change at a much lower wage. His company, Performance Enhancement for Professional Athletes in Alameda, had already established a reputation among players and agents of elevating vertical leaps and lowering sprint times.

And yet in 2003, when Weatherspoon met with Kyle Boller, a potential middle-round draft pick, and his father and told them that his training methods would make the Cal quarterback a first-round pick, Boller's father laughed.

"I guarantee it," Weatherspoon said. "Mike Vick was a superstar last year and now every damn coach in the NFL is looking for a fast quarterback. I can make your kid fast.... Your kid is going to go in the first round."

Weatherspoon delivered Boller to the annual predraft combine in Indianapolis with precious little body fat on his 234-pound frame. The Cal quarterback posted a 20-yard shuttle time that beat the speed posted by all of the quarterbacks and running backs and most of the cornerbacks and wide receivers. Though Boller completed at least 50 percent of his passes only once in his four seasons in Berkeley, and though he led teams that finished a combined 15-30, the Baltimore Ravens made him the nineteenth overall pick in the draft.

"When he got into the league after his first season," Weatherspoon recalled, "people came up to me and said, 'The kid can't even play football. What the fuck?' I said, 'That's not my job. You watched that boy for four years. My job is to get him ready for the combine.'"

And such was his job when he started training Aaron Rodgers, another Cal quarterback in need of upgraded wheels. Weatherspoon had become a good friend of Cal coach Jeff Tedford and had watched Rodgers play his two seasons at Berkeley. The trainer thought the quarterback was an ordinary athlete with a superhuman arm.

"I'd never seen anything like it," Weatherspoon said. "He's got to be the most accurate quarterback I've ever seen."

Weatherspoon got results by training his clients in the sand and the water to improve their agility, strength, and balance, and by running them to the point of fatigue. Within two months, he could surgically shave three-tenths of a second from a 40 time while adding four to six inches to a vertical leap.

The trainer helped put seven players in the first two rounds of the 2003 draft. Lorenzo Alexander, a Cal defensive lineman who had been working out with Weatherspoon since his high school days, recommended him to Rodgers. The quarterback had the trainer at hello.

"I fell in love immediately with Aaron," Weatherspoon said. "He's got this quirky sense of humor that cracks him up, and he doesn't care that you don't get it. He walks away with that smile on his face like, 'I just got one over on him.' I really liked that about him."

Weatherspoon quickly discovered that Rodgers was among the most competitive people he had ever met. The trainer had rented two 50,000-square-foot facilities on the shuttered naval air base on San Francisco Bay, along with an indoor turf field, to prepare his athletes for the beauty pageant that was the combine.

The first time Weatherspoon watched Rodgers in the 40-yard dash, he came away thinking, *Boy, he cannot run*. The trainer recalled that the quarterback initially tested out in the 4.9s.

"Aaron's whole thing in training was that he wanted to outdo Boller in everything that Kyle did," Weatherspoon said. "He was chasing Kyle Boller. He wanted to eclipse him from the record books.

"Kyle ran in the 4.5s, and Aaron was like, 'I gotta run 4.5. I gotta run 4.5.' I said, 'No problem, I'll get you there.' And by the end of camp, he was running 4.5s all day long."

It took Weatherspoon six to seven weeks to get him there; Rodgers had started the program with a short gait and without much in the way of knee drive. Weatherspoon wanted to open up his hips and get him to run the 40 in nineteen strides or less. It worked.

So did the excruciating Rolfing technique used to help Rodgers get taller. Yes, taller.

Weatherspoon claimed that his client, on arrival, was a shade taller than six feet, as opposed to the listed six foot two. "That was an issue," the trainer said. "And Aaron was like, 'What can I do about that?'"

Weatherspoon explained that weightlifting compresses the body, and that nobody stands up completely straight, and that if Rodgers were willing to undergo a once-a-week, twenty-minute session of deep tissue manipulation, he could lengthen connective tissues, improve his alignment, and gain a half inch to an inch in height.

The only downside was the pain. By using their hands, knuckles, and elbows to release tension and balance the body, therapists made these elite athletes cry for their mothers.

"Nobody wanted to get on the table with our therapist. Nobody," Weatherspoon said.

Rodgers was willing to submit to the pain.

"He might have been biting his tongue, but nobody else could deal with it," Weatherspoon recalled. "I never heard him complain about it or told her to stop."

Rodgers's height was indeed an issue with some NFL scouts, so even a half inch could be a difference maker in an evaluation. And Weatherspoon claimed that the quarterback would not have been measured at six foot two without his Rolfing sessions.

"People were like, 'Holy shit, how did he get taller?'" the trainer said.

THE PLUNGE

Rodgers still had to outshine Utah's Alex Smith, who stood six foot four, in their workouts and interviews to land the coveted prize—selection as the No. 1 overall pick by his childhood team, the San Francisco 49ers.

Rodgers and Smith had introduced themselves to America in the same nationally televised college game in 2003, won by the Utes. Off the bench, Rodgers was the more effective passer while Smith, making his first start, was the more effective runner. Scouts saw them the same way at the start of the February 2005 combine. They questioned the Cal quarterback's athleticism, just as they questioned the Utah quarterback's ability to throw the deep ball against secondaries with NFL closing speed.

Smith had to answer for what he was not asked to do in Urban Meyer's spread offense. Rodgers had to answer for his robotic-looking mechanics and earhole-level ball placement in Cal's West Coast offense, along with the underwhelming history of Tedford's first-round quarterbacks. Though Trent Dilfer, whom Tedford had coached as a Fresno State assistant, had game-managed his way to a Super Bowl ring with the 2000 Baltimore Ravens, none of Tedford's high picks had thrown more touchdowns than interceptions in their NFL careers.

Rodgers was not about to quiet those concerns over four days in Indianapolis, where more than three hundred prospects gathered to be timed and tested, poked and prodded, by team reps trying to piece together a profile of the young men who might someday win them a Super Bowl. Each team was allowed fifteen-minute interviews with as many as sixty combine invitees, and those interviews ranged from informational to interrogative, biographical to bizarre. Prospects were often asked to break down plays on video.

The top quarterbacks in the 2005 draft did not match up with the 2004 class, which featured Eli Manning, Philip Rivers, and Ben Roethlisberger. But the 49ers needed help at the sport's signature position, and they made it clear that either Rodgers or Smith would be their guy.

They met with both in Indianapolis. "You expect a quarterback is going to know a lot about football," said rookie head coach Mike Nolan. "But I was surprised by how much they knew about the game."

Rodgers scored a 35 out of a possible 50 on the Wonderlic test, which measured cognitive ability via fifty multiple-choice questions that needed to be answered in twelve minutes. The good news? This was an excellent score, far north of the reported Wonderlic average of 20.

The bad news? Alex Smith scored a 40. Between the combine and the April 23 draft, he was going to be a tough man to beat.

Smith had the requisite brains, and he had the requisite size. Rodgers was the same height as his quarterbacking heroes, Joe Montana and Steve Young, but few scouts seemed to care.

"I actually prayed to God last night to give me a couple more inches," Rodgers joked with reporters at the combine. "But I don't really think that's a factor. A friend emailed me the other night that the average size of the Hall of Fame quarterbacks was 6-1, 200 pounds."

Nobody was going to earn induction into Canton at the combine, so, like Smith, Rodgers decided against throwing with the quarterbacks who were rated lower on the early draft boards. The top two prospects chose to make NFL evaluators wait to watch them perform at their workouts in the middle of March.

Meanwhile, Rodgers and Smith took part in drills inside the RCA Dome that measured their speed and agility, including the all-important 40-yard dash. Smith showed off his athleticism in the three-cone and 20-yard shuttle tests, posting the best quarterback times in both. His 32-inch vertical leap was two and a half inches shorter than the mark set by Rodgers, who matched the best performance at his position.

Evaluators were more interested in how fast Rodgers could run than in how high he could jump. Wearing a white shirt carrying the number 24, blue shorts, and yellow shoes, Rodgers made his way to the 40 starting line, doubled over, and put his hands on the turf between two small orange cones. He swung his left arm backward and toward the dome roof, and then took off.

Ideally, Weatherspoon said, a sprinter should stay down for the first six to eight steps as if he were pushing a sled. To the uneducated eye, it seemed Rodgers did what he could to cover the assigned distance as quickly as his body would allow. His arms and knees were pumping like mad, and while he wasn't quite moving with the grace of an Olympic sprinter, he looked a whole lot better than Tom Brady did five years earlier, when the Michigan quarterback ran the 40 as if he were an out-of-shape broker chasing his runaway dog.

To the educated eye, Rodgers's execution was sloppy and potentially harmful.

"What, you forgot everything you learned?" Weatherspoon asked him.

"I just stood straight up," Rodgers confessed. "I got excited."

His official time was actually a very respectable 4.71, the same time posted by Smith. Rodgers had proven he could go step for step with an accomplished runner who also happened to be his chief competition for the first pick.

But Weatherspoon had been expecting something in the 4.6s and had even held out hope for something in the 4.5s. "I was mad at him," the trainer said. And yet Weatherspoon knew that his client had closed the athleticism gap on Smith in Indianapolis, and that Rodgers would get to unleash his most lethal weapon—his right arm—the following month in Berkeley.

Smith put on a clinic for NFL teams at his own campus workout on March 16. The Utah quarterback threw eighty passes to receivers Steve Savoy and Paris Warren during his hourlong audition inside his team's facility, and a mere three hit the ground. He took some snaps from under center—he spent his college career in shotgun formation—and showed the kind of arm strength on deep balls that he wasn't often asked to show in the spread. Smith was good enough to compel the attending scouts to give him a standing ovation. Scouts are no more inclined to give those ovations at personal Pro Days than reporters are to give them at press conferences.

Every NFL team was represented in Salt Lake City. The teams with the top three picks—San Francisco, Miami, and Cleveland—all had their chief decision-makers on hand to study Smith, including Mike Nolan, new Dolphins coach Nick Saban, and Browns general manager Phil Savage. They had spent time talking to Smith, who had led Utah to a 12-0 season, and had all come away impressed with him as a young man.

As for how Smith looked when he took the dropbacks and executed the rollouts and throws needed in the NFL, Nolan of the Niners said, "He did a lot of things he didn't do as a college player, and he did them well." Nolan added that Smith impressed him with "the consistency of his personality."

Knowing that Nolan was among dozens of NFL evaluators who had boarded planes for the Bay Area thinking Smith had just vaulted to the top of the draft, Rodgers was facing intense pressure in his workout.

On St. Patrick's Day, the Cal quarterback delivered a command performance to the NFL executives, coaches, and scouts who gathered at Memorial Stadium to watch him spin it. In an explosive counterpunch to Smith's eighty-pass performance, Rodgers threw ninety-two passes, including ninety-one accurate ones.

"He is as polished as I've seen," said Nolan, who had final say on the top draft pick.

Rodgers completed rollout passes to his right and left with relative ease, tempering concerns about his mobility. Nolan watched it all with Niners offensive coordinator Mike McCarthy, quarterbacks coach Jim Hostler, and vice president of player personnel Scot McCloughan.

"I did not know he had that much arm strength," Nolan said. "We had him stand at the 50 and take a step and put as much height on the ball as he could while getting it to the end zone. . . . It was effortless for him to throw the ball up. He had a great deep ball that just came out of his hands so easily. Without question Aaron had the best arm strength and ability to throw the ball of all the guys we looked at.

"But there's a lot more to playing quarterback than throwing the football."

Was this startling exhibition of arm strength, accuracy, and poise enough for the Niners to move Rodgers ahead of Smith on their draft board?

The league still had a tough time getting past the history of Tedford's NFL quarterbacks. It seemed his system was making the player, rather than the other way around, and some evaluators believed Rodgers was an extension of that trend.

The quarterback thought that he was better than the other first-rounders mentored by his Cal coach (and did not hesitate to share that opinion), and that it was ridiculous to penalize him for the sins of others.

"I really don't believe in the Tedford curse," he said. Rodgers maintained that one team gave more credence to the curse than any other.

The Green Bay Packers.

Rodgers was finding out the hard way that the process of judging talent before the draft was a full-contact sport. One NFC scout provided this assessment of him to Bob McGinn of the *Milwaukee Journal Sentinel*:

"I think he has a good chance of being a bust. Just like every other Tedford-coached quarterback. Thing I struggle with [with] him is he gets sacked a lot. He doesn't have great ability to change the release of the football. He's mechanically very rigid. . . . There will be more growing pains with Alex Smith but in the end, he has a much better chance to be much better."

A scout from the AFC offered up this Rodgers report: "The Tedford quarterbacks never made it. They carried the ball too high. His delivery was a little unconventional and it was, 'Yeah, this just doesn't transfer to the league.'"

Those scouts were hardly alone in thinking that Rodgers was a system creation. The Niners talked a lot about the Tedford curse, Nolan said, because it struck them as odd.

But then again, at the workout, Nolan said to himself, "Oh my God. I know you've got this [Tedford] thing, but son of a gun, nobody throws the ball like that. Nobody can flick his wrist like that."

McCarthy was surprised by Rodgers's execution in his Pro Day drills because he had not been blown away by what he had seen on film. The Niners' offensive coordinator thought it was the best workout he had seen live, in any year.

Nolan recalled that the San Francisco group did discuss Rodgers's earhole position of the ball and wondered if that could be changed. During one workout drill, Rodgers was asked to take snaps and get rid of the ball quickly, and he managed the task effortlessly without raising the ball to his ear. Nolan remembered walking away thinking that ball position "doesn't need to be a negative on the guy."

After Rodgers's near-perfect showing in Memorial Stadium, the Niners' four representatives arranged to meet him for lunch at a Berkeley restaurant. The San Francisco contingent was sitting at a table on the outside patio when Rodgers pulled up in what Nolan recalled as a big, black SUV.

As the new caretakers of a dreadful 2-14 roster, Nolan, McCloughan, McCarthy, and Hostler were on the verge of a career-shaping decision. The son of Dick Nolan, former NFL player and former Niners and Saints head coach, Mike had been an NFL assistant with six franchises since 1987 before getting his first crack at running his own team—the Niners granted him complete control of football operations. McCloughan, a former minor-league baseball player and the son and brother of former NFL players, was making the jump from scouting into a senior personnel role that could lead to bigger, better things. McCarthy had been in the league since 1993 and was itching for his first head coaching job. And Hostler had been a position coach for several teams—including the 2012 Super Bowl champion Baltimore Ravens—who was looking for his first coordinator's job.

If they made the right pick between Rodgers and Smith, their professional goals could be achieved . . . and then some. So, this lunch with the Cal quarterback was important, especially since Nolan and the Niners put more emphasis on leadership, character, intelligence, and mental toughness than they put on physical skill. In fact, reported Kevin Lynch of the *San Francisco Chronicle*, seven of their ten criteria used to evaluate a quarterback dealt with "the mental aspect."

Widely known as one of this blood sport's finer gentlemen, Nolan fell hard for Alex Smith, the human being. He saw the Utah quarterback as a polite and respectful kid. A pleaser. A safe pick. Years later, Rodgers would tell a story that he admitted he could not verify—Nolan favored Smith because he saw him open a car door for his mother.

"I think it's nice to show respect. I'm big on respect," Nolan said. "It's a funny story, but it's not true. I don't put much credence in that. Aaron was Aaron. He was respectful too, like Alex, but he had a lot of Cal in him, which was not a bad thing."

A lot of Cal in him. That came through during lunch in Berkeley. Nolan had been a Stanford assistant—he was on the 1982 staff victimized by The Play, Cal's winning last-second, five-lateral kickoff return that unfolded with the Cardinal marching band on the field. He believed he was a leading scholar in the mindset of the prototypical Cal and Stanford student.

If Rodgers happened to pat Nolan on his ass during their meeting or refer to him as "Mike" instead of "Coach Nolan," well, Mike grew up in California too. "And that's kind of the California way, it really is," Nolan said. "They teach their kids to say adults' first names, and I was probably that way as a kid too. I realized later that you don't get anything in life until you say 'Sir' or 'Ma'am.'"

At age twenty, Alex Smith was already a "Sir" and "Ma'am" guy.

"I remember rumors of certain things Alex did and Aaron did not," Nolan said, "and they're just good, laughable stories. There's not a lot of truth to them. . . . Cal and Stanford kids have a lot of confidence, and Aaron was a Cal guy. He was extremely intelligent. He was not showing it off, but he was smart all the time. Whatever the conversation, he was smart."

Though Nolan did describe Rodgers as "very cocky, very confident, arrogant," he insisted those traits were not viewed as negatives. Nolan had competed with and against many distinguished quarterbacks over the years.

"And the thing the really good ones always are," he said, "is extremely confident to that point of arrogance. Every one of them. . . . Aaron was not afraid to speak up on any matter there. He was easy to talk with, respectful. You're not going to stump him. If you asked him a question, he had an answer for you. He was very impressive in every regard."

The Niners left their lunch with a ton to think about. In Rodgers and Smith, they were choosing between two extremely bright quarterbacks who were lights out in their workouts while NFL teams scrutinized their every move.

Rodgers's roots could not be dismissed in the debate. Pro football was showbiz, after all, and the San Francisco 49ers could have done a lot worse in the draft than picking a lifelong fan from Chico (only three hours away) who wore a Joe Montana T-shirt under his college uniform, and who had turned his bedroom into a Montana shrine, complete with Joe Cool posters, bobblehead dolls, and football cards. Rodgers's father, Ed, predicted that his son would be worth ten thousand extra tickets to the Niners if they drafted him.

Ten days before the April 23 start of the draft, Rodgers visited the Niners' facility in Santa Clara for more than eight hours and sounded like a politician stumping for votes. He called his unique mechanics "one of my best attributes" and said he had no interest in changing his top-shelf ball position.

"I love it now; I wouldn't change it," Rodgers said. "Being able to hold the ball that high and getting the ball out of my hands that quick I think is a real advantage I have over other quarterbacks."

Rodgers also reminded people he had excelled in the West Coast offense that San Francisco was going to run, while Smith was busy doing his thing in the spread.

"Dropping back and making a read is a lot different than catching the ball and being in the pocket already, I think," Rodgers said. "No offense to him, he's a great quarterback, and he put up some great numbers. But it's going to take a little bit of time for him, I think, to get adjusted to doing that."

On that same day, Rodgers's representative was meeting with the 49ers' chief negotiator, Paraag Marathe, to talk contract terms in the event the team selected his client. Mike Sullivan was his name. He knew how to get a guy drafted No. 1 overall.

• • •

IN 2001, AFTER the San Diego Chargers rejected his contract demands and traded the first pick in the draft to Atlanta, Mike Sullivan persuaded the Falcons to give his client, Virginia Tech sensation Michael Vick, the richest rookie deal in league history at $62 million over six years, including $15.3 million guaranteed in the first three years. The following year, Sullivan went back-to-back with Fresno State quarterback David Carr, who broke Vick's rookie record with $16.25 million guaranteed by the Houston Texans in his first three years.

In the spring of 2005, the Octagon agent was hoping to make Aaron Rodgers his next record-breaking No. 1 pick.

Like many top prospects trying to secure representation, Rodgers had grown weary of the recruiting blitz. "He was getting calls from agents left and right," said his coach at Butte, Craig Rigsbee. "It was, 'Hey, do you want to talk to Joe Montana? Hey, do you want to talk to Steve Young?'

"One day he came over my house and he was laying on my couch and he says, 'All these goddamn agents are calling me. They're having their guys call me.'"

Rodgers eventually narrowed his choices to Sullivan and David Dunn, who had negotiated Drew Bledsoe's league-record deal of ten years, $103 million, with the New England Patriots. Sullivan had a clear advantage in this derby, as he represented Jeff Tedford and a number of Tedford players including Carr, Trent Dilfer, and Kyle Boller.

Rodgers chose Sullivan, in large part because Dilfer had given him such a strong recommendation. The agent had a good working relationship with San Francisco's Marathe, and he felt confident that Rodgers would indeed go first.

If the Niners decided to draft Smith instead, at least three other teams in the top five had an apparent need for quarterback help. The Miami Dolphins, picking second, had thirty-three-year-old Gus Frerotte atop their depth chart, a man who had made a combined seven starts in the prior four seasons. The Cleveland Browns, picking third, were going with the thirty-three-year-old Dilfer, who would be an ideal full-time mentor for Rodgers. The Tampa Bay Buccaneers, picking fifth and searching for a franchise quarterback, were interested enough in Rodgers to work him out in Berkeley.

A couple of weeks before the draft, Tampa Bay head coach Jon Gruden ran Smith through drills in Salt Lake City before meeting up with the Cal quarterback the next morning. Rodgers sat across from Gruden, Buccaneers general manager Bruce Allen, and quarterbacks coach Paul Hackett in the school's football offices as he started the interview stiffly and nervously, according to Jerry McDonald of the *East Bay Times*, who had been invited to the session by Gruden.

Wearing a hooded sweatshirt and sweatpants and holding a computer clicker, Rodgers loosened up as he diagrammed plays on a grease board and reviewed Cal game film with Gruden, including plays from the USC loss. "Before long," McDonald wrote, "Rodgers' feet were up on a chair, and the two were trading good-natured barbs."

The coach asked the quarterback why he held the ball so high above his shoulder, and Rodgers responded that he was taught to hold it near his ear and was comfortable with that approach. At one point Rodgers pointed to a teammate on the film and said, "That guy right there is the best running back in the country."

"He doesn't look that fast to me," Gruden responded.

The back was Marshawn Lynch, who had praised Rodgers for taking the blame after a practice handoff screwup so the coaches would go easier on the freshman.

"No, this guy is the best," Rodgers assured Gruden. "You watch."

McDonald later said that Gruden and Rodgers put on the same kind of classroom show that the coach popularized later on ESPN's *Gruden's QB Camp*. One exchange between the two involved a *People* magazine distinction in 2001.

Rodgers: "I heard you were one of the fifty most beautiful people in the world."

Gruden: "I'm still in the top sixty-five."

During the hourlong interview, Gruden and Allen teased the quarterback about the pending arrival of a mystery man at the workout to follow. Rodgers thought it might be Joe Montana, his hero, and instead it turned out to be Jerry Rice, another one of his favorites, still hoping to find one last NFL job at age forty-two.

As the thirteen-time Pro Bowler walked down the steps of Memorial Stadium, Rodgers grabbed Gruden and said, "Holy cow, that's Jerry Rice!"

"Hey Aaron," Gruden said, "you tell Rice what routes to run."

The Tampa Bay coach wanted to see how the quarterback reacted to that kind of pressure. Rodgers was floored by the presence of the greatest receiver of all time, and actually had more success throwing the ball to Cal teammate Chase Lyman than to the titan who was twice his age. On his final pass, Rodgers missed Rice in the end zone on a 50-yard fade and, McDonald wrote, punctuated his audition by "cupping his hands to his head and turning away in disgust."

All in all, it was still quite a morning. Rodgers called the experience "surreal." Rice said the kid had "a very strong arm" and that his delivery made it seem "almost like it's no effort at all." Gruden sounded like he had just spent ninety minutes in the company of the next Montana.

"He communicates the system well, and his skill level is tremendous," Gruden said. "He's got touch, he's got zip, he's got mobility, he's durable. He's complete."

It sure sounded like the Buccaneers were going to be there for Rodgers if his hometown team fumbled the ball. But then again, as much as the days and weeks before the draft were about hopes and dreams, the main currency of the process was pure, unadulterated bullshit.

And Jon Gruden could bullshit with the best of them.

• • •

AARON RODGERS WAS in New York City at the invitation of Gil Brandt. A longtime Dallas Cowboys executive who was among the founding fathers of the modern scouting and drafting apparatus, Brandt was the league official who determined which prospects were worthy of being on-site for the annual NFL Draft spectacle.

In the spring of 2005, he decided that six players, Rodgers among them, should be present at the Jacob K. Javits Convention Center when NFL commissioner Paul Tagliabue announced the names of the college stars who had been selected.

"I recruited him to come to New York," Brandt recalled. "He was apprehensive about coming."

Brandt assured the Cal quarterback that he had a strong chance of being among the top five players drafted. Rodgers conferred with his agent, Mike Sullivan, and both agreed that Brandt's projection made sense. The reward of Rodgers being there when his improbable dream came true was worth the risk of being embarrassed by an improbable plunge down the draft board on national TV. New York City, here he'd come.

On Thursday afternoon, two days before the draft, Rodgers was in his hotel lobby when his phone rang. Jon Gruden was calling.

"If you're there at five," said the Bucs coach, "we're taking you."

Sullivan was standing next to Rodgers when that message was relayed. This was great news, though not surprising, given how Rodgers's recent morning with Tampa Bay went down.

Earlier that week, a report surfaced that San Francisco was leaning toward picking Alex Smith. Sullivan also fielded a call from a trusted league source warning him that, no matter what they were saying, the Niners had already decided on Smith. Suddenly it seemed Rodgers might need a safety net like the one Gruden was apparently providing.

Sullivan did have one advantage over Smith's representative, Tom Condon, whose client list included Peyton and Eli Manning, both No. 1 overall picks. Rodgers's agent had already agreed to the parameters of a contract with the Niners, as the team desired, and Condon had not. Would that be enough for the Cal quarterback to come from behind and nip Smith at the wire?

Rodgers did not even understand why this was a close call to begin with. "This is a no-brainer," he said. "I'm from Chico, three hours away, went to Berkeley, I'm the best quarterback in the draft. I mean, let's make it happen."

He had spent forty-five minutes with San Francisco offensive coordinator Mike McCarthy during his visit and felt better about that interview than any other.

"I really felt like after my interview with the 49ers that there was no way that they wouldn't pick me," Rodgers said. "It was going to be a perfect pick, me and San Francisco, my childhood team, and I was going to be wearing red and gold. . . . I know I asked them straight up what they were going to do, and he said, 'I think we're going to pick you,' which I never forgot."

McCarthy said he spent the entire weekend before the draft with Mc-Cloughan studying every available college quarterback, thinking San Francisco might draft two of them to build depth at that position. By Friday, the eve of the draft, the Niners appeared to have settled on Smith with their first pick.

Sullivan was growing concerned because Nick Saban of the Dolphins, holder of the second pick, was believed to covet a running back to replace the (temporarily) retired Ricky Williams. Saban loved Smith, and Smith alone, at the quarterback position. "For some reason Saban didn't like Rodgers at No. 2," Brandt said.

Of greater concern to Sullivan was the word he had received from the

Cleveland Browns that they would not select a quarterback with the third pick. The Browns always seemed a good fit, and now they were off the board entirely. Rodgers needed Tampa Bay to come through.

Sullivan had a good relationship with Buccaneers GM Bruce Allen, so after Allen's coach had called to inform Rodgers of the team's intentions, the agent asked Allen to let him know at midnight whether the Bucs were still definitely in. Sullivan knew Gruden might be leaking information—credible or otherwise—to better position Tampa Bay for a trade. The agent did not want to meet with Rodgers and his family Saturday morning, a couple of hours before the draft started, without knowing if his client would be among the top five picks.

Meanwhile, the man responsible for Rodgers's trip to New York, Gil Brandt, said he met the quarterback for dinner at the famous Italian restaurant Carmine's, second level. "I had a contact there," Brandt said. "Got us seated right away."

The occasion was not as festive as it should have been. Brandt had been working his sources and had discovered that Rodgers was plunging, and rapidly. He invited the Cal star to the city, and now he did not think the kid was going top five or top ten or even top twenty.

The draft guru felt responsible for putting Rodgers in this situation. He had seen the quarterback with the other invitees earlier on a tour bus, taking pictures of city landmarks with his flip phone. Brandt thought Rodgers looked oblivious to what was about to hit him.

"I actually saw it coming, like the headlights of a locomotive going at top speed with no brakes," Brandt would write. "I even tried stopping it, but it was a runaway destined to crash."

Just before his dinner with Rodgers, as he was scurrying to find his invited quarterback a home, Brandt placed a call to a friend in Green Bay, John Dorsey, the director of college scouting for the Packers, who held the twenty-fourth pick. Brandt told him that Brett Favre's heir apparent, Aaron Rodgers, was about to fall into his lap.

"Don't pass him up," Brandt said.

"Don't worry," Dorsey responded. "We won't."

Bruce Allen's call came in as scheduled, while Mike Sullivan was in the VIP area of a Manhattan club with a client who was in dire need of good news.

Sullivan had been nervously counting the minutes until midnight. He answered his cell, walked out into the street, and asked Allen for the club's final decision.

"We're not taking him," the GM said.

Sullivan's heart sank along with his client's stock.

"I had to go back in and tell Aaron the Bucs were a 'no,'" the agent recalled for this book. "I've had top quarterbacks before, but this was, 'Oh my God, I don't know if I can do anything about this.'"

As far as the agent knew, no NFL team was committed to hiring his guy. The draft was twelve hours away.

It was going to be a sleepless night.

• • •

NICK SABAN CALLED Gil Brandt early Saturday morning to tell him that he was definitely drafting a running back with the second pick, and that he wanted to hear his preference between Auburn's Ronnie Brown and Texas's Cedric Benson. Brandt told him he thought Brown deserved the nod.

The two backs joined Aaron Rodgers, Alex Smith, Michigan receiver Braylon Edwards, and Miami cornerback Antrel Rolle as the only prospects invited by Brandt to sit in the Javits Center green room until their names were called. Five of these young men were fairly confident that Paul Tagliabue would be calling them to the stage in short order.

Rodgers had no idea how long his wait would last.

Before he met with the quarterback and his family Saturday morning for a predraft debriefing, Sullivan lobbied Tennessee Titans GM Floyd Reese to use the sixth overall pick on his guy as an understudy to veteran Steve McNair. Reese explained that he was a Rodgers fan but that he needed to draft a fast cornerback.

It was fourth and long, and Sullivan was running dangerously low on options. "This could be rough," he told Rodgers. "I don't have a team saying they'll take you if you're there. I'm really sorry to tell you that I don't know where you might go or how far you will fall, and I apologize."

Why was this happening? One prominent NFL head coach had told Sullivan that Jeff Tedford's offense at Cal used a lot of maximum protection, that Rodgers was not asked to make many third and fourth reads, and that he held the ball too high. Some coaches thought these issues were not fixable. Others were too desperate to win immediately to invest the time necessary to fix them.

Rodgers's supposedly robotic dropbacks were still a concern in league circles. Contrary to some scouting reports, Sullivan never thought his client's personality—that is, cockiness—was a deterrent for the Niners or anyone else.

When Sullivan presented his grim Saturday morning report to Rodgers and his family, well, Rodgers and his family had seen this movie before. No scholarship offers out of high school. Asked to sit out a year by Division III Occidental. Recruited by a local community college coach who walked to his house to make the pitch.

Now Rodgers was at the NFL Draft, all dressed up and nowhere to go. He wore a blue pinstriped suit, a week's worth of gel in his hair, and a flavor saver tucked below his bottom lip when he took his seat at a round table in a packed area backstage. He spoke with his best friend and Cal roommate, Jordan Russell, seated to his left, as kickoff drew near, while ESPN's draft expert Mel Kiper Jr. was reminding America that a week and a half earlier, Rodgers looked like San Francisco's pick. Kiper said the kid was going to be "a fine, solid starting quarterback," but not a franchise quarterback.

A few minutes later, Tagliabue walked to the podium and made it official. "With the first selection in the 2005 NFL Draft," he said, "the San Francisco 49ers select Alex Smith, quarterback, Utah."

Smith rose from his table, hugged family members, grabbed his Niners jersey and cap, and posed for photos with the commissioner. Mike Nolan later conceded that Rodgers was the more NFL-ready player, but as *Sports Illustrated*'s Peter King would write, "Some in the front office thought Rodgers came across as too much like a big man on campus."

So much for arrogance being a desired trait.

Smith was drafted for leadership and communication skills, for the way he carried himself. Now the interminable journey was on for his rival. Teams were on the clock for fifteen minutes between first-round picks, and each interval seemed to move at half speed for Rodgers.

Ronnie Brown was called out of the green room by Miami at No. 2. Braylon Edwards was summoned by Cleveland at No. 3. Cedric Benson was picked by the Chicago Bears at No. 4.

On the broadcast, ESPN's Chris Berman said, "Now, Tampa on the clock next. Is this Aaron Rodgers's time? He's in the green room."

He was there to stay, given what Bruce Allen had told Sullivan at midnight. Sure enough, the Bucs picked Auburn's Cadillac Williams, making it three running backs in the first five picks, including two from the same school. Williams was surrounded by family in his Alabama home when he got the call. Now guys who weren't even in the green room were getting drafted ahead of Rodgers.

The Tennessee Titans were up at No. 6, but their GM had already given Sullivan the bad news. On ESPN, Berman called Rodgers "still a quarterback waiting to happen" and reported that he had "taken a walk out of the green room a little bit. I don't blame him."

The so-called green room was not a room at all, but a cramped waiting area cordoned off by colorless curtains, tarps, and metal poles, with tight spaces to navigate between the tables, monitors, and camera lights. This was not a comfortable place to wait for anything.

Arizona selected Miami's Rolle with the eighth pick, setting off a celebration at a table next to the Cal quarterback's. The player who was once the popular choice to go first was now officially the last man sitting.

As if to comfort Rodgers, Mel Kiper mentioned on the broadcast that Dan Marino, Miami Dolphins Hall of Famer, was the second-to-last player drafted in the first round in 1983. But as the picks kept coming off the board, and Rodgers kept being told by NFL decision-makers that he was not good enough to play for their teams, comfort was nowhere to be found.

His parents, Ed and Darla, were sitting right there with him, quietly hurting for their son and trying their damnedest not to look embarrassed. With San Diego on the clock for the twelfth pick, ESPN's Suzy Kolber sat with Aaron and asked him why in a couple of weeks he had gone from a clear-cut No. 1 overall pick to a guy tumbling down a five-story staircase.

"Yeah, I wish I could tell you," Rodgers responded. "I haven't changed anything. It's just perceptions of me, or maybe the needs of the teams at the spots. I'm not too worried. I'm excited about going to a team that wants me and making an impact right away."

Darla Rodgers was not happy with Kolber's visits to their table, though the reporter was merely doing her job. "She was trying to get a meltdown," Darla said, "and Aaron was just stoic. . . . It was really awkward, because your heart is breaking for him and you think, 'Seriously, this whole room's empty and they got it so wrong and we're sitting here and now it's a public humiliation.'"

Darla did not care that all this made for compelling TV—that was her own flesh and blood's suffering on display. When Kolber asked Aaron how he was handling the free fall, he replied, "It's building character, I think, as we speak."

On the very first day that a video was uploaded to YouTube, Aaron Rodgers was starring in pro football's first reality show. The cameras kept zooming in on that dazed face crowned with spiked hair, his blue eyes betraying the pain.

The NFL Draft had come a long way from its debut in 1936, when teams gathered in a Philadelphia hotel and, without the benefit of any scouting department intel, largely selected players based on newspaper accounts of their feats. Many draft picks turned down the NFL for better paydays in less violent and more lucrative professions. The first overall pick and first Heisman Trophy winner, Jay Berwanger of the University of Chicago, decided he would rather be a foam rubber salesman than a running back.

But now the draft was a blockbuster Hollywood production with multigenerational wealth on the line for the college candidates who had been scouted and tested to death. Millions of viewers were watching these close-ups of Rodgers shaking his head, lowering his eyes, and exhaling in exasperation. Were there any foam rubber sales jobs available in Chico?

The ordeal passed the four-hour mark. The day before, Rodgers had joked with his fellow invitees that they should put money in a pool to see who would be the last player left in the green room. Now the joke was on him.

Friends and supporters three thousand miles away were fuming as Rodgers kept getting bypassed and ESPN kept beaming his beaten-down image into their living rooms. Craig Rigsbee, the juco coach. Thomas Weatherspoon, the trainer. Jeff Tedford, the Cal coach. They were feeling his torment too.

"It was painful to watch," Tedford said, "because I could see it on Aaron's face."

Rodgers's flip phone kept buzzing in the Javits Center, and he kept checking it and hoping a general manager or head coach was reaching out to end the nightmare. But it was just his longtime buddies, like Joey Kaempf from his Oregon days, busting his balls as a way of lightening the mood.

It didn't work. "It's embarrassing," Rodgers said. "You know the whole world is watching. . . . It's hard to laugh in a situation where you know everybody is laughing at you."

Rodgers started questioning every aspect of his predraft plan. His father, Ed, leaned hard on the Rodgers' belief system. "As a faith-based family," he said, "you figure God's got it in control. Whatever is going to happen is supposed to happen. I probably didn't get a chance to tell Aaron that."

Soon enough, an impatient-looking cleaning staff emerged to break down tables and to disassemble the backstage area. The workers were eyeing the Rodgers clan and wearing the same look on their faces. *Won't some damn team please draft this poor kid already so we can get home to our families?* The league's event operations guy, Eric Finkelstein, put in a call to get the crew to stand down.

Out of left field, Wilma McNabb, mother of Philadelphia Eagles quarterback Donovan McNabb, took a seat beside Darla and offered words of mom-to-mom comfort—Donovan had been booed by Eagles fans after Philly selected him second overall in 1999.

Darla's sister Cheryl Pittman was up in the Javits Center crowd as part of a Rodgers contingent that included friends from Chico, the Rottschalk family and the Ruby family. Cheryl had won a round-trip ticket to anywhere in the country in a contest at a teachers conference and had used the ticket for the draft.

Cheryl arrived in the big city still thinking her nephew would get drafted by her favorite team, the Niners, or at least get drafted by someone early. "We were up in the stands flabbergasted," she recalled. "I was heartbroken. We were all heartbroken."

Family members and friends were so certain that Aaron would be selected among the top picks, they did not bother to eat in the morning. Given their plans to celebrate after the short-and-sweet formalities, they weren't just flabbergasted and heartbroken. "We were starving too," Cheryl said.

The Oakland Raiders caused a hopeful stir by trading with Seattle to secure the twenty-third pick, inspiring Rodgers to wonder if they were moving up three spots to get him. The Raiders played twenty minutes away from Cal.

Smith had given the best combine interview that longtime Raiders scout Bruce Kebric had ever conducted—"I thought the guy was going to be the CEO of a big company some day," Kebric said—but the scout believed Rodgers was the superior player. Before Niners VP of player personnel Scot McCloughan had notarized the team's No. 1 overall pick, Kebric told

McCloughan's father, Kent, and brother, Dave—both Raiders scouts—to advise Scot that he was making a mistake by drafting Smith over Rodgers.

"I saw both of them," Kebric said, "and I thought there was no comparison between the two."

In his official scouting report on Rodgers, Kebric listed his strong points as "arm strength, accuracy, movement, mobility," and his weak points as, simply, "height." The Raiders liked their quarterbacks to be six foot three or taller.

Kebric's summary of Rodgers read like this: "Right-handed. Square frame. Solid lower body. Athletic, mobile quarterback with excellent arm strength, patience, movement, poise, judgment, downfield focus, resourcefulness. Throws tight ball with good timing. Accuracy at all levels. Quick away from center, good feet. . . . Carries ball high, short throwing motion, quick release. Doesn't need body or step-up to throw deep. Excellent feel [for] pressure . . . First Round. More talented than Raider quarterbacks."

But when decision time arrived, Raiders overlord Al Davis, a blind believer in blinding speed, picked a burner in Nebraska cornerback Fabian Washington and stuck with veteran Kerry Collins at quarterback.

The Green Bay Packers were on the clock at No. 24. Unaware of their intentions, San Francisco started thinking the unthinkable with its first pick in the second round, No. 33 overall. "Maybe we get both of them and let them fight it out," said Niners coach Mike Nolan, "and then you trade one of them for a good pick. . . . As Aaron kept going, I said, 'Oh my goodness, let's consider maybe taking the other one.'"

But new Green Bay GM Ted Thompson, running a draft for the first time, had been thinking days earlier that the possibility of Rodgers being available at No. 24 was real, and that the Packers should take him. Brett Favre was thirty-five years old and had been openly and constantly pondering the pros and cons of retirement.

That morning, Packers head coach Mike Sherman had watched the tape of Rodgers completing twenty-three consecutive passes against USC. A former Packers executive hired back from Seattle, Thompson believed in revealing virtually nothing about his intentions on any draft or personnel front to the news media or anyone else. He also believed in taking the best college player left on his big board.

So, when the first round moved into the late teens, the GM approached longtime Packers president Bob Harlan in their Lambeau Field draft room and asked if they could speak outside in the hall. Thompson needed to discuss the magnitude of a decision that would jolt the only community-owned major sports franchise in North America.

"If Rodgers is there, I've got to take him," he told Harlan. "It won't be pretty. The fans won't be happy if Aaron's coming in with Brett already here. Are you OK with this?"

Just as he had promised the previous GM, Ron Wolf, Harlan had assured Thompson that he would face no interference in football decisions from the franchise's forty-five-member board of directors and seven-member executive committee.

"Ted, it's your ball club to run," Harlan told him. "You make your choice."

Packers vice president Andrew Brandt was in the middle of the room when the picks were coming off the board and the team's turn was closing like a freight train. Rodgers was the last first-round name still up there, ready to be claimed and placed right behind the most durable player at his position in the history of the sport.

To Brandt's left were the scouts and executives, and to his right were the coaches. Sherman was bouncing from group to group. The Packers were about to get a shot at hiring arguably the best player in the draft, at the sport's most important position . . . with the twenty-fourth pick!

"But I was getting a strong feeling from the coaches side that they were whispering, 'We can't do this,'" Brandt recalled. "Coaches are judged much more immediately than general managers, so they felt we were going to use this precious asset of a first-round pick on a player who wouldn't help us that year, or the next year. He may never help us.

"On the other side of the room, our scouting staff and general manager are like, 'Guys, what do we always say? Trust the board. Trust the board.' The room was becoming combustible. I remember it was, 'Hey, let's cool the tension and have a discussion here.' I was not making myself the arbiter. It was just each side making its case, and ultimately Ted was the decision-maker. He just kept coming back to, 'Trust the board.'"

Thompson had reminded people that in 1984, a year after the Portland Trail Blazers had drafted shooting guard Clyde Drexler in the first round, they passed on Michael Jordan in favor of Sam Bowie to fill a need at center. "I never want to be that guy," Thompson said.

Truth was, his Packers were desperate for help on the other side of the ball. "I was thinking we were going to take a defensive player because we had Brett Favre," said new defensive coordinator Jim Bates. "I said, 'Gosh, Aaron Rodgers, it came out of nowhere.'"

Though most of the coaches wanted to plug other holes on the roster to give Favre (and themselves) a better chance at a Super Bowl run in the 2005 season, Packers offensive coordinator Tom Rossley had a different take. He had attended Rodgers's workout at Cal and came away thinking he had never seen a more accurate passer. He thought Rodgers had a little magic to him, too.

"So, when I was in the draft room I'm thinking, 'Keep falling. Come to us,'" Rossley recalled. "I know there was a lot of discussion about other players in the room, but I was jumping up and down for Aaron, knowing you can't let a guy like that pass."

Thompson knew what he was going to do, but he wanted to use part of his fifteen-minute window to wait for a potential trade offer to come in. Meanwhile, Rodgers was conferring with his agent at the table. At one point earlier, needing to clear his head, the quarterback told Sullivan, "I'm outta here," and left the green room for the hallway.

Sullivan followed him out and said, "I know this sucks, but there are teams out there looking to see how you handle this. You're going to have a lot of adversity in life, and this is going to be a test. You've got to show the mental toughness to handle this."

Back in the green room, Aaron Rodgers's phone rang. Andrew Brandt thought he was calling Sullivan and got the quarterback instead. He apologized to Rodgers for dialing the wrong number and asked for the agent.

"I felt so bad," Brandt said. "And poor Mike, now the family's looking at him cross-eyed, nobody else is in the room. . . . Now Mike's talking out of the side of his mouth to me because he didn't want Aaron and his family to know what's going on. He's whispering to me, 'Are you going to take him?'

"I said, 'Mike, you've just got to trust me. Hold on.' It was the longest twelve minutes of their lives when I couldn't say anything."

Thompson finally gave Brandt clearance to tell Sullivan that the Packers were drafting his client. The GM announced to the room, "Fellas, I'm going to take Rodgers." He got on the phone with Rodgers and told him that maybe divine intervention had brought the two parties together.

The Green Bay Packers, the very team that had pressed Rodgers about Tedford's track record more than any other, had decided he was the one to reverse the curse.

THE PLUNGE

Paul Tagliabue, NFL commissioner, walked to the podium with a white card in his hand and a mischievous grin on his face. "With the twenty-fourth selection in the 2005 NFL Draft," Tagliabue announced, "the Green Bay Packers select Aaron Rodgers, quarterback from California."

Liberated after four hours and thirty-five minutes, passed over twenty-three times by twenty-one teams (Dallas and Minnesota ignored him twice), Rodgers rose from his chair with that flip phone still attached to his ear and shook Sullivan's hand. He embraced his mother, Darla, and his friend Jordan Russell as the Javits Center crowd of about 1,800 cheered wildly for him.

"You're a cult hero already," Sullivan told him.

The quarterback hugged his brothers, Luke and Jordan, and his father, Ed. Giants fans, Jets fans, and Packers fans wearing cheeseheads and Favre jerseys started chanting, "Aa-ron Rod-gers . . . Aa-ron Rod-gers." On his walk to meet the commissioner, Rodgers put on a Packers cap before he was stopped by a league official, Merton Hanks.

A four-time Pro Bowl safety with San Francisco after getting drafted in the fifth round in 1991, Hanks wrapped Rodgers in a hug and whispered into his ear, "I played my whole career with a chip on my shoulder. You should do the same."

Rodgers walked up to the stage and held his Green Bay jersey—No. 1—while posing for photos with Tagliabue, the camera lights flashing around him.

The Javits Center workers could finally finish cleaning the green room.

• • •

AARON RODGERS CITED his faith in the moments after the Packers picked him. "The Lord has been teaching me a lot about humility and patience," he said, "and He kind of threw both of those in my face today."

The Javits Center fans were loving him, but in Titletown USA, at a Green Bay draft party of a couple of thousand fans in the Lambeau Field Atrium, the reaction was entirely different.

"The atrium erupted in boos," recalled Bill Michaels, host of the Packers' radio network.

"The boos of that crowd were thunderous," said Wayne Larrivee, who was also hosting in the atrium for WTMJ in Milwaukee. Packers executives could feel the walls of their draft room reverberate from the din.

"The booing literally, and I say *literally* with emphasis, shook our souls, and shook me personally," Brandt said. "It physically moved us. It was like a thunderclap below our feet."

Larrivee recalled that he tried to calm the fans by telling them that there will come a day when they loved this draft pick. Most of the audience didn't want to hear it.

"I never heard a reaction that vociferous," Larrivee said.

Thompson joined the radio show live and moved to defuse the situation, talking up the young quarterback's potential behind the aging Favre. In New York, nobody was doing a better job of talking up Rodgers's potential than Rodgers.

Asked how disappointed he was to not go No. 1 to the 49ers, the twenty-fourth pick said, "Not as disappointed as the 49ers will be that they didn't draft me."

Rodgers was not angry over the millions of guaranteed dollars he lost in the plunge. He was furious over the lack of awareness of his talent. One more time, nobody wanted to offer him a scholarship.

"A lot of teams passed on me," Rodgers said. "And when my time comes to play, I'm going to show those teams they made a mistake. And if we play the 49ers at their place, I'm going to make sure the entire city of Chico comes down there to watch us beat them."

His anger was powerful and raw, and yet there was one invested observer who was just as upset about the way the afternoon went down, maybe more so.

Brett Lorenzo Favre.

Ninety seconds after Favre watched his team draft his replacement, his agent called Packers VP Andrew Brandt and set the tone for the next three years with these three words:

What the fuck?

7

BRETT

John Gee was waiting outside of Lambeau Field with a Cal cap on his head and a mountain bike by his side. He was part of a long-standing training-camp tradition of local kids shepherding the Green Bay Packers from their dressing room to the practice field and back again.

It started under Vince Lombardi—children carrying their heroes' helmets while race-walking alongside the players who pedaled their bicycles a couple hundred yards to work. The ritual was meant to strengthen the bond between community and team.

This could only happen in Green Bay, with a franchise and stadium plunked down in the middle of a middle-class neighborhood, the last survivor among the Duluths, Daytons, Cantons, and Pottsvilles that were a proud part of the National Football League's origin story.

Now it was Green Bay all alone against the heavyweight markets in the modern NFL, Chicago and New York and the rest. The Packers' championship past had earned their home the nickname of "Titletown," which was small-town America's middle finger to the big boys. And part of the Titletown charm was a community that treated the Packers as if they were teenagers trying to win a high school state championship.

The Packers did not have a billionaire owner who had made a fortune in oil, paper, retail, or finance. This was the only franchise owned by the ham-and-eggers, in this case 112,000 stockholders, a network that outnumbered the population of Green Bay (101,000). If the rest of the NFL had gone hopelessly corporate, it still seemed that the Packers were supported by car washes, bake sales, and 50/50 raffles.

And by backpack-wearing middle-school kids like John Gee waiting to give his new blue-and-silver Trek 3500 to Aaron Rodgers so the rookie could ride his bike to work.

As the twenty-fourth pick in the draft, Rodgers had just signed his contract with the Packers for five years and $7.7 million, including $5.4 million guaranteed and escalators and incentives that could push the total sum to $24.5 million. It was a far cry from the six-year, $49.5 million deal landed by San Francisco's No. 1 overall pick, Alex Smith, who got $24 million guaranteed.

At least Rodgers was getting to play with Brett Favre, his all-time favorite quarterback not named Joe Montana or Steve Young. Rodgers had worn his jersey number, 4, at Butte. Favre was a living legend among the citizens of Green Bay, not to mention untold millions worldwide.

After the Packers won five championships under Lombardi in the 1960s, including the first two Super Bowls, they made a grand total of two postseason appearances (and won only one playoff game) over the twenty-four seasons preceding Favre's arrival. Green Bay general manager Ron Wolf, who had coveted the Southern Mississippi quarterback in the 1991 draft as a New York Jets executive (Wolf had him rated as the No. 1 prospect in the country), finally got his man when he sent a first-round pick to Atlanta for Favre.

Falcons coach Jerry Glanville saw the talent in his young quarterback but said, "I could not sober him up." Favre admitted to "trying to drink up Atlanta," leaving his coach no choice but to make him someone else's problem.

"I sent him to a city," Glanville said, "where at nine o'clock at night the only thing that's open is Chili [John's]."

Undaunted, Favre found plenty of places to party in Green Bay. He lived his life with the same reckless abandon that he played with, at least until his binge drinking and dangerous painkiller addiction compelled him to seek treatment three different times. Favre led the Packers to twelve winning seasons in his first thirteen (the team was 8-8 the other year), made back-to-back trips to the Super Bowl, and won Green Bay's first title in nearly thirty years by beating the New England Patriots in Super Bowl XXXI.

And no matter how hard he drank or how late he stayed out early in his career, raising hell in a pre–social media age, Favre never missed a start from the fourth week of the 1992 season onward. He was always ready by kickoff to play like the fearless country boy he was, scrambling around with his hair on fire, pointing this way and that and pumping fastballs on the run.

The locals adopted him. Favre was one of them—a hunter and a fisherman who was forever dressed in a ball cap, T-shirt, and jeans, and who relaxed with a pinch of Copenhagen chewing tobacco between his cheek and gum.

"Everybody looked up to him," John Gee said. "We all wanted to sling it like him or have any interaction with him that we could. That was the goal. To have an interaction with Brett Favre."

In the summer of 2005, at age thirteen, Gee figured the ongoing fascination with Favre might give him an opening to meet Aaron Rodgers and become his bicycle kid. The tradition, Gee said, "signals the start of football season."

The rookie finished his contract negotiations late and missed four practices over the first two days of camp. The bike kids were already assigned to other players by the time Rodgers reported, at least until Gee, an enterprising middle schooler, got the blessing of his assigned player (undrafted linebacker Zac Woodfin) to offer his mountain bike to the quarterback. Smartly wearing his Cal cap for the occasion, Gee, a USC fan, walked right up to Rodgers on his first day, introduced himself, and won the job without much competition.

"I would say when it's normal there's a bunch of kids that would rush a first-round draft pick," Gee said. "But I think there was probably some hesitation because Brett was still the starting quarterback, and people were unsure whether or not to go for Aaron, and if he would even pan out."

They hit it off instantly, the boy who had moved to Green Bay from Southern California and the quarterback who had moved there from Northern California. Gee made the twenty-minute journey from his home to Lambeau on his bike every day, down Oneida Street. He met up with Rodgers after the Packers had bussed in from nearby St. Norbert College, a school on the Fox River where Lombardi first housed the team during training camp, and regularly attended morning Mass at Old St. Joseph.

Rodgers and Gee talked about football and school and their mutual love of music. The boy was struck by how genuinely curious this NFL player was about his life; Rodgers even attended a couple of his youth football games. Gee had struggled to make new friends and to maintain his grades after his family moved back to Wisconsin from Huntington Beach, California, but Rodgers's friendship was a difference maker.

"My grades shot up from a B average to straight As from seventh to eighth grade after I met Aaron," he recalled.

Gee was an only child who suddenly felt like he had a big brother in his life. He picked up Rodgers before and after practice, summer day after summer day, introducing him to his parents along the way. Gee would ultimately wear Rodgers's jersey number, 12, in his own games.

Some fans were excited to have a new quarterback in town, the heir apparent. Others thought the Packers had made a mistake by not drafting a playmaking receiver or a stud on defense. But they were all asking themselves a variation of this question that Gee asked Rodgers one day at camp:

"Are you going to be the next Brett Favre?"

"I'm going to be the next Aaron Rodgers," he replied.

A perfect answer for a rookie whose relationship with the folk hero was as imperfect as they come.

• • •

WHAT THE FUCK?

Andrew Brandt, Packers vice president, had explained to Brett Favre's irate agent on draft day that the team was not replacing his client, that it was only picking the best player available in Aaron Rodgers.

That wasn't going to be good enough for ol' Bus Cook from Ole Miss, the country lawyer who had secured the NFL's first $100 million contract for Favre, a Super Bowl winner and three-time league MVP, in 2001. Brandt heard from Bus all the time about how unfair the Packers were being to the man who brought back the glory days all by himself.

"Andrew, do you know what it's like to come into work every day and sit with your replacement?" the agent repeatedly asked the executive.

No, Brandt did not know the feeling.

"It fuckin' sucks," Cook assured him.

The Packers allowed Cook access to areas that were off-limits to other agents because he represented their franchise player. But when Cook pressed general manager Ted Thompson to draft someone other than Rodgers, the GM did what he had to do for the long-term health of the team. And on his first morning of practice, Rodgers moved to validate that choice.

"He's playing with the second-team offense," Brandt recalled, "and he rolls right and lets go a 65-yarder in the air that hits Donald Driver in the breadbasket. Ted's eyes and mine locked and he just gave me a look that said, 'We got our guy.'"

Rodgers did not help his cause when minicamp opened in late April at Green Bay's practice facility, the Don Hutson Center. The rookie had described Favre as "lazy" when asked about the veteran's absence from camp in a TV interview and had to explain it away as a joke gone awry. "Bad sense of humor," Rodgers conceded. He had been joking about a player who had made 225 consecutive starts, including the postseason. "I just hope he didn't take it the wrong way," Rodgers said.

Favre never took things the right way when it came to his backups—if he believed they were threats to his standing as the starter. If he thought another quarterback on the roster had no realistic chance of unseating him (Doug Pederson, Craig Nall), Favre could be his loyal friend.

Rodgers represented a clear and present danger and had to be dealt with accordingly. Eliminated, if necessary. The popular postdraft narrative that had the Cal quarterback learning from Favre was silly given that Favre had no intention of teaching anything to anyone. His job was not to mentor Rodgers or to effectively expedite his own firing. Favre's job was to lead the Packers to victory and to play with a child's joy for as long as his aging body allowed.

By design, his mission made Rodgers's first year in Green Bay the longest year of his football life. It wasn't supposed to go that way, according to the rookie's most ardent supporters.

After Rodgers's free fall in the draft, Craig Rigsbee called him to say, "I know you're pissed. I know it's not what you wanted. But I'm going to tell you this is the best thing that's ever happened to you. Everyone who gets drafted first goes to a shitty team. The coaches are shitty, the players are shitty, and as a quarterback you get the shit kicked out of you. . . . Alex Smith is going to make the money now, but in the long run you'll play behind Favre, you're going to stay in the league a lot longer and make a lot more money."

Trainer Thomas Weatherspoon, who grew up in Wisconsin a Packers fan, told his predraft client from Chico, California, "You're going to another Chico. There's nothing for you to do in Green Bay but football. They love their quarterbacks in Green Bay and you're going to be there forever. They're going to name streets after you."

It all sounded good. Better than good. After listening to Rodgers talk about his appreciation of Lombardi and Bart Starr and other Packers greats, and about how he prepared himself for NFL success, at a media luncheon, Bill Michaels of Milwaukee's WTMJ shook his hand and told him, "If your talent is half as good as your mind, you'll be a Hall of Famer."

As it turned out, the new quarterback played to mixed reviews during the spring minicamp and organized team activities (OTA) season. Six days after the draft, in his first practice as a pro, Rodgers impressed one of the few Packers assistants who wanted him picked—offensive coordinator Tom Rossley—with his quick release, velocity, and mobility.

"He's better than I thought he would be," Rossley said, "and I thought he would be good."

In June, however, Rodgers began sailing balls over his receivers' heads. Rossley observed that he wasn't finishing his throws. The quarterback explained that he wasn't confident in his reads, making him late in his process and leaving his feet out of position. In one June practice, Rodgers was intercepted three times, including once in the end zone. All fixable first-year stuff as he was learning the playbook and system.

Rodgers again looked mechanical with his top-shelf ball position, but Packers head coach Mike Sherman, a fifty-year-old Bostonian, did not try to alter his approach. In his first NFL head coaching job, with an impressive 53-27 record over five seasons, Sherman never wanted Rodgers on his team. Nothing personal, just business.

Sherman had rightfully concluded that a young quarterback was not about to help him win a championship, and if he had not been stripped of his GM duties after Favre ended the 2004 season by throwing 4 interceptions in a wild-card playoff loss to Minnesota, he could have done something about it.

Sherman had excused Favre for the spring program to give him a chance to recharge after a devastating eighteen-month period that saw his father die of a heart attack, his brother-in-law die in an ATV crash on Favre's Mississippi property, his incomparable teammate Reggie White die of a respiratory disease, and his wife Deanna receive a diagnosis of breast cancer.

But Favre did make appearances at the team facility and, on June 2, met his eventual successor on the practice field. As Rodgers recalled it, Favre was wearing a golf hat and golf shirt when he approached the rookie. "I said 'Hi' to him," Rodgers said. "I would be so terrified as a twenty-one-year-old to say anything, and this was like my idol. It was Joe Montana, Steve Young, and then Brett."

Author Jeff Pearlman reported in his bestselling biography of Favre, *Gunslinger*, that Rodgers first met the franchise player in the team cafeteria and greeted him by saying, "Good morning, Grandpa," a story corroborated by Craig Nall.

Rodgers denied the timing of that account yet conceded that he likely called Favre "Grandpa" at some later point as a joke—one the veteran quarterback did not find funny in the least. Nor did Favre appreciate Rodgers's antics in his annual celebrity softball game, which raised more than $100,000 for the Favre foundation that supported children's charities.

Before nearly nine thousand fans in Fox Cities Stadium, Rodgers showed off his youth baseball skills by slugging two balls over the wall. He also celebrated by doing a cartwheel into second base on his first home run trot, and by jumping on a teammate for a piggyback ride from third base to home to punctuate his second home run trot.

Favre made it clear to teammates that he had no use for the rookie's act. This was going to be a long, hot summer at Lambeau.

• • •

WHILE HIS AGENT Mike Sullivan was trying to get his guy signed and into training camp by the end of July, Aaron Rodgers was keeping his arm in shape in his new backyard by throwing two hundred passes a day to his older brother, Luke, who had moved to Green Bay to live with Aaron. Inside their walk-in closet, Luke stumbled upon his kid brother's rejection letters from Illinois and Purdue tacked to the wall—directly above a lithograph of Joe Montana.

"He's got a bigger chip on his shoulder now than ever," Luke said.

Rodgers finally signed his deal and reported to camp. He threw the ball better in the afternoon practice than he did in the morning, and the coaches sounded pleased enough with what they saw. Now that Rodgers was done buying and furnishing his new house, he was asked by a media member what he hoped to do with the rest of his newfound cash.

"Take care of Mom and Dad," he replied, "and sock the rest away."

As he tried to find his footing during camp, Rodgers maintained a good working relationship with one reporter in particular, Dylan Tomlinson of Gannett Wisconsin newspapers, who had visited the quarterback in Chico and, over lunch, had inquired about Favre.

Tomlinson thought of Favre as a great quarterback and, well, a not-so-great person and did not think this teacher-student thing was going to work. Suspecting the worst, he asked Rodgers how the veteran was treating him.

"We haven't talked much," the rookie replied. "How do you think he'll be?"

"I don't think it's going to go well," Tomlinson said. "I think he's going to treat you like shit, basically."

Rodgers remembered that warning. And sure enough, when he saw Tomlinson during training camp, he told him, "Every time I ask [Favre] something, it's, 'Well, you're the first-rounder. You tell me.'" No. 4 wanted nothing to do with No. 12.

It was a shame too, since Rodgers studied every move Favre made and intentionally sat almost directly in front of him in the team meeting room, just to soak up what he could.

In the end, the two quarterbacks were all but meant to be opponents in a boxing ring, where contrasting styles made for great fights. In this corner you had a wild child from the backwater South who never grew up and lived his life as an open book. In that corner you had a sensitive and private gamer nerd from Northern California who would much rather watch *Jeopardy!* than chug beers with the locals.

And again, Rodgers occasionally said or did things that lit Favre's fuse. He was fond of boasting about his Wonderlic score of 35, five points lower than Alex Smith's but thirteen points higher than Favre's. The old man stewed when the kid pointed out the discrepancy.

The incumbent also didn't appreciate Rodgers kicking his ass on the golf course, which happened in front of at least one of Favre's regular playing partners, kicker Ryan Longwell.

At the end of camp, while Rodgers was jogging off the practice field, he tapped Tomlinson on the shoulder. "Hey," Rodgers said to the reporter, "everything you told me about Favre was true."

Rodgers made his NFL debut in the preseason opener against the San Diego Chargers and looked dreadful. He was sacked twice and completed 2 of 6 passes for a mere 7 yards. Twice his radio device failed, and once he tripped and fell on his back after taking the snap from center.

"It was pretty embarrassing," Rodgers said. He led Green Bay on only one scoring drive in twenty full preseason possessions.

Favre's 2005 Packers would not fare much better during the regular season. They lost their first four games and seven of their first eight on the way to a 4-12 season. Favre had the worst season of his career, throwing a league-high 29 interceptions and making like a guy who might soon follow through on his repeated threats to retire.

He could still sling it—that wasn't up for debate. On a dare, Favre once threw a ball about fifty yards through a small camera hole in a wall about thirty-five yards above the practice facility field while Rodgers and assistants Tom Rossley and Darrell Bevell watched in awe. "Brett wasn't the most accurate guy, but he had that magic," Rossley said. "He could throw another thousand balls and never again get through that hole."

And yet those who watched closely noticed that Rodgers was capable of similar feats. Tomlinson had seen one spring practice that pitted the quarterbacks against each other in the indoor facility, the two of them trying to throw footballs into garbage cans placed forty yards away.

"Favre's throwing it twenty yards over the thing every time," the reporter said, "and Rodgers hits three out of four."

• • •

AARON RODGERS TOOK the field for the first time in a regular-season game on October 9, a sunny day at Lambeau, early in the fourth quarter of Green Bay's 52–3 victory over New Orleans. While the bearded Favre watched from the sideline a day before his thirty-sixth birthday, his twenty-one-year-old backup got under center from his own 3-yard line. Thrown by Rodgers's cadence (and non-Mississippi accent), lineman Will Whitticker flinched, drawing a false-start penalty.

The quarterback barked at the right guard, a fellow rookie, through an incredulous smile. He was asked to throw only one pass in this blowout, on a third-and-7 from his own 33 with a little more than five minutes to play. Rodgers's first official NFL completion was a swing pass to fullback Vonta Leach for no gain.

Rodgers's only other meaningful playing time came during a game much more representative of his team's season—Baltimore's 48–3 December wipeout of the Packers on *Monday Night Football*, a disgraceful result in light of the Ravens' standing as the league's lowest-scoring team. Mike Sherman replaced Favre with Rodgers near the end of the third quarter.

On the first snap of the fourth, Rodgers dropped back for his second pass attempt of the year, only to be sacked from the blind side and stripped of the ball. He would throw an interception in the end zone and, with Baltimore leading 41–3 in the closing seconds, suffer one final indignity—another blind-side sack and fumble, this one returned for a touchdown. Linebacker Adalius Thomas struck a Heisman pose in the end zone before Rodgers unbuckled his chinstrap and staggered off the field.

The final game mercifully arrived on New Year's Day at Lambeau, with the 12-3 Seahawks in town. Even with Seattle prepping for the playoffs, the game's main storyline was Favre's potential farewell. Just as injuries to skill-position players and free-agent departures on the offensive line had conspired against the Packers, age and gravity had conspired against their quarterback. Favre had thrown 9 interceptions against no touchdowns in his previous four games, and he ranked twenty-ninth in the league in passer rating (70.5).

The Packers had gone on record saying they wanted him back, yet again. Favre conceded of his employers, "Maybe . . . they don't know how to tell Brett Favre, 'We want to go in a different direction.'"

With cameras flashing around him on every snap, and with fans chanting "one . . . more . . . year," Favre finally threw a touchdown pass and beat a Seattle team coached by the man who helped him win a Super Bowl. Mike Holmgren threw his guy one last bone—he pulled key starters in the second half to protect them for the postseason.

Favre himself was pulled with forty-one seconds left, just so the Lambeau crowd of 69,928 could say goodbye . . . if this was indeed a goodbye. The quarterback raised his arms and saluted the fans as he headed for the sideline. After Rodgers took a knee to end the game, Favre made his way to midfield for handshakes and hugs with Holmgren and the rest. Rodgers did something quite thoughtful—he handed Favre the game ball. The legend was surrounded by photographers and camera operators as he walked toward the Lambeau tunnel, stopping and turning for one last big wave to the crowd.

Of course, Rodgers wanted Favre to get on his tractor in Hattiesburg, Mississippi, and stay there forever. This wasn't only about the rookie's desire to take the starting job in Year 2. It was also about Rodgers wanting to liberate himself from the never-ending Favre freeze-out.

"I didn't know ninety percent of what went on, but Aaron did tell us a few things about how [Favre] wasn't very welcoming," said Rodgers's father, Ed. "He'd have the other quarterback go on hunting trips and fishing trips and Aaron would never get invited."

Another person close to Rodgers said his family feared the long-term impact Favre's behavior would have on the rookie. "He was actually cruel to Aaron," the person said. "Aaron is twenty-one, twenty-two, and Coach Sherman doesn't know what to do with this renegade who plays lousy and talks about retiring and then comes back. It was bad."

How bad? One day late in the season, Favre eyed the table in the locker room that was often reserved for items to be signed by players for charity (helmets, footballs, pennants, etc.) and decided it would be fun to substitute Rodgers's actual helmet—complete with his radio device—for one of the replicas on the table. Favre told his backup that, on this day, all the quarterbacks were to pick up their helmets in the practice facility, while secretly recruiting as many teammates as possible to sign Rodgers's with a black Sharpie. Even an oblivious Aaron signed his own helmet.

"Favre was walking around the locker room and said to me, 'Hey, sign this helmet,'" said Brady Poppinga, a rookie linebacker. "I'm like, 'Man, that's one authentic-looking helmet. It looks like one of ours.' But I didn't look into it much more than that; I signed it and had to get out to practice."

The Packers were on the field when Rodgers noticed that Favre and coconspirator Craig Nall, the third-string quarterback, were already wearing their helmets. They pointed to an equipment staffer who was walking toward Rodgers carrying a helmet that was covered in black scribblings. Aaron's helmet.

The rookie reluctantly pulled it down over his head.

"We were all in our stretching lines," Poppinga recalled, "and there was this roar of laughter."

Mike Sherman looked at Favre and Nall and shook his head, then turned his attention to Rodgers. "Aaron," the coach said, "what do you think, you're back in high school and you're getting everybody to sign your yearbook at the end of the year?"

When the practice ended, the rookie approached someone in the locker room and said, "Do you know what that motherfucker did to me?"

This, Poppinga said, was a prime example of how Favre treated Rodgers. "He treated him like his little brother," the linebacker said. "It was, 'I want to bug him as much as I can to delay the inevitable.'"

During practices, Favre's cold shoulder did not diminish Rodgers's appetite for attacking and defeating the first-team defense while he ran the scout team. "They wanted me to throw a pick every play," Rodgers said, "which I refused to do." Some players and coaches grumbled that Rodgers did not run the upcoming opponent's plays the way they were drawn up, and instead threw some unscripted curveballs that were designed to make him look good.

Rodgers wasn't getting in the game, so your average NFL weekday was his Sunday showcase. The rookie had been impressed by Favre's no-look passes and wanted to throw some of his own. After a few weeks of this Showtime act, Sherman sent a stern message to his quarterbacks coach, Darrell Bevell: *Tell the rook to stop fuckin' throwing no-look passes.*

Rodgers was going to temper his act only so much. He liked to go deep to an undrafted receiver from Alabama State, Chad Lucas, who noticed that defenders such as veteran cornerback Al Harris complained that Rodgers wasn't giving the first-stringers the assigned looks.

"Aaron wanted to showcase his arm talent," Lucas said. "There were times the ball was supposed to get checked down and he threw it deep anyway. It might have pissed off the coach, but it made those guys play harder and get ready for Sunday. Aaron always had this quiet fire about himself that if you pushed him, it would come out."

Another receiver, Terrence Murphy, Rodgers's roommate during training camp, saw that fire when starting linebacker Nick Barnett gave the quarterback a hard time in practice about constantly throwing to Murphy. Rodgers and the second-round pick from Texas A&M had natural chemistry as members of the class of 2005 who fell in the draft, and as movie buffs who went together to the local theater and grabbed a bite at a Red Robin.

"All you do is throw to Murph," Barnett barked.

"Well shit, stop him," Rodgers responded. "Fuck, he's open, I'm throwing him the ball."

This was an interesting time in Green Bay to study quarterback-receiver dynamics across the board. In May, Favre had criticized Pro Bowl receiver

Javon Walker for holding out of minicamp in hopes of landing a contract more lucrative than his existing five-year, $7.485 million deal. The quarterback had committed a clear violation of locker-room protocol that angered Walker and fellow star receiver Donald Driver.

And yet those same receivers only wanted to catch passes from Favre in camp and in early-season practices.

"There was a time Donald Driver and Javon Walker didn't halfway want to get into the huddle with Aaron," Murphy recalled. "It's the NFL. That's how guys are.... I do remember times when Brett had some reps he might not want to take, Aaron would go in, and I would see guys' faces change and they'd say little stuff to him.

"They used to treat him like shit at times for sure."

Of course, the same could be said of Favre, who never conceded anything to the only true competition for his job since 1992.

"My contract doesn't say I have to get Aaron Rodgers ready to play," Favre said. "Now, hopefully, he watches me and gets something from that."

Truth was, Favre never wanted his backup to get much of anything out of watching him.

"At first Favre ignored him," said Craig Rigsbee, who remained close to Rodgers. "Aaron thought he'd be strong, and when they said, 'You're going to be mentored by Favre,' he said, 'I've got a quarterback coach. I don't need him to mentor me at all.' That pissed Favre off. It was very awkward."

It was also a problem that Mike Sherman no longer had to worry about. Thompson fired him for going 4-12 and found a replacement who, like many other evaluators in Rodgers's football life, was not a true believer. In fact, he was among those chiefly responsible for denying the Cal quarterback his boyhood dream.

• • •

MIKE MCCARTHY WAS a tough guy from a tough town.

"I like that Pittsburgh macho stuff," general manager Ted Thompson said of his new head coach.

As a firefighter, cop, and bar owner, McCarthy's old man, Joe, had hit the Irish American trifecta in the Steel City. Mike used to clean the bathroom in the basement of Joe McCarthy's Bar and Grill. He hated that walk downstairs, the smell of urine growing more powerful with each step he took after a full house of beer-pounding steelworkers had cycled through.

"Being the oldest son, I got the short end of the stick on many Sunday mornings," McCarthy said. "Saturday night was the least accurate night of the week."

He was a Catholic boy from the Greenfield neighborhood who attended St. Rosalia Church and Bishop Boyle High School. He was an accomplished tight end at an NAIA school in Kansas, Baker University, before he got into coaching. He had been the quarterbacks coach of the Packers in 1999—not a good season for Brett Favre, hampered by an injured thumb—and then the offensive coordinator in New Orleans (for five years) and in San Francisco (for one year).

In the spring of 2005, McCarthy was in on the 49ers' decision to draft Alex Smith, and not Aaron Rodgers, with the first overall pick. McCarthy and Niners quarterbacks coach Jim Hostler had spent time at a team meet-and-greet with the media inside a Santa Clara pizza shop trying to convince *San Jose Mercury News* columnist Tim Kawakami that his preferred choice for the No. 1 pick—Rodgers—was the wrong one.

"They were like, 'You're an idiot' and went off on me," Kawakami recalled. Hostler was the one doing most of the talking, but McCarthy also made it clear that he had no use for the columnist's printed opinion that the Cal star should be the Niners' next quarterback. Kawakami covered Rodgers's signature performance—his twenty-three consecutive completions in the loss to USC—and later wrote that McCarthy supported Hostler's bashing of the Cal quarterback, "telling me that my praise of Rodgers' performance against USC should've been largely directed at [Jeff] Tedford's coaching. Not to Rodgers' play."

This matched up with Mike Nolan's recollection of a process that led San Francisco's new staff to Alex Smith. "It was my first head coaching job," he said, "and Mike was the guy who was most knowledgeable on quarterbacks of the group, and as a group that's what we decided."

McCarthy pushed back on the idea that he was a driving force behind the Smith selection. "I'd like to sit here and tell you I was in the big meeting," he said for this book. "I was the offensive coordinator, and I did express my opinion. But those selections are made by a group of people, and ultimately a lot of information goes into that. I thought both quarterbacks were very young, talented guys who you could win with."

Nolan insisted that he deserved the blame as the Niners official who had final say on the draft pick. But the head coach did recall that McCarthy was concerned about Rodgers's ball position and was unsure if he could change it.

"There are things on my mind that still bother me to this day," Nolan told me many years later. "I'll let Mike tell you the truth. Mike was just with me one year and he got the Green Bay job. We were thirty-second in offense, and Mike got the Green Bay job."

That's right—the 49ers ranked dead last in the NFL in total yards in 2005. They ranked dead last in passing yards. They ranked thirtieth out of thirty-two in total points.

And Mike got the Green Bay job.

"He had a lot to do with picking the other one [Smith]," Nolan said for this book, "and in the end he got the one [Rodgers] that he didn't pick, and it elevated his career."

Not right away it didn't.

Shortly after Green Bay hired him, McCarthy visited Brett Favre at his Hattiesburg estate, where the quarterback had been out in the woods cutting down trees with his chainsaw. They met for nearly three hours and the new coach told the old gunslinger that he would love for him to return for a fifteenth Packers season.

Favre thanked the man for coming, danced his tired retirement two-step for three months, and finally informed the team he was indeed running it back. Favre was already on record saying that if he did return for the 2006 season, that would be his last year. "There's no doubt about that," he said.

Meanwhile, McCarthy was busy coaching the No. 2 quarterback on the roster, the one he did not want in San Francisco. "Mike got an earful from Aaron about that," Nolan said, "and deservedly so."

Rodgers was known to read and hear whatever was said about him by a coach, player, broadcaster, or columnist, so there was almost no chance he missed McCarthy's stated assessment of him in November, when recalling his feelings about Rodgers as a draft prospect.

"I thought he was a real good football player," McCarthy said. "I think he went where he was supposed to go. I think it was a good pick for [Green Bay]. We just didn't look at him as the first pick. We're happy with the guy we drafted."

Ouch.

Now McCarthy had to make peace with Rodgers. He admitted to the second-year quarterback that he had underestimated his athleticism, but that he felt fortunate to have been granted this mulligan.

"I pulled him into a meeting and said, 'Hey, the last time I saw you was during draft prep,'" McCarthy recalled. "We talked about it. I thought it was important that him and I talk about it. I kind of said, 'That's the way the league goes.'"

Rodgers did not forgive, and Rodgers did not forget. He did agree to move forward with a man who was prepared to coach him in a way that Mike Sherman did not.

A few days a week, McCarthy had Rodgers on the field and in the classroom for what the coach called "Quarterback School." Previously uncertain that he could lower Rodgers's ball position and release point, McCarthy did just that, breaking down the Tedford approach to make the quarterback's delivery more relaxed and fluid. The earhole days were over. It worked at Cal, but it was not going to work in the NFL. Among the moves McCarthy made in the development of Rodgers, this was a particularly wise one.

"We felt the ball should be lower because . . . we always thought he could move easier with it that way," McCarthy said, "and in the framework of the body it was better protected than higher ball carriage. . . . It was an opportunity to take advantage of his athletic ability."

McCarthy also ran Rodgers through a series of footwork and hand-eye coordination drills to enhance his mechanics and started pestering the second-year quarterback about lowering his body fat.

With Favre excused, Rodgers went through Quarterback School with Tom Arth, an undrafted quarterback from Division III John Carroll. By minicamp in May, Rodgers was praising McCarthy's lighter and looser tone and explaining how it "breeds an atmosphere of communication." Rodgers also said the sessions had already made him a significantly better player.

McCarthy had brought in Atlanta Falcons assistant Jeff Jagodzinski as his offensive coordinator and former Buffalo Bills offensive coordinator Tom Clements, another Pittsburgh area guy, as his quarterbacks coach. Clements had quarterbacked Notre Dame to the 1973 national championship and had won two Grey Cup titles in the Canadian Football League. McCarthy wanted a former player to tutor Rodgers, someone who had faced and conquered big-game pressure.

Rodgers hit it off with the quarterbacks coach, who would turn out to be one of McCarthy's best hires. In training camp, more and more people around the team started observing that Rodgers could make every throw that Favre could make, and maybe even a couple that Favre couldn't.

"Aaron was outperforming Favre in a lot of drills," said radio man Bill Michaels. "He could throw it seventy yards downfield into a basket." Michaels recalled that newly signed cornerback Charles Woodson, a four-time Pro Bowler, told him that the Packers were going to be just fine whenever Favre actually did retire.

"That guy is beating us," Woodson said of Rodgers. "That guy is for real. He's putting it in places that we can't get to."

Rodgers's belief in himself—never a problem—was growing teeth by the hour. Before he was drafted, he told Packers GM Ted Thompson that he was better than all the other Tedford quarterbacks he was being compared to. After he was drafted, Rodgers said that he felt he shared Favre's fearlessness and his mental and physical toughness.

Now he was telling friends that he felt he could go toe-to-toe with a first-ballot Hall of Famer. "I remember having calls with him when he was the backup," said his childhood friend in Oregon, Joey Kaempf, a Division I basketball player at Santa Clara. "Aaron would say, 'I'm better than Favre right now. I should be playing.'... He wasn't happy just sitting in the room with Favre. He wanted to start."

Though he publicly supported Favre's decision to return to the team, Rodgers was privately disappointed. He wasn't the only Packer who felt that way. As much as they admired Favre's durability and appreciated everything he meant to the franchise, people throughout the organization were worn to the nub by the protracted drama.

Former Packers tight end Mark Chmura, who won a Super Bowl with Favre, was not speaking only for himself when he shredded his former quarterback for being selfish and hypocritical during his latest prolonged flirtation with retirement. Chmura pointed out that Favre had criticized Javon Walker the previous year for supposedly putting himself ahead of the team, only to do the same thing times ten.

But out in the parking lots, the tailgating men, women, and children who filled Lambeau Field to capacity for every home game still adored Favre. "There are fans out there," Chmura said, "[who] could find out that

Brett Favre could run over fourteen puppies, and they still wouldn't care. These people would think he was still the greatest thing since sliced bread."

Rodgers was always going up against the people's champ, and it wasn't a fair fight. As long as he had a pulse and a functioning right arm, Favre was going to be on the field. Only injury or retirement could end his streak of consecutive starts.

Knowing he would rarely get any playing time in a regular-season game at Lambeau, Rodgers tried to show the locals what he had in the team's annual scrimmage on Family Night, a training-camp tradition that drew tens of thousands of fans.

Leading the second-team offense against the first-team defense, Rodgers noticed that when he carried out his fakes on one particular running play, no defender was there to stop him on the back side. He was wearing a red jersey, the universal "Do Not Disturb" sign for all linebackers and strong safeties who might otherwise consider taking a run at a quarterback's ribs.

Even though he could not be hit in this live scrimmage, Rodgers asked for permission from Jagodzinski to fake one to the running back and carry it himself. The quarterback promised he wouldn't tell anyone that he had received Jagodzinski's blessing, and the offensive coordinator gave him the green light.

After throwing a short touchdown pass to Marc Boerigter, Rodgers was charged to carry out "98 Strike," that running play to one of his backs, on a two-point conversion attempt. Instead of handing off the ball, he kept it and ran a bootleg into the end zone.

"Nobody tried to tackle him," said linebacker Brady Poppinga, "but he's avoiding guys, spinning. It was like he was trying to avoid would-be tacklers, but there were none there. He was off-limits. He scores, the crowd goes crazy, and he spikes the ball. I thought it was goofy because we can't tackle the guy and he knows it. Maybe it was just a showman move."

A year after he struggled in a Family Night scrimmage against Buffalo in a grim first preseason, Rodgers had overcome a few drops by his receivers to lead the second-team offense on a 75-yard touchdown drive and to thrill a record Family Night crowd of 62,701 by completing three straight fourth-down throws. The next day, while waiting for a debriefing in the team meeting room, players were stunned when their burly head coach came barreling through the door.

"He's hot," Poppinga said of Mike McCarthy. "He blasts through there and his face is red."

Poppinga was sitting one row behind Rodgers, to the backup's left, and one row ahead of Favre, to the starter's right. McCarthy turned on the film and immediately jumped on Rodgers's unscripted romp into the end zone.

"Aaron, what are you supposed to do?" the coach barked. "You know what you're supposed to do, hand the ball off." McCarthy told the quarterback that "there are no solo soldiers on this team" and warned Rodgers to abandon his rogue maneuvers.

"I've never seen him rip anyone like this," Poppinga said. "He was tearing him apart. Aaron was sinking in his seat, his face was beet red. He was completely embarrassed."

Rodgers could have told McCarthy that his offensive coordinator had approved his little audible, but he had given his word. He owned the prank. Jagodzinski was spared.

And just as McCarthy finished blitzing Rodgers, Favre leaned forward, as close to Poppinga's ear as he could get, and gave his own little lecture on how his backup was carrying himself.

"That Aaron," Favre said. "He is *sooooo* cocky."

Rodgers played much better in his second preseason than he did in his first, completing 22 of 38 passes with 3 touchdowns and 1 interception in four games. He had taken many first-team reps in the spring, with Favre away, and the game was no longer moving at a breakneck speed. Rodgers noted that a number of fans and media had gotten down on him in his rookie year. "After this past spring," he said, "it was pretty funny because it was like, 'Oh, wow! He actually is pretty decent.'"

As Rodgers got more decisive, Packers teammates began to believe in him. "A-Rod's earned our respect," said sixth-year receiver Robert Ferguson. Some Berkeley guys had called Rodgers "A-Rod" too, including Marshawn Lynch.

At the start of his 2006 season, the original A-Rod, Alex Rodriguez, was coming off a 48-homer, 130-RBI season for the New York Yankees as American League MVP. Rodgers was opening his 2006 season as an untested player who had looked lost in Year 1.

If nothing else, he made a preseason stir with a much-ridiculed mustache (the remnants of a full beard) that he called "a tribute to all the great people in history that had mustaches—guys like Tom Selleck and Chuck

Norris and Jesus and Ron Burgundy," before shaving it. With or without the facial hair, Rodgers thought he had become a much better quarterback.

The only way to truly improve, however, was through experience in games that mattered. And that was a major problem when the man in front of Rodgers opened 2006 with a record 241 consecutive starts, including playoffs.

In Week 11 of the season, Favre's thirty-seven-year-old body finally broke down, clearing a pathway for his twenty-two-year-old backup. Late in the first half of Green Bay's game against New England, as three-time Super Bowl champ Tom Brady was staging his weekly clinic, Favre was grabbed low by the Patriots' Tully Banta-Cain and driven into the ground by Tedy Bruschi for a 10-yard loss.

The Packers' starter got up slowly, grabbed his right elbow, and appeared in extreme pain while holding his arm as trainers led him off the field. Rodgers entered a game that his 4-5 team was already trailing by 21 points to a dynastic opponent and an all-time great defensive mind, Bill Belichick. He had thrown a mere three passes all year.

"And Aaron Rodgers comes onto the field," Greg Gumbel announced on the CBS broadcast. The Lambeau crowd cheered, and as he entered the huddle Rodgers quickly motioned for the fans to lower the volume. Gumble's partner Dan Dierdorf said that the backup had benefited from "a chance to study at the feet of the master."

It was second down and twenty at midfield, and Rodgers went into shotgun formation, his left foot forward (the opposite of how he positioned himself at Butte College, the result of a Tom Clements adjustment to improve his rhythm and balance). He barked out his signals, took the snap cleanly, stepped into the pressure, and fired to the right sideline and over the head of receiver Ruvell Martin.

On the next play, back in the shotgun, Rodgers threw to the left sideline, where no Packer was even remotely available to catch the ball. The pass sailed so high that it was hard to tell if it was intended for Greg Jennings or Donald Driver. Rodgers pointed to one of the receivers and walked off the field.

Favre was loaded into a cart and driven to the locker room in the final seconds of the half. The crowd stood and cheered when he walked through the tunnel and back onto the field a minute into the second half. "Well, they love him like no other," Dierdorf said on the air, "and justifiably so."

The fans did not know that Favre was done for the day, that this was the backup's game the rest of the way. On his first snap of the second half, Rodgers rolled right and hit tight end Donald Lee for sixteen yards and a round of applause. It went downhill from there.

Rodgers was sacked and stripped of the ball on his final play of this 35–0 defeat, a fitting end to an afternoon that derailed his big-picture designs. He completed 4 of 12 passes for 32 yards and got sacked three times. The news got worse after the game.

An X-ray showed that Rodgers had broken his left foot and needed season-ending surgery.

Aaron had limped out of the locker room and had refused to speak with reporters because he had just gotten the crushing news and couldn't bear to talk about it. McCarthy believed that he broke his foot on a scramble in the middle of the third quarter. Though Rodgers had a trainer tape his ankle to support the foot, he did not have a good feeling about it.

"Man, it feels like my foot's broken," he told third-string quarterback Ingle Martin. "But I'm not coming out of the game."

Rodgers won points with his teammates and coaches by playing the entire fourth quarter with a fractured fifth metatarsal bone that now needed to be stabilized by a surgically implanted screw. Brett Favre would have done that. Bart Starr too.

Vince Lombardi's quarterback had won the famous 1967 Ice Bowl in the final seconds by asking his coach for the ball and then somehow throwing his frozen, swollen body across the Lambeau goal line to beat the Dallas Cowboys for the NFL title.

Tough men played that position for the Green Bay Packers. Rodgers said that by persevering through his broken foot, he showed the fans "what kind of guy they're getting in the future."

Assuming there would be a future.

• • •

BRETT FAVRE DID everyone a favor on February 2, 2007, by announcing that he was ending his annual retirement saga earlier than he normally did and, once again, returning to work at 1265 Lombardi Avenue. When

Mike McCarthy got the word from GM Ted Thompson, his first order of business was to call Favre's backup.

Aaron Rodgers was not surprised. Naturally, he was bitterly disappointed.

The two quarterbacks had actually improved their relationship, even if, as Rodgers pointed out, he was closer in age to Favre's teenage daughter than he was to No. 4. Favre could see how hard Rodgers worked, and how eager he was to share information with the starter from his film work, and how helpful the backup was in teaching him everything he missed in McCarthy's Quarterback School. Rodgers even printed out reports on the opposing defensive backs every week—their strengths and weaknesses—and gave them to Favre.

"I always joked that he just tossed them in the bin on the way out," Rodgers said.

On his end, Favre said that whenever his backup asked to watch film together, he would agree. "He was a heck of a lot smarter than I was," Favre said, "but I would help him out."

Despite the evidence to the contrary—Rodgers told the *Green Bay Press-Gazette*'s Rob Demovsky that he did not even have his teammate's phone number—Favre swore he had no animosity toward his backup. He said he enjoyed their one-on-one time together in the film and meeting rooms.

After Rodgers's foot surgery, Favre had to notice that his backup did not go home to heal. While using crutches and wearing a boot on his foot, Rodgers attended team meetings, watched film, and wore a headset on the sidelines to help out during games. How could an ultimate gamer like Favre not appreciate that?

"I think a mutual respect grew into the friendship we have right now," Rodgers said, as he headed into another uncertain offseason. He would spend part of that offseason watching his Oregon childhood buddies Joey Kaempf and Scott Dougherty play basketball at Santa Clara.

The Packers had won their last four games to finish 8-8, giving Favre another reason to come back. When people asked Rodgers about the uncertainty of it all, and what it was like to endure another will-he-or-won't-he soap opera, he compared it to one of his darkest football days.

"It's like sitting in that green room [on draft day]," he said. "I couldn't do anything about dropping, dropping, dropping."

Favre had outlasted all of his knockaround buddies on the team and had admittedly become more of a loner—he was doing most of his hunting and fishing these days with a rookie quarterback, Ingle Martin, another product of the South. And yet he couldn't resist getting off that tractor and getting out of those woods for another go-around with the Packers, his sixteenth.

On cue, the masses couldn't resist standing and cheering for him; Favre was a regular atop the Harris Poll of fans as America's favorite football player. The ratified 2000 plan to renovate Lambeau Field likely would not have happened without him.

Rodgers was up against a monster, and he knew it. But while attending Cal's game at UCLA during the Packers' October bye week, Rodgers told his former Berkeley teammate Vinny Strang, "I see what Brett's doing, and I know I can make all those throws. I can do that."

Strang was a little taken aback. *You're two or three years removed from college, you're behind a Hall of Famer*, he thought to himself, *and you're telling me you can make all the throws he can?*

On Thursday night, November 29, Rodgers got his shot to walk that talk inside Texas Stadium. The 10-1 Dallas Cowboys and 10-1 Packers were battling as credible Super Bowl contenders when Favre got knocked out of the game in the second quarter with elbow and shoulder injuries. Rodgers entered this heavyweight fight with the home team leading, 27–10.

He could not afford to deliver another uninspiring performance. As Pete Dougherty of the *Press-Gazette* wrote in the summer, "Rodgers has done nothing to eliminate himself from the succession line, but he's done nothing to push Favre toward retirement."

Rodgers took the field with rock-star hair flowing out of the bottom of his helmet, and with large white wristbands pulled up near his elbows. He stepped into the Green Bay huddle and addressed his teammates.

"Guys, trust me," he said. "Believe in me."

On his first series, Rodgers attacked a third-and-7 situation by accepting a big hit that sent him helicoptering to the ground for an 8-yard gain. "A little John Elway–esque at the end of that one," NFL Network analyst Cris Collinsworth said on the broadcast. "When you sit on the bench for year after year behind Brett Favre [and] you finally get a chance to play, why not?"

Rodgers popped up and emphatically signaled for a first down. The rest of the game was his. On his second series, Collinsworth claimed that the

Packers "aren't going to win a whole lot with Aaron Rodgers playing quarterback, unless things change drastically."

Rodgers forever remembered that rip because he filed away every real or imagined slight. He managed the next play as if his radio device was picking up the broadcast—by completing a pass to Greg Jennings for a 43-yard gain.

"Well," Collinsworth said, "I knew I could get the Packers going if I just insulted their quarterback."

With thirty-one seconds left in the half, Rodgers hit Jennings for an 11-yard score and the first touchdown pass of his career. As the receiver celebrated with teammates, the quarterback ran to the back of the end zone to secure the ball. Rodgers carried it to the sideline, and as he slapped hands with teammates and hugged them, the camera cut to a shot of the injured starter.

Favre had a towel draped over his left shoulder. He looked less than thrilled as he lowered his head and walked toward the bench.

The Cowboys won the game, 37–27, but Rodgers won the night. He completed 18 of 26 attempts for 201 yards and ran for 30 yards and three first downs. After the Packers cut the deficit to 27–24, the NFL Network's Bryant Gumbel was moved to say, "My goodness, young Aaron Rodgers." His partner Collinsworth said, "We got a story going on right here."

As Rodgers was dealing, starting linebacker and draft classmate Brady Poppinga was among the Packers at least mildly surprised by what they were seeing. They had been unsure Rodgers could ever ascend to this level of play.

"The Aaron I had faced on the practice squad, he had moments when he was absolutely horrendous," Poppinga said. "He just wasn't good. It was a small sample size, and it wasn't like, 'He sucks.' It was more that I didn't know what he was capable of until that game."

Near the visitors' bench, while watching No. 12 make like a healthy No. 4 in his prime, Favre was holding his wounded right arm. Poppinga approached him and said with all seriousness, "Man, you've done a heck of a job teaching him."

Favre was not at all happy to hear it. "He was like, 'It's not over yet, Brady,' and he walks away," Poppinga recalled. "We were down 3 points. He was chapped about this because he sees the writing on the wall."

The graying Favre remained in control of the narrative—always. If he could drag his body out there, the Packers were going to keep Rodgers on the bench. As Gumbel said on the air, "In any other community they'd say this is the start of a quarterback controversy. But that won't happen in Green Bay."

Favre said after the Dallas defeat that he planned to be ready for the next game against Oakland, his 270th consecutive start. He had appeared on forty-nine injury lists during his absurd streak and had never missed an opening snap. He had a separated left shoulder along with his reinjured right elbow and it did not matter. He was playing.

To his credit, Favre was gracious when asked about Rodgers's performance. "I thought he played great," the starter said. "He gave us a chance to win. I've been saying that all along. I thought he was ready to play."

In the offseason, Favre was angered when the superstar Raiders receiver he had pushed Green Bay to acquire, Randy Moss, was dealt to New England. That feeling was only hardened by the fact that Moss was currently on his way to a 23-touchdown, 1,493-yard season for the unbeaten Patriots and by the fact that Favre's unproven (at the time) understudy was rumored to be part of the Packers' trade talks with Oakland. Ted Thompson shot down the notion that he had ever considered trading Rodgers, but still, enough Packers diehards harbored doubts about the twenty-fourth overall draft choice to make his Dallas breakthrough feel crucial.

Mike McCarthy said that he talked with Thompson on the flight back from the Dallas game, and that they agreed the kid was ready to play. And yet Rodgers did not play another relevant snap the rest of the season.

He injured his hamstring in practice, missing the final four games, before returning to the field in the closing minutes of an already-secured playoff victory over Seattle in the Lambeau snow. Back on the frozen tundra the following week, with a wind chill of minus twenty-three at kickoff, Rodgers watched as a stiff Favre floated a ball into the hands of New York Giants cornerback Corey Webster in overtime.

That interception helped gift the NFC Championship to the New York Giants, who sealed it on a 47-yard field goal that Lawrence Tynes made in impossible conditions. For the tenth straight season with an all-time great quarterback, the Packers fell short of the Super Bowl.

On the way out of Lambeau, one member of the Packers' board of directors punched an elevator wall and shouted, "We can lose these games with that son of a bitch or without him. And I'm tired of losing these games."

For the better part of three years the Packers had absorbed criticism for drafting Rodgers. So much so, said Packers VP Andrew Brandt, "that when people talked about replacing Favre when he eventually retired, it was always, 'You're not actually going to replace him with Aaron, right?'"

At the same time over those years, Brandt was fielding calls from Rodgers's agent, Mike Sullivan, who kept asking the Packers executive, "What are we doing? Is Aaron ever going to play? You and I both know Brett is never going to retire."

But something had changed after the Dallas game. The following day, Poppinga and his wife attended a party hosted by a friend who had also invited Packers executives Brandt and John Schneider, a top personnel aide to the GM.

As Poppinga recalled it, Schneider was in quite the talkative mood. Maybe he had downed a couple of cold ones, maybe not. Either way, the man was on a roll. "And he does not have a filter at all," the linebacker said.

Poppinga was not there to talk business, but Schneider wanted to share a piece of intel about the team's future. He wanted to point out that something valuable was gained in the loss to the Cowboys.

"Brady," he said, "we got our guy."

Poppinga shot him a look. "What do you mean 'our guy'?"

"No more, 'Is Brett Favre retiring, or is he coming back?'" the executive replied. "Aaron is our guy."

"Really?"

"We're done with Brett, man," Schneider told him. "Aaron was awesome yesterday."

Poppinga put his head on a swivel to see if anyone else was hearing what this Packers personnel man was saying about arguably the best player in franchise history. Schneider added that Poppinga was going to get a contract extension, which sounded awfully good to the linebacker.

That Monday, Schneider hunted down Poppinga, looked him in the eye and said, "Brady, what happens in Vegas, stays in Vegas." Poppinga agreed. He shared his inside information only with his fellow linebacker, A. J. Hawk.

"This is Brett's last year," he told Hawk. "They're over him."

"Wow" was Hawk's response.

For the first time, the Green Bay Packers wanted Brett Favre to retire. They wanted Aaron Rodgers to be the new face of their franchise, and they were not about to let the old face get in their way.

8

A STAR IS BORN

AARON RODGERS COULD not even get through one scrimmage as the undisputed starting quarterback of the 2008 Green Bay Packers. On August 3, Family Night at Lambeau Field, the sold-out crowd included a thirty-eight-year-old fan who was hoping to get a tryout to make this team.

Brett Favre.

The bogeyman was back. Five months after he retired in an emotional press conference, Favre was in the building and fixing to play football. Aaron Rodgers could not kill him off.

That's the way it seemed, anyway. The Packers had never said the word "no" to Favre on anything, and now that he had decided to resume his career, many assumed they would cave and send Rodgers back to the bench.

But after the devastating overtime loss to the Giants in the NFC Championship Game, Packers executives concluded that Favre was no longer capable of leading the team to a Super Bowl. This time around, Ted Thompson did not approach Favre after the season to assure him that the Packers wanted him back. He never said anything to his quarterback, and Favre got the message. He retired on March 4.

Over time rumors and reports gave way to Favre making it official that he was launching a comeback. Heated words were exchanged between the team and the quarterback and his agent, Bus Cook. New Packers president Mark Murphy actually traveled to Hattiesburg to offer Favre as much as $25 million to stay retired.

The Packers wanted to give Favre a lucrative, long-term marketing deal just to keep him on the sidelines. That was how much they did not want him playing for their team.

Favre did not take the deal. Green Bay was unwilling to release him, which would have allowed Favre to sign with his preferred alternative, Minnesota, nor was it willing to trade him to the Vikings or any other NFC North foe. Thwarted, the quarterback boarded a private jet with his wife, Deanna, and Cook, and flew to Austin Straubel International Airport in Green Bay, all while Rodgers was preparing to play on a Family Night that should have been renamed Dysfunctional Family Night.

Favre landed at 7:06 p.m. and deplaned to a hero's welcome. "Here is Brett Favre!" exclaimed one local TV anchor broadcasting live. "He's back! Brett Favre is back as the starting quarterback of the Green Bay Packers!" Some fans had been waiting three hours for his plane to show up at the Executive Air terminal, ignoring the rain and the lightning in the sky. "It was like Lombardi was coming home," said longtime Packers CEO Bob Harlan.

Wearing a Nike T-shirt and cargo shorts, Favre waved to a couple hundred cheering fans who had been tipped off to his arrival. They held up welcoming signs and chanted, "We want Brett." Favre and his wife drove off in a burgundy Escalade that was followed by a Milwaukee TV station helicopter. The trailing copter, wrote Tony Walter of the *Press-Gazette*, "gave the entire episode an O. J. Simpson flavor."

The televised images of this surreal journey played on the monitors in the Lambeau Field press box, where reporters were waiting out the thunderstorms that delayed Rodgers's debut by an hour.

"It was an incredible juxtaposition," said *Press-Gazette* beat writer Rob Demovsky.

Favre made it to the stadium in time for part of the show, only it wasn't much of a performance. Rodgers was terrible in the scrimmage, hitting on 7 of 20 throws for 84 yards (including 9 straight incompletions), and throwing a ghastly interception in the end zone in a two-minute drill.

The crowd of fifty-six thousand was not happy. As much as the organization did not want Favre back, the fans could not get enough of him. Everywhere Rodgers went during the summer, people asked him if he thought Favre was about to unretire.

Some booed Rodgers during training camp and cheered his lousy throws. "A total disaster," starting safety Nick Collins called it. "I mean, we had little kids out there calling A-Rod trash."

Rodgers heard it again from Family Night fans who would have been happy to reimburse Favre for the jet fuel he burned from Mississippi to Green Bay. "They're booing all of us, probably me mostly," he said. "So yeah, I take it personally."

NFL commissioner Roger Goodell had agreed to reinstate Favre, but he wanted a quick resolution to his status. Privately, Rodgers was incensed that Favre was back in his life. Publicly, he stayed above the fray.

Fans chanted "We want Favre" and "Bring back Brett" during practices at Clarke Hinkle Field, next to the indoor Don Hutson Center. At one camp session a young couple wore shirts that mocked Thompson, who was unfairly portrayed by Favre supporters as the villain in this drama.

Favre used to drink beers with Thompson at the 50 Yard Line, across the street from Lambeau, in the 1990s, when the former Houston Oilers linebacker and special teamer was a personnel man on his way to a bigger job in Seattle. After Thompson returned to Green Bay as general manager, he did not grant Favre the same favored-nation treatment that was afforded by Mike Sherman. The quarterback and GM had no use for each other in the end.

The Packers did leak word that Favre would be allowed to compete for the first-string job, after repeatedly telling him that would not be the case. Rodgers said, "It's going to be a dogfight," when handicapping the competition with the three-time league MVP.

"But we were not giving the job back to Brett," said former Packers VP Andrew Brandt, "and Aaron knew that."

Even if Aaron did not act like he knew that.

Brandt had recently left the organization as its lead contract negotiator and salary cap manager, but he remained in contact with Rodgers and team officials. A Stanford guy, Brandt had gotten along with the Cal guy during their three years together.

"He'd come over my house; I think he babysat our kids once," the executive said. "Aaron had that Northern California chill that I experienced at Stanford. He had that ability to not get rattled. Off the field he had a preternatural calm. Brett was all highs and lows, and Aaron was completely different."

Brandt advised Rodgers to keep his head down during the Favre standoff and stay focused on the job. It was much easier said than done. Erick and Adam Rolfson, two brothers from the Milwaukee suburb of Pewaukee, had created a website, www.bringbackBrettFavre.com, and organized a rally outside of Lambeau in July that was attended by nearly two hundred people—many dressed in No. 4 jerseys—who chanted for Favre and demanded that the Packers make him the starter in 2008.

"This is a hot-button issue that surpasses anything I've ever gone through," Thompson said. The Packers were so overwhelmed that they asked former White House press secretary Ari Fleischer to come up with a public relations game plan. Seriously.

Rodgers was getting his own PR advice from Adam Woullard, a young member of the team's media relations department who had developed a strong rapport with the former backup. In addition to being the point man for all of Rodgers's media requests, Woullard volunteered to take phone calls from aggrieved shareholders who sometimes identified themselves as team owners and who thought their $200 investment in a share entitled them to have a say in the selection of the starting quarterback.

"People were calling every day about the Favre situation," Woullard said. "And a majority of those calls, almost exclusively, were in support of Brett."

Along with Brandt, the current management team of Murphy, Thompson, and Mike McCarthy was trying to assure Rodgers that he had the franchise's full support. "But with Aaron," Woullard said, "it was more like, 'What if they fuck me? What if Brett convinces them to take him back?'"

Despite that Northern California chill and preternatural calm, and despite those reassuring voices within the building, Rodgers could not fully exorcise the ghost. Woullard recalled how No. 12 felt when No. 4 had stated that it was not his job to prepare his backup to replace him.

"The fact that Brett said that publicly really bothered Aaron," Woullard said. "He said something to the effect of 'What did I ever do to this guy to make him dislike me like that?'"

Training camp had devolved into something of a circus. Around the campus of St. Norbert, where the Packers bunked for camp, linebacker Brady Poppinga said he saw the toll it had taken on his fellow draftee from the class of 2005.

"He was not sleeping at all," Poppinga said. "He was very, very worn out. He was very, very, very tired and fatigued. But the fact that he was able to barrel through that . . . was the moment I knew Aaron was going to make it. He's going to be phenomenal."

On Family Night, the Rolfson brothers staged another Favre rally outside the stadium, at the foot of the Vince Lombardi statue. Erick Rolfson walked around with a megaphone and announced, "We won," before thanking the supporters "who picked up the torch that we lit." One female fan held a sign that read, "Yes, Brett Did Build This House."

But Favre knew that even he could not possibly play in Green Bay if the team's general manager and head coach did not want him there. When he arrived at Lambeau, Favre found that his passcode into the building did not work. The organization's security chief and longtime Favre friend, Doug Collins, escorted him to see McCarthy and asked him not to speak to any teammates. "Right away I was like, 'I'm not playing here,'" Favre said.

He had finally accepted reality. When the Packers first told him in June, "We've moved on," they actually meant it.

Favre and the Packers met for six hours over two days in what McCarthy called "brutally honest" conversations. The Green Bay legend could not get past how he felt he had been treated, after everything he had done for the team. The Packers told Favre that he had put them in an impossible spot.

It was time to sign the divorce papers in blood.

The Packers were holding serious trade talks with the Tampa Bay Buccaneers and New York Jets. Favre wanted to play within the division he had ruled for so long, ideally for the Minnesota Vikings. No way Thompson was keeping him in the NFC North. Of the two teams negotiating for his services, Favre preferred Jon Gruden's Bucs over the big-city Jets.

Naturally, near midnight on Wednesday, August 6, Green Bay traded him to New York for a conditional draft pick.

Aaron Charles Rodgers was a free man.

• • •

ON THE NIGHT of September 8, 2008, Aaron Rodgers took the field to face the Minnesota Vikings in his first career regular-season start. His tumultuous summer now behind him had not only been about Brett Favre and his Favre-ness.

Rodgers fired his agent, Mike Sullivan of Octagon, in favor of David Dunn of Athletes First, the runner-up for the quarterback when he left Cal. Rodgers made the same jump from Sullivan to Dunn that had earlier been made by one of his mentors, Trent Dilfer, whose recommendation three and a half years earlier had steered the Cal star to Sullivan.

Rodgers had been outraged by Nike's decision to exercise a clause in his $300,000-a-year sponsorship deal that allowed the company to subtract money from the contract in the event the player was not dressing for games. The shoe giant had signed Rodgers to that deal on the belief that he would be a high draft choice and a starter early in his career. After he fell in the draft, sat behind Favre, and landed on injured reserve with his broken foot in 2006, Nike official Bill Kellar informed Sullivan that the company was prorating his client's payout.

Sullivan did not know if that was a factor in Rodgers's decision, or if the quarterback ultimately held his agent responsible for what went down on draft day. He tried to get an explanation from his client after he received his termination letter, but Rodgers would not take his calls.

Dunn was now in charge of guiding and protecting Rodgers as he entered the second phase of his career, as an NFL starter. The Packers had little doubt they had made the right call in putting the fourth-year quarterback in charge of Favre's team. In fact, when the Green Bay staff was coaching the NFC team at the Pro Bowl in Honolulu, offensive coordinator Joe Philbin walked up to quarterbacks coach Tom Clements and said, "Tom, not for nothing, but Aaron Rodgers can throw the ball every bit as good and probably better than all the guys here."

Those "guys" included the Colts' Peyton Manning, the Steelers' Ben Roethlisberger, and the Cowboys' Tony Romo. Philbin shared that assessment with Rodgers in the spring.

"It was true," the coach said. "I grew up in Massachusetts. You don't have to be smart to figure out that Roger Clemens has a good fastball."

As much as the Packers swore they had complete faith in Rodgers's four-seamer—receivers Greg Jennings and James Jones even thought he packed a little more heat than Favre did—they did use a second-round draft choice on a quarterback, Louisville's Brian Brohm (and also took LSU's Matt Flynn in the seventh round). The Packers were in dire need of depth at that position, but still, a second-rounder in the NFL was expected to become a starter, and quickly.

Rodgers was assured by his bosses that he was The Guy, yet he knew he had to earn that title and that trust. A constant reminder was staring back at him a few yards from his locker—Favre's old locker, with No. 4's nameplate still in place.

"I know the pressure I'm under," Rodgers said.

Rodgers did not do anything to relieve the pressure with an interview he gave *Sports Illustrated*. Asked if he thought he needed to appeal to fans the way Favre did, Rodgers told the magazine, "I don't feel I need to sell myself to the fans. They need to get on board now or keep their mouths shut."

That quote sparked an unnecessary fire that Rodgers scrambled to put out. By training camp, the kid who had lent his bicycle to the quarterback for three summers as part of Green Bay's camp tradition, John Gee, said the quarterback "was getting threats, and there was a lot going on security-wise. It wasn't safe for him to ride anymore." Gee had stopped riding himself, as he was busy preparing for his high school football season. He said it was difficult watching from a distance as his friend dealt with the negativity that surrounded Favre's comeback attempt.

Rodgers's personal PR adviser and friend, Adam Woullard, had called Steve Young and Jay Fiedler, who replaced Joe Montana and Dan Marino, respectively, for advice on how to follow a legend. As a Niners fan who idolized their star quarterbacks, Rodgers remembered Young's volatile journey to the Hall of Fame. He recalled that family members and friends who adored Montana could never root for Young, no matter how good he was at his job.

"I remember Steve Young told me, 'The biggest regret I have, after I won the Super Bowl, is that clip that showed me wanting a teammate to take the monkey off my back,'" Woullard said. "He said, 'Up until then, I hadn't shown that any of this bothered me, and it did.' That was the plan with Aaron. Never let them see you sweat."

Good luck with that: Rodgers was holding one of the biggest jobs in sports. Playing quarterback for the Green Bay Packers was much like playing center field for the New York Yankees—it was a storied position for a storied franchise in a storied building.

Lambeau was pro football's Field of Dreams, sold out on game day every week since 1960, with more than sixty thousand people on the season-ticket waiting list. Andrew Brandt looked out his office window and saw drivers get out of their cars to genuflect, as if completing a football pilgrimage. Requests poured in from people saying they needed tickets for a sick relative or friend whose lifelong dream was to attend a game in Vince Lombardi's ballpark.

"And it's such a unique place to work," said Packers offensive coordinator Joe Philbin. "You live in the neighborhood and you've got great neighbors. You take two lefts, a right, and then you go through two sets of lights and all of a sudden Lambeau appears right in front of you."

The mystique never disappointed. A walk into Lambeau and a survey of the bleachers made seventy-year-old men feel like they were twelve years old.

"Other teams have tried to duplicate it," said former GM Ron Wolf. "But you can't duplicate Lambeau Field because it's a walking history book. You just walk in the stadium and look up and see all the magical names above the bowl."

To attend a big game there, especially in bone-chilling temperatures, was to imagine Lombardi leading the home team out of that tunnel in his fedora and camel-hair coat, in all his gap-toothed glory. After facing the Packers in Milwaukee as the starting quarterback of the New Orleans Saints, Archie Manning finally got a chance to play at Lambeau as a Vikings backup near the end of his career. He said he felt like a little kid at age thirty-four.

A coach who started his career by turning little St. Cecilia High School in Englewood, New Jersey, into a national powerhouse, the Brooklyn-born Lombardi created a coast-to-coast fan base by molding the little Green Bay Packers into an NFL dynasty, quarterbacked by Bart Starr. It's why a man born in the early 1950s who lived in New York Giants country, Joseph Aloi, had a shrine to the Packers in his northern New Jersey home, a room stuffed with Packers memorabilia. He had a sign on the door informing visitors that Lambeau was 1,004 miles away. He had a framed certificate on the wall proving that he bought a share of the franchise for $250.

"It's worthless," he said, "but not to me. I'm an owner of the Green Bay Packers."

When he saw his first game at Lambeau, Aloi told himself, "This is heaven." The reality was better than the dream.

There were countless Joseph Alois all across the country and around the world. Bart Starr was their quarterback. Brett Favre was their quarterback.

And now Aaron Rodgers was their quarterback. Starr and his wife, Cherry, had been writing him letters of support as the new starter, and Rodgers said it meant the world to him. He had watched old tapes of those iconic Packers teams. He looked around and saw the names on the building's façade. That was the standard. Rodgers now had his chance to put his name up there with them.

On the night of September 8, under a fading sun, Rodgers trotted onto the Lambeau field to cheers from a crowd of 71,004. He was not wearing a mouth guard, just like his predecessor. Rodgers thought Favre's decision to go without a mouthpiece projected a vibe of old-school toughness. He also thought a mouthpiece could diminish his command voice in the huddle and at the line.

On his first snap, out of the shotgun, Rodgers hit Donald Lee for three yards. A baby step, but a productive one. This was a night to play like he had at Cal, dissecting a defense with mostly short and intermediate passes.

But on the first play of his third possession, early in the second quarter, Rodgers entered the huddle and told Greg Jennings, "I'm putting it up no matter what." Rodgers then faked a handoff, rolled right, and showed off his powerful arm with a 56-yard, down-the-middle strike to Jennings to the Vikings' 6-yard line. Rodgers jogged down the field pumping his right fist as the crowd went wild.

Just before that deep ball, a bygone prediction came true on national TV. In the summer before Rodgers attended Butte College, he told his high school girlfriend Micala Drews that he was going to play in the NFL. Drews responded by saying that he had a great name for the league.

"Someday people will refer to your home stadium as Mister Rodgers' Neighborhood," she said.

And sure enough, a little more than six years later, ESPN showed two Packers fans—including one wearing a cheesehead and a Favre jersey—holding up signs that said, "Monday Night Football at . . . Mr. Rodgers Neighborhood."

On third-and-goal at the 1-yard line, Rodgers dropped back and shifted to his left to avoid pressure and then, with another Minnesota pass rusher charging straight at him, fired a low, off-balance fastball off his back foot before spinning around. Fullback Korey Hall dove and made a remarkable catch, securing the touchdown. It was a schoolyard throw ripped from the Favre playbook.

The game still hung in the balance in the middle of the fourth quarter. The Packers led 17–12 when Ryan Grant's 57-yard run put the home team on the 2-yard line. After Rodgers failed to score on a quarterback sneak, he succeeded on the second try and then bounced up from the pile and emphatically spiked the ball. Rodgers then ran toward the stands and jumped into the crowd for his first career Lambeau Leap, the signature touchdown celebration started by LeRoy Butler in 1993.

Rodgers soon took a couple of knees to run out the clock on a 24–19 victory, then shook hands with his opponents. He was then escorted by Woullard to an on-field interview with Michele Tafoya, who asked about the Lambeau Leap. "I've been dreaming about that for four years," Rodgers said.

He was a study in supreme efficiency, connecting on 81.8 percent of his passes (18 of 22), the second-best percentage for a first-time starter in league history. Rodgers was good for 178 passing yards, 2 touchdowns (including the one with his feet), and no turnovers or sacks.

This was the night that the Packers were supposed to retire Favre's No. 4, at least until he tried to muscle his way back onto the team. (Favre had beaten Miami the day before in his New York Jets debut.) Given everything that unfolded over the summer, Rodgers carried a heavy burden into Lambeau Field, and impressed his teammates with how he handled it.

"You can't imagine the amount of pressure he has on his shoulders right now," Hall said, "and he went out and he was collected and calm.... I think he won the respect of a lot of people."

Rodgers was the most liberated 1-0 quarterback on the planet. "It feels good," he said. "You've got to remind yourself that it's just one win, but it was a big one."

No. 12 was on the board. But as far as hunting down the hunter, Favre, Rodgers was hardly out of the woods.

• • •

THE LAMBEAU CROWD was murmuring, a sound that betrayed its anxiety. The 0-15 Detroit Lions had just scored to cut their deficit to 24–21 in the middle of the fourth quarter, and the idea of finishing the season on a six-game losing streak punctuated by a defeat at the hands of one of the sorriest teams in the history of North American sports had the stadium on edge.

A year ago, the Packers had gone 13-3 in the regular season and had nearly earned a Super Bowl trip with Old Man Favre at the helm. And now Aaron Rodgers was in danger of launching his era with a 5-11 record and a failure to make Detroit the league's first 0-16 team.

The 2008 Packers had started out 4-3—with Rodgers twice exceeding 300 passing yards, making 157 consecutive throws without an interception, blowing out Peyton Manning's Colts, and playing through a painful shoulder injury. The team had rewarded the promise its quarterback showed in the first seven games with a six-year, $65 million contract that made up for some of that draft-day cash he lost to San Francisco's Alex Smith, who was injured and out for the year after posting an 11-19 record over his first three seasons. Rodgers landed the new contract eleven days after the man who did not draft him No. 1 overall, Mike Nolan, was fired by the 49ers.

"If I can get to the end of this [deal] I'd be very successful," he said. "I plan on proving that their giving me an extension was the correct thing to do."

Rodgers had come a long, long way.

"It was hard on him," said his mother, Darla. She recalled wearing her son's jersey into a convenience store during his first year on the team, and the man behind the counter having the nerve to say, "Why are you wearing that? He's nothing. We shouldn't have taken him."

Darla did not tell the man that she was Rodgers's mother. She did tell him, "I think I know something that you don't know about Aaron's capabilities." Darla and her husband, Ed, and a handful of others, including Craig Rigsbee, joked that there were about a half dozen believers who were "the keepers of the secret."

Rodgers burned to become the best quarterback the Green Bay Packers ever had. Better than Starr. Better than Favre.

To be fair, Rodgers had learned things from Favre that made him a more effective leader and complete player. Though the selection of Utah's Smith helped cost him his job, Nolan said it was a blessing for Rodgers to have watched Favre scramble around and wing it for three years.

"That freelance thing Favre did to extend plays, Aaron picked up on that right away," Nolan said. "He never did that in college. Never, as in zero."

Rodgers also saw how Favre interacted with teammates on the practice field, making the grind as fun as possible, and how he interacted with lower-level staffers in the back rooms of Lambeau—the equipment and security people, the trainers and cafeteria workers—and treated them like neighbors from back home. Those people cried with Favre when they huddled right before the legend was effectively booted out of the place.

But Rodgers wanted to lead his own way, too, not simply pick up where Favre left off. He trusted Adam Woullard to give him sound advice, in part because the PR man turned down an opportunity a couple of years earlier to leave the backup and become Favre's point man. Woullard might have been the first person in the organization to pick Aaron over Brett, and Rodgers never forgot it.

During the final Favre comeback crisis—media relations staffers had their vacations blown up every year by a Favre development—Woullard met with Rodgers at his locker at 6 a.m. every day to review news reports and the proper responses to those reports. As good as the PR man was at his job, the quarterback took Woullard's talking points, put them in his own voice, and sometimes improved them.

Woullard had a general policy of not socializing with players but made an exception for Rodgers. A-Rod was his guy. They went out to dinner about once a month, often at Rodgers's favorite restaurant, Chives, in Suamico, where the quarterback liked to order a White Russian for dessert. Rodgers even attended Woullard's in-season wedding ceremony in Appleton in 2006 when, for once in his life, he might have had a little too much to drink.

Two days later, Woullard was lining up players in the stadium tunnel before kickoff against the St. Louis Rams when Favre looked at him with a twinkle in his eye and said, "Aaron showed up pretty hungover to our quarterbacks meeting yesterday."

"Yeah, sorry about that," Woullard responded.

"No problem," Favre said, before charging onto the field.

In 2008, Woullard talked to Mike McCarthy about allowing Rodgers to do his weekly Wednesday press availability at his locker, and not at the auditorium podium that his predecessor used. Favre became a loner, an outsider, in his final years, a product of the age gap between the quarterback and the rest of the roster. He dressed in his own designated area near the locker room, and he was rarely in that locker room when reporters were present. Rodgers told his father that Favre did not know the names of any of his linemen's wives. "Aaron would know all of them," Ed Rodgers said.

Aaron declined to conduct his interviews on a bigger platform, aiming to send a message to his teammates that he was not above them in any way. "It was my idea," Woullard said. "It wasn't manufactured in a sense of, 'Oh, we're doing this to make him seem humble.' No, unlike Favre, these are Aaron's peers. He's the same age as his teammates."

Rodgers also regularly had teammates over to his Suamico home as a way of bonding off the field. "It was exciting, a new sense of culture here," Woullard said. "There was a sense of fun and camaraderie in that locker room that made me feel giddy."

But Rodgers had to win over the fans, too, and to do that he had to win games. One such fan was Kyle Cousineau, a former bicycle kid at Packers training camp who grew into such a recognizable fixture among the die-hards that he became known as the unofficial mayor of Green Bay. "There's nothing other than the Packers in our fair city," Cousineau said. "They are the driving force behind everything here."

He lived for the college atmosphere that defined the pregame hours at Lambeau; his home was practically next door, right there in the middle of a residential neighborhood. When Rodgers replaced Favre, the bearded fan was torn because, well, like the rest of Green Bay, he felt a certain kinship with No. 4.

"We knew his parents and his brothers and sister by their names and faces," Cousineau said. "We saw them at every game. We saw them at the bar after the game, whereas when Aaron came in, it was different. I like him as a person and a quarterback, but he was a kid from California who was way more private."

Cousineau said that five-game losing streak late in the 2008 season had a lot of fans (himself included) wondering why the franchise was in such a rush to give Rodgers a lucrative contract extension, calling it "a head-scratcher."

One Packers fan who had cut against the grain of the vast majority by backing the decision to trade Favre, Ryan Glasspiegel, recalled the late November loss to the Carolina Panthers as "rock bottom" for the pro-Rodgers people at Lambeau. The first-year starter was brilliant in the second half that day, but the Packers still fell to 5-7 on a late Carolina touchdown and a later Rodgers interception.

"There were more people in Favre Jets jerseys, not just Packers jerseys, than in the jersey of any other current or former Packer," Glasspiegel said. "A third of the crowd was wearing blaze orange because it was hunting season. I've never been in Lambeau when it seemed people didn't want to be there, but I got a surreal sense that day that a lot of people would've rather been deer hunting than at that game.

"At that time Favre was 8-3 with the Jets and a favorite for MVP. It was disdain from the audience at the situation."

Four weeks later, back at Lambeau, the 0-15 Lions had stunned the home crowd. They just needed one late defensive stop for a chance to score and reduce Rodgers's Packers to a national punch line.

In March, as part of a trip arranged by a Christian outreach group, Rodgers had trained with service members at Fort Wainwright in Fairbanks, Alaska. He was struck by how the troops were unfazed by scrutiny, completely unafraid to fail. Rodgers acknowledged that football adversity does not even remotely approach battlefield adversity, but he learned a lesson that he found applicable to his craft.

"A lot of people are going to say stuff about me," he said, "but I should not be afraid to fail."

Rodgers knew people were going to say unkind things about him if he could not beat the Lions. So, right after Detroit's touchdown cut Green Bay's lead to 3 points, Rodgers gathered his fellow offensive starters on the field and called the first play, a deep pass to Donald Driver. "Go get it," he told the receiver.

The quarterback ran a play-action fake to the left before rolling to his right. He fired the ball fifty yards in the air to the wide-open Driver, who had beaten cornerback Leigh Bodden on a double move. Driver ran into the end zone for a 71-yard score and a Lambeau Leap as the crowd exploded around him.

It was a devastating counterpunch delivered sixteen seconds after Detroit pulled close. "It was a great call," Rodgers said of his head coach. "I just told Mike [McCarthy] I appreciate the call. It shows a lot of confidence for him to call a play like that in a running set with two tight ends on the field."

The Packers won the game, 31–21, and Rodgers walked off with a series of critical individual accomplishments. He started all sixteen games. He finished 2008 as the second first-year starter in NFL history to throw for at least 4,000 yards. He also finished fourth in the league in touchdown passes (28) and sixth in passer rating (93.8).

Meanwhile, Favre missed the playoffs with the Jets after injuring his arm and losing four of his final five starts. He threw for 566 fewer yards and 6 fewer touchdowns than Rodgers did while throwing 9 more interceptions.

A STAR IS BORN

The Packers had made the right choice. Jennings said his quarterback's overall performance "says a lot to everybody across the United States and the NFL that he is the real deal."

At the team's Christmas party, Bob Harlan, a Packers administrator since 1979 and the chairman and CEO when he retired in January 2008, approached Rodgers to congratulate him on handling the Favre chaos and Year 1 as a starter with a lot of class.

Rodgers thanked the former executive before saying, "Bob, it . . . was . . . TOUGH."

When Rodgers left the field for the last time in 2008, the same Packers fans who booed him on Family Night chanted his name. He was a 6-10 starter, and he did not expect the crowd to support him like that. For the first time, he felt what Favre had experienced. Rodgers maintained years later that it was one of the most profound moments of his football life.

• • •

AARON RODGERS HAD grown much as a pro by the time he entered the Georgia Dome on Saturday night, January 15, 2011, for a divisional playoff game against the top-seeded Atlanta Falcons. He had led Green Bay back to the playoffs in 2009 by becoming the first quarterback to throw for at least 4,000 yards in each of his first two seasons as a starter, overcoming 50 sacks (and a penchant for holding the ball too long) and a pair of losses to Brett Favre and his new team, the Minnesota Vikings, to earn a Pro Bowl berth and a playoff matchup with the Arizona Cardinals.

As much as the Favre defeats stung, Rodgers understood that it would have been tough to beat a strong Vikings team on the road under any circumstances. He knew that Favre was never going to lose his Lambeau comeback game any more than he was going to lose that 2003 *Monday Night Football* game against Oakland in the immediate wake of his father's death. In addition, Rodgers threw for a combined 671 yards and 5 touchdowns in those defeats while showing Favre-like toughness in absorbing 14 sacks.

None of that meant Rodgers was completely over the ice-cold shoulder his predecessor often gave him. While appearing in person on *The Michael Irvin Show* with Irvin and Kevin Kiley at the Super Bowl following the '08 season, Rodgers paused and got emotional when the Hall of Fame receiver asked him if he had talked to Favre since he had left Green Bay for the Jets.

Rodgers said that he had reached out to Favre but had never heard back.

He said that they joked around a lot during their third and final season together and that they parted on good terms. "And to not have talked to him in over a year is disappointing," Rodgers said. He would get over Favre soon enough, and so would all of Green Bay.

Mike McCarthy had made sweeping changes on his staff after his 2008 team went 6-10, mostly on the defensive side of the ball. His decision to keep offensive coordinator Joe Philbin and quarterbacks coach Tom Clements as Rodgers's chief consultants in 2009 and beyond was a smart one.

The Packers suffered a dispiriting defeat at the hands of the 0-7 Tampa Bay Buccaneers to fall to 4-4 but won seven of their last eight regular-season games, including a sweet 30–24 victory over San Francisco and Alex Smith. "It's fun to play against a team that you idolized growing up, and watched every Sunday after church," Rodgers said after passing for 344 yards and 2 scores in his first meeting with the team and player that wrecked his draft day. Green Bay's only loss in that stretch came at the hands of the defending champion Steelers, 37–36, on a 19-yard touchdown pass from Ben Roethlisberger to Mike Wallace (and ensuing extra-point kick) with no time on the clock.

In the wild-card game with the Cardinals, Rodgers would lose an overtime shootout with Kurt Warner on a strip sack, a noncall on a potential face mask penalty, and a recovered fumble by Karlos Dansby, whose walk-off 17-yard touchdown run inspired the losing quarterback to fire his helmet to the ground. Arizona had missed a short field-goal attempt for the victory at the end of regulation, and Rodgers had given that break right back by missing an open Greg Jennings deep for what would have been a walk-off touchdown on the first play of overtime.

Of greater big-picture consequence, Rodgers opened his playoff career by throwing for 423 yards—a Packers postseason record—and 4 touchdowns while running for another score. He was ready to ascend to a new level of stardom.

Rodgers helped send Favre careening toward permanent retirement in 2010 by beating him twice, including a 31–3 smackdown in Minneapolis. After recovering from a concussion that benched him for the Week 15 game against New England's Tom Brady, Rodgers led the Packers back to the playoffs with victories over the Giants and the Bears that earned the NFC's last tournament seed.

In the wild-card round, Rodgers secured his first career playoff victory at

Michael Vick's expense in Philadelphia to set up the divisional-round game in Atlanta. Rodgers had twice outplayed Falcons quarterback Matt Ryan in his three seasons as a starter only to have an 0-2 record to show for it.

The Packers were so confident they would prevail because they had No. 12 on their side. Following Favre, said fullback John Kuhn, "was a pressure only a few people in sports history could have overcome." Rodgers gave his team belief in 2009 that it could do special things, making the overtime defeat in the desert all the more devastating. "We went into those playoffs thinking we would win it all," Kuhn said. "It was, 'Wow, this guy is going to take us to the Super Bowl and win it.' That was all him. That was all Aaron Rodgers."

The following winter, Rodgers put on an exhibition of quarterbacking in the Georgia Dome that was hard to believe. He completed 31 of 36 passes, threw touchdown passes to three different receivers, and ran one in himself. His athleticism was on full display whenever Atlanta pass rushers had point-blank shots at him, frustrating Falcons on the field and on the sideline.

With Green Bay leading 28–14, Atlanta's John Abraham sacked Rodgers on the first play of the second half and mimicked what had become the quarterback's signature championship-belt celebration—Rodgers would bring his two open hands together, palms facing his waist, and then quickly wrap those hands to his hips to punctuate a touchdown. The Falcons were poised to seize the momentum.

Two plays later, on third-and-13, linebacker Stephen Nicholas blitzed from Rodgers's left side and raced in untouched for what appeared to be a certain sack. The quarterback took a half hop forward at his own 11-yard line to slightly alter Nicholas's path, and then executed an abrupt spin that sent the linebacker on a lunging flyby.

Rodgers then scrambled to his left, chased by two defenders, before unleashing a dart to James Jones on the sideline for 15 yards and a first down. On the opposing sideline, an inactive Falcons player in street clothes recoiled from the scene and angrily snapped a towel to the turf. A play that should have led to a punt and good field position for the home team instead allowed for Green Bay's 80-yard drive, Rodgers's 7-yard touchdown run, and a championship-belt celebration.

"It was one of those nights," Rodgers said after the 48–21 victory.

It was one of those nights that made San Francisco look foolish for using the No. 1 overall pick on Alex Smith, who was 19-31 as a starter with no playoff appearances.

It was one of those nights for Packers fans who rallied for Brett Favre's return and sent hostile notes to team executives in 2008 to go find themselves another cause.

The Packers advanced to the NFC Championship Game without punting the ball once. Of all those sacks he avoided, Rodgers said, "I had eyes in the back of my head."

Players on both sides of the field talked about this performance for years to come. "It's the best game I've ever seen a quarterback play in the playoffs, ever," said John Kuhn, who scored 2 touchdowns. "He did a lot of that with his legs. . . . There were moments of near flawlessness.

"Early on in his career, Aaron had some gambler to him. He would hold on to the ball sometimes to the dismay of his linemen and a lot of times to the satisfaction of the crowd. He let a play develop until the very last minute, because he could get in and out of messes as good as any running quarterback that's ever played."

Kuhn was not arguing that A-Rod was Michael Vick. He was saying that Rodgers knew when to lean on his mobility to buy extra time to throw the ball, and to run it when necessary. What Rodgers could do with his arm and legs was mesmerizing even to those out on the field with him.

"I'll be honest with you, we do watch him when we're playing," Kuhn said. "There are opponents of Aaron Rodgers who get off the bench to watch him. They can't believe the stuff they see from him on TV, but it's so much more entertaining to see it in live form.

"You know you're watching something in the moment that is absolutely exceptional. You know you're watching Tiger Woods at the Masters as the ball trickles into the cup."

Rodgers still had to survive a couple of Sunday rounds to win his green jacket. But 150 miles from Augusta National, the Atlanta masterpiece advanced the idea that Rodgers was well on his way to becoming the best player in the NFL.

He needed a ring to notarize it.

• • •

THE NIGHT BEFORE Super Bowl XLV at Cowboys Stadium in Arlington, Texas, Aaron Rodgers was enjoying a quiet dinner with family and friends in a private room in Pappas Bros. Steakhouse.

Joe Thatcher, major league pitcher, was among the twenty or so people in the room. He was not there to celebrate his 1.29 ERA in sixty-five relief appearances with the 2010 San Diego Padres. He was representative of Rodgers's impressive ability to collect friends through disparate connections. Thatcher stayed at Rodgers's offseason home in Del Mar, north of San Diego, whenever he needed a place to crash, free of charge.

Rodgers was generous that way. He had one of the Packers' young trainers, Nate Weir, living with him in Suamico free of charge too.

On this night, Thatcher was celebrating his friend's appearance on the biggest stage in American sports. Rodgers had earned this trip the hard way, on the road against a rival the Packers had started playing in 1921, when the Chicago Bears—then known as the Chicago Staleys—pounded them, 20–0.

Rodgers was not brilliant in the 182nd clash between the two franchises (only their second in the postseason), doing just enough in Green Bay's 21–14 victory for the NFC title. But he did score the first touchdown and did stop the Bears' Brian Urlacher from turning an interception at his own 6-yard line into a 94-yard touchdown return by tracking him down and tripping him up near midfield. The quarterback also showed some Ray Nitschke–Dick Butkus level toughness in Soldier Field by overcoming a vicious fourth-quarter hit to the side of his face, courtesy of Julius Peppers's helmet, which left him spitting blood.

Rodgers had suffered his second concussion of the season only six weeks earlier, forcing him to wear a helmet with additional padding, and yet he was hell-bent on finishing this game. When it was over, Pam Oliver of Fox said to him on the field, simply, "You're heading to the Super Bowl."

"It's a dream come true," Rodgers replied.

As a sixth seed that played the entire year without its star running back, Ryan Grant, and that lost ascending tight end Jermichael Finley after five weeks, Green Bay had managed to win three road playoff games to reach the Super Bowl. It was a testament to Mike McCarthy's coaching, and to Ted Thompson's roster building, and to the organization's decision to believe in Rodgers almost as much as he believed in himself.

And that's what Joe Thatcher saw that night in the restaurant—his friend's unyielding faith in his own abilities. Even though Thatcher was a professional athlete, he was struck by how calm Rodgers was as the storm approached.

"He had the biggest game of his life the next day," Thatcher said, "and it was just another night together with family and friends. I remember how impressed I was walking away from there. He was going to go back to the hotel, finish scouting, and go to bed. You would have never known he was starting the Super Bowl the next day."

Rodgers had been like this all week, at peace with the magnitude of it all, and unfazed by the ice and snow that brought Lambeau's frozen tundra to the Dallas–Fort Worth area, making the Super Bowl logistics even more challenging than usual. Rodgers had this trip all mapped out as far back as early September, when he came up with the idea of dressing in a cowboy hat and a bolo tie for the Welcome Back Packers luncheon to send a Super Bowl–here-we-come message to all comers. He persuaded some Packers to follow his sartorial lead. Mike McCarthy signed his name to it too at the start of training camp.

"I have every intention and belief that we have the capability of winning the Super Bowl," he said. In his first team meeting of camp, the head coach talked to his players about winning the whole thing.

"We talked about where [the Super Bowl's] played at and the relevance of our team meeting room," McCarthy said. "The only team pictures in that room are the team pictures of the world champions of the Green Bay Packers. And everything we've done throughout the offseason and everything we'll do starting [today] will be taking a step to being the next team up on that wall."

Down in Texas five months later, based at the 421-room Omni Mandalay at Las Colinas in Irving, McCarthy had the nerve to get his players measured for Super Bowl rings. It was a major gamble. If word got back to the Steelers and their players cited the move as a source of inspiration in a winning effort, McCarthy never would have lived it down.

But he was not coaching scared, not even against a Pittsburgh defense that had allowed the fewest points in the league. "I felt that the measurement of the rings, the timing of it, would be special," he said. "It would have a significant effect on our players doing it the night before the game."

McCarthy's team could not have been more confident and relaxed. Before their final team meeting, the Packers gathered and sang songs as C.J. Wilson, rookie defensive end, played the hotel's baby grand piano. "It was the most united I'd ever seen us as a team," Greg Jennings said.

Now there was only one giant step left to take against the team that Mc-

Carthy rooted for as a boy. He had Rodgers on his side, the best reason to believe that those ring measurements would come in handy.

Rodgers seemed poised to take over the league. Back at Pleasant Valley High School in Chico, the message on the school's marquee read like this: "Excellence Is Not an Act. But a Habit. There's a PV Viking in the Super Bowl!"

The somewhat goofy kid who did not have a single major-college scholarship offer out of PV, and who was effectively forced to play ball at the local community college, was about to enjoy the sweetest revenge of the nerd. Growing up, Aaron spent Super Bowl Sunday with family members, including his maternal grandparents, Chuck and Barbara Pittman.

In the first days of February 2011, the family had taken the show on the road. Aaron's parents and brothers were on-site, and his grandfather Chuck was driving 1,800 miles with his wife because Barbara did not fly. Good thing Chuck loved to drive. As a twenty-one-year-old kid in 1949, Chuck and a couple of good friends bought brand-new Mercury Club Coupe cars in Santa Rosa and raced their way back home to Ukiah. As an older man, Chuck used to tease the kids that he could drive to El Paso and back in the same weekend to see Barbara's relatives.

Unlike counterpart Big Ben Roethlisberger, who, on Tuesday night, was seen drinking with his linemen in a bar and singing Billy Joel's "Piano Man" into the small hours of Wednesday, Rodgers wanted to stick to the routine that had served him well for his entire football life.

"For a guy who was just embarking on superstardom, he wanted to be incredibly low-key," said John Kuhn. "Every night we got together and played cards. . . . He wanted to keep things that simple that week. Media obligations were through the roof for him, and he could've done a million engagements, but he kept it low. His purpose that week was to win the Super Bowl."

Rodgers landed in Texas knowing he was playing better football than anyone in the league. He carried himself as an uncrowned league MVP, and his cocksure gait had become a familiar tell to teammates and friends.

A. J. Hawk, starting linebacker, had seen it on a regular basis. "Aaron's got a distinct walk," he said. "You can pick it out from a mile away, especially when he's going good. He had that walk the whole postseason. . . . He's got some little rhythm to it. He's always walking like slightly downhill. I don't know what it is or how he moves his feet and arms, but you can see it on the golf course all the time if he's playing well."

After he missed the New England game in December, and before he made his next start against the Giants, Rodgers told Wayne Larrivee, the radio voice of the Packers, that the week off left him feeling refreshed. He then threw for 404 yards and 4 touchdowns against the Giants and was off to the races from there.

Now Rodgers was universally respected and admired by the entire Packers fan base. Brett Favre had finished his career in Minnesota with a 5-8 record. He walked away at age forty-one injured and hurt by allegations that he sent obscene photos and messages to a female Jets employee in 2008; the NFL fined him $50,000 for failing to cooperate with its investigation "in a forthcoming manner," but could not determine if he had violated the league's policies involving workplace conduct.

Rodgers would never again compete against Favre, the player. But he still had to compete against Favre, the legacy. He had never won a championship in high school, in junior college, or in Division I. To match No. 4, No. 12 had to win the big one in the pros.

• • •

THE PACKERS FELT their world championship being pulled from their grasp, slowly but very surely. They had scored the first two touchdowns of the Super Bowl, the first on a perfect 29-yard pass from Aaron Rodgers over the top of Pittsburgh's William Gay into the hands of Jordy Nelson, the second on Nick Collins's pick-six of Ben Roethlisberger. On the pass to Nelson, Rodgers tapped the right side of his helmet to signal a go-route to the receiver, opting out of the screen pass to a back that he almost always threw on that play.

Green Bay took a 21–3 lead in the second quarter on a Rodgers heater over the middle that barely got past a diving Ryan Clark and found Pro Bowl receiver Greg Jennings, who held on despite getting blasted by Troy Polamalu from behind. Rodgers later called over to Pittsburgh's Clark, referring to him by number by saying, "Hey, two-five," and then showing the safety his thumb and index finger placed a fraction of an inch apart.

Who said number one-two wasn't cocky?

Though the Packers took a 28–17 lead in the fourth quarter on another Rodgers-to-Jennings touchdown, the Steelers had changed the feel of the game in the second half. On the ensuing possession, Roethlisberger completed 7 of 8 throws and found Mike Wallace for a 25-yard touchdown before Antwaan Randle El scored the two-point conversion.

It was 28–25 with 6:19 to go, and the Packers were threatening to come undone before 103,219 on-site witnesses and 111 million viewers, the biggest audience in the history of American television. More people were watching Aaron Rodgers and Big Ben than had watched the last episode of *M*A*S*H* in 1983.

Green Bay had lost its all-world cornerback, Charles Woodson, to a broken collarbone and the team's all-time leading receiver, Donald Driver, to an ankle injury earlier in the game. Rodgers had also been victimized by a series of dropped passes, including three by Nelson (though he finished with 140 receiving yards) and one by James Jones early in the third quarter, on third down, that likely would have resulted in a 75-yard touchdown. Rodgers grabbed his helmet with both hands after the Jones drop and yanked them downward in disgust.

Later in that quarter, when the quarterback threw a short pass behind rookie tight end Andrew Quarless, a Fox camera caught Driver on the sideline saying, "Come on, A-Rod."

By the time he faced a third-and-10 with those six minutes and nineteen seconds left, Rodgers had been hit sixteen times by the Steelers, including 10 knockdowns and 3 sacks. McCarthy had prepared for this onslaught. He had told Joe Philbin during the week that if the Steelers stayed in their base defense he might ask Rodgers to throw the ball forty times. (He threw thirty-nine passes.)

"I'm gonna put the ball in his hands," McCarthy said. "The downside is he's going to take some hits. . . . He took a lot of hits in that game and he just kept firing."

Rodgers had just been sacked on first down, and it was a wonder that he held on to the ball after getting hit from the rear. To further complicate matters, left guard Daryn Colledge committed a false-start penalty to put the Packers in that third-and-10 hole.

"You could just feel the game starting to slip from us there," said Kuhn.

The Steelers were working with well-developed Super Bowl muscle memory; this was their third trip to the big game in six years. Roethlisberger had already won two rings, and he had teammates up and down the roster with Super Bowl experience. Across the ball, the Packers were all new to this.

"Well, the longer that this game goes," said Fox analyst Troy Aikman, three-time champion quarterback of the Cowboys, "with it being as close as it is, I think the more nervous you've got to get then if you're the Green Bay Packers."

The legions of Steelers fans in this cavernous building were getting louder and louder, drowning out the famed Green Bay chant of "Go Pack Go." This was a clash of NFL titans—Pittsburgh had won six Super Bowls, and Green Bay had won 12 NFL championships, including three Super Bowls—and of two of the biggest, most fervent fan bases in the sport. The Packers had been holding their training camp at tiny St. Norbert College in De Pere, Wisconsin, since 1958, and the Steelers had been holding theirs at tiny Saint Vincent College in Latrobe, Pennsylvania, since 1966. These franchises shared an ethos and a deep connection to their communities.

Now it was all on the line for Rodgers, in shotgun formation, wearing his dark green Packers jersey and classic gold helmet. He had three receivers to his left, one to his right. Jennings was lined up tight left, on the line of scrimmage, with two teammates outside of him off the ball.

At the start of this drive, Rodgers told the men in his huddle, "Hey, let's take it down and score, and we're the champs." Punting to the Steelers at that point was tantamount to kicking away the Lombardi Trophy.

Rodgers took the snap with 5:59 left, dropped back as he looked toward the left seam, and let loose one of his patented fastballs that grazed the outstretched fingers belonging to Pittsburgh's Ike Taylor and found Jennings's hands just as the receiver hit the NFL logo at midfield. A diving Polamalu made the stop, but not before Jennings gained 31 yards. The play—"Strong Left, Trips 27 Tampa"—would become a forever part of Packers lore.

Green Bay fans exhaled, then stood and cheered. "When Aaron made that throw," Kuhn said, "it was like he pumped breath back into our lungs at a time when we were just gasping for air."

Off the biggest pass of his career, Rodgers hit Jones three plays later for 21 yards to the Steelers' 8-yard line. On third-and-goal with 2:14 to go, he lofted a ball toward the right corner for Nelson, who was tightly covered by Anthony Madison. It was precisely the pass Rodgers had to make. He could not leave the ball short and risk an interception, and a potential damaging return. He had to go a bit long and force Nelson to go get it with every last inch of his wingspan, leaving an incomplete as the worst-case scenario.

The ball bounced off the diving receiver's fingertips. The Packers settled for the field goal and a 31–25 lead, forcing Pittsburgh to score a touchdown to dodge defeat.

"I was just praying our guys would come up with one more stop," Rodgers said.

Two years earlier, Roethlisberger led the Steelers on a 78-yard drive in the closing minutes to beat Arizona in Super Bowl XLIII. One Packers fan who knew better than most what Big Ben could do was A. J. Hawk's brother, Ryan, who had been Roethlisberger's college backup and roommate at Miami of Ohio. Ryan was sweating it in the Cowboys Stadium stands. He had seen Roethlisberger make magical things happen so many times.

Only Pittsburgh was no longer riding a wave of momentum. Keyaron Fox's personal foul on the kickoff return compromised the Steelers' mission, as it put the ball on their 13-yard line with only 1:59 on the clock and only one time-out to call.

Big Ben opened the drive with a promising pass to Heath Miller for 15 yards. But the Steelers gained a mere 5 yards on the next three plays, putting Roethlisberger in a fourth-and-5 situation at his own 33 with 0:56 left. On the Green Bay sideline, Rodgers faced the stands and waved a towel in a bid for more noise from Packers fans.

Roethlisberger called for the snap with one second on the play clock, backpedaled as he immediately looked to his left, and fired 11 yards downfield to Wallace, who had to go up high for the attempted catch. Cornerback Tramon Williams closed hard on the ball and did a tremendous job avoiding early contact with Wallace. The receiver had his hands on the ball for an instant but could not keep it under control. The ball fell to the turf, and the Green Bay celebration was on.

Rodgers threw his towel in the air and started hopping about, hugging teammates and pumping his fists before looking skyward as he took the field. Two kneel-downs later, Fox's Joe Buck made it official with this bulletin:

"The Green Bay Packers have won the Super Bowl. The Lombardi Trophy is coming home."

Rodgers was mobbed by his teammates and surrounded by photographers. He handed his helmet to a staffer and slapped on his Super Bowl championship cap. Despite all the drops, he finished with 304 yards passing, 3 touchdowns, and no turnovers. He earned all that confetti and those streamers raining down around him.

Of course, Rodgers was named Super Bowl MVP. He held the Lombardi Trophy over his head to great cheers after winning four consecutive sudden-death games, none of them played at Lambeau. He won a red Chevy Camaro convertible for being the best player in the game.

Rodgers's family was on the field during the postgame celebration, all of them wearing Packers gear and credentials that granted them access. The quarterback's father, Ed, remembered looking up during the game to see former president George W. Bush sitting in Jerry Jones's box, and thinking how surreal the whole event was, including the sight and sound of Terry Bradshaw introducing his son as MVP.

The quarterback's mother, Darla, was wearing her son's No. 12. She recalled watching players making snow angels out of the fallen confetti, and thinking about her three sons' boyhood love for pro wrestling and Hulk Hogan when Packers linebacker Clay Matthews placed a championship belt down on the quarterback's shoulder.

"It was amazing, wonderful," Darla said. "We've never missed a game. We've watched Aaron elevate. If he had the ball in his hands, be it as the point guard or the guy on the mound, it always worked great for the team. He could inspire confidence and get people to do things at a certain level.... I thought in the back of my memory arsenal, Aaron may take this whole game on his shoulders.

"And then he's up there [on the podium] and he's done it. They're world champions and this is the epitome of his goal, and it was crazy to be there."

Rodgers had won it all near the old Dallas home of his paternal grandparents, Kathryn and Edward Wesley Rodgers, before Edward went off to become an American hero overseas. How proud would the decorated combat pilot have been to have seen all this?

As proud as Aaron's maternal grandparents were, as they stood amid the confetti and took it all in. Chuck and Barbara Pittman posed for pictures with Ed and Darla and Aaron, dressed in his championship T-shirt and cap, and with their fellow grandsons Luke and Jordan, all three generations basking in the glow.

On the morning of game day, in high school, college, and the pros, Aaron had been in the habit of calling Chuck and Barbara in their Ukiah home. As a Packer he called during his drive to the stadium, just as the Pittmans were brewing their early morning coffee on the West Coast.

"He always gave us his thoughts on the game plan," Barbara Pittman

A STAR IS BORN

wrote to me years later. "I know the three of us looked forward to this time together—it started our day out just right, and Aaron said it did his, also."

But no football Sunday in the Rodgers and Pittman families had ever been like this football Sunday.

"It was a venture once in a lifetime from beginning to end," the quarterback's grandmother recalled. "It was priceless to see Aaron's dream come true. I can still see the joy and happiness on his face."

He had delivered one of the greatest postseasons ever—1,094 yards passing, a 68.2 completion percentage, 9 passing touchdowns, only 2 interceptions, and 2 rushing touchdowns. Rodgers won the Super Bowl MVP award that Brett Favre did not win fourteen years earlier. He was the chief reason that Green Bay became the NFC's first six seed to win a title.

After he was done with the ceremony and his media obligations, Rodgers sat at his corner locker, wiped out. While teammates were hooting and hollering and drinking champagne, Rodgers remained at his locker and did about a ten-minute photo shoot while cradling the Lombardi Trophy in his lap. Mike Clemens, longtime Packers radio reporter, figured that the quarterback must have prearranged this session, that he wanted these pictures to forever savor this moment.

"It was like he was making sure he had it for his scrapbook for himself," Clemens said.

Rodgers and the Packers showered while singing Queen's "We Are the Champions." Back in Chico, Craig Rigsbee was already thinking of sending an article about the Packers' victory to the mother of the Butte backup who had blasted him for starting Rodgers over her son.

On-site, Rodgers had some Pleasant Valley teammates in the Cowboys Stadium crowd, including Casey Helmick, Nick Rosemann, and Tim Bushard. Unbeknownst to Rodgers, his boyhood friend from his Oregon days, Joey Kaempf, was there with his father, Dr. Joe Kaempf, the youth coach who taught Aaron to visualize success on the athletic fields before competing.

Back at the Omni Mandalay, Kid Rock performed at the Packers' championship party, telling the crowd that he did not down even one beer during the Super Bowl. He asked the fans, "Are you ready to do some drinking, have a little party, get this thing cranked up a little bit, yeah?" The fans cheered, Kid Rock started singing his biggest hit, "All Summer Long," and a memorable time was had by all.

The Packers had earned their postgame party the hard way. A. J. Hawk's brother, Ryan, was among the few hundred people in the room, and he said that the postgame party was "absolutely wild" and "not slowing down" at 4 a.m.

"I'm a fullback," said John Kuhn, "so I'm going to take it deep into the night, and I did, and the linemen did too. Aaron was quick. He went up, waved to everybody, got introduced, and then he was gone. He wanted to be low-key and go back to his room to celebrate with family and friends. He was gone. He celebrated in his own way."

On the bus ride from his Super Bowl victory to the hotel, Rodgers had reflected on his entire career, from PV to Butte to Cal to Green Bay. He was booked for a morning trip to Disney World, and for an appearance on the *Late Show with David Letterman* that night. A couple of hours after his biggest victory, the quarterback thought to himself, *I'm on top of the world. We just accomplished the most amazing goal in football.*

And yet he felt almost empty inside because he wondered if there were any more mountains for him to climb in life, or if this was it.

Until he found that second calling, Rodgers wanted to preside over the league's next dynasty. He wanted to do with the Packers what Tom Brady had already done with the Patriots from 2001 to 2004—win three out of four. Or something to that effect.

"I remember Aaron talking about how life was now going to change," McCarthy recalled. "I felt after that game, he had walked through the door of greatness and his life was going to be different."

Going forward, it seemed Rodgers wanted to win a different way than he had in his third year as a starter. From the outside looking in, his fired agent, Mike Sullivan, thought the chip on Rodgers's shoulder from his draft-day plunge had taken on a new form.

"I believe it got converted when he won the Super Bowl," Sullivan said. "There was a gradual change in 'I'm in charge now.' There was a sense that he was going to do things his way now, because he felt let down by everybody who evaluated him.

"Now he felt, 'I don't have to answer to anybody anymore.'"

9

PAIN

OFF HIS MVP trip to Disney World, Aaron Rodgers was a Cinderella story no more. The kid from Chico, overlooked and undervalued, was now living the life of the rich and famous.

Even before he had delivered his championship season, Rodgers had built his parents a spacious home in Chico, and he had bought himself a five-bedroom, six-bathroom sanctuary in the San Diego area for a couple million bucks. He invited his big brother and his buddies to move in with him.

As a guitar player fixing to chase greatness in an industry outside of pro football, Rodgers started his own record label, Suspended Sunrise Recordings, with his friend Ryan Zachary, when he signed a Chico-based indie pop rock band, the Make. He hired Murphy Karges of the multiplatinum band Sugar Ray to produce, direct, and find talent.

Athletes wanted to be musicians, and musicians wanted to be athletes, and Rodgers wanted to be both. Nobody believed he could ever win the Lombardi Trophy. Why couldn't he shock the world again by fielding a band that won a Grammy?

The football star and would-be music mogul had no trouble persuading a series of successful and beautiful women to spend time by his side, including the lead singer of Lady Antebellum, Hillary Scott, and a Packers fan from Wisconsin, actress Jessica Szohr. At some point in 2011, the Super Bowl MVP got serious with Destiny Newton, an attractive Chico woman whom he had known—and had a crush on—for years.

Committed to bachelorhood for the time being, the quarterback turned his Mediterranean-style offseason home in Del Mar into a 5,770-square-foot man cave. His brother Luke, who had lived with Rodgers at the start in Green Bay, moved into the house with his roommate Ryan West, a senior electronic technician supervisor with the Coast Guard. At various times Aaron's close friends—Zachary, Andrew Jeter, and Keola Pang—lived at the Del Mar home on Rancho Nuevo, as did West's brother Jacob and West's cousin Michael Mygrant, who grew up in Indiana with his best friend Joe Thatcher, the Padres reliever and yet another Rodgers guest.

"It was kind of a frat house," Thatcher said.

Only the men in the house were all professionals. Though they knew how to have a good time, their home environment was not defined by debauchery, but rather by competition.

It was A-Rod against the world in Ping-Pong, basketball, pool baseball, golf, home run derby, volleyball, you name it. The half-court basketball court was by the garage out front, and the Ping-Pong table was on the outside patio. The backyard had a putting green that could be converted into a volleyball court. Rodgers had a batting cage—sometimes guys who had downed a cold one or three might walk in there and try (and fail) to hit Thatcher's nasty stuff. Inside the front door and to the left, the pool table could be found in the family room.

Games were being played at all hours in all corners of the property. "It was just like we were ten-year-old kids again, diving around," Thatcher recalled. "At one point I'm thinking, 'This is Aaron Rodgers playing pool baseball with us.'"

And if one of Rodgers's houseguests happened to beat him in the pool or in the cage or on the court—a rare event—he might mock the quarterback with his championship-belt celebration.

"We all did it," Thatcher said. "I don't know how it started. Maybe it was a Ping-Pong or a pool table gesture in the heat of the moment. When Aaron did it on the [NFL] stage, it took on a life of its own."

Rodgers got a major State Farm ad campaign out of it, and suddenly people everywhere were doing his "Discount Double Check" move. But as far as TV acts go, Rodgers and his crew best aligned with the cast of *Entourage*, and they knew it. They talked about it. They joked about it. If there was some discussion over which friend was Turtle (Zachary was the popular pick), nobody wasted a second debating the identity of this cast's Vincent Chase.

"We weren't crazy like *Entourage*," Thatcher said, "but it was a lot of fun."

Rodgers attended a good number of Padres games to watch the reliever and, on a couple of occasions, to visit with him in the clubhouse. Thatcher's baseball friends started hanging with Rodgers's Del Mar boys, and the crew kept growing. The quarterback saw that Thatcher was living out of his suitcase when being sent back and forth from San Diego to the Triple-A affiliate in Portland and offered a steady roof over his head. Free of charge.

In fact, according to another friend who stayed in Rodgers's home, the host did not charge rent to anyone who lived there. "If you were in his circle, he took care of you," that friend said. "The guys just paid utilities."

Thatcher put a bed in the library in Rodgers's home and lived there until he proved himself as a big leaguer. He would pitch in more than four hundred games over nine years to a career ERA of 3.38.

"I do believe having Aaron open his house to me really helped me to focus on baseball and establish myself," Thatcher said. "That was a big turning point for me. . . . I don't think people necessarily know that it takes a special person to open up a house to a group of friends."

The pitcher normally rented a beach house with a handful of teammates after the endless major league season to wind down before heading home. Thatcher recalled that Rodgers once showed up at their beach place to talk baseball, a sport he loved, after having just played a physical game against the Vikings. Jared Allen had gotten to Rodgers more than once, and Thatcher was struck by just how banged up the quarterback was a day or two later.

To prepare his body for the 2011 season, and to enhance his chances of winning back-to-back Super Bowl titles, Rodgers began working with a young Chico trainer, Angelo Poli, who specialized in neuromuscular reeducation, or posture and alignment mechanics. People did not go to Poli for brute strength as much as they did for fine-tuning and finesse. The trainer had worked with Aaron's parents and with his younger brother, Jordan, a quarterback at Vanderbilt who had followed Aaron's path from Pleasant Valley to Butte.

Poli ran Whole Body Fitness on Highway 32, right next door to Rodgers Chiropractic, Ed's office. He worked with Aaron during the NFL lockout that ran from the spring into summer.

"The main thing I want is to be able to take a hit on the field and get up after and keep playing," Rodgers told Poli.

The quarterback had a secondary goal that matched up with the timing of the lockout. "I want to be able to see my abs," he told the trainer.

Poli worked on Rodgers's diet—the quarterback had a notorious sweet tooth. Fiber. High-quality proteins. Slow-burning complex carbohydrates. Spreading out meals frequently throughout the day. Rodgers eventually settled on a daily diet plan that he described as 80 percent healthy, 20 percent fun.

"I wanted to take him to a point where he could really be proud of his physique . . . and we got a really rewarding outcome for that," Poli said.

But the NFL was not a beach-bod competition. It was the ultimate battle of attrition and, as the likes of Brett Favre and Peyton Manning and Tom Brady proved, durability and availability were everything at the game's signature position. There was no bigger drop-off in sports than the drop-off from the first-string NFL quarterback to the backup.

When Rodgers first arrived at Poli's doorstep, his feet, shoulders, and arms were out of alignment. The trainer focused on his posterior chain to make his body more erect. Rodgers had internally rotated shoulders that needed readjustment. He also wanted to work on his core stability and flexibility.

"He wanted to be injury-proof," Poli said. This was an exciting assignment that did not come without its burdens.

"When the MVP and the national American football sweetheart comes to you," Poli said, "you can't injure him in training. . . . There's no coming back from that."

Poli had trained everyone from Olympic-level strength athletes to NFL position players to action pistol shooters to mountain climbers and hunters, and nobody could match Rodgers's proprioception, or body awareness. His innate ability to multitask, calculate his movements, and process information quickly was as impressive as his arm strength.

"Aaron's unique edge," Poli said, "was his mind."

Poli put targets on the gym walls and had Rodgers throw balls at them while performing drills. The trainer pointed a laser beam at random targets while his client was doing a footwork exercise and expected him to hit the spot with a throw. He had Rodgers bounce a tennis ball off the wall, over and over, at warp speed. He also had him put on boxing gloves and fire punches at his focus mitts.

To keep Rodgers on his toes, literally, during workouts, Poli taped po-

Edward W. Rodgers, Aaron's grandfather, was a decorated World War II pilot who flew dozens of successful missions against Hitler's war machine before he became a POW.
COURTESY OF ED AND DARLA RODGERS

Aaron Rodgers, born in 1983, was obsessed with football practically right out of the crib.
COURTESY OF ED AND DARLA RODGERS

In happier, more unified times, the Rodgers family struck quite a pose.
COURTESY OF ED AND DARLA RODGERS

Young Aaron was a soccer and baseball star before his parents let him play football.
COURTESY OF ED AND DARLA RODGERS

Aaron's dream was to play for the local NFL team and to become the next Joe Montana and Steve Young.
COURTESY OF ED AND DARLA RODGERS

The first known time that Aaron Rodgers was pictured with the colors of the Green Bay Packers.
COURTESY OF ED AND DARLA RODGERS

As an eighth-grader in 1997, Aaron finally got the green light to play tackle football—with the Chico Jaguars.
COURTESY OF ED AND DARLA RODGERS

Despite being a standout quarterback at Pleasant Valley High School, Rodgers did not receive a single Division I scholarship offer.
COURTESY OF ED AND DARLA RODGERS

A junior college transfer, Rodgers lifted Cal to new heights in 2004.
© SAN FRANCISCO CHRONICLE/HEARST NEWSPAPERS VIA GETTY IMAGES

Rodgers was relieved when the Packers finally ended his draft-day plunge in 2005.
© AP IMAGES/JULIE JACOBSON

Brett Favre was not terribly interested in educating his talented backup.
© AP IMAGES/ MORRY GASH

Despite their success, Rodgers and Mike McCarthy were not always on the same page.
© JIM BRYANT/ALAMY STOCK PHOTO

Aaron Rodgers, named Super Bowl MVP in February 2011, became the best player in the NFL.
© AP IMAGES/GREG TROTT

Rodgers celebrated his biggest victory with his parents, brothers, and maternal grandparents about four years before the family estrangement.
© AP IMAGES/DAVID STLUKA

Actress Olivia Munn was dating Rodgers in 2014 and 2015 when he stopped communicating with his family.
© ABACA PRESS/ALAMY STOCK PHOTO

Racing star Danica Patrick was among the quarterback's high-profile romances.
© ZUMA PRESS/ALAMY STOCK PHOTO

Rodgers had more talent than Tom Brady, but Brady ended up as the lord of the rings.
© MATTHEW HEALEY/ALAMY STOCK PHOTO

Matt LaFleur got two MVP seasons out of Rodgers before giving the ball to his replacement, Jordan Love, in 2023.
© CAL SPORT MEDIA/ALAMY STOCK PHOTO

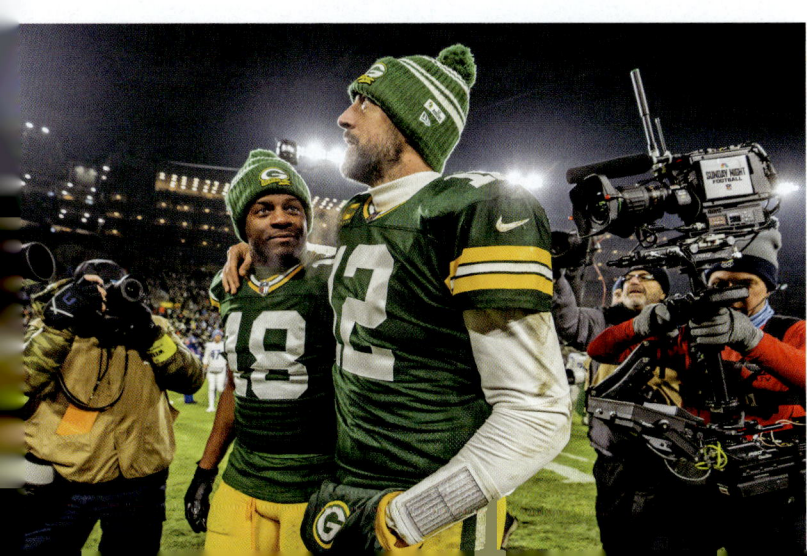

Rodgers says farewell to Lambeau Field on January 8, 2023, walking out with his good friend Randall Cobb.
© AP IMAGES/ TODD ROSENBERG

Rodgers declined Joe Namath's invitation to wear his retired Jets jersey, No. 12, and picked his Cal number instead.
© ELSA/GETTY IMAGES

Ed and Darla Rodgers were dressed appropriately for their son's big 2023 debut at MetLife Stadium.
COURTESY OF IAN O'CONNOR

A surreal pregame scene on the 9/11 anniversary, with Rodgers carrying out the American flag. His first Jets season lasted four snaps.
© MICHAEL OWENS/GETTY IMAGES

tato chips to the back of his heels. For kicks, the trainer drove his motorcycle through the parking lot and had Aaron and Jordan fire spirals at the raised net attached to its rear.

Poli put in two hours of preparation for every hour he spent with Rodgers in the gym. The quarterback was a full-time job, and Poli loved every part of the gig. Rodgers thanked the man for his dedication with an annual act of kindness—one year he had a van drop off a state-of-the-art refrigerator to replace the small, beat-up one in the gym.

As part of his duties, Poli occasionally recruited locals to catch passes from Rodgers in a nearby field at DeGarmo Park. One day the trainer called his brother, an IT manager at a critical-access hospital, in need of someone to run post patterns and curls for perhaps the greatest thrower of the football on the planet.

Gino Poli had not played the game in high school or college, but he was a good recreational athlete who had caught his share of passes in pickup games. He knew it would be a challenge to catch a throw from an NFL star, but he figured, *you know, how hard could it be?*

On arrival at the field, Gino made his first mistake. As he approached Rodgers for a fist bump, he accidentally stepped on the quarterback's sunglasses. Gino told Rodgers that he hoped they were a two-dollar pair from Dollar Tree.

"They are not," Rodgers replied.

He got his revenge when Gino lined up to the left and ran a little square-in about twenty-five yards downfield. Angelo had asked his client to take it easy on his brother, but Rodgers promised only that he would put the ball right in Gino's chest. And then the quarterback fired his first laser at his average-Joe wideout.

"It was like I would imagine a torpedo, just a sizzling sound as soon as it came in," Gino said. "I reached for it and grabbed it, but the power is difficult to explain. It hit me—I had to jump up as I was turning the corner for it—and it knocked me straight on my butt. Just knocked me down."

Gino did hold on to the ball. He was proud of that too. Years later, Gino still had the remnants of the bruise that ball left in the middle of his chest.

"I had never heard that sound from a football approaching as I received it," Gino said. "That's what was terrifying, just whistling all the way to the point where it drilled me. It was glorious."

Rodgers kept aiming at the same spot in Gino's chest, all but trying to make that bruise bigger. He threw about fifteen passes, and the trainer's brother caught three of them. "That was very discouraging," Gino said. "I thought I was good at catching footballs."

Before he headed back to his IT job, Gino Poli had this one question for Aaron Rodgers:

"Do you ever have any challenges when connecting with your receiver after he gets off the line of scrimmage?"

"It's easy," the quarterback replied. "It becomes easy the moment the cornerback turns his back. The moment he turns his back, then I know I've got him. And then I can make my connection."

• • •

AS A VETERAN defensive coach, Perry Fewell never had more fun competing against a quarterback than he did when competing against Brett Favre. He thoroughly enjoyed how Favre talked to him during the gameday action—"Oh, you got me on that one"—or winked at him while running by the sideline to celebrate a big play.

Preparing for Aaron Rodgers, and a divisional playoff game between the Packers and Fewell's New York Giants on January 15, 2012, was a different experience. Rodgers was not only the best player in football, soon to be named a near-unanimous league MVP. He was also the newly crowned Associated Press Male Athlete of the Year, and a quarterback who had just produced the greatest regular season in NFL history with a record 122.5 passer rating and an absurd 45 touchdowns against 6 interceptions.

"A-Rod sets the bar so high, he makes players play better," Fewell said. "He was like Magic Johnson. When you play with Magic, you have to play at his level."

It was no fun playing against Magic Johnson.

As defensive coordinator of the Giants, Fewell had a front-row seat for Rodgers's version of Showtime in December 2011, when the defending champs were in New Jersey to claim their eighteenth consecutive victory. (They won nineteen straight.) Rodgers threw for 4 touchdowns and 369 yards that day and, with fifty-eight seconds left in a 35–35 game, started the winning drive at his own 20 by delivering the first of four straight completions for 68 yards. He set up Mason Crosby's chip-shot field goal that went through with no time on the clock.

Fewell knew he had to alter his strategy against Rodgers in the sudden-death rematch. The coordinator was on a mission of sorts after taking considerable heat for the performance of a Giants defense that had struggled. The message boards were cruel, and even Fewell's ten-year-old son was subjected to the occasional unkind remark.

As a Black man who had been the interim head coach of the Buffalo Bills for seven games but had never landed the big full-time job, Fewell was angry about several Rooney Rule interviews that he believed were meant only to satisfy the rule's minority-candidate requirements. He saw it in the body language of the white executives who interviewed him.

Fewell knew that a championship might change all that, and after shutting down Atlanta's Matt Ryan in the wild-card round, a road triumph over the top-seeded Packers, winners of twenty-one of their last twenty-two games, would make that championship seem awfully attainable.

The Giants had learned plenty from their 38–35 regular-season loss to the unbeaten Patriots in 2007 and applied it in their epic Super Bowl XLII upset of those same unbeaten Patriots. Four years later, the Giants believed their 38–35 regular-season loss to the unbeaten Packers provided the intel and confidence needed for a divisional-round upset of those same 15-1 Packers.

Fewell remembered that Rodgers had been Green Bay's leading rusher in December with 32 yards, so he was not terribly concerned about defending the run game the second time around. He knew his defense had gotten healthier and faster. He knew he wanted to make Rodgers scramble and expend as much energy as possible.

"We wanted to rush five people," Fewell recalled for this book. "We wanted to make Aaron move up in the pocket. We called it a level rush. If we get to Aaron's level and make him step up in the pocket, we could retrace our steps and capture him. Sometimes we're not going to get him, but we could hit and harass him.

"In the secondary, what we learned from the first contest was you couldn't show him the correct coverage alignments. We tried to falsify our coverage alignments. We aligned at the halfway points of where we aligned the first time we played him so he couldn't get a look at it. In Green Bay's offense . . . his throwing game from under center was the quick game. But in the shotgun, it was intermediate and deep routes. So, we would try to show him different looks, and then jump his routes."

Nobody had a sensible plan for defending Rodgers all year. Green

Bay had scored 560 points and 70 touchdowns in the regular season, the second-most in NFL history (the 2007 Patriots went for 589 and 75). The Packers' offense had set all kinds of franchise records, and Rodgers was playing at a level never touched by Favre or Bart Starr. As great as Tom Brady was in 2007 and Peyton Manning was in 2004, neither could quite match Rodgers's rating in 2011, or even remotely approach his ability to scramble.

Fewell was facing a quarterbacking machine unlike any before it, and as a game planner he needed to pitch a perfect game.

"We put our corners halfway between a Cover 2 and Cover 3 look," the coordinator said, "and [free safety] Antrel Rolle was the key. He played nickel and safety, and we allowed him to roam around and say, 'Aaron, find me. I'm going to be lurking everywhere you're looking.' . . . We played in between, and just got to our spots on the snap of the ball.

"We used the play clock to time it. We had to hold our disguise until seven or eight seconds were left on the clock. We knew the snap would be between five and six seconds. . . . That was our thought going in. It was, 'Hey, you can't let him get the look.'

"Here's another thing that, when you watched him on TV, if he started talking to his receivers or he got a little frustrated, you felt like that was to your advantage because you threw his thought process off just a little bit. He would second-guess himself. You wanted to see that look of frustration on his face because that would give us confidence."

The Packers knew this was not going to be any cakewalk into the NFC Championship Game. Eli Manning and Tom Coughlin, quarterback and coach, had already beaten Brady and Bill Belichick in a Super Bowl, and had nearly beaten Green Bay six weeks earlier. The Giants still had their championship core intact and, after sitting out the regular-season finale and resting up during the wild-card round bye, Rodgers had not played since Christmas night.

The Packers were also playing in the shadow of a profound human tragedy. Joe Philbin, offensive coordinator, had lost his twenty-one-year-old son, Michael, who had drowned in the Fox River in Oshkosh, where his body had been discovered the previous Monday. Packers coaches and players attended the Friday funeral Mass at St. Elizabeth Ann Seton Catholic Church to support Philbin, his wife, Diane, and their five children. The offensive coordinator missed much of the week, spoke to the team Saturday, and on Sunday took his spot upstairs in a Lambeau booth.

The players wanted to beat the Giants for Philbin, badly. They wanted to give him the game ball afterward. They wanted to cry with him in the winning locker room.

"I don't think people understood what we were going through," said running back Ryan Grant. "It took a lot out of a lot of guys. It's not an excuse, because we're professionals.

"But my mom calls me before every game and says, 'What do you think?' And that year, every week, I told her, 'We're going to destroy them.' When she called that week and asked, I said, 'Yeah, we'll see.' She was like, 'What do you mean?' I told her there was a different energy around the organization. We were trying to balance the energy of a massive opportunity and a massive game with real feelings for a coach who was beloved. A lot of us were very close to Joe, and we knew his son. It was hard."

They played the football game because that was what professional football players did. It was a cold afternoon at Lambeau, and yet it felt like a midsummer day in Chico compared to that January 2008 night that saw the Giants end Favre's Green Bay career.

As he took the field, Fewell thought of Vince Lombardi and the old Packers teams. "It's nostalgic when you go into Green Bay," he said. "The atmosphere was just electric. . . . The crowd was at a fever pitch. They were the No. 1 seed coming in, and we were the 9-7 regular-season team coming in to get their butts whooped."

In all seriousness, the Giants had firm belief in their ability to win again at Lambeau. Manning was an opportunistic big-game player. Giants general manager Jerry Reese recalled that Peyton's kid brother was one of two people on the frozen tundra in the NFC Championship Game four years earlier (Plaxico Burress was the other) who acted like the Arctic conditions were hardly a bother. "Eli looked like he was playing in a park," Reese said.

Manning actually had more postseason experience at Lambeau than Rodgers did—the Packers' franchise player was making his home playoff debut. And perhaps it showed on the home team's first possession, after the visitors opened with a field goal. On third-and-long from the Giants' 29, Rodgers, wearing a white long-sleeved shirt under his green jersey, overthrew a wide-open Greg Jennings for what would have been a touchdown. The Packers tied it with their own field goal.

On the next possession, Manning found Hakeem Nicks, who bounced hard off Green Bay's Charlie Peprah and outraced several Packers down the left side for a 66-yard score. The crowd of 72,080 sounded alarmed.

Rodgers moved to ease the tension and settle the crowd by taking advantage of a major break—officials failed to award the Giants a recovered fumble after replays clearly showed that Jennings had indeed lost the ball. Five plays later, on the first snap of the second quarter, Rodgers hit John Kuhn for an 8-yard touchdown and a much-needed Lambeau Leap.

But Mike McCarthy responded by making the first of two unforced errors before the end of the half. He tried to catch the Giants by surprise by having Mason Crosby attempt an onside kick, only for the visitors to recover it for excellent field position. The Giants did nothing with it, rendering McCarthy's strange gamble moot.

His second mistake was not washed away by circumstance. The Giants had kicked a field goal off a Kuhn fumble and were prepared to run out the clock and take a 13–10 lead into halftime when McCarthy called time-out with fifteen seconds left and the Giants on their own 40-yard line. Right after the whistles blew the play dead, Manning handed off to Ahmad Bradshaw for what would have been an inside run designed to bleed down the clock. The visitors had no time-outs left to use.

Given a chance to reconsider their options, the Giants decided to send Bradshaw to the outside and hope he gained enough yards for a Hail Mary heave. Manning reminded the running back that he needed to get out of bounds before time expired. "So, the [Packers'] time-out did change the play," Eli said.

Manning pitched the ball left to Bradshaw, who used the Packers' pursuit against them by cutting across the field and sprinting all the way to the right sideline, getting out of bounds at the Green Bay 37 as if he were following the lead of the gesturing Manning to his rear.

Six seconds to go. Manning called the play in the huddle, "Flood Tip," and went into shotgun formation, with one receiver to his right and three to his left. He dropped back, stepped up to avoid pressure, and launched the ball toward the left side of the end zone, with four Giants and four Packers in the neighborhood. The six-foot Nicks went up high and in front of Peprah. It was as close to an uncontested Hail Mary catch as you will ever see, and it was also the first completed Hail Mary of Eli Manning's life, all the way back to his grade-school days.

The fans booed the Packers off the field and into the tunnel. McCarthy swore that his team was not deflated at the start of the second half. Human nature strongly suggested otherwise.

On the first possession of the third quarter, Rodgers made a great escape from the pocket and an even greater throw to Donald Driver while scrambling to his left, putting the ball on the Giants' 30. Maybe McCarthy was right. Maybe not.

On the very next play, just as Jennings was breaking into the clear on a slant-and-go (or sluggo) route on the left, and just as Rodgers was about to unleash a sure touchdown pass, Osi Umenyiora stripped him of the ball and the Giants recovered. While still down, Rodgers slammed his right hand three times into the grass.

Down 20–13 early in the fourth quarter, the Packers started to crack under the pressure. On third-and-5 from the Giants' 39, Rodgers let rip a fastball at a wide-open Jermichael Finley, only to lead him too much into the middle of the field. From a sitting position, Finley slammed both hands down in anger while looking back at Rodgers, who was doing his own animated gesturing. On the Fox broadcast, Hall of Famer Troy Aikman questioned why the quarterback needed to put so much zip on the ball with his receiver that open.

"That play would have taken us there," Finley said. "That would have gotten us rolling. That's why we call it a game of inches. One play can stop you from getting a ring. I thought he was going to throw me a cupcake ball . . . but that's Aaron Rodgers. That's his style of play."

Feeling desperate, McCarthy chose to go for it on fourth-and-5. Rodgers was sacked by Michael Boley, who celebrated by performing the quarterback's championship-belt move. Twice.

"Players came over and said, 'Perry, he's confused,'" Fewell said. The coordinator made a mental note and said, "Yeah, we got him."

Down 10 again in the middle of the fourth quarter, Grant fumbled, and the Giants' Chase Blackburn returned it to the Packers' 4-yard line, where he was tackled by Rodgers. Manning ended Green Bay's dynastic hopes on the next play, hitting Mario Manningham in the back of the end zone.

Before his season was officially over, Rodgers took a nasty hit from Umenyiora on his final, futile touchdown drive, and watched his last throw get deflected and then picked off by Deon Grant. The Giants intercepted the last pass of Rodgers's magical Green Bay year, just like they had picked off the last pass of Favre's magical Green Bay career.

Rodgers removed his helmet near the bench and pulled a team beanie down over his ears. "This is going to be a long offseason for the Green Bay Packers and Mike McCarthy and Aaron Rodgers," Aikman said.

It was no surprise that Manning had put up 330 yards and 3 touchdowns against a Green Bay defense that had surrendered a league-worst 411.6 yards per game, and that had consistently failed to generate a pass rush. But the Packers had not played loose with the ball all year—they had fewer turnovers (14) than victories, and yet they committed 4 when it mattered most.

Rodgers was victimized by as many as seven or eight drops, depending on how you kept score, and he did his damnedest to work the problem, again leading his team with 66 rushing yards on 7 carries. But he was sacked four times and harassed enough to reduce an offense that had averaged 35 points per game to one that barely scored 20.

"It played out exactly as we game-planned it," Fewell said.

This was all a crushing turn of events for Rodgers, who lost a chance to claim a second ring at age twenty-eight.

"You win a championship," he said, "and you're kind of at the top of the mountain. And you forget how bad this feeling is."

Rodgers would not be suiting up in Lucas Oil Stadium in Indianapolis for Super Bowl XLVI on February 5. He would be appearing in Indy the night before at the Murat Theatre with his good friend and Green Bay roommate Kevin Lanflisi to receive his first NFL MVP award. Rodgers earned forty-eight of fifty votes in an Associated Press poll of media members who cover the sport.

Peyton Manning introduced him, and Rodgers thanked his parents for their support. He acknowledged San Francisco 49er legends Steve Young, Jerry Rice, and Joe Montana, and quipped, "Big Niner fan when I was a kid. Thanks for drafting me."

He got a laugh from Young and others in the crowd. It was a glorious night, yet Rodgers would have traded a hundred of these nights for Eli Manning's spot opposite Tom Brady on Sunday. As much as he coveted the MVP distinction, Rodgers knew he would be judged by his number of Super Bowl rings.

So, this was about to be a longer offseason than Aikman said it would be. No Lombardi Trophy meant no reprieve from the misery of defeat. No sanctuary from the pain.

Imagine if someone told Aaron Rodgers that he would play another eleven years in Green Bay, and never step foot inside the big game again.

• • •

THE QUARTERBACK SIGNED up for a weekly radio gig with ESPN's Milwaukee station, 540 WAUK-AM, in 2011, with sportswriter Jason Wilde in the role of host and point guard, charged to get Aaron Rodgers the ball where he needed it and then to get out of the way.

Wilde was good at it. Rodgers was even better. Packers fans and beat writers treated it as appointment radio. If you wanted to hear a superstar athlete talk like your next-door neighbor might at a barbecue, and not as a fearful, cliché-spewing automaton at the podium, *Tuesdays with Aaron* was the right place to turn.

Rodgers regularly pulled back the curtain on his professional life, providing listeners with back-room snapshots of what success at his level looks like. And though he was a public figure who believed that his private life should remain off limits to the news media and to amateur internet sleuths, Rodgers was not afraid to get personal on his own show.

Forty minutes deep into his December 31, 2013, episode, Rodgers got as personal as he ever did when he took a question about his sexuality from Wilde. It was stunning to hear the subject raised and addressed.

On the other hand, if you were an NFL player, a coach, an executive, an agent, or a reporter assigned to cover the league, you likely had heard the rumor that Rodgers was gay. It was out there, as they say. Jeff Pearlman reported in his definitive biography of Brett Favre, *Gunslinger*, that the rumor circulated through the Packers' locker room because Rodgers "didn't boast of sexual conquests." Years later, when Rodgers walked into a Milwaukee restaurant with a woman he was dating, a prominent Green Bay player turned to the longtime sports executive he was eating with and said he was surprised to see the quarterback with the woman because many Packers believed him to be gay.

For whatever reason, Rodgers picked the Tuesday after a dramatic, season-saving victory over the Bears to put this one in play. He talked about the rumor with Wilde before their show and decided he wanted it publicly addressed. On the air, Rodgers brought up the downside of his celebrity and mentioned "crazy rumors that swirl around from time to time that get silly."

Wilde responded sarcastically, "I have no idea what you could be referring to." He paused for effect before adding, "Oh, you mean the Aaron Rodgers–is-gay story?"

Rodgers laughed while confirming that was indeed the story he was talking about. "So, you're aware?" Wilde asked. "You saw this out there?"

"Yeah, I'm just going to say, I'm not gay," Rodgers replied. "I really, really like women. That's all I can say about that.

"There's always going to be silly stuff out there in the media, and you can't worry too much about [it], and I don't. . . . I think there should be, professional is professional, and personal is personal. And that's just how I'm going to keep it."

Years later, when I asked him why someone who fiercely protected his privacy would answer a question about his sexuality on a radio show, Rodgers said for this book: "I think I was upset at the framing [of the rumor] because it was meant to shame the idea of being gay, and I have so many friends that are gay in the community.

"And right before that, [Wilde] and I actually have talked about this multiple times, and I said, 'I want to go after them, the people saying this.' Not in relation to me, because I could give a shit what they thought about me, but that they're using this to shame, like it's a bad thing to be gay. Like it's a negative.

"That's what I wanted to go after. And [Wilde] said, 'You should just let it go and just say no.' I wish I had done the former because that's how I really felt. I'm like, say anything you want about me, but do you understand these people are using this to shame the idea of being gay? That's just disrespectful to all my friends who are in the community who don't believe that it's a choice. They were making it seem like you're shaming people for being gay, when a lot of them, if you ask them, they didn't ask for this life. 'This is who I am.' So, I wished I would have handled it that way, and I don't blame Jason. We've talked it out."

Rodgers did often use his platform to send messages to his teammates and fans, and to promote the admirable work he was doing in the community. During his September 23, 2014, show, he spoke of his advocacy for Midwest Athletes Against Childhood Cancer (MACC Fund) and a partnership with Milwaukee attorney David Gruber that produced a series of "it's Aaron" videos of Rodgers arriving at homes unannounced to visit family members touched by tragedy and moved to make a difference.

In one video, the quarterback visited the twin sister of a young boy he had grown close to, Jack Bartosz, who suffered for years from neuroblastoma before his 2012 death at age ten. At age eleven, Annie Bartosz launched the Gold in September (G9) foundation to defeat childhood cancer.

Rodgers went door-to-door with Annie to spread the word to stunned locals who were not expecting a future first-ballot Hall of Famer to end up on their porches. "It's fun to be able to raise awareness for these causes," Rodgers said.

Of course, that September show had to navigate its way back to football, and to the Packers' 19–7 loss to the Lions and third consecutive 1-2 start to a season. Wilde said he wanted to ask Rodgers the two questions everyone had been asking him: "What's wrong with the offense? And what's wrong with you?"

The conversation bounced from how close Rodgers thought the offense was to clicking to why he had little use for putting receivers in motion (evolving defenses adjust to motion and sometimes play "more vanilla" without it) to his appreciation of soccer goalkeeper Tim Howard to his enduring love for the movie *The Princess Bride*.

Somewhere in the middle of all that, Rodgers had a message to send to the fan base. "Five letters here," he said. "Just for everybody out there in Packerland."

"Panic?" Wilde asked through a laugh.

"R-E-L-A-X. Relax," Rodgers said. "OK? We're going to be OK."

Soon enough, the audio and the printed words were everywhere. Rodgers's brother Luke had his apparel company, Pro Merch, print up stylish green "Relax" T-shirts with images of the quarterback's face and signature within a few days, and sold twenty-five hundred in one week. Oh, and Rodgers responded to his own call for calm by throwing 4 touchdown passes in a blowout road victory over the Bears.

"That's what I want to do as a leader," Rodgers said. "I like to put pressure on myself."

He explained on his show two days later that some questions from the previous week that he described as "ridiculous" inspired his "Relax" bit.

Rodgers had taken exception to the notion that the fractured left collarbone that caused him to miss seven games in 2013 and/or his relationship with actress Olivia Munn, whom he had started dating in the spring of 2014, had negatively impacted his play.

"Those are so idiotic," Rodgers said, "it's not even worth responding to either one of those."

And yet the fans had a right to be concerned about where their Packers were heading. After winning it all in Rodgers's third season as a starter, the fans had expected a second ring by now.

Instead, they were dealt two more years of postseason despair. After opening 2012 by losing to the 49ers and his old friend Alex Smith, Rodgers closed the year by losing a divisional-round game to the 49ers and Smith's replacement, Colin Kaepernick, who shredded Green Bay's defense with a quarterback-record 181 rushing yards, 263 passing yards, and 4 combined touchdowns.

Rodgers agreed to a five-year, $110 million extension in April, months before his 2013 season came down to one flick of the wrist. On December 29, needing to win the final game to make the playoffs as NFC North champs, Rodgers returned from his broken collarbone to defeat the very rival that had injured him eight weeks earlier, the Chicago Bears, on a fourth-and-8, 48-yard touchdown pass to Randall Cobb with thirty-eight seconds left. The Bears were leading by a point when they rushed seven against Green Bay's six blockers, only to get beaten by Rodgers's remarkable escape to his left, aided by a diving block from John Kuhn on Julius Peppers.

The Packers' sideline was turned upside down. This was inarguably Rodgers's all-time finest regular-season play, dismissing the blitz, shedding his rusty-looking form, and nailing the third fourth-down conversion of this sudden-death drive. Cobb had just returned from his own extended absence—ten weeks on injured reserve with a fractured tibia. Mike McCarthy said the play "will be running on the highlight reel for the rest of my time on this Earth." Bob McGinn of the *Milwaukee Journal Sentinel* said the touchdown stood "among the greatest plays in the franchise's 93-year history."

How many quarterbacks in the history of the NFL—never mind the history of the Packers—could have made this throw after being out so long with a serious injury?

"It was a lot of joy and excitement," Rodgers said. "This has been a wild season. I feel very blessed to have this job."

The quarterback and his friends did not have long to celebrate. The following Sunday, back in freezing conditions at Lambeau, Rodgers and the Packers lost another playoff game to Kaepernick and the Niners, this time on a last-second field goal, leaving them 1-3 in the postseason since their Super Bowl victory.

Alex Smith had been traded to Kansas City, and the people who had drafted him instead of Rodgers were long gone. But still, after promising payback for rejecting him, Rodgers was hurt by his back-to-back failure to eliminate the Niners from the tournament.

"Very disappointing, personally," Rodgers said that night.

"I thought there was something special about this year. I thought we'd make a run."

The Packers returned to form in 2014 after their quarterback told their fan base to calm down, winning 11 of their last 13 regular-season games, including a stirring comeback victory over Miami and his former coordinator Joe Philbin (courtesy of a Dan Marino fake-spike special against Dan Marino's old team) and a 55–14 thrashing of the Bears that saw Rodgers tie an NFL record with 6 touchdown passes in the first half. *Six.*

The NFC's No. 2 seed beat the Dallas Cowboys in the divisional round because the refs took away a fourth-down catch by Dez Bryant near the goal line, and because Rodgers played through the pain yet again, hobbling about with a left calf injury while still somehow throwing for 316 yards, 3 touchdowns, and a couple of late third-down conversions that ran out the clock on a 26–21 victory.

"I think I got a hundred and twenty minutes left in me," Rodgers said. That included the Super Bowl. The first sixty of those minutes were to be spent in Seattle, site of the NFC Championship Game.

At thirty-one years old, on the verge of winning his second league MVP award, Rodgers entered this duel carrying some heavy CenturyLink Field baggage. He had been blown out in this building in the season opener by the Seahawks' Russell Wilson and Marshawn Lynch, his old Cal teammate, and he had come out on the wrong end of the Fail Mary fiasco here in 2012, when replacement refs defined the NFL's labor standoff with the regular officials by missing an offensive pass interference call and rewarding Seattle with a surreal walk-off touchdown.

For all of the special things he had done on NFL fields, Rodgers had his fair share of scar tissue. The stinging playoff defeats left permanent marks, but the quarterback had also absorbed shots to the ribs in recent years from a few teammates and people closely associated with them.

In 2012, a month after Jermichael Finley's agent tweeted that Rodgers was an ineffective leader who failed to "take the blame & make every1 better," Finley said that his chemistry with Rodgers was "not good enough at all," that he needed "the quarterback on my side," and that "it takes two people" to fix the problem.

After he signed with the Vikings in 2013, Greg Jennings spent considerable time referring to Rodgers as "12" or "the guy they have now" rather than by name and painted him in a *Minneapolis Star Tribune* interview as a me-first, team-second star.

"A lot of times when you have a guy who creates that spotlight for himself and establishes that and takes a lot of that, it becomes so-and-so and the team," Jennings told the paper. "It should always be the team. . . . I'm going to defer to the team, to the team, to the team. And I think when you reach a point when you're not deferring any longer, it's no longer really about the team.

"Don't get me wrong, '12' is a great person. But when you hear all positives, all positives, all positives all the time, it's hard for you to sit down when one of your teammates says, 'Man, come on, you've got to hold yourself accountable for this.' It's hard for someone to see that now because all they've heard is, 'I'm doing it the right way. I'm perfect.' In actuality, we all have flaws."

Jennings had been angry over an in-game comment Rodgers made to San Francisco's Carlos Rogers in 2012, when he told the cornerback that the Niners should try to sign Jennings in free agency. The quarterback said he meant it as a joke; his receiver didn't take it that way. Nor did Jennings's sister Valyncia, who blasted Rodgers later that season with a series of tweets that included the claim that he was "the most overrated QB in the league!"

A more credible voice, retired three-time Pro Bowler Donald Driver, backed up Jennings when he said, "We've always been in the room, and we've always said that the quarterback is the one who needs to take the pressure off of everyone else. If a guy runs the wrong route, it's easy for the quarterback to say, 'Hey, I told him to run that route,' than the guy to say, 'Hey, I ran the wrong route.'

"Sometimes you ask Aaron to take the pressure off those guys so we don't look bad. He didn't want to do that. He felt like if you did something bad, you do it. That's the difference. You want that leadership."

Rodgers absorbed the body blows like a pro, like he once absorbed a towel full of shaving cream to his face from his buddy John Kuhn while the cameras rolled at his locker. Perhaps a man widely perceived as sensitive to a fault—an observation embraced by a *60 Minutes* profile that annoyed Rodgers—was attempting to grow a thicker layer of skin. On the other hand, as Jennings said on the show, "He's going to be sensitive to the fact that we're saying he's sensitive."

In the end, Rodgers was surprised that his approach to leadership was being challenged. He had started regularly inviting teammates to his home for catered dinners right after replacing Brett Favre, and he had been in the habit of gifting teammates laptops and flat-screen TVs. He had also made himself available to rookies, joking with them to make them feel at home the way some players (not named Favre) had made him feel comfortable in 2005, veterans such as Javon Walker, Na'il Diggs, and Grey Ruegamer. As he got older, Rodgers did so much talking in the meetings—about an offense he knew better than everyone—that he felt like an assistant coach.

He thought he was a good leader. He did not see much reason to change.

Rodgers was confused by Finley's stance on their chemistry, or lack thereof, since the two met in one-on-one bonding sessions on Saturday nights to talk about football and life. But the quarterback did not publicly assail him. Rodgers declined to return fire on Jennings (or his sister) for the short term when he reported to camp in 2013. On the Driver front, McCarthy stepped in and picked up the blitzer for his quarterback, countering that "Aaron manages his job responsibility very well" and that "accountability is throughout your whole football team."

It had gotten awfully noisy around Rodgers, even though he had made peace with Favre at the 2013 NFL awards show, where they appeared as copresenters and shook hands and made awkward conversation about the pros and cons of comebacks, all in good fun. "A time for healing," Rodgers called it.

Now it was late in the 2014 season, and the Packers were in the NFC Championship Game for the first time since they won it all. They needed leadership from the franchise player whose management style had been questioned.

On one good leg, Aaron Rodgers needed to be Aaron Rodgers to get a second crack at bringing the Lombardi Trophy back to Lombardi's home.

• • •

JOEY KAEMPF WAS sitting in the stands at CenturyLink Field, long known as perhaps the loudest building in the NFL. Seattle Seahawks fans were called the Twelfth Man for a reason.

A close Rodgers friend since their boyhood days in Oregon, Kaempf was a Seattle-area attorney who had intimate knowledge of the eardrum-shattering capacity of a Seahawks crowd. And when Rodgers took the field with 1:19 left in the NFC title game and the home team leading, 22–19, Kaempf heard the fans get louder than he had ever heard them get before.

On this windy, rainy day, the Packers were on the verge of an unfathomable collapse. They were leading 16–0 in the middle of the third quarter, and they were leading 19–7 with less than five minutes to play and in possession of the ball. Only a series of bizarre events and dreadful decisions had landed them in this dire endgame position.

Desperate to get on the board in the third quarter, and tired of watching Russell Wilson throw the ball to the wrong team, Seattle faked a field-goal attempt and had holder Jon Ryan, a punter, run hard to his left as if keeping the ball, suck in Packers linebacker A. J. Hawk, and then shot-put the ball to a rookie tackle, Garry Gilliam. The former Penn State tight end was all alone in the end zone for the touchdown. The crowd went wild.

Down a dozen points late, Wilson scored from the 1-yard line, setting up an onside kick. Stephen Hauschka aligned his body and the ball for a kick to the right side, where six Seahawks were stationed at the 30-yard line in three-point stances. The Packers merely had to recover the ball to virtually seal a trip to the Super Bowl.

Hauschka hit a high hopper toward Brandon Bostick, a second-year tight end from Division II Newberry College in South Carolina. Instead of blocking a Seahawk and clearing a lane for the Pro Bowl receiver behind him, Jordy Nelson, Bostick went up high like a power forward rising for a rebound. The ball dropped through his hands, bounced off his helmet, and fell into the arms of Seattle's Chris Matthews. Four plays later, Marshawn Lynch ran off left tackle for a 24-yard touchdown and a 1-point lead with 1:25 left. The crowd went wilder.

The Packers all looked like they had seen a ghost. On the two-point conversion attempt, Wilson rolled right, spun hard left away from pressure, immediately turned right again, and then threw up a moon ball across his body to the left side of the end zone while getting hit. Green Bay's Ha Ha Clinton-Dix seemed to have a good shot at the ball, yet somehow misplayed it. Luke Willson made the catch for the three-point lead.

Most opposing quarterbacks would have crumbled in this situation. The Seahawks were the defending champs, and they fielded by far the best defense in the league. They had beaten up Peyton Manning and his Broncos so thoroughly in the previous Super Bowl in New Jersey that Peyton's famous father, Archie, said outside the Denver locker room, "That's why I hate football."

Now this was why Aaron Rodgers hated football. In addition to the trick play and the fluke play that changed everything, he knew the Packers had wasted numerous opportunities to put away Seattle and book that trip to the big game. They had two possessions in the middle of the fourth quarter that could have secured victory, and Mike McCarthy called five running plays and one passing play that led to a pair of three-and-outs, saving the Seahawks precious time. In between those possessions, Green Bay's Morgan Burnett claimed Wilson's fourth interception and, instead of racing for the open field in front of him and a possible clinching pick-six, took a baseball slide at his own 43 with 5:04 to go. Players and coaches were smiling and hugging on the sideline after that one.

The Packers also left a busload of points on the field in the first half, when Rodgers was picked off by Richard Sherman in the end zone on the opening drive, and when McCarthy was moved to kick field goals rather than go for it on back-to-back fourth-and-goals at the 1-yard line.

"We weren't playing as aggressive as we usually are," Rodgers said later. Did he mean "playing," or "coaching"? The quarterback declined to elaborate.

Rodgers had said the previous season that McCarthy usually supplied him only the play call and formation—as opposed to play call, formation, and audibles in earlier years—and then let the quarterback take it from there. Given that the Seattle crowd was as loud as a 747 at takeoff, any opposing quarterback's ability to check at the line was severely compromised.

On the Fox broadcast, Joe Buck said his booth and the entire stadium were shaking. A tidal wave of momentum was crashing against the visiting side. So, when Rodgers faced the Seahawks' famed Legion of Boom with seventy-nine seconds to play and the ball on his own 22, he was staring at an impossible proposition. He had to make it possible with his left calf screaming at him.

"I felt it the whole game," Rodgers said.

And yet he immediately attacked the situation with 15-yard passes to Jordy Nelson and Randall Cobb, and then with a 12-yard hobble to the right sideline that included a one-legged hop to spare his left leg a landing it did not need. Rodgers had gained 42 yards in forty-four seconds to move into field-goal range without using one of his three time-outs.

On the next play, granted room for another meaningful gain on the run, Rodgers's injured leg instead forced him to attempt a push pass to running back Eddie Lacy, who wasn't looking for it. The quarterback could squeeze only another six yards out of this drive before turning it over to his kicker, Mason Crosby, who had been 18 for 20 on field-goal attempts in his postseason career, including 6 for 6 in these playoffs. And when he made it 7 for 7 on his tying 48-yarder, Rodgers jumped with his arms and his index fingers pointed to the sky.

It was a 22–22 game when Rodgers led a contingent of six Packers out to midfield for the coin toss; the Seahawks sent a delegation of three. The referee, Tony Corrente, announced that the visiting team had the honor of calling heads or tails before showing his coin to the bearded man in the striped Packers beanie, his hands stuffed in his hand-warming pouch.

"Tails," Rodgers said.

Tails never fails.

Corrente flipped his coin in the air and, wouldn't you know it, the damn thing turned up heads. Rodgers turned away in annoyance. He knew there was a reasonable chance he had touched the ball for the last time in the 2014 season. He knew Wilson was 9-0 against Super Bowl–winning quarterbacks and fully capable of going 10-0 on the first possession of overtime.

On the fifth snap of the extra session, Wilson converted a third down with an over-the-top throw to Doug Baldwin down the right sideline for

35 yards. On the next play, Wilson took the shotgun snap and lofted another aesthetically pleasing pass down the middle to a tightly covered Jermaine Kearse, who caught it at the 1-yard line just as Green Bay's Tramon Williams climbed onto his back. Receiver and cornerback tumbled into the end zone as one, with the ball in Kearse's breadbasket for a 35-yard score.

"Seattle's going to the Super Bowl," Buck shouted on the air.

The Packers staggered about the field, looking broken and lost. Normally, this would qualify as a suitable time to rant about one of the dumbest rules in sports, the rule that allowed the whims of a coin toss to hand a lucky team the opportunity to win a championship game without the unlucky team possessing the ball. But given all their execution breakdowns, the Packers were not worthy of that excuse. Green Bay was like a golfer just trying to hold on to a lead in the final round of a major, just trying to get it to the house, only to play too cautiously to earn the trophy.

Up in the stands, Rodgers's friend Joey Kaempf had already decided, "That's the most devastating game I've ever been to in my life." Years later he thought of his friend's last stand on this day, his rally against all odds to tie the game in the closing seconds of regulation.

"It's one of the most impressive drives of his career," Kaempf said, "but nobody remembers it."

History was written by the victors. The Packers did not wait long to fire their special teams coach, Shawn Slocum, or to waive Brandon Bostick, the men most responsible for the onside kick from hell. Only there was no deleting this meltdown from anyone's memory bank.

"It's going to be a missed opportunity that we'll probably think about for the rest of my career," a deflated Rodgers said. "We were the better team today, we played well enough to win. We can't blame anybody but ourselves."

A lot of questions could not be adequately answered, such as: Why didn't the Packers spend more time targeting an injured Richard Sherman late when it was clear he was essentially playing with one arm? Why didn't McCarthy show more faith in the sport's best player by letting him throw more in the middle of the fourth quarter?

The Packers gave away this Super Bowl trip and now had to live with the consequences. "You can't let them complete a pass for a touchdown on a fake field goal," Rodgers said. "You can't give up an onside kick, and you can't not get any first downs in the fourth quarter and expect to win. And that's on top of being really poor in the red zone in the first half. So, put it all together and that's how you lose games.

"This was a great opportunity. We were on the cusp."

Rodgers missed out on a classic duel with Tom Brady and the Patriots in Super Bowl XLIX, which would be decided by the mother of all end-game gaffes. Seattle's heartbreaking defeat on the goal line—via Wilson's interception—did little to ease Rodgers's pain.

"We had the best team in the league," Green Bay's quarterback maintained. The Packers had beaten the Patriots at home during the regular season. "I felt like we could beat them again," Rodgers said.

Either way, he would start the 2015 season as a two-time NFL MVP and one-time Super Bowl MVP, and as the instantly recognizable face of a legendary franchise that was fielding a playoff team every year. Rodgers's side gig, his record label, never really took off, and that was OK.

He had that lucrative State Farm deal that made him a crossover celebrity, not to mention a victory over Kevin O'Leary of *Shark Tank* and astronaut Mark Kelly in a round of *Celebrity Jeopardy!* Aaron Rodgers was still living large. His professional life was still one to die for.

But behind his wildly successful public existence was a shattered family unit, and a story of how fame and fortune can separate loved ones in ways they had never thought possible.

10

THE ISLAND

JORDAN RUSSELL WAS right there on draft day, sitting by Aaron Rodgers's side, the only person not related to the quarterback—outside of his agent—who had a place at the table in the green room.

Russell was right there as Rodgers's teammate and punter on the Pleasant Valley High School freshman team. He was right there with Aaron on a San Diego beach during spring break, blasting him from behind and bragging that the tackle was among his finest athletic feats.

He was right there as his roommate and personal chef at Cal, in their duplex apartment on Tyler Street, off of Ashby. Years later, he was right there in the foursome when Rodgers made his first hole-in-one at Canyon Oaks Country Club, hitting a 6-iron over a lake and into the cup tucked in the back right corner of the sixth green, 170 yards away, mere weeks after being named Super Bowl MVP.

They played nickel-dime-quarter poker as ninth graders, and they played $2 and $8 online-poker tournaments into the early-morning hours after Rodgers's football games at Cal. Russell loved how his roommate did not fit the Big Man on Campus archetype that suggested a major-college quarterback should be partying at a frat house deep into the night. Rodgers wanted to win those low-stakes poker tournaments as badly as he wanted to beat USC.

Over the years, Russell enjoyed pole-position status among their group. He was effectively Aaron's best friend. Russell had not fancied life as a PV punter, so he quit football and joined the school's golf team and bonded with Rodgers over rounds at the Bidwell Park course.

Rodgers had complete faith in Russell, or else he never would have had him there at that draft table for the most stressful day of his football life.

"It was me sitting there almost feeling like I was there to comfort him," Russell recalled. "He'd get up and walk around and . . . grab a bottle of water and just take a lap, and the whole time he was like, 'This is bullshit. I don't know why this is happening.' . . . It was like this fuck-the-world mentality. 'I'm going to show everyone that they're wrong.'"

They had been through a lot together, so when Rodgers heard that Russell was about to buy a Honda Prelude, it came as no surprise that the quarterback offered him a loan because he felt his boy should be driving something more luxurious—like a used BMW 328i Coupe. Russell borrowed about $15,000 with a better interest rate than he could get at a bank.

"He's got the biggest heart of anybody I've ever met," Russell said years later. The cash offer, Russell added, "was the true spirit of him wanting to prop me up."

But over time, the chef who was not making much money while studying his craft fell behind on his loan payments. He met Rodgers for breakfast and asked if he could cut those payments in half and extend the loan, and the quarterback told him he needed to take up the matter with his marketing agent at the time, H Koal. Russell instead took out a personal loan at a credit union to cover the balance and handed his friend a check for the full amount. Rodgers ripped it up. He had been angered by word that Russell had been supposedly bad-mouthing him to mutual friends.

"I don't need your money or your friendship," Rodgers told him.

"That was the first time I experienced him saying, 'Don't bite the hand that feeds,'" Russell said.

Rodgers was never one to move past perceived slights easily. He held on to grudges like he held on to a football—with a firm grip. If he thought that you had wronged him, he could surgically cut you out of his life on the spot.

"I was the first guy in his whole friend group to get exiled," Russell said for this book. "The first guy to be put on 'the Island.'"

Nobody ever wanted to end up on Aaron's island. It was a cold and lonely place, with no cell or internet access to the man who put you there. All of Aaron's friends knew that to communicate with anyone sentenced to the Island was to risk landing on the Island yourself.

THE ISLAND

Nobody was exempt from Rodgers's draconian dogma. Not even the people who loved him the most, including the man and woman who brought him into the world.

• • •

AARON RODGERS'S FAMILY had quite a history. His maternal grandmother, Barbara (Blair) Pittman, did extensive genealogy work and wrote that she found that her side of the family "is mostly Scotch-Irish and our ancestors go back hundreds of years. [The] Boyds-Blairs and Crawfords fought in the battles we saw in the movie 'Braveheart' and . . . they were among the fierce brand of brave Protestants who ran the hills of Scotland and shed their blood and gave their lives for FREEDOM."

Pittman wrote that she walked in the footsteps of her ancestors, and those of her husband, Chuck, "everywhere they walked in the United States," by taking numerous trips to the eastern part of the country and to Salt Lake City to visit towns, libraries, and cemeteries while trying to contact every living relative.

Aaron Rodgers's American family tree can be traced to the *Mayflower*'s departure from the English port city of Plymouth and arrival in the New World, at Cape Cod, in 1620. Among the 102 passengers on board was a young boy named Resolved White, along with his parents, William and Susanna White. Susanna remarried after William's death and is believed to have been among four women to have cooked the first Thanksgiving dinner for the Pilgrims and the Wampanoag tribe in 1621. Susanna was Aaron Rodgers's tenth great-grandmother. Her son Resolved, later a soldier in King Philip's War, was Rodgers's ninth great-grandfather.

Rodgers had another tenth great-grandmother in Elizabeth Clason, or Clawson, a Connecticut woman who was accused of being a witch and tried in a Fairfield courtroom in 1692. Elizabeth's body was searched for satanic markings, and she was tied up and thrown into a pool of water to determine if she would float (a supposed indication of guilt, with water, a pure and central part of baptism, believed to reject anyone who had made a deal with the devil). Though two eyewitness accounts suggested that she might have floated, Elizabeth was found not guilty of the witchcraft charges after dozens of fellow Stamford residents signed an affidavit attesting to her character.

Before his death in 1863, the quarterback's fourth great-grand-uncle, Dr. Arba Blair, was an Oneida County, New York, abolitionist who provided sanctuary for escaped slaves in his home as part of the Underground Railroad movement. The founding officer of the New York State Anti-Slavery Society, Blair was once clubbed over the head and pelted with brickbats and stones by a proslavery mob. Many years later, evidence emerged that Aaron Rodgers's ancestors had fought on opposite sides of the Civil War, according to the quarterback's father, Ed.

After leading the effort to research and relive her family's history, Barbara (Blair) Pittman described herself as a storyteller who went beyond collecting facts in an effort to "put flesh on the bones." She called her process "an awesome journey."

One of her eleven grandchildren, Aaron, created his own special part of the family's journey. He went from his boyhood Super Bowl Sunday gatherings at his grandparents' house on West Mill Street in Ukiah—the one he called "the Forever House"—to his own Super Bowl Sunday party as a grown-up quarterback, phoning Barbara and her dear Chuck before every game along the way.

"Aaron was always a kind, sweet boy," Barbara wrote to me, "and I always thought of him as a man of God when he was older, with a heart of gold. . . . He could not have loved and honored his grandfather more, and from his notes and calls, he loved me. He always said he wanted to do just like we did when he is a grandfather and have each of his grandchildren spend a week every summer."

But ten years into his NFL career, Rodgers stopped calling Barbara and Chuck before games. He stopped calling them at all. He was no longer speaking to his immediate family members, or to many of his extended family members.

"Words cannot express how I miss my Aaron," Barbara wrote in 2023. "One never stops loving and if the words I hear in the Sermons I listen to come true, I will hold him once more. . . .

"I love my Aaron and maybe some day we will understand what happened to make him want nothing to do with us."

Aaron stopped speaking with his parents in the winter of 2014, when his girlfriend, actress Olivia Munn, among the stars of the HBO drama series *The Newsroom*, had been living with him in Green Bay. Ed and Darla Rodgers had visited their son before an early December 2014 Packers home game, along with their friends Larry and Diane Ruby, and enjoyed a pleasant conversation with the actress. They left town believing there were no problems among them.

Rodgers then played a dreadful game at Buffalo, connecting on only 17 of 42 passes, throwing 2 interceptions, and posting a career-worst 34.3 quarterback rating in a 21–13 defeat. According to sources, Munn called Ed and Darla that night and blindsided them with an angry rant about their plans to see Aaron again when the Packers played at Tampa Bay before Christmas, a game that Rodgers family members planned to attend as part of a Disney World trip. The actress made it clear that she did not want her boyfriend's parents meeting them or attending the game. Ed and Darla explained that they had been attending Aaron's games since he was a kid and did not need her permission to continue doing so.

Munn declined comment for this book through a representative. Ed and Darla said they did not make any disparaging remark that might have set off the actress. "The only thing I said was, 'You haven't been on the scene very long. You're just his girlfriend. We're his parents,'" Ed recalled.

If Ed and Darla figured their son would call and apologize for his girlfriend's behavior, well, that call never came. They made the trip to the Tampa Bay game, anyway, and did not see their son. According to sources, Aaron later sent an email to family members that effectively said, "Don't attack the woman I love."

Ed and Darla had been sent to the Island. They would not have another conversation with their middle child for at least another nine years.

Aaron's parents were not fans of Munn even before the blowup. They had privately hoped that their son would marry his ex-fiancée Destiny Newton, the local woman who had first caught his eye years earlier. But Aaron ended the engagement in 2013.

"We all loved her," said one Rodgers friend. "We knew Destiny. We trusted her. She would have kept the crew tighter."

That same person also said that Rodgers did not just excommunicate family members, but a number of friends as well. "It was more or less a clean sweep of people that were close to him," the person said.

Three years after he hired his close friend Andrew Jeter to replace H Koal as his marketing agent, Rodgers parted ways with Jeter and signed with Tiger Woods's agent, Mark Steinberg, at Excel Sports Management. Keola Pang, his former Pleasant Valley teammate and Del Mar guest, was also cut out of his life, Jordan Russell style. Russell made a comeback. Not many did.

It certainly was not fair to solely blame Munn—or, perhaps, to blame her at all—for personal and business decisions made by her boyfriend. Rodgers had temporarily removed Russell from his life before he ever met Munn. He was his own man, and nobody was forcing him to do anything. Rodgers never needed much help in determining when to end a relationship.

"You get on his bad side, you cross him once, you are dead to him," said someone who knew him for many years in Green Bay.

So perhaps too many people close to the quarterback were too quick to finger a convenient fall guy, or fall gal, rather than hold him fully responsible for his own choices. Or maybe they were unwilling to consider that Munn had merely opened her boyfriend's eyes to the fact that, yes, some were taking advantage of Rodgers and trying to capitalize on his success.

"She was with me during the season and having her around meant so much to me," the quarterback told his radio cohost Jason Wilde. "To be able to have that stability off the field just allows you to play with a clear mind, I think, on the field, and not having to deal with any of those burdens that can come along if you're not dating the right person. So, thankfully I am."

At the same time, Munn did not help her own cause. The Christmas gifts that Ed and Darla had sent to their son and his girlfriend? Rather than regift them to someone else or offer them up for charity, Munn insulted her boyfriend's parents by sending the presents back to them in Chico. Sources said they coincidentally arrived at the Rodgers home on Ed's birthday, making him think initially that he had received a present from his son.

Given her devout religious views—Aaron's mother disapproved of premarital sex and was opposed to her middle child sharing a hotel room with his girlfriend even as an NFL player—Darla did not appreciate how Munn had joked about oral sex in an interview, or how she had publicly talked about her sex life with Aaron just before that fateful loss at Buffalo.

"She was saying all that shit and it pissed Darla off, really pissed her off," said someone close to the family.

Over the years, Darla and Ed believed they had reason to get livid again and again. Munn claimed in an interview on Andy Cohen's SiriusXM radio show that she had actually encouraged her boyfriend to build a bridge back to his parents, and also that Aaron had stopped speaking to Ed and Darla and his older brother, Luke, eight months before he started dating the actress.

"It's a lie," Ed Rodgers said.

With Ed as a sports chiropractor on staff at Whole Body Fitness, where Angelo Poli trained Aaron next door to Ed's office, and with Luke using his brother's image to sell sports-themed T-shirts for his apparel company, and with Jordan following in Aaron's quarterbacking footsteps, Munn had this to say to Cohen about the Rodgers family dynamic:

"I do believe that family and fame and success can be really complicated if their dreams are connected to your success. . . . Their work has a direct connection to what he does. At the end of the day, there's a lot of complications. I don't think either side of the road is clean, but I do think it's not OK when you try to stand on someone's shoulders and then throw dirt in their face, which is what I think they did with him."

No, Ed and Darla did not want to let those comments stand for this book.

Ed: "She just made stuff up to make herself look good. . . . She said the family was dysfunctional before she met Aaron, which is bull. We were going to all of his games; we were staying at his house. We had a great relationship. Nothing bad was going on."

Darla: "I can think about showbiz families that, like the Kardashians, climb all over each other for fame and stuff like that. But that's not our family. Nobody did that."

Aaron had been generous with his family for years, starting with his purchase of a new home for his parents before he was making killer NFL money. Ed and Darla had always wanted to live next to their good friends, the Rubys, in Chico, so when a piece of property opened up next to them on Donald Drive, Aaron bought it for his parents as a surprise for $330,000 and built a house for them for more than $1 million. The home came complete with solar panels to dramatically reduce electric bills.

Aaron provided cars to multiple family members and at times paid for vacations, private jet travel, and hotel bills. He gave his parents annual cash gifts of approximately $15,000 each, up to the federal maximum allowed without a tax imposed. Aaron helped his younger brother, Jordan, land an upgraded apartment for his final year at Vanderbilt and allowed his older brother, Luke, to live with him rent-free.

Did Aaron sense that his generosity was being taken for granted? And does a child or sibling who makes it big have an obligation to share his or her wealth with relatives until the end of time?

"If Aaron feels his family or other people in his life have laid claim to something based on his efforts," Jordan Russell told me, "Aaron will then go out of his way to make sure they earn their own way."

Munn agreed with that approach. She agreed that her boyfriend should not let his family do any fame-and-fortune chasing through him.

Munn had no interest in allowing Rodgers's family members access to her boyfriend's Lambeau Field suite. Aaron had grown up around strong, unyielding women—his mother was much like Darla's mother, Barbara Pittman, when it came to setting ground rules—and Munn was a presence in her own right.

Over time, Ed and Darla told others that they saw the actress as a chief culprit in the family division. Luke did the same. Rodgers's family members and friends were still citing Munn as a primary cause of the family division years after the actress and the quarterback broke up in 2017.

And yet Aaron never accepted the narrative that Olivia was a divisive force. In fact, Rodgers told me he absolved his ex-girlfriend of blame in the estrangement and said the actress "has nothing to do with all the years before." He said that his family issues are deep-rooted, though he declined to discuss the specifics of those issues for public consumption.

Given his history of not commenting on his family fractures, Aaron said he has been distressed over the years by the occasional leak or comment from a family member. He said he wishes he was granted the same respect he had shown his parents and siblings.

"I have questions about why they feel the need to talk about it, because it's like a game of poker," Rodgers said. "When you are holding all the cards, you don't have to bluff. There's nothing they can say other than make up stories, but look at the facts."

One regrettable fact in particular was all on Aaron and nobody else. In 2015, he had agreed to serve as a groomsman in the wedding of his former Cal teammate and roommate Francis Blay-Miezah, who later became a captain in the Alameda County Fire Department, and his Pleasant Valley schoolmate and friend Randi Coppage. Aaron's family had been invited. Blay-Miezah was close to Ed and Darla, who likened the former linebacker to a fourth son.

The May 23 wedding was held at Thomas Fogarty Winery and Vineyards in Woodside, California, in the Santa Cruz Mountains two thousand feet above Silicon Valley. "It was a cold and foggy day which made it that much more dreamy and romantic," Brent Holland Studios wrote in a Facebook post, with photos of a radiant bride and dignified groom.

Facing his new wife, dressed in a light, yellow-colored suit, Blay-Miezah cried during the ceremony when telling Randi how much she had changed his life, and how proud her late father was of the woman she had become. It was a moving scene in a beautiful event, and it was a shame Rodgers missed it.

He had sent word to Blay-Miezah the day before, the night before, or the morning of the wedding—depending on the source—that he would not be attending. (Rodgers denied that he notified the groom that late in the process.) Aaron and Olivia were scheduled to sit at his family's table, and those seats remained empty.

Luke posted photos on Instagram that included these hashtags in the caption: *#truefriendsshowup* . . . *#wouldntmissitfortheworld* . . . *#rememberwhereyoucamefrom*.

Aaron felt that his college roommate and teammate could have and should have honored his request to not invite his family to the wedding—Aaron was closest to Blay-Miezah, after all. But that day was about Francis and Randi, not Aaron, and still Rodgers could not rise above his issues with his family to honor that truth.

"I respect that opinion," Aaron said before describing it as wrong and lacking an understanding of "the complexity of the whole situation."

Some Rodgers family members did not see anything complex about Aaron's decision. "I think that was the last straw for Luke," said one family friend. "It was like, 'Who are you? I don't even want to fuckin' know you anymore.'"

Luke was likely the first man down in the family dispute. He was the best natural athlete among the Rodgers boys, and yet the one who did not become a major-college football star. On his LinkedIn page, Luke described himself as a three-time intramural basketball champ and two-time intramural flag-football champ at Chico State, where he studied premed before earning his MBA at San Diego State.

Bonded by their boyhood battles on the athletic fields, Luke and Aaron had been close enough to live together in Green Bay and in Del Mar. Luke worked as a bartender, as a sports marketing consultant, and as a participant in the Fuel TV adventure series *Clean Break* before his apparel company, Pro Merch, took off. Luke and business partner Austin Casselman cut an impressive deal with the Target chain.

Soon enough, in addition to Aaron and the Bears' Devin Hester, Pro Merch reached agreements with Seattle's Marshawn Lynch, Houston's Arian Foster, and San Francisco's Patrick Willis; landed required licensing deals with the NFL Players Association and Major League Baseball Players Association; and signed deals with legacy Hall of Famers in both sports. They were selling T-shirts designed to focus on the players' personalities in more than 1,600 Target stores nationwide, and contributing profits to charitable foundations and causes such as breast cancer awareness.

Aaron seemed to be on board with Pro Merch early on, until he wasn't. The quarterback said he helped his older brother land a group licensing agreement with the NFLPA but that he did not want to be named as a company founder "because I had nothing to do with it, and [Luke] was selling shirts with my picture on it."

Casselman said the T-shirt with the word "Relax" above Rodgers's face that Pro Merch put out in 2014 "sold tens of thousands in a short amount of time, which proves the theory of what we're doing." Asked about that T-shirt before the playoffs, Rodgers said, "Well, I can tell you I've seen zero of that money."

Luke had grown frustrated over Aaron's failure to get back to him on design approval in a timely fashion while he was in-season with the Packers. Aaron was not a fan of his brother using his likeness on shirts, though he dismissed Pro Merch as a nonfactor in the family dispute and said his issues with Luke "started way before that." (Luke declined to be interviewed for this book.)

Aaron was known to be unhappy that Luke appeared in the 2012 *Clean Break* series, which was advertised as a competition for men leaving behind the rut of their everyday routines for exotic adventures in Hawaii. The quarterback was annoyed by the notion that Luke needed to break free from his shadow after he provided him with financial support. Someone close to the family said this was an example of Aaron being too sensitive about a nonexistent slight.

Either way, Luke said in 2017, "It's hard not talking to your brother. It's not fun. It sucks."

Jordan was likely the last immediate family member who had been communicating with Aaron, since he was there with Munn in Phoenix on January 31, 2015, to see his brother win his second league MVP award, more than a month after the quarterback had cut off his parents. Jordan also spent a full day that spring on set with Aaron while he taped *Celebrity Jeopardy!*

Luke was attempting to arrange a sit-down with Aaron for the following day. The quarterback was scheduled to spend that day driving Munn to a filming session in the desert, so he texted Luke word that he was committed to his girlfriend and unavailable to meet. It was believed to be the last communication between the two for years.

Jordan might have had a shot at getting the brothers back together again, the way they were when Jordan was in eighth grade at Marsh Junior High and Aaron and Luke were coaching his basketball team. But sources said the possibility of the three brothers meeting with Ed and Darla in Chico for a family summit died when Aaron and Jordan had a blowup during a phone call. (Jordan did not respond to requests to be interviewed for this book.)

Meanwhile, Jordan was trying to navigate his own professional football journey. After his successful college career at Butte and Vanderbilt, Jordan had been signed and cut by three NFL teams within thirteen months of going undrafted in 2013. He was then signed by the Canadian Football League's BC Lions, who would be coached in 2015 by none other than Jeff Tedford, Aaron's coach at Cal. Tedford had been fired by Cal in 2012, angering his former star to the nth degree.

Jordan did not put on an impressive minicamp performance for the BC Lions. "He was trying to do some of Aaron's stuff," Tedford recalled. "I said, 'Hey Jordan, there's only one Aaron Rodgers in the world. You've got to fix your mechanics. You can't manufacture velocity on the ball like Aaron can.'"

Tedford invited Jordan to training camp anyway. Right after he attended the Blay-Miezah wedding, and right before the start of camp, Jordan called to report that he was retiring from football to pursue a career in TV.

And that career got a major boost in 2016, when Jordan appeared on the ABC dating-game series *The Bachelorette*. On his way to winning over a Dallas real estate developer named JoJo Fletcher on a date in an Argentine vineyard, Jordan told her and nearly seven million American viewers that his famous brother would not be joining them for their hometown date with his family in Chico on the next episode.

"I have a great relationship with my brother Luke," he said. "Me and Aaron don't really have that much of a relationship. It's just kind of the way he's chosen to do life, and I chose to stay close to my family and my parents and my brother and, yeah, it's not ideal. And I love him.

"I can't imagine what it's like to be in his shoes and have the pressure he has and the demands from people that he has. Don't have hard feelings against him. It's just how things go right now."

Jordan told Fletcher that he did not think Aaron was aware that he was appearing in this show. He conceded that his own football career had been a struggle under the weight of being a certain someone's little brother.

"Frankly at every step of my life I was just kind of disappointed," Jordan told Fletcher. "And no matter what I did, it was never good enough for a coach or for a teammate because I was being compared to someone who did it the best."

Their hometown date the following week in Chico featured Jordan and Fletcher, Ed and Darla, and Luke and his girlfriend.

Jordan said he missed Aaron a lot "especially in moments like this, because my family means so much." Luke said he missed Aaron too, and explained why neither he nor Jordan liked to discuss the estrangement this way:

"It pains both of us like, not to have that relationship. . . . I trust that God brings things full circle and that everything would just get back to us being a family."

During the show, the dinner table was set for a party of eight, with only six people seated. The two empty chairs at one end of the table, opposite Jordan and Fletcher, were not meant to suggest that the neighbors would be arriving late. They served as reminders that the famous quarterback and actress had cut themselves out of the script.

Aaron was irritated by his family's decision to film that scene, empty chairs and all, especially when he was not invited to participate. Not that he would have shown up. Aaron did not appreciate that Jordan was using their personal issues to increase his visibility for a potential TV career.

Back in Green Bay, when addressing reporters at training camp, Rodgers talked about Jordan's disclosures on *The Bachelorette* without talking about Jordan's disclosures on *The Bachelorette*.

"I haven't seen the show, to be honest with you, so it hasn't really affected me a whole lot," he said. "I've always found that it's a little inappropriate to talk publicly about some family matters, so I'm not going to speak on those things. But I wish him well in the competition."

If any human being was capable of performing conflict-resolution magic, and of leading the Rodgers family back to a unified place, it was probably Craig Rigsbee. He was the juco coach who restored everything for Aaron, and in return Aaron sometimes wore Butte gear and identified himself on *Sunday Night Football* telecasts as a product of Butte football, irritating the people at Cal. Rigsbee was also the juco athletic director who supported Jordan as he helped the 2008 Roadrunners go unbeaten and finish first in the JC Grid-wire national poll.

Rigsbee had strong relationships with Ed, Darla, and Luke too. They all knew him as an agenda-free advocate of the Rodgers family, and as one of the best communicators in the business, a guy who could connect with people of all ages, races, and socioeconomic backgrounds. Aaron could never try to tell him to stop talking and telling stories, because it would be like trying to tell Charles Barkley to stop talking and telling stories.

When Rigsbee's son Jordan signed with the Carolina Panthers in 2016, his father jokingly asked if he was planning on cutting off communication with him. "Dad, I'm a backup lineman," Jordan Rigsbee replied. "Nobody cares about me. We're never going to be estranged."

Many would have said the same of the Rodgers clan back in the day, as family members happily bounced from one athletic conquest to the next. Times and people change. In the summer of 2016, Rigsbee was attending the celebrity golf tournament at Lake Tahoe, the American Century Championship, when Aaron was introduced on the first tee.

This was just days after those back-to-back *Bachelorette* episodes aired. "And someone goes, 'Hey, are you Jordan Rodgers's brother?'" Rigsbee recalled. "Fucking he looked over there and he was legitimately pissed off and shook his head. . . . So, Jordan's more famous than him now?"

Rigsbee laughed. He was no more afraid to tell a story on Aaron than he was to tell his former quarterback what was right and what was wrong. After Rodgers won the Super Bowl, he was named Chico Sportsperson of the Year and was scheduled to receive his award at the Chico Sports Hall of Fame and Senior Athletes Banquet. When the quarterback told his former coach that he did not plan on attending, Rigsbee shot back, "Get your ass over here and sit at my table. You need to go."

"OK," Rodgers replied.

According to his hometown newspaper that was sponsoring the Sportsperson of the Year event, Rodgers was honored and humbled "while the crowd of 400 gave a rousing standing ovation." The man of the hour said all the right things and thanked all the right people, including the *Enterprise-Record* "for all the stories they've written and for the way they've treated me and my family."

Rodgers ended his speech by saying, "I have two hopes, one, that I can be a role model to younger athletes, and that I can properly thank all the teammates and the city of Chico for what they've meant to me and my family. Thank you."

And then Rodgers slipped out a back door, on Rigsbee's instructions, and disappeared into the night.

So many times, the old coach had witnessed the price of Rodgers's fame firsthand. Once a woman approached their table at the Tea Bar & Fusion Café in Chico and was going on and on about how Rodgers was the greatest before the quarterback replied, "Wait a minute, you don't even know me. You're making me uncomfortable. Please stop." Aaron signed a napkin for the woman to make her go away.

When it came to the star quarterback, Rigsbee said, people did not know (or care) when enough was enough. The old juco coach was not naming names, but he was no fan of those he perceived to be barnacles attached to the Rodgers cruise liner.

"They just can't be hanging on your coattails their whole lives," he said. "People try to take advantage of you and pretty soon they do other shit, and then you get pissed off, and it's a tough thing. Then they talk bad about you like, 'Oh, he's stuck up,' or, 'Oh, he abandoned me.' No, he's fuckin' tired of taking care of your ass."

In his early NFL days, when Rodgers was around Chico more, Rigsbee and his former juco star would meet up at The Bear, where Aaron had announced he was committing to Cal. Inevitably patrons would start looking and pointing and pulling out their phones to take pictures or to call buddies to tell them to get to The Bear ASAP. When people showed up with jerseys to sign, sometimes Aaron had to tell them, "Hey man, I'm just trying to have dinner."

Rodgers was never much of a drinker, of course, though Rigsbee got him going a few times on a double Stoli or three. One night at the 5th Street Steakhouse, one of Rodgers's local favorites, the quarterback decided he was going to have a drink.

"He goes, 'Get me one. No, two,'" Rigsbee recalled. "OK, so I order him two Stoli tonics with lime and he drinks it, and he says, 'This is pretty good. What is this?' I say, 'Stoli tonic with lime.' We ended up drinking five of them and got shitfaced. We get a taxi and we're singing Counting Crows songs because he's good friends with Adam Duritz."

Rigsbee would indeed be the best candidate to broker peace between Aaron and his family, if only he was up for the job. He was not. He did not believe it appropriate to inject himself into the drama.

"I don't get in between all that," Rigsbee told me. "I don't ask Aaron questions. The only thing I ever did is, I kind of got on his brothers' asses when they were down-talking him one time when they were in town. I said, 'That's enough of that shit. Do not say that shit in public, and don't talk about it now.'"

If Rigsbee was going to be most protective of one family member, it was Aaron. That was his guy. His quarterback. Rigsbee bristled when people who did not know Rodgers described him as selfish and arrogant from afar. He saw Aaron as his own man, nothing more or less, a guy who was never afraid to cut against the grain for what he believed in.

"And when you're super successful, now everybody wants a piece of you," Rigsbee said. "Everybody wants you to give them shit. Everyone says you owe them shit."

Like many fellow friends, Rigsbee did not feel that Rodgers got enough credit for his charitable deeds. In November 2018, when the Camp Fire raged across Paradise, a town in the Sierra Nevada foothills, and other Butte County communities as the most devastating wildfire in state history, Rodgers wore a "Butte Strong" hoodie in a Twitter video while pledging a million-dollar donation to the relief effort.

The quarterback was stepping up for his people. And no matter how much money he made or how much money he was worth, a million bucks was still a million bucks. It was a really thoughtful thing to do, while also helping one of his chief sponsors, State Farm, raise additional funds for victims of the fire.

But his younger brother, Jordan, who had become a college football analyst for the SEC Network, responded to that tweet with this post of his own: "PLEASE DONATE, SPREAD AWARENESS & SEND LOVE. But when your own Mom is home alone during the fires, car packed ready to evacuate, & you miss the fundamental first step of compassion; calling your parents to make sure they are safe. . . . Everything else just feels like an act." (The post was later deleted.)

Older brother Luke added his own response, writing, "Smells like cowardice this morning . . ." He also retweeted Jordan's post and went back and forth with another poster who called him out for putting a family matter in the public arena, telling the man that he had donated to the cause and checked on his parents.

These were cheap shots that deserved to be flagged for unnecessary roughness. No matter the circumstances, when you try to turn a positive into a negative, you are the problem.

"Well, [Aaron] had already bought them a house," Rigsbee said of Rodgers's parents, "and he's done a lot for them and a lot for his brothers too." Rigsbee called Jordan "a super nice kid" but criticized his decision to broadcast the family's issues with Aaron on *The Bachelorette* as a "terrible" move.

Over the years it was clear where the brothers stood on social media. In 2015, when Aaron jabbed Seattle quarterback Russell Wilson after a victory over the Seahawks by saying, "I think God was a Packers fan tonight" (Wilson had credited God after Seattle's stunning NFC title game victory in overtime eight months earlier), Jordan responded by praising Wilson for saying that he would remain humble and that everybody was entitled to their opinions.

"My parents taught us this as well," Jordan tweeted. "Way to take the high road @DangeRussWilson."

On National Siblings Day, 2018, Jordan posted a tribute to Luke on Instagram with a picture of them together and a caption that included this line: "I've looked up to this guy since I was a little kid." No sight or mention of the middle brother.

Jordan married JoJo Fletcher years later, after Luke had married Aimee Wathen, and Aaron was nowhere to be found in the photos because he was nowhere to be found at the weddings. When Luke announced the birth of his son Jack Jordan Rodgers on Instagram, he wrote to his pictured newborn (with his parents in the delivery room), "Your middle name is for @jrodgers11 and we can only pray you grow up to be as generous, kind, loyal (and tan) and an amazing man of character as your uncle Jordan."

Aaron had taken himself out of these moments with his extended radio silence, and with his series of no-shows at significant family events. He did not attend services for his grandfather Chuck Pittman, who died at eighty-seven in 2016, despite the fact, Barbara said, that her grandson "wrote many times over the years that he wanted to be the man Grandpa was. [Aaron] was a very loving person."

One family member who attended the graveside service was hoping against hope to spot Aaron sitting under a distant tree. Barbara Pittman did say that her grandson called her after Chuck's death "to tell me how sorry he was and how much he loved him and me. [He] also sent an e-mail. It really touched me."

Six months later, sportswriter Tyler Dunne, in a well-sourced *Bleacher Report* piece, questioned whether a struggling Rodgers was a leader capable of elevating his team. He reported fresh details on the family division and wondered if that division was impacting Rodgers's performance. A couple months after that, before Green Bay faced Dallas in a divisional playoff game, Karen Crouse of the *New York Times* quoted Ed Rodgers describing the *Bleacher Report* story as accurate and saying, "Fame can change things." Aaron's father told the *Times* that while he would not have chosen to make public the family's problems, "It's good to have it all come out."

Aaron definitely did not agree with that assessment. He protected his privacy the way a left tackle was supposed to protect him. Few things were more "inner" than Rodgers's inner circle. He was never comfortable with family and friends talking about him for the record, or with reporters who sought them out without seeking his blessing in advance.

One person in Green Bay who broke through that wall for a sneak peek was Kyle Cousineau, a real estate appraiser who was recognized by Cheesehead TV and other go-to team sources as the ultimate Packers superfan.

Cousineau hung out with Rodgers a handful of times. They had a mutual friend in Packers tight end Tom Crabtree, and the superfan would see the quarterback at a local karaoke place or bowling alley. Cousineau used to tend bar at the Abbey Bar & Grill, across the street from the team's training camp at St. Norbert College. Once, in the middle of a blizzard that had him thinking he'd close up early, Cousineau emerged from a swinging door in the back to find "this poor dude sitting at the bar with three buddies. It was Aaron Rodgers celebrating his birthday.

"Before I knew it there were thirty guys at the bar, twenty-five of them from the Packers, and I partied with them all night. We had a blast."

Cousineau figured Rodgers had picked this time to go out knowing that almost nobody else would be in this college joint on a stormy weeknight. The bartender knew that Brett Favre would have never picked a night like this to party, at least before he quit drinking. Favre needed people around him. They were his lifeblood.

Rodgers was a small-town quarterback who was comfortable in small-town Green Bay, which was basically Chico with snow blowers. But unlike his predecessor, he never wanted everyone to know everything about him. "Just a very guarded individual," Cousineau said.

He called Rodgers "the most calculated person I've ever talked to, even in private settings. When you talk to him and ask questions, he studies every syllable, and he knows what his answer will be and he will never miss a beat."

Cousineau attended a Foo Fighters concert with Rodgers and Crabtree in Madison in 2017 and ended up backstage, where the quarterback mingled with drummer Taylor Hawkins, had himself a beer, and did a shot of whiskey with Dave Grohl, the band's founder and lead singer.

"Then we went out to watch the show, and Aaron was drinking water," Cousineau said. "He didn't want people to see him drinking during the season."

Rodgers wanted people to see what he wanted them to see, nothing more. Four years into the family estrangement, he hated it when a mere mention in the press of being at home "with my folks in town for my birthday"—right after his brother Jordan had ripped him on social media for not contacting their parents during the wildfires—created headlines for major outlets everywhere. "Aaron Rodgers Making Peace with Parents After Nasty Public Feud," read the TMZ headline.

As it turned out, Rodgers didn't mean "folks" as in parents, but "folks" as in friends. Ed and Darla shared no such birthday reunion with their son.

Aaron's decision to divorce his family impacted more than his parents, brothers, and grandparents. He cut off communication with other relatives who had been part of his life, including Darla's two sisters, Valerie and Cheryl, who were around their nephew a lot when he was growing up. They had the sweetest memories of him too.

Valerie said a newborn Aaron played the role of Baby Jesus in that family Christmas Eve program and played other roles over the years in Christmastime performances—shaped by themes from a movie, a book, a painting, or an international custom—that the family had put on with as many as fourteen participants.

On Super Bowl Sunday, Valerie recalled how a preschool Aaron played with the other kids in the bedroom only during pregame festivities and warmups. After the opening kickoff, Aaron was sitting on the floor in front of the TV mesmerized by the big game and commenting (a lot) on the action.

"Auntie," little Aaron said to his aunt Cheryl, who went by Auntie Myrl (her middle name), "someday I'm going to play football. Someday I'm going to be on TV."

Auntie Myrl patted him on the head and promised Aaron that she would watch him. "You'd never think in a million years it would happen," she recalled.

The cute kid with the pleasant disposition turned out to be one in a million. One in fifty million.

Aaron was a great cousin to her triplets, he really was, and they all loved watching him play at Pleasant Valley High. "My kids were in third grade, and we didn't miss a football game," Auntie Myrl said.

"Every Friday we'd get in the car and go to Chico and meet everyone there. It was family night in the stands with Darla and Ed. We'd watch the game, see Aaron after the game, then leave to go home. My kids were sound asleep in the car when we got home Friday night. We did that every home game when Aaron and Jordan played ball and played at Butte too. . . . We would not have missed it for the world."

Aaron cosigned all the student loans for one of the triplets, Annie, so she could attend Emerson College in Massachusetts, where she played softball, interned at the New England Sports Network, and worked weekends on the *Boston Globe*'s sports desk. When Annie was younger and the triplets either attended Cal games or listened to them on the radio, they all wore Cal jerseys bearing the Rodgers name. When Annie and her brother, Willie, and sister, Emily, watched Green Bay games at home, they all wore Packers gear.

Aaron appreciated the support. "He always contacted the kids on their birthdays," Auntie Myrl said. "Until we didn't hear from him anymore."

Auntie Myrl had her theories as to why it all fell apart the way it did, why Aaron, in her words, "just disappeared" from all of their lives.

"I think that what happened with Aaron," she said for this book, "being raised so Christian . . . was he got to Cal and met kids from different countries and cultures, and they worshipped their own god their own way, and he realized they were good people. . . . And he started to make his own choices."

One person close to Rodgers described the extended family's code of conduct as black-and-white, with no room for shades of gray. "If you don't march along to the same guidelines of what you were taught to do, or instructed to do," that person said, "you were the black sheep."

Slowly but surely, Aaron did pull away from the strict religious dogma at the center of his upbringing and, eventually, from the people who still embraced it.

And then he met Olivia Munn. "I think Aaron took Olivia's side with whatever happened on a phone call or with Christmas presents," said one person close to the family. "They were a couple and he stood by her. . . . Aaron found a comrade [in Munn] who said, 'I see it the same way you see it.'"

Aaron did not cut off communication with all family members. He maintained a relationship with his uncle Chuck, the youngest of the four Pittman children, who was not communicating with his sisters. Aaron also stayed in contact with Uncle Chuck's two children.

But one of Chuck's sisters, Aunt Valerie, had been on the radio-silence side of it long enough to understand what her nephew's choices had done to the people who loved him most.

"All of my fond memories of Aaron predate at least 2014, when fame and fortune, for lack of a more plausible reason, must have had a major impact on him," Valerie wrote to me. "I understand that it is an inherent danger but thought my nephew, who had grown into a man exhibiting both exceptionally strong moral character and leadership, and had deep family values, would be able to remain steady and rise above the fray. He began to show disappointing signs of no longer being the same Aaron (which I do not want to elaborate on).

"It goes without saying that his 'lack of communication,' with no rational explanation or effort to overcome any misunderstandings, has caused untold pain and grief. Naturally, the hurt has been felt most deeply by his parents and brothers, who had always shared a very close relationship with him. How devastating to have a son and brother shut you out of his life, seemingly so suddenly, with no apparent reason.

"To my knowledge, he has made no effort to work things out. . . . I struggle to find a cause, or excuse, for turning your back on a loving family that always supported you, sacrificed for you, and helped you achieve your biggest dream. Surely the huge loss cannot be worth it in the long run.

"Both my mom and sister Darla seem to have always held onto hope and continued to pray for an eventual reconciliation, believing in the Parable of the Prodigal Son, ever ready to forgive. In my opinion, a reconciliation would mean the world to Aaron's immediate family, but not so much to his extended family, who have suffered from whatever angers him and [from] subsequent disinterest simply by association."

If given the opportunity, Valerie's sister Cheryl, Auntie Myrl, said she would tell her nephew to draw a line in the sand "and then let's step over it and not look back and enjoy the last part of our lives." Denied that opportunity for direct communication, she asked that one message be delivered to that little kid who promised her that he would someday play football on TV.

"Just tell him his auntie loves him," Auntie Myrl said.

• • •

JORDAN RUSSELL GOT a phone call out of left field while he was boarding a plane to Indonesia. Aaron Rodgers was on the line and hoping to end one of the many estrangements in his life.

"Hey man, I missed you," Rodgers told his old friend. "I need you back in my life."

Why in the world did the quarterback suddenly need the chef?

"I missed his friendship," Rodgers said for this book. "The way my life was going, I felt more a call to spirituality and that was what I felt like he was always talking about and interested in."

Paroled from the Island, Russell did not expect a full accounting from Rodgers of why he found it necessary to cut off all communication with the man who had been his best friend since they had met in their Pleasant Valley High Spanish class during their freshman year.

The conversation, Russell explained, "was more like, 'Hey man, look, the past is the past. I love you. You mean a lot to me. You've been there from the beginning. You're my brother. Let's move on.'"

Russell was prepared to move on under one condition. "If you want me back in your life," he said, "I'll be there. But I demand your respect."

Russell wanted it known that for all of their uplifting ups and distressing downs, he viewed his famous friend as an exceptional human being. Aaron Rodgers was a master of his craft, Russell reasoned, and he had been focused on the pursuit of perfection since the day Russell met him. The Cal roommate saw that pursuit up close, when all the other players were out doing what college kids do to have fun. But Aaron?

"He was in the lab," Russell said.

And nobody was allowed to interrupt him.

"Part of what it takes to become a master is to be myopic," Russell said, "to say the hell with everyone else and everything else who is not mission aligned.

"He has been single-focused on that mission, and if you're not there to help him in the direction that he's going . . . you'd better get out of the way."

• • •

AARON RODGERS'S FIRST agent, Mike Sullivan, was not the only observer who believed the quarterback was going to do things his way, and only his way, after he won the Super Bowl. As Sullivan said, Rodgers had felt "let down by everybody who evaluated him." It was time to trust his own instincts.

Rodgers had maintained his standing as a masterful NFL player after he won his second league MVP award, even if Tom Brady was winning the championships that his more talented counterpart was not winning.

Rodgers recovered from a 20–0 third-quarter deficit to beat the Detroit Lions in a December 2015 game decided on the final play—his 61-yard

Hail Mary touchdown heave to a fellow Cal player, Richard Rodgers. After Aaron Rodgers showed off his athleticism on a 17-yard scoring run, the Packers tried a lateral play in the final seconds before the Lions stopped it with a facemask tackle of the quarterback, who got the flag, 15 yards, and one more snap. Packers ball at their own 39, down 23–21, with nothing but zeroes on the clock.

"How far can Rodgers throw it?" CBS play-by-play man Jim Nantz said on the Thursday night broadcast. His partner, Phil Simms, said Rodgers could reach the end zone if he could get out of the pocket and give himself a running start.

Rodgers took the shotgun snap and started moving left before hitting the brakes and heading back to his right, barely avoiding a pass rusher. Then he gave himself that running start before launching a pass so high it looked like he was trying to throw it over the top of the Empire State Building from a spot on Thirty-Fourth Street.

"He turned thirty-two yesterday," Nantz said as the ball ascended toward the Ford Field ceiling. "Does he have a vintage moment in him?"

Richard Rodgers timed his jump perfectly in front of a scrum of jostling bodies and came down with the ball in the end zone. Aaron Rodgers took off his helmet as he ran down the field, making like Brett Favre in the Super Bowl.

The quarterback called "the Miracle in Motown" one of the greatest joys the Packers had ever experienced on the field. "I've never had a completed Hail Mary before," he said.

He would complete another one in a divisional-round playoff game at Arizona that finished off about as improbable a postseason drive as any quarterback had ever led. The Packers were down 20–13 with fifty-five seconds to go, facing a fourth-and-20 from their own 4-yard line. Their quarterback was standing in the end zone when he caught the snap and quickly executed his signature spin-out move to his left to avoid pressure. Rodgers took another running start and, as he hit the goal line, fired a half Hail Mary to Jeff Janis, a seventh-round draft pick from Saginaw Valley State and second-year receiver who had caught two passes the entire regular season.

Janis pulled in the strike for a 60-yard gain. Three snaps later, with four seconds on the clock and the ball at the Cardinals' 41, there was nothing halfway about the Hail Mary throw to come. Rodgers was initially supposed to roll right, according to left tackle David Bakhtiari, who said the quarterback had forgotten to give the protection assignment to his offensive linemen.

"He just told us to get to the line," the tackle recalled. The play clock was running down and Bakhtiari and guard Josh Sitton were yelling at center Corey Linsley to snap the ball. "It was an absolute fuckery of a play," Bakhtiari said.

But Rodgers knew the Cardinals were bringing pressure from his right, and just as Bakhtiari was shoving defensive end Calais Campbell to the turf, the quarterback executed that spin to his left again, this time unscripted.

"He was running like a chicken with its head cut off behind me," Bakhtiari said. "I was like, 'What the hell is going on?' That's when I became a spectator."

Rodgers then launched another moon shot just before he got hit and fell to the ground. Nobody had ever delivered a Hail Mary with as much arc and accuracy as A-Rod did.

Remarkably enough, in the middle of the Arizona end-zone logo, Janis rose high and beat two Cardinals for the ball—including five-time Pro Bowler Patrick Peterson—before crash-landing on his back. He had possession, and Packers fans who had escaped the Green Bay winter for the desert climate exploded in response.

"That's insane," Al Michaels shouted on NBC.

"That may be one of the great throws ever made," said his partner, Cris Collinsworth.

Bakhtiari ran up to Rodgers and screamed obscenities into his face, telling him that he was the man and the best of the best. "Quintessential Aaron," the tackle said.

With Green Bay riding high, this would have been the perfect time to go for 2 points and the victory. The Packers had never touched the ball in overtime the previous year in Seattle after Mike McCarthy coached too conservatively with the fourth-quarter lead. Could the Packers really take the chance of losing another coin toss and another season without the sport's best player seeing the field?

Yes, they could, McCarthy decided, as he charged Mason Crosby to kick the extra point and send the game into overtime. Both sides gathered for the midfield coin toss and, for the second straight year, Rodgers called tails.

Tails never fails.

Referee Clete Blakeman tossed the coin and nearly caused a riot when it landed on heads without ever flipping. Blakeman gave himself a mulligan and, wouldn't you know it, the coin came up heads again.

Tails had failed Rodgers two years in a row, and the quarterback waved his right arm in disgust.

On the Arizona sideline, Cardinals executive Terry McDonough walked up to star receiver Larry Fitzgerald and said, "Fitzy, you gotta win this game for us."

The receiver replied, "Come on, T, you know me. Don't worry, I got it."

On the first play of overtime, Arizona quarterback Carson Palmer bounced out of trouble and threw across his body toward the left side to Fitzgerald, who cut across the field, broke a couple of tackles, and raced all the way to the Green Bay 5-yard line for a 75-yard gain.

Two snaps later, Fitzgerald was in the end zone and the Packers were heading home early for a fifth consecutive postseason. McCarthy's last three playoff losses had been decided on the final play.

• • •

THE FOLLOWING SEASON, the Packers were reeling at 4-6 before their franchise player had the audacity to say, "I feel like we can run the table, I really do." The Packers ran the table, finishing the regular season 6-0 and then beating the Giants by 25 points in a wild-card playoff game. Rodgers threw 19 touchdown passes in those games, and had no interceptions in his 240 pass attempts. He even connected on yet another Hail Mary pass against the Giants at the end of the first half that set the blowout in motion and booked a divisional-round matchup with Dallas on the road.

It looked like overtime again with twelve seconds left and the score tied, 31–31. Rodgers, who actually threw a pick in this game, had just been blasted from the blind side by a blitzing Jeff Heath, and somehow did not fumble the ball. The Packers faced a third-and-20 after the sack and an incompletion, ball on their own 32.

"I first thought he was going to try to just throw another Hail Mary," Packers president Mark Murphy said. "I just didn't think there was any way he could get it to the end zone."

It didn't matter. Rodgers needed only a field goal, so this was going to be more of a laser. He did not even call a play in the huddle. With the play clock running out, A-Rod had to go streetball on this one.

He asked for dash protection on his rollout, with left guard Lane Taylor leaking out with him in bodyguard mode. They had talked about it a bit the previous morning. Rodgers quickly assigned routes to tight end Jared Cook and wideout Davante Adams, and told the other receivers to freelance their way over to the left side of the field and find a hole. McCarthy deserved credit for giving Rodgers a menu of plays to pick from in a crisis like this and for giving him the freedom to improvise on the fly.

Out of shotgun formation, Rodgers rolled left, looked for an open man in the secondary, scrambled closer to the Dallas sideline, and then, while on the move, fired down that sideline to Cook, who somehow kept his toes inbound as he fell across the line for a 36-yard gain. If it was not the finest throw of Aaron Rodgers's career, it was close enough.

"It's incredible watching him," said rookie Cowboys quarterback Dak Prescott. "I hate it in this circumstance, but he is an incredible quarterback."

Mason Crosby nailed the 51-yarder to send the Packers to an NFC Championship Game that they would lose, 44–21, to the Atlanta Falcons, who would later suffer a devastating Super Bowl collapse to the benefit of—who else?—the New England Patriots. Rodgers had lost yet another chance to stop Tom Brady, who now owned five championship rings.

But in a team sport, it was hard to diminish Rodgers's individual greatness. He had made so many clutch plays, enough to own multiple rings himself, only to be done in by suspect coaching and defense and special-teams play . . . and bad coin-toss luck.

"At the end of the day," Cowboys coach Jason Garrett said of Rodgers, "they're going to talk about that guy as one of the top three quarterbacks who ever laced them up. Someone said earlier this week, 'He's been hot for the last seven or eight weeks.' He's been hot since 2008."

Rodgers was thirty-three. McCarthy was now officially running out of time to maximize his superstar's prime. The stress of the failed chase for the second Super Bowl title was impacting the coach-quarterback relationship. The missed opportunities were stacking up, one on top of the other, creating a mountain of evidence that this partnership needed to be broken up.

Divorce was in the air. Aaron Rodgers was getting ready to send his head coach to the Island.

11

NO LOVE LOST

AARON RODGERS STEPPED to the podium, tugged at the arms of his sweater, and faced a conference room full of reporters ready to flex his considerable muscle.

This was the late afternoon of September 30, 2018, Lambeau Field, and Rodgers was in the early hours of a contract extension scheduled to pay him $176 million over six years. He had just beaten the Buffalo Bills despite playing with a bad knee and a broken leg.

Rodgers suffered the injury on a first-half sack in the Sunday night season opener against the Chicago Bears. He grabbed his left leg on the ground and got carted off the field with a distant look in his eye. Mike McCarthy was told on his headset that Rodgers was done for the year, a season after Minnesota linebacker Anthony Barr broke the quarterback's right collarbone and limited him to seven games.

Rodgers was tested at halftime before somehow talking himself back into action. When the crowd cheered him on his return from the locker room, Rodgers told himself, "We might as well win this thing." And win it the Packers did, 24–23, with their quarterback passing for 273 yards in the second half.

Hopping about in the pocket on one good wheel, Rodgers erased a 20–0 third-quarter deficit by throwing 3 touchdown passes in the fourth quarter for the first time in his career, earning his sixteenth victory over the Bears—his most over any opponent. In the one hundredth season of Green Bay Packers football, Rodgers had just scripted the greatest fourth-quarter comeback in franchise history.

It was another stunning display of physical and mental toughness from Rodgers, as was his ability to play through the pain of a tibial plateau fracture (a break in the top of the shinbone, involving the knee) and a sprained medial collateral ligament for the rest of the year.

"I thought the season was over for him," said offensive coordinator Joe Philbin, who had returned to Green Bay after his time as Dolphins head coach and Colts assistant. "What he was able to do the first four or five weeks, he had to live in the training room. I was shocked he was able to play. We had to play the whole game in the pistol and shotgun because he couldn't get under center for a while."

Given the circumstances, every victory was a cause for a postseason-like celebration. And yet when Rodgers was done beating the Bills, 22–0, to raise Green Bay's record to 2-1-1, he did the strangest thing in his postgame press conference.

He called an all-out blitz on McCarthy.

In a give-and-take that lasted six minutes and thirty seconds, Rodgers did not cite McCarthy's name when describing an offense that had gained 423 yards as "terrible," or when saying the performance "was as bad as we've played on offense with that many yards in a long time."

Rodgers complained that there was "no flow to the game." He said Green Bay's defense competed at a championship level, and that the offense competed at a nonplayoff level. He said that the Packers needed to put their playmakers in position to make a greater difference, and that star receiver Davante Adams, who was targeted fourteen times, should have been targeted twenty times.

The quarterback was not blaming himself for these flaws in approach. Asked how the team should go about putting Adams and others in better position to succeed, Rodgers said, "It's by the plan."

Mike McCarthy's plan.

Though it produced 423 yards and 22 points, Rodgers felt the Packers should have been good for 600 yards and 45 points against Buffalo, even with the franchise player wearing a knee brace. Rodgers was asked about his level of input.

"Coaches put the plan together," he said. "I tell them what calls I like, and we go."

And with that Rodgers exited stage right, leaving behind a group of reporters that was not expecting such a negative assessment after Green Bay's first shutout since 2010. Those reporters figured that first-year defensive coordinator Mike Pettine, who had replaced the fired Dom Capers, might qualify as the story of the day.

Rodgers called an audible on all of that. On his way out of the room, ESPN's Packers beat reporter, Rob Demovsky, looked at Pete Dougherty of the *Press-Gazette* and said, "Holy shit. He's trying to get McCarthy fired."

After thirteen years together, Rodgers wanted to end the partnership. It was clear. It was happening.

The signs of discontent had been there for a while. During an overtime victory over Cincinnati in 2017, Rodgers was seen staring at his sideline from the field and twice shouting, "Stupid fucking call." During a loss to the Bengals in 2013, the quarterback and McCarthy had an intense argument over a play call, which both later dismissed as a normal, heat-of-the-moment interaction.

At that point, the Packers were 6-18 in games decided by 4 points or fewer in the five-plus years Rodgers had served as McCarthy's starter. Their failures in close games and in postseason games since winning the Super Bowl naturally created tension in the relationship that only worsened with time.

It was hard not to measure Rodgers and McCarthy against the NFL's standard, Tom Brady and Bill Belichick, since New England's partnership had won five Super Bowls and had appeared in eight by the start of the 2018 season, including two titles in four trips to the big game since Rodgers became Green Bay's starter in 2008.

McCarthy was certainly not a bad coach; he had won at least ten games eight times in his first twelve years with the Packers. But he was not a great coach either, while Belichick was arguably the greatest of all time. Brady had a major advantage over Rodgers at the second-most important position in the sport (head coach), and in Josh McDaniels he also had perhaps the best offensive coordinator of his generation.

In 2016, Brady had told one NFL head coach that if Rodgers had the benefit of the Patriots' system and advance intel on opposing defenses, "he'd throw for seven thousand yards every year. He's so much more talented than me." Brady later said Rodgers inspired him to practice harder because of how brilliantly he managed his pocket game. "His ability to throw the football is unlike anyone in probably the history of the league," Brady said. "It's pretty awesome to watch. He throws some of the best incompletions I've ever seen."

That was a hell of a way to put it. Like Rodgers, Brady's inner fire was fueled by past doubts and slights—he was a former seventh-stringer at Michigan who was drafted in 2000 after 198 players were picked ahead of him. But for all of his winning intangibles, and his Michael Jordan–esque hunger to conquer all, Brady never had Rodgers's physical ability. So why were Belichick's Patriots getting so much more out of their quarterback than McCarthy's Packers were getting out of theirs?

"I think Aaron is the greatest thrower of the football ever . . . though Patrick Mahomes is starting to challenge that," NBC analyst Chris Simms, a former NFL quarterback and Belichick assistant, said for this book. "I always fight the critics and say, 'You don't think Aaron Rodgers would've won six Super Bowls with the Patriots?' I'm a guy who thinks they would have won ten in a row with Aaron Rodgers as quarterback of the Patriots. Has there ever been an organization that has failed a guy more than the Green Bay Packers have failed him?"

Simms pointed out that Belichick, long known as a defensive mastermind, was ahead of the field offensively in using the slot receiver position as a lethal weapon and in developing the two–tight end set. Given that Rodgers had elite mobility and one of the quickest releases and strongest arms the game had seen, and that he owned the all-time best touchdown-interception ratio, Simms argued that McCarthy's West Coast system suffered from a failure of imagination.

"The offense is elementary," said Simms, whose father, Phil, a longtime CBS analyst, was a Super Bowl MVP with the Giants. "Me and Dad would be watching Packers film during the season and going, 'This offense couldn't be any more basic. It couldn't be any more elementary if it were the third day of training camp.' Really, what they've been asking [Rodgers] to do for a long period of time is drop back, make a bunch of people miss, and throw a laser across the field that almost nobody else can throw.

"Then it's 'He can't win the big game.' Nobody looks at Green Bay's offense and says, 'This is creative.' . . . And he doesn't have that Belichick defense. It's always, 'Aaron Rodgers can't win the big game.' Green Bay is not even in the playoffs without Aaron Rodgers."

Simms argued that the New England system created immense opportunity for its franchise quarterback. "Nobody threw to more wide-open receivers in the history of football than Tom Brady," he told me.

"If Aaron Rodgers went to New England, oh my God, even Aaron doesn't know how good he'd be in that system.... If you put Brady and Rodgers on the practice field together, there's not one thing Brady will ever do better than Rodgers. Brady is a great leader, we know that. But Brady was also taught how to be that, how to be part of the culture and system. In Green Bay, that was never there.... Brady had Belichick to teach him how to lead and how to work."

Before Packers president Mark Murphy replaced him in 2018 with Brian Gutekunst, GM Ted Thompson also consistently failed to field a top-ten defense to supplement his all-world quarterback. The Packers were fifth in the league in yards allowed in their 2010 championship season, but in 2018 found themselves near the end of a run of nine straight years outside of the top ten in that defensive category, which included only one season better than a ranking of fifteenth.

Thompson believed in the old-school, draft-'em-and-develop-'em approach to building a roster, but his success rate in selecting college prospects was hit-or-miss at best. The Packers were rarely significant players in free agency, and the big veteran names they had signed over the years were found on the defensive side of the ball (Reggie White, Charles Woodson, Julius Peppers).

"At one point Aaron Rodgers was as close to the greatest one-man show ever seen in the history of the sport," Simms said. "But that's where football is fucked up. It's not basketball. You can't carry a team to a championship if you don't have the right support."

Or the right head coach. Rodgers did not personally dislike McCarthy; he thoroughly enjoyed their weekly Thursday meetings that could go on for hours, two football guys talking about far more than route trees and blitz pickups.

"Those were fifty percent football, the other fifty percent life," McCarthy said. "I got to watch him grow up. He was just a young kid who could go to the mall on Fridays, then he became the starter, and then his life became what it is now."

Rodgers and McCarthy did win a Super Bowl together. Nobody could take that away from either man.

Coach and quarterback subscribed to the notion that conflict was good and resolution was even better in maintaining and growing a relationship in a highly competitive arena. They argued, and then they hugged it out. They both wanted to know what, exactly, was wrong with that?

"From my perspective, it was clearly just two competitive individuals who had worked together a long time," McCarthy said for this book. "And when those things happen, when we were always pushing the envelope offensively, there was urgency to win another Super Bowl as time grew on. I think it's part of our industry that you can do ninety-eight positive things but the two things that get interest are the arguments or disagreements. . . . Aaron is super competitive and wears his emotions on his sleeve."

But through his actions and the words he shared with people close to him, Rodgers clearly did not see McCarthy as his intellectual equal. And whether he was in a meeting room with a coach or in a pregame debrief with network broadcasters and producers, Rodgers had a hard time hiding it when he felt he was dealing with someone who was not seeing or thinking the game on his level.

Of course, his feelings about McCarthy's offense and how he called plays were shaped, to some degree, by their relative lack of postseason success. Brady and Belichick had their problems, especially after the coach drafted the quarterback's would-be successor, Jimmy Garoppolo, in 2014. But in New England, the championships and the coach's near-maniacal work ethic and attention to detail kept putting those problems in a box to be stored in the facility basement, for the time being anyway.

"I respected [Belichick's] work ethic so much because I knew he was combing through every single bit of film every single week to try to put us in a position to succeed," Brady said. "So, when someone critiques you, 'OK, I'll embrace that.' Now, if you're not putting in the work and you're critiquing me, ehh, I may not listen to it."

Was McCarthy grinding at a Belichickian pace? Or was he getting massages in his office during meetings, as Tyler Dunne of *Bleacher Report* would write? One Packers source said the coach did book some massages during Saturday meetings that were called "Rodgers Presents," a one-man Broadway show which featured the quarterback discussing with teammates the plays and checks he planned to use the following day, with some of Aaron's whimsical humor sprinkled in. McCarthy called the massage stories "ridiculous" and "utterly absurd" and "a cheap shot" that he did not deserve.

"I do have a work ethic," McCarthy said. "That's one thing I have."

In Green Bay, the postseason failures inspired a blame game that framed Rodgers as the anti-Brady in the clutch. The quarterback needed to take that out on someone. At times McCarthy was that someone.

Even the people who loved the Packers the most could see how Rodgers felt about his head coach as a 7-9 season in 2017 (with Rodgers missing nine games) started veering into a 6-9-1 season in 2018 (with Rodgers playing hurt all year). Bob Harlan began working in the team's front office in 1971—a dozen years after he interviewed a rookie Packers coach named Vince Lombardi as a young United Press International reporter—and was still serving as chairman emeritus more than a half century later when he recalled how his friend Rodgers interacted with McCarthy.

"I don't think they were as close at the end," Harlan said, "and it's too bad because I think Mike had a lot to do with Aaron's development. I'd watch Aaron come to the sideline and there was not a lot of talk between the two of them, and then I watched that confrontation. It wasn't really warm.... In watching them come off the field, sometimes Aaron just walked by Mike when it looked like Mike wanted to talk to him. And that's not good."

Wayne Larrivee grew up a Packers fan in western Massachusetts, near the New York state border, carrying to school a metal lunchbox graced by the image of franchise great Jim Taylor, and yet the team's longtime radio voice was not blind to the inevitable Rodgers-McCarthy endgame unfolding before him.

"From my seat I sensed they were growing apart as coach and player," Larrivee said. "In the end there was frustration with the playoff losses, and one began to wonder if they could get it done together again. I just sensed that they were growing apart."

Sixth-year left tackle David Bakhtiari, a close friend of Rodgers and a Pro Bowler in 2016, thought the partnership between the quarterback and the head coach had grown a little stale. "I think probably egos were involved," he told me, "and they just started fracturing the relationship."

Rodgers had been telling people for years that he had issues with McCarthy that went beyond his Pittsburgh accent. In fact, even before he became a starter, Rodgers had issues with his head coach, starting with the fact that McCarthy did not think that the Cal quarterback was good enough for his employer in 2005, the San Francisco 49ers, who were holding the first pick in the draft.

Rodgers said he would joke with McCarthy about that botched evaluation, and the coach called those jabs nothing more than "busting chops." But there was always a surplus of truth in the quarterback's humor. Rodgers randomly brought up McCarthy's bygone love for Alex Smith in this meeting or that meeting, just to remind his head coach that he had not forgotten.

As former 49ers head coach Mike Nolan had said, Rodgers gave McCarthy an earful and McCarthy deserved that earful. "Those two butted heads a lot," said one Packers source who had daily interactions with both men. "Mike picked Alex Smith, and you had this Pittsburgh tough guy dealing with an intellectual tough guy from California, and Aaron's arrogance did show up at the time.

"They used to try to get Aaron to do power lifts [for his legs], and he was like, 'I don't want to do that.' He had a very specified vision for the kind of player he wanted to be and the preparation that went into that, and probably to his own detriment. He didn't want to listen at times to people. He knew what he wanted. . . . So, it would not be unusual to see [Rodgers and McCarthy] in the hallway having a talk that sometimes got pretty intense, both before and after Aaron became a starter. . . . There were quite a few talks between McCarthy and Aaron, not all of them positive."

One person close to Rodgers criticized the head coach for not soliciting more input from his most valuable player and for not calling more of the plays that the quarterback was most comfortable with. "McCarthy was known to scratch things out and expect [the Packers] to implement them on Sunday after the Thursday night meeting, when he always met with Aaron and asked, 'What are you most comfortable with in this game plan?'" the person said. "And Aaron would tell him A, B, and C, and then they'd get to the game and never run them."

McCarthy denied the claims that he did not call Rodgers's preferred plays and that he tried to install plays very late in the work week. "I think that's all a reach," he said. "That's totally different from what I believe in. Everything I do offensively is built around the quarterback being successful." For a Sunday game, McCarthy said he always made sure his players left the building on Thursdays with a full command of the game plan that could be tweaked and cleaned up in the Saturday dress rehearsals.

A Packers source contended that McCarthy did occasionally come away from a televised Thursday night NFL game or a Saturday afternoon college game with a play or plays he wanted to implement.

"Yeah, that definitely happened," said the source, who pointed out that other NFL head coaches did the same thing.

One longtime friend of Rodgers said that as much as the quarterback loved Tom Clements, the position coach and offensive coordinator who left Green Bay after the 2016 season, "he was always dissatisfied with [McCarthy's] play calling."

Another former teammate and friend said that he never heard Rodgers complain about McCarthy on a personal level. It was always business. Strictly business. "He complained like, 'We should be doing X, Y, and Z and we're over here doing this,'" that person said. "Especially at a crucial time of the game, if the clock was an issue, Aaron was like, 'Let me take care of it and handle it.'"

Veteran tight end Marcedes Lewis, who entered the league in 2006 and joined the Packers in 2018, remembered a time when McCarthy called a play and Rodgers dismissed it in the huddle, came up with his own script for the receivers and protection for the linemen, and completed a 40-yard pass.

"I'm like, 'What's really going on?'" Lewis said. "I've never seen anything like that before in my life. . . . I feel like Aaron had his own set of things that he wanted to do, then obviously McCarthy had his things that he wanted to do. I just think there was a little dysfunction."

To talk to people who knew Rodgers and to family members who talked football with him before the estrangement was to hear the same observations about McCarthy over and over. His offense was unimaginative. He was too conservative a play caller. He was a nice man who was overmatched.

A veteran Packers player said that one of Rodgers's biggest problems with McCarthy involved the game plan for Green Bay's devastating 2014 NFC Championship Game loss to Seattle. Rodgers had apparently done a deep-dive study of the Seahawks that year and found that Dallas Cowboys quarterback Tony Romo had hurt their defense in a 30–23 victory with a half dozen plays that seemed indefensible. The player said Rodgers wanted those plays called over and over against Seattle, and McCarthy called only a few of them one time each.

Maura Mandt, executive producer of ESPN's ESPY Awards show and a close friend of Rodgers (he sometimes stayed at her Hollywood area home), often privately complained to people about McCarthy, seemingly echoing the quarterback's thoughts. Another longtime friend of Rodgers swore that he would have matched Brady's number of championship rings if only he had Belichick in his corner.

Young receivers who listened to Rodgers's revised directions in the huddle, instead of running the particular play that McCarthy called, were sometimes confronted on the sideline about why they did what they did, putting them in the uncomfortable position of either fingering the franchise quarterback or taking one for the team. A-Rod's team.

Rodgers did have the right to audible away from his head coach's call. "I don't care, if you have two ten-years-plus guys working together, they're not always going to agree on choices you make," McCarthy said. "We did a tremendous amount at the line of scrimmage. I trusted him to make those decisions."

And yet, as Kalyn Kahler wrote for *Sports Illustrated*, Rodgers changed plays so often that it could be difficult for McCarthy "to get into a rhythm as the play caller. McCarthy might call the same play three times in a game, without the play actually being run as he called it. And if McCarthy calls a play that Rodgers doesn't like early in the game, that can sour the mood for the rest of the game."

Or for the rest of the season. Something was off about the 2018 Packers right from the start, and one of McCarthy's chief lieutenants, Philbin, sensed it. He was a Rodgers favorite who used to entertain the quarterback in his early Green Bay years with his Saturday "Cup of Joe" speeches, talking about colonial life in his home state of Massachusetts, telling the players about the shot of Jameson or the Guinness beer he drank the previous night, and once even dressing up as a pilgrim before a Thanksgiving Day game at Detroit.

"Some of it was off the wall," Philbin conceded. His players were under so much pressure that occasionally it made sense to keep things light.

The offensive coordinator had been away from the Packers since the end of the 2011 season, and when he rejoined the staff in 2018, he thought he was more or less walking back into the same organization that had won the Super Bowl and had gone 15-1 in his last two seasons in Green Bay. He was mistaken.

"Sometimes it's hard to go back," Philbin said for this book. "You think everything is going to be the same, and that was probably a mistake on my part. It was a different vibe. I don't think it was necessarily Mike McCarthy and Aaron Rodgers. It was a different vibe organizationally and in the locker room. It was just different.

"I don't know if there was pressure on everybody because Aaron got hurt in 2017. I can't really put my finger on it. . . . I could feel some differences even before we had OTAs."

Two weeks after Rodgers essentially ripped McCarthy in his postgame presser, prompting an hourlong clear-the-air session in the coach's office the following day, the Packers looked like the Packers and Rodgers looked like Rodgers. Starting at his own 10-yard line with no time-outs left and 1:07 to play, and with Green Bay and San Francisco locked in a 30–30 *Monday Night Football* game, Rodgers executed a brilliant drive defined by his athleticism (a 21-yard run on his bad knee) and his precision. He completed 19-yard sideline throws to rookie Equanimeous St. Brown and to Davante Adams inside the final fifteen seconds that led them directly out of bounds.

His second straight game of at least 400 passing yards set up Mason Crosby, who kicked the winning 27-yard field goal with no time on the clock, making up for his four misses (and one extra-point miss) the previous week at Detroit. The Packers appeared fine at 3-2-1 heading into their bye week.

And then they lost five of their next six games, including one to Brady and Belichick in New England. In the middle of that stretch, the Packers lost at Seattle after Rodgers misfired on an easy third-down throw and McCarthy chose to punt on fourth-and-2 from his own 33-yard line with 4:20 to play and the home team leading, 27–24. The Packers never again touched the ball, falling to 1-5 at CenturyLink Field under McCarthy.

"It was definitely a consideration," the losing coach said of going for it on fourth down. "But with the one time-out and the clock stopped at two minutes, we played the numbers."

The numbers actually supported a play from scrimmage—teams converted on fourth-and-2 more than 50 percent of the time, and Rodgers threw for a first down on third- and fourth-and-2 more than 62 percent of the time, according to Football Outsiders.

The coach revealed that his initial thought was to try to get the first down before a conversation with his staff persuaded him to punt the ball to the league's best rushing offense, which proceeded to gain the two first downs necessary to run out the clock. Given his history in that building, including his disastrously conservative calls in an NFC Championship Game that Green Bay just handed away, McCarthy should have trusted his first instinct.

His decision summoned the comments made by Greg Jennings the previous summer, when the former Packers receiver said the head coach's cautious approach had hurt past teams. "If you watch New England play, when they have a lead," Jennings said, "they go for your throat."

On December 2, Aaron Rodgers's thirty-fifth birthday, the Packers fired McCarthy after they lost to the 2-9 Arizona Cardinals at Lambeau, falling to 4-7-1 on the year. Philbin was named the interim coach for the final four games.

"The 2018 season has not lived up to the expectations and standards of the Green Bay Packers," Mark Murphy said in a statement. "As a result, I made the difficult decision to relieve Mike McCarthy of his role as head coach, effective immediately. Mike has been a terrific head coach and leader of the Packers for thirteen seasons, during which time we experienced a great deal of success on and off the field."

It was a cruel way to fire a man who had a nearby street named after him. Murphy, a former NFL safety for Washington and college athletic director who became the Packers' president and CEO in 2007, had increased his own power when replacing GM Ted Thompson, who had been suffering from an autonomic disorder, with Brian Gutekunst after the 2017 season. Against the grain of franchise tradition, Murphy decided that the GM would no longer have autonomy over football operations. Gutekunst would report to him, as would McCarthy and the newly promoted executive VP of football operations (Russ Ball).

The publicly owned Packers did not have a traditional overlord atop the organization, so at league meetings the billionaires who ran the other clubs did not view Green Bay's representative the same way. "We were not treated as equals, or shown the same level of deference," said one longtime team official, who described "an inferiority complex" that Packers reps felt at those meetings. Though the billionaires said they loved Green Bay's underdog story, they did not see Mark Murphy as one of them.

But now Murphy was at least carrying a bigger stick in-house. He should not have swung it at McCarthy, who deserved the courtesy of a full season before he was let go. He had earned that much. "It couldn't have been handled any worse," said McCarthy, who later added: "It's the only negative thing I can say about the Packers."

By any measure, McCarthy had a good run in Green Bay. "I can't complain a whole lot about Mike," Rodgers told me, "because I had so much freedom at the line of scrimmage. Even if he called something that I didn't like, we had a ton of stuff we could get to. . . .

"You can nitpick all you want. We had a lot of success, we butted heads from time to time, but you look back at it, I can't complain about the freedom that I had. And we lit it up for a lot of years."

McCarthy left Green Bay with a career regular-season record of 125-77-2, a postseason record of 10-8, and a place among only four NFL coaches to ever lead their teams to a streak of at least eight consecutive playoff appearances. Many football coaches would kill for those numbers, especially if they came packaged with a Lombardi Trophy.

And yet the McCarthy era was recalled more for what did not happen, as opposed to what did happen. He was 1-3 in the NFC Championship Game. He won "only" one championship with a quarterback and team that seemed destined for multiple rings.

Rodgers said he was shocked when he learned the news. This was a strange season for him, all across the board. He was angered when the quarterbacks coach he had grown close to, Alex Van Pelt, was not retained after the 2017 season—a move made without Rodgers's input—and was replaced by one of McCarthy's old Pittsburgh buddies, Frank Cignetti, who was not embraced by the franchise player.

Receiver Jordy Nelson had been released in the offseason, and Randall Cobb had been limited by injury, compelling Rodgers to force-feed Adams (111 receptions) while struggling to build a rapport with rookies Marquez Valdes-Scantling and St. Brown. Rodgers broke Tom Brady's NFL record by throwing 402 consecutive passes without an interception (he threw only two picks all year), but his touchdown percentage (4.2) was a career low and less than half his peak 2011 standard, and he was sacked 49 times.

McCarthy wasn't around for the finish, and Murphy wanted it made clear that the quarterback had nothing to do with the coach's termination. No matter how the Packers wanted to frame it, Rodgers had won the long-game battle of wills with McCarthy, as expected.

Rodgers was hoping Philbin would get a serious look as McCarthy's potential successor but knew that was a long shot. He played for Philbin anyway, even with the Packers out of it, and ended up with a concussion and a temporary loss of vision suffered in the season-ending 31–0 loss to Detroit.

Nobody ever said that Rodgers wasn't tough.

The quarterback maintained that he did not need to be involved in the hiring of McCarthy's replacement, while noting that he always had productive communication with Murphy and Gutekunst and that "their offices, like they say, are always open."

Just not quite as open as Rodgers might have thought. The Green Bay Packers were always old-school thinkers who believed that players play, coaches coach, and decision-makers decision-make.

Mark Murphy might not have belonged to the billionaire boys club of NFL owners, but he was the one running Titletown. And he did not anoint himself power broker in chief to hand off his power to a quarterback. So, the team president set clear boundaries in the search for the next head coach.

"Obviously Aaron is free to provide input and talk to us," Murphy said. "But he won't be part of the process."

• • •

AARON RODGERS HAD eight yards to go. Eight yards to score a touchdown in the closing minutes of the NFC Championship Game against Tom Brady and his new team, the Tampa Bay Buccaneers, and then he would get a shot at a two-point conversion and overtime and a potential trip to the Super Bowl, at last.

The Buccaneers were holding a 31–23 lead in front of 7,772 fans at Lambeau Field, what passed for a big crowd in the era of COVID-19 restrictions. Coaches and personnel were wearing masks on the sidelines, adding to the surreal scene. It was first down, 2:22 left on the clock, and Rodgers had a chance to wipe away so much more than the unforced errors committed by his team earlier in this game.

These final 142 seconds were everything for Rodgers, and that fact had little to do with Green Bay's blowout loss in Tampa in October, when Rodgers put on his only truly bad performance of the 2020 season and one of the worst of his career, checking in with a quarterback rating of 35.4 that Brady nearly tripled.

Avenging a regular-season loss, even one to Brady, did not make Rodgers's top-twenty-five list of concerns on this day. This was about his legacy. Rodgers was 1-3 in his NFC Championship Game appearances, and 7-7 in the playoffs since winning the only Super Bowl he had ever played in. Brady had advanced to nine Super Bowls in New England, winning six. Now he was threatening to advance to a tenth without the help of Bill Belichick and the Patriot Way.

Rodgers had Brady right where he wanted him, at Lambeau, stripped of his dynastic mystique and aura. Tampa Bay was the losingest organization in North American sports when Brady signed on. Bruce Arians was coaching him now, and his philosophy would not have worked in Foxborough, Massachusetts. "Win or lose, we booze," Arians said.

This was what Rodgers wanted: a chance to beat Brady when the playing field was level. This was not Belichick vs. Mike McCarthy. This was Arians vs. Matt LaFleur, a pretty fair fight.

Unlike his predecessor, McCarthy, who was built like a beer keg, LaFleur did not fit the football coach prototype. At first glance, he looked more like a golf pro who bounced between the PGA and Korn Ferry tours.

Fittingly, Rodgers learned about LaFleur while driving to a Scottsdale golf club. Gutekunst called to tell Rodgers about the Tennessee Titans' offensive coordinator, a product of the Mike and Kyle Shanahan system, and asked him to give the coach a call. Rodgers and LaFleur had a conversation while the quarterback was waiting on the sixth tee at Estancia. When Rodgers called Gutekunst to tell him that he enjoyed the conversation, the quarterback learned from the GM that the Packers had already decided to offer LaFleur the job.

As Murphy had promised, Rodgers was not part of the process.

The quarterback told me that during one of the first conversations he had with LaFleur, the new coach told him, "I just want you to turn your brain off."

A coach was telling one of the league's smartest and quickest on-field thinkers to turn his brain off?

"Matt, that's not how I play," Rodgers replied. "I play with my mind. I win the games Monday to Saturday. I win the games on the field with my reactions. I need my guys with their brains turned on."

The first year of the LaFleur-Rodgers partnership was a success—a 13-3 regular season and another NFC North title—though its ending was ripped from the pages of the McCarthy-Rodgers partnership. Once again the defense cracked, surrendering 37 points to San Francisco in the NFC Championship Game, including 4 touchdowns and 220 rushing yards to a fifth-year back, Raheem Mostert, an undrafted player who had only once rushed for more than 100 yards. Rodgers had now been eliminated from the playoffs three times by the franchise that did not draft him.

But in 2020, when he turned thirty-seven, Rodgers was back at his 2011 peak, dominating the league and breaking his own franchise record with 48 touchdown passes (against only 5 interceptions), his third season of at least 40 (Brett Favre never topped 39). He completed a career-best 70.7 percent of his throws while leading the league's top-scoring offense. His offseason Zoom sessions with LaFleur and his offensive coordinator and quarterbacks coach, Nathaniel Hackett and Luke Getsy, had paid off.

"We just spent so many hours just talking," Rodgers said. "I think it was great for us all to really kind of feel into that, get some strength in the grounding of our friendship and our working relationship. I think it's really changed the way we've kind of installed plays and are communicating things."

Rodgers had also been inspired by a draft-day decision that enraged him like no other. Entering the 2020 draft, the Packers had not picked a skill-position offensive player in the first round since they had selected Rodgers himself in 2005. They had used all nine of their first-round picks in the previous eight years on defensive prospects.

And then, after again falling one game short of the Super Bowl, the Packers made a trade with Miami to move up from the thirtieth pick to the twenty-sixth. They were finally taking a bold first-round step to get some skill-position help on offense.

Only Jordan Love of Utah State was not drafted to help Aaron Rodgers. He was drafted to replace Aaron Rodgers, without the Packers ever giving A-Rod a heads-up that this move was a distinct possibility.

Rodgers could not believe it.

What the fuck? he texted someone after the pick was made.

Fifteen years earlier, those were the exact words that Favre's agent, Bus Cook, used with a Packers official after they had drafted Rodgers to ultimately succeed his client.

But the Love selection was different. In 2005, Rodgers did a free-fall into Green Bay's lap, leaving Ted Thompson with little choice but to make the best player on his board the first draft choice of his tenure as GM.

This time around, Gutekunst ignored his roster needs and chased after another quarterback. His franchise player nearly fell out of his chair. Rodgers was living a comfortable professional and personal life before that draft, with seemingly no threats looming outside the gates of his privileged existence. He was still competing at a high level on the field, and off the field he was enjoying a serious relationship with the former professional racing star Danica Patrick that started in early 2018; they were living together in the $28 million Malibu mansion that Rodgers bought from British pop star Robbie Williams, prompting talk of a potential engagement and marriage.

And then his own team blindsided him, knocked him on his ass. Rodgers had been watching the draft feed with former teammate A. J. Hawk and former Indianapolis Colts punter and current radio and TV personality Pat McAfee and wondering what wide receiver might be there for Green Bay to complement Davante Adams, the three-time Pro Bowler. He then got a text from his marketing agent that just said, simply, "Quarterback," a bulletin that sent the fifteen-year veteran to his pantry to pour himself four fingers of tequila.

Jordan Love? Craig Rigsbee, a former Utah State player, had returned to campus for an alumni event and, as an honorary captain, walked out with Love for the coin toss before a rout of Stony Brook. "I didn't even know who he was," Rigsbee said.

He knew now. So did everyone in Rodgers's orbit, from Chico to Green Bay and back.

"I wasn't thrilled by the pick, obviously," Rodgers said, "but the organization is thinking about the present and the future. . . . I think it was more the surprise of the pick, based on my own feelings of wanting to play into my forties, and really the realization that it does change the controllables a little bit. Because as much as I feel confident in my abilities and what I can accomplish and what we can accomplish, there are some new factors that are out of my control."

Rodgers called Love to let him know that he had nothing against the kid, that he knew exactly what Love was feeling, and that he did not want anything negative attached to the realization of his boyhood dream. It was the right thing to do, and something Favre would not have done in a million years.

As much as people wanted to compare his situation to Favre's fifteen years earlier, Rodgers pointed out that the 2004 Packers were 10-6 and first-round playoff losers while the 2019 Packers were 13-3 and among the final four. Rodgers also reminded people that Favre had already talked of retiring before 2005, while his successor had talked recently of playing on and on.

"My sincere desire to start and finish with the same organization," Rodgers said, "just as it has with many other players over the years, may not be a reality at this point."

Actually, Rodgers did have control over the situation. Upon drafting Jimmy Garoppolo in the second round in 2014, Belichick told reporters the following: "We know what Tom's age and contract situation is." For a coach who never disclosed anything publicly, it was a stunningly candid admission. Brady was being put on notice before his thirty-seventh birthday.

Brady then went out and won the Super Bowl at the end of the 2014 season and won another at the end of the 2016 season, effectively forcing Belichick (with a push from owner Robert Kraft) to trade away Garoppolo in 2017. Brady took control of those loose controllables that Rodgers was talking about. It was time, in 2020, for Rodgers to do the same.

He started that process with a remarkable regular season, and with a convincing 32–18 victory over the Los Angeles Rams in the divisional round of the playoffs that put him in this all-time heavyweight fight with Brady for control of the sport. Late in that fight, trailing on all cards, Rodgers still had a chance to land the decisive roundhouse right.

The Packers' eight-point deficit in the closing minutes of the NFC Championship Game was largely due to mistakes made by their finest players. Adams, All-Pro receiver, dropped a back-shoulder touchdown pass in the second quarter before the Packers settled for a field goal. Rodgers, all-world quarterback, threw his only interception in what turned out to be an impactful sequence near the end of the first half.

On third down, with eighteen seconds to go and the ball on the Green Bay 45, it appeared the best the Buccaneers could hope for was a meaningful gain or two and a field goal to add to their 14–10 lead. Under pressure, Brady lobbed a ball down the right sideline to tight end Cameron Brate that was headed straight for the Packers' Will Redmond. The defensive back dropped the interception at the Green Bay 20 that would have given Rodgers a chance to kneel out the clock.

To the untrained eye, that development might have seemed inconsequential. The Bucs were expected to punt on fourth down. No harm, no foul.

To the educated follower of Brady's career, this was an opportunity to be seized. Brady had made a cottage industry out of capitalizing on unexpected openings granted by the opposition.

Arians sent out his punt team, a reassuring sight for Packers fans. From behind his face shield, Arians thought about it some more during a time-out and decided to take a chance on his six-time champ.

"B. A. wanted to go for it," Brady said. "I liked the call, and I'm going to do whatever he asked me to do."

On cue, Brady hit Leonard Fournette for 6 yards and a first down at the Green Bay 39 before the Bucs called their final time-out with eight seconds left. The Packers were expecting Brady to try to connect on a quick pass to the sideline to stop the clock and shorten the field-goal attempt. Mike Pettine, Green Bay's defensive coordinator, put his unit in man-to-man coverage.

"When we lined up," Arians said, "you could tell it was going to be a touchdown."

Scott Miller, a smallish wide receiver with blazing speed, lined up on the left side and ran an old-fashioned fly pattern right by cornerback Kevin King. Brady hit him in stride in the end zone for a 39-yard score with one second left. It felt like a dagger straight through Green Bay's heart.

"Definitely not the right call for the situation," LaFleur conceded about the man coverage. "You can't do stuff like that against a good football team and expect to win."

Worse yet, on the third play of the third quarter, Aaron Jones committed a ghastly turnover. A fifth-round pick out of Texas–El Paso in 2017, Jones had made himself a Pro Bowl running back. He was good for more than 3,000 rushing and receiving yards and 30 combined touchdowns in the 2019 and 2020 regular seasons. But after making this third-down reception that left him well short of the first-down marker, Jones needed to protect the ball.

He fumbled it on contact instead, and Tampa Bay's Devin White returned it to the Packers' 8-yard line. Brady then did what Brady so often does. He executed a play-action fake on first-and-goal and found Brate for a touchdown. The Bucs had a 28–10 lead.

Plenty of accomplished teams have folded under such duress. Rodgers wasn't going to let the Packers do that. He fought back with two long touchdown drives sandwiched around a Brady interception, though a St. Brown drop of a two-point conversion attempt turned what should have been a 28–25 deficit heading into the fourth quarter into a 28–23 deficit.

And then the strangest thing happened in that final quarter. Brady was picked off on back-to-back possessions by Packers cornerback Jaire Alexander. The NFL's greatest winner ever had suddenly positioned his team to lose.

LaFleur responded in a perfectly reasonable way. On both ensuing series, with a chance to finally take the lead, the Packers' coach asked Rodgers to throw the ball on every play. The result?

Two sacks. Four incompletes. Two punts.

"We had the ball there with all the momentum," Rodgers said. "We just kind of needed one first down to get going. We just didn't get it, which was disappointing."

The Packers let Brady escape, and the Bucs kicked the field goal that created the late eight-point spread that confronted Rodgers, who had hit Marquez Valdes-Scantling for 29 yards and Adams for 9 and 11 yards to give Green Bay that first-and-goal at the Tampa 8.

The COVID-sized Lambeau crowd was doing the best it could to push the Packers across the goal line. On first down, with three receivers to his right, Rodgers fired a quick pass to the middle wideout, Allen Lazard, who was not looking for the ball when it whistled past his helmet. Rodgers thought the undrafted third-year receiver was going to make a less severe cut into the heart of the Tampa defense. "I don't blame him for that," the quarterback said.

On second-and-goal, Rodgers took the shotgun snap and, for some reason, abandoned a relatively clean pocket as he scrambled through the right tackle gap. With Ndamukong Suh about to knock him down, Rodgers threw to the back of the end zone, over Adams's head. Third-and-goal.

The crowd was murmuring nervously, thinking this was not trending in the right direction. Rodgers was alone in the backfield, with three receivers to his right, two to his left. He called for the snap with 2:15 to go. On his left, tight end Robert Tonyan ran toward the left flag in the end zone, while Jamaal Williams planted himself at the 4-yard line. On Rodgers's right, Valdes-Scantling ran toward the right flag while the middle man, Adams, and the outside man, Lazard, planted and cut to the quarterback's left.

All of Tampa Bay's defensive backs were fully occupied with the task of smothering their receivers. As Rodgers held the ball on the 17-yard line and danced a bit, he felt the pressure and again scrambled forward to the right side with 2:12 left.

At the 13-yard line, he pointed his left arm toward Adams, who was in the front of the end zone, with two defenders closing on him. Meanwhile, the whole right corner of the field was wide-open. Rodgers could have run the ball for a touchdown, or at least run it close to the goal line to make the fourth-down play much more manageable.

Jason Pierre-Paul, an athletic defensive end, was in pursuit from Rodgers's left. The mammoth Suh was bearing down on him from the rear. From the comfort of a press box, while eating a soft, heated pretzel, it was always easy to say that the man in the arena should have done this, or should have done that, when making a split-second decision while chaos raged around him.

That qualifier aside, yes, Rodgers should have raced those bigger men to the end zone, even at age thirty-seven. He was no longer the quarterback who had rushed for more than 300 yards in four different years. His regular-season total this time around was a modest 149.

But he was still an athlete, and a playmaker. Coaches preached that you take what the defense gives you, and the Tampa Bay defense gave Rodgers that lane. He didn't take it. At the 10-yard line, he fired a low fastball against his body to Adams, who never had a chance. The Bucs' Mike Edwards dove in front of him to knock down the ball, and if Edwards had not gotten to it, his teammate Andrew Adams would have made the play.

The fans' collective groan was loud enough to suggest that the crowd was five times its actual size. Fourth-and-goal, 2:09 to go. LaFleur could have been aggressive and granted one more shot to the quarterback who was expected to be a near-unanimous winner of his third league MVP award. Or he could have done what Mike McCarthy would have done.

LaFleur chose McCarthyism. Mason Crosby kicked the 26-yard field goal to make it 31–26, and counted on his three time-outs, the two-minute warning, and an improved Packers defense that had finished ninth in the league in yards allowed—its first top-ten finish since 2010—to stop Brady and return the ball to Rodgers.

Predictably, in a Groundhog Day tribute to past postseason failures, Green Bay's offense never again touched the ball. The Packers caught a bad break on a third-down pass from Brady to Tyler Johnson—a ball that was overthrown and not catchable—when the officials called defensive pass interference on Kevin King. It was a call that should not have been made, and the fans let the officials know it.

Not that it mattered. The Bucs ran for another first down and Brady took a knee on the final play, and that was that. Hard as it might have been to believe, Rodgers passed for 346 yards and Brady threw 3 interceptions, and the Packers still lost.

The dueling No. 12s came together for a hug.

"Great playing, buddy," Brady said.

"Good job, buddy," Rodgers said. "See you, buddy. Take care now."

"You too," Brady replied.

This defeat might have been more crushing than the loss to the Giants after the 2011 season, and the loss to the Seahawks after the 2014 season. Much of the postgame talk revolved around LaFleur's decision to kick a field goal on that final Packers drive.

The losing coach explained that the offense's failure to gain any yards on the three preceding plays, and the need to convert a two-point conversion on top of the touchdown, shaped his choice to rely on his defense and the time-outs. In hindsight, LaFleur admitted regretting his call. "Any time it doesn't work out," he said, "you always regret it, right?"

Asked about his coach's decision to take the ball out of his hands on fourth down, Rodgers said, "That wasn't my decision. But [I] understand the thinking, above two minutes with all of our time-outs. But yeah, that wasn't my decision."

The play call on third down was his decision. Wearing a dark wool hat pulled down tight over his forehead and ears, and a dark patterned bandana wrapped around his neck, Rodgers sat alone in a room while telling reporters, via Zoom, that LaFleur allowed him to reject his call in favor of the quarterback's preference. Rodgers also revealed that he assumed the Packers would go for it on fourth down and that he might have called a different third-down play had he known a field goal was the plan.

"Obviously," LaFleur said, "we've got to come up with a better way of communicating."

One question needed to be asked and answered: could Rodgers have simply run it for a score on that third-down play and wiped away all these uncomfortable truths?

"I felt like I had a chance maybe to run it," he replied, "but I felt like there was a guy kind of closing on me."

LaFleur admitted that he was not on his A-game and that he had a hand in sending Brady to his tenth Super Bowl appearance, on his home field in Tampa. The second-year head coach said that he did not call the right plays and that he had let a lot of people down.

Rodgers criticized the late pass-interference call and described himself as "pretty gutted." He did not agree that his endgame failure would *haunt* him, but conceded, "This one definitely stings, and is going to for a long time."

LaFleur called his quarterback "the heart and soul of our football team," and all but demanded that he return for his seventeenth season in Green Bay. But four days after calling his future "a beautiful mystery," Rodgers said that a lot of the Packers' futures were uncertain, "myself included. That's what's sad about it most, getting this far.

"It's really tough to get to this point . . . and that makes the finality of it all kind of hit you like a ton of bricks."

Rodgers thanked the distant reporters on the other side of this Zoom exchange for the work they had done all year and said he appreciated his interactions with them. He finished by saying, "I'll always be thankful for this season. Thank you."

It sure sounded like goodbye. Rodgers had now lost four of his five trips to the NFC Championship Game. The guy who had won the Super Bowl had morphed into the Guy Who Couldn't Win the Big One. Something had to give. Something had to change.

Brett Favre, of all people, seemed to agree. Favre had talked to Rodgers after Green Bay drafted Jordan Love, and found a man who knew, deep down, that he could not finish his career with the Packers.

"I think Aaron will finish somewhere else," Favre told Rich Eisen. "That's my gut. I guarantee you this: It's got the wheels turning in Aaron's mind. If that's the case, then that means there's a chip on his shoulder toward the organization that otherwise was not there. And so, all he needs is a reason other than this reason to expedite that."

A reason like hiring Matt LaFleur without his input. A reason like drafting Love without advance notice. A reason like failing to retain distinguished core veterans whose intangible value was ignored on departure. A reason like failing to draft and acquire championship-level offensive weapons that, according to Favre, "just sends a disrespect message to Aaron Rodgers."

Off his conversation with his successor, Favre said of the Packers, "I think they burned a bridge that's going to be hard to overcome. At some point, I think it will rear its ugly head."

As it turned out, Aaron Rodgers had indeed reached the beginning of his end in Green Bay. And his eventual exit would end up looking like Favre's in more ways than one.

12
DIVORCE

Aaron Rodgers was always one of the best interviews in the league. At his locker or at the podium, he was consistent in delivering thoughtful, long-form opinions about the sport and his place in it.

He could rise to meet a great question with a greater answer, and he could elevate a mediocre question the way he elevated mediocre teammates. At a time when media access to superstars was dwindling, when athletes were more inclined to send unfiltered messages to fans on social media platforms, Rodgers was an exception. He was candid and relatively available, at least in-season. He seemed to enjoy the give-and-take with reporters, even when a tough question might turn it into a sparring session.

On Thursday, August 26, 2021, Rodgers was very much in his element. One of his stated goals was to learn as much about as many subjects as possible so he could "hang in any conversation," so he was bouncing easily from topic to topic with the reporters seated before him.

The plays that were developed in the quarterback room. The books he bought at Barnes & Noble for Marquez Valdes-Scantling. The importance of good mental health. The amazing acupuncturist who had helped him relieve stress through box-breathing techniques. The team's special group of receivers. The state of Jordan Love's health and development. The pressure of winning it all.

"It's Titletown," Rodgers said. "It's championship or disappointment just about every year."

As he held court, Rodgers was wearing a Packers cap over the hair he had already started growing out for his John Wick Halloween costume.

The whole process was as easy for him as a quick pass to the flat. The Packers posted the video from this presser with the Valdes-Scantling headline, "Rodgers Believes MVS Has Become 'a True Professional.'"

No, that was not going to be the headline anywhere else. After the conversation turned to the offensive line, Rodgers was hit with this question from Ryan Wood of the *Green Bay Press-Gazette*:

"Are you vaccinated, and what's your stance on vaccinations?"

After Wood said the words, "Are you vaccinated," Rodgers subtly nodded his head. He had been prepared for this question and, he later said, for a particular follow-up that did not come. His response ultimately changed the way he was perceived by an untold number of people and defined a tumultuous offseason and preseason in a most unfortunate way.

That offseason started in February, when Rodgers told the Packers that he wanted to be more involved in decisions that impacted his ability to do his job. One example: Green Bay released receiver Jake Kumerow immediately after Rodgers raved about him, making the quarterback look foolish and powerless.

The Packers were not adopting the approach of the team that had just beaten them in the NFC Championship Game. The Tampa Bay Buccaneers had called their all-out pursuit of free agent Tom Brady "Operation Shoeless Joe Jackson"—Bucs executive and *Field of Dreams* fan John Spytek, a former Brady teammate at Michigan, came up with the name—and then used Brady as a lead recruiter in improving the roster that dominated Kansas City in Super Bowl LV.

Tampa Bay GM Jason Licht acquired the playmaking assets that Brady wanted, including Rob Gronkowski, Leonard Fournette, and Antonio Brown, who accounted for all four touchdowns that the Bucs scored against Kansas City to land Brady his record seventh Super Bowl ring. Rodgers, with one ring, watched that go down and told himself he was done sitting out all roster-building exercises.

In November 2020, GM Brian Gutekunst did Rodgers a solid by signing his good friend, left tackle David Bakhtiari, to a four-year extension worth $23 million per year, making him the highest-paid offensive lineman ever. The quarterback was not terribly impressed.

Feeling that his past advice on potential acquisitions had been ignored by Gutekunst and his predecessor, Ted Thompson, Rodgers asked to be directly involved in conversations about free agents and to be used as a recruiter to help land high-end talent. He also said that he wanted to help the front office "maybe learn from some of the mistakes in the past, in my opinion, about the way some of the outgoing veterans were treated, and just the fact we didn't retain a number of players that I felt like were core players to our foundation, our locker room, high-character guys."

Rodgers listed a dozen such players, including Charles Woodson, Jordy Nelson, Julius Peppers, Clay Matthews, Randall Cobb, and James Jones. The reigning league MVP and three-time winner of that award also told the Packers that he wanted contractual guarantees beyond the 2021 season—providing him protection against Gutekunst running him out in favor of Love.

Talks with management and Matt LaFleur went nowhere. The response was not exactly "shut up and play," but close enough.

In March, Rodgers told the only team he had ever played for that if it could not commit to him beyond 2021, and could not include him in personnel conversations, to go ahead and trade him. He considered retirement a viable option, at least for a while. A past *Celebrity Jeopardy!* champ, Rodgers had fared well as guest host of *Jeopardy!* for a couple of weeks in April, a dream side gig that had some full-time potential. Ratings were up 14 percent when he hosted, and Rodgers had legitimate interest in replacing the late, great Alex Trebek, if the tapings could be scheduled around his football season.

If he was going to play another football season. ESPN's Adam Schefter reported on April 29, the day of the draft, that Rodgers had told people in the organization that he did not want to return to the Packers. Rodgers wanted to finish his career with San Francisco, the original team that had passed on him, and he wanted Gutekunst and Mark Murphy to close on a deal that would put him there.

"We're not going to trade Aaron Rodgers," Gutekunst promised hours after the Schefter report, and a few months after Murphy had said, "We're not idiots. Aaron Rodgers will be back. He's our leader."

Only Aaron Rodgers had something to say about that. He could not envision staying in Green Bay unless Gutekunst was fired, according to Charles Robinson of Yahoo! Sports. Bob McGinn of *The Athletic* later reported that Rodgers had mocked Gutekunst in group chats with Packers teammates by calling him "Jerry Krause," the GM of the six-time champion Chicago Bulls who, for various reasons (some of them silly), had been despised by Michael Jordan, Scottie Pippen, and Phil Jackson.

It wasn't as if Gutekunst did not fully appreciate Rodgers's greatness. Bakhtiari said the GM told scouts that they should not bother comparing quarterback prospects to Rodgers, that it wasn't fair to them. "When you see Aaron touch his back foot and an absolute missile comes out of his hand, it's disgusting," Bakhtiari said. "Aaron will make one throw a day that will absolutely blow your mind."

When it came down to it, Gutekunst was just another face in the endless parade of small-college grinders who, absent the necessary skill to play ball for a living, worked connections to piece together lucrative front-office and coaching careers in the NFL. Would the Packers really pick him over an all-time great player?

Green Bay fans everywhere were in a panic. Cherry Starr, the widow of Bart Starr and a friend of Rodgers who used to make him brownies, was right there with them. "I have Aaron's cell number," Cherry told me, "so I sent him a text that read, 'Please, please, finish out your career with the Packers.'" Cherry said the quarterback sent her a sweet reply.

At least Rodgers was exchanging pleasantries with one significant member of the Packers family. Seeing the opportunity, 49ers coach Kyle Shanahan called Packers coach Matt LaFleur the night before the draft to inquire about Rodgers's availability. "You're talking about the MVP of our league last year.... Yeah, we inquired," said 49ers GM John Lynch.

The Packers said they were not interested; they later tried to throw money at the problem by offering their quarterback a two-year extension, which he rejected. Rodgers skipped the team's entire offseason program, and his fiancée, actress Shailene Woodley, supported his personal boycott. (Rodgers and Danica Patrick had broken up in 2020; the quarterback announced his engagement to his latest high-profile girlfriend during his MVP acceptance speech in February.) Woodley retweeted a Twitter video posted by Stephen A. Smith in which the ESPN personality shredded the Packers for disrespecting their franchise player.

Rodgers was threatening to skip training camp before his employer made some concessions, according to Schefter, including a willingness to trade him after the 2021 season if he remained unhappy with how the organization was treating him. Satisfied for the time being, Rodgers reported to camp for his seventeenth season, knowing that Brett Favre and Bart Starr did not make it past sixteen seasons in Green Bay.

"I'm not a victim here at all," he said. "I just want to reiterate that. I've been paid a ton of money by this organization." Yes, over sixteen years, he had been paid a reported $241 million in salary alone.

Rodgers was back without a firm assurance that his voice would be heard in personnel decisions going forward. The Packers were not about to turn over the franchise to Rodgers the way, say, the Brooklyn Nets had turned over theirs to Kevin Durant and Kyrie Irving. The quarterback reminded reporters that he was not consulted on the LaFleur hire and many other major moves, and that he felt management officials just wanted him to throw the football and stay out of their business.

"In my opinion, based on what I've accomplished in this league, the way I show up in the locker room, the way I lead, the way I conduct myself in the community, you should tie myself to a little bit more input," Rodgers said. "The rules are the same for most people, but every now and then there are some outlier guys who have been in organizations for 17 years and won a few MVPs, where they can be in conversations at a different level.

"I'm not asking for anything that other great quarterbacks across the last few decades have not gotten. The opportunity to just be in a conversation, so if you're going to cut a guy who, based on a meritocracy, was our second-best receiver in training camp last year for the majority of camp, maybe run it by me, see what I feel. I might be able to change your mind."

As a show of good faith, the Packers reacquired Rodgers's close friend Randall Cobb, whose presence lowered the volume on his buddy's noisiest summer since the home fans booed him in 2008. Rodgers was going to be a quarterback after all, not a game show host.

He was also going to be a contentious figure in the national debate over the methods to combat the spread of COVID-19. That became a fact on August 26, the moment he answered the question that he had been waiting for, the question about whether he had been vaccinated.

"Yeah, I've been immunized," Rodgers said that day. "There's a lot of conversation around it, around the league, and a lot of guys who have made statements, have not made statements, owners who made statements. There's guys on the team that haven't been vaccinated. I think it's a personal decision. I'm not going to judge those guys. There's guys who have been vaccinated and have contracted COVID. So, it's an interesting issue. I think we're going to see it play out the entire season."

Rodgers talked about the testing schedule and wondered if the protocols would change at some point, before he was asked a follow-up by Jason Wilde, who was acting under the reasonable assumption that his former radio cohost had just confirmed that he was vaccinated. Wilde brought up two quarterbacks who were reportedly unvaccinated, Minnesota's Kirk Cousins and New England's Cam Newton, and asked if Rodgers was motivated to make sure he was available to play and to set a good example for others.

"No, it wasn't about that at all," Rodgers replied. "I like to learn about everything that I am doing and there was a lot of research that even went into that. . . . There [have] been people that have tested positive. I think it is only vaccinated people here, so it's going to be interesting to see how things work moving forward. Obviously, there could be some issues with vaccinated people only testing every couple weeks and nonvaccinated testing every day. . . . I think this is going to continue to evolve as we get into the season."

On that note, Rodgers started to leave the media auditorium before he was asked to field one last question from a reporter participating by Zoom. The man wanted to ask about the New Orleans Saints, the opponent in the season opener, so a relieved Rodgers was done talking about the pandemic for the time being.

• • •

ON NOVEMBER 3, NEWS broke that Aaron Rodgers had tested positive for COVID-19, that he was unvaccinated against the virus, and that he would miss at least one game—against the Chiefs on November 7—as he sat out a minimum of ten days. People who had assumed "immunized" in the summer meant vaccinated in the fall suddenly felt duped.

For good reason. They *had* been duped.

Rodgers's claim in August that he had been immunized against the virus inspired headlines such as "Aaron Rodgers Says He's Vaccinated but Won't Judge Teammates Who Aren't." He had called a trick play in the worst possible arena at the worst possible time. On the same day he was sidelined and reported to be unvaccinated, Johns Hopkins University revealed that the COVID-19 death toll in the United States had surpassed 750,000.

While teammates and everyone else in the organization knew of Rodgers's unvaccinated status, and while the quarterback had been fulfilling the vast majority of his daily masking and testing obligations inside the team facility, he was not wearing a mask, as required, while taking questions from reporters during his weekly availability in the auditorium.

This was not good. This was not good at all. The news created a shitstorm that raged throughout the league and in all corners of society. Even people who did not follow the NFL, or who did not know much about Rodgers, weighed in with blistering takes. The quarterback got pummeled for what some described as a dangerously misleading position and others described as an outright lie.

"I realize I'm in the crosshairs of the woke mob right now," Rodgers said two days later on *The Pat McAfee Show*, his weekly go-to forum that was growing in significance by the day. "So, before my final nail gets put in my cancel-culture casket, I think I'd like to set the record straight on so many of the blatant lies that are out there about myself right now."

Though he had become fond of mocking "cancel culture" and "woke culture," Rodgers had been among the most socially aware players in the NFL. He was the rare white star to say out loud what was obvious about Colin Kaepernick—telling ESPN's Mina Kimes in 2017 that teams were keeping him out of the league because he protested racial injustice and systemic inequities during the pregame playing of the national anthem—and to remain fully supportive of players who chose to kneel during the anthem.

Rodgers spoke out against the horrors of war in the Democratic Republic of the Congo, and he denounced a fan who shouted an anti-Muslim slur during a moment of silence in 2015 following the terrorist attacks in Paris that killed 130. President Barack Obama wrote a letter of appreciation to Rodgers, which, the quarterback told Kimes, he kept because it meant a lot to him.

But in defending his vaccination beliefs, Rodgers veered off course. He told McAfee, "The great MLK said, 'You have a moral obligation to object to unjust rules and rules that make no sense,'" taking liberties with the letter and spirit of Dr. Martin Luther King Jr.'s actual quote—delivered from a

Birmingham, Alabama, prison cell in his fight for racial equality—that he never should have taken. Instead of simply apologizing for his obvious mistake in how he initially handled his vaccination status, Rodgers was making a bigger mess.

Not many people in Rodgers's life had ever heard him say the words "I'm sorry," and that impressive streak was not about to be broken on McAfee's show. The quarterback said the media was conducting a witch hunt to shame unvaccinated players. He said that he did not lie in his August press conference, and that when it came to his statement that he had been immunized, "there was nothing deceptive about it."

Rodgers said this with a straight face. "Had there been a follow-up to my statement that I had been immunized," he claimed, "I would have responded with this: I would have said, 'Look, I'm not some sort of anti-vax flat-Earther. I am somebody who's a critical thinker. You guys know me, I march to the beat of my own drum. I believe strongly in bodily autonomy, and the ability to make choices for your body, not to have to acquiesce to some woke culture or crazed group of individuals who say you have to do something.'"

Rodgers said he consulted medical professionals and conducted extensive research that showed he was allergic to an ingredient in the Moderna and Pfizer vaccines. He also said he was concerned enough about reports of adverse medical reactions—including blood clotting—associated with the Johnson & Johnson vaccine to seek an alternative immunization protocol that covered multiple months.

When the NFL rejected his petition to review his personal homeopathic treatment program and grant him the status of a vaccinated player, Rodgers appealed the ruling and presented the league with more than five hundred pages of research on the efficacy of vaccines and masks. The appeal was denied. "I think they thought I was a quack," Rodgers said.

He mentioned fatherhood "as the next great chapter in my life," and said he was concerned about the lack of study on what effect, if any, vaccination could have on sterility. "I made a decision that was in the best interests of my body," he said. Rodgers wanted to make this point clear: "I'm not a COVID denier or any bullshit like that."

But his unforced error here was in not coming clean with the public in the first place. Had he merely explained in August that he was allergic to the polyethylene glycol, or PEG, in both mRNA vaccines, and that he was concerned about how the Johnson & Johnson vaccine might negatively affect his body, many consumers of that response would have found it to be a fairly rational position. Why wait for a follow-up question that was not asked? Not everyone would have loved Rodgers's straight-up answer, but he would have gotten some points for honesty and he would not have received a third of the criticism he absorbed for his deceit.

He outsmarted himself, and after his *McAfee* appearance fueled another heavy round of unfriendly fire, Rodgers seemed to realize it. During his next appearance in his regular Tuesday slot, he spoke of the empathy he had for those who died from COVID-19, and for those whose lives and businesses were irreparably harmed. He acknowledged that, as a sports superstar, he was a role model to many people.

"And so, I just wanted to start off the show by acknowledging that I made some comments that people might have felt were misleading," Rodgers said. "And to anybody who felt misled by those comments, I take full responsibility for those comments."

He later repeated that sentiment. He never said he was sorry, and it sounded more like one of those "if anyone was offended" apologies than a genuine expression of contrition. So be it. Rodgers had already demonstrated his compassion for COVID victims by donating $500,000 to the Barstool Sports relief fund, and by donating $1 million to eighty small businesses in his hometown of Chico and surrounding Butte County.

"But in the end," Rodgers said, "I have to stay true to who I am and what I'm about. And I stand behind the things that I said."

Years later, when I asked him if he would have gotten vaccinated if a local mandate had sidelined him like New York's had sidelined Brooklyn Nets star Kyrie Irving, Rodgers said, "I wouldn't have done it." He would not have gotten vaccinated to make himself eligible to play for the Packers and help his teammates win games? "No," he said.

Rodgers did make an important concession and did express one significant regret over how he handled his vaccination status in that August press conference. He admitted that he should have just told the news media the truth up front about his Moderna and Pfizer allergy and his Johnson & Johnson fears.

"If there's one thing I wish could have gone different, it's that," Rodgers said for this book, "because that's the only thing they could hit me with. And the reason I said [that I was immunized] is because that was the crux of my appeal. That statement was the crux of my appeal—that I've been immunized.

"I had an immunization card from my holistic doctor, which looked similar. I wasn't trying to pawn it off as a vaccine card, but I said, 'Listen, here's my protocol. Here's what you can follow to look this up.' And it was an ongoing appeal. So, if I had just said that in the moment, there's no chance that the appeal would have been handled the same exact way."

Rodgers believed the truth would have negatively affected his chances to win an appeal that he ended up losing anyway.

"Why should I have to give my medical history or issues to the press?" he asked me. "They were fuckin' killing everybody.... But if I could do it again, I would have said, 'Fuck the appeal, I'm just going to tell them I'm allergic to PEG, I'm not getting Johnson & Johnson, I'm not going to be vaxxed.' But I really thought my appeal had a chance to win, because I came in there, and one of the main issues was, they were saying the vax stops transmission and contraction. And I said, 'We have five scouts, day one, out with COVID [who were] all fully vaxxed.' I said, 'What are we talking about here?'"

Rodgers faced consequences for his stand, starting with his lost nine-year partnership with Prevea Health, headquartered in Green Bay. The health care organization announced in a joint statement that it encouraged all eligible populations to get vaccinated, and deleted tweets and removed videos that promoted its ties to Rodgers.

The NFL also fined the Packers $300,000 and Rodgers and receiver Allen Lazard $14,650 each for COVID protocol violations. The league determined that Rodgers and Lazard had, on occasion, neglected to wear masks inside the team facility, and that Rodgers should have worn a mask at his press conferences. The quarterback and receiver were fined for attending a team-sponsored Halloween party, a no-no for unvaccinated players forbidden from gathering in groups of more than three.

It was too bad, because Rodgers looked great all dressed up as the lead Keanu Reeves character in *John Wick*, with fake blood smeared across his face. Fittingly enough, Wick was a fascinating figure who was hard to nail down. Was he a good guy? Bad guy? Antihero?

The same questions could be asked about Rodgers, one of America's most recognizable men and a figure prominent enough to once get an audience with the Dalai Lama. Who the hell was this guy when he was out of his costume? And what, exactly, was behind that mask that he often refused to wear?

• • •

TEAM PRESIDENT MARK Murphy was speaking at a Lambeau Field event during the Aaron Rodgers standoff when he quoted former GM Ted Thompson, who had died in January, as calling the quarterback "a complicated fella."

It was an apt assessment. A-Rod, the masterfully playful photobomber of everything from the team captains' pictures to the Academy Awards ceremonies, had no shortage of friends, including loyal ones from his boyhood days in Oregon and Chico. And yet many NFL people were surprised at how often Rodgers showed up alone at events and thought of him as a loner, going back to the early days of his career. "Aaron Rodgers, party of one," was how someone who knew him well in Green Bay described his customary arrival status.

Rodgers was known to scan every room he entered, left to right, right to left, as if reading a defense at the line. He wanted to know who was in the room and who he needed to avoid.

Jerry Kramer, the Hall of Fame Packers guard who made the famously decisive block for Bart Starr in the epic Ice Bowl in 1967, spoke of how Rodgers did not interact with the old-timers the way that Brett Favre did. "Brett would spend more time bullshitting with you, and he had a giggle generally," Kramer said. "Brett would shake hands and smile at you and chat with you."

Rodgers talked often about his love for the game's history, for Packers history. He watched those films of Lombardi's teams, and Kramer was a walking, talking library, a gifted storyteller who was always willing to share what it was like to be in that locker room and to be on that field.

And yet the former Packers great did not get to know Rodgers.

"I got to know his handshake," Kramer said.

His handshake?

Kramer explained that Rodgers was polite during their interactions, but always brief and borderline eager to keep it moving. Rodgers did not let anyone in without a struggle. Anyone. He was always on high alert for those packing an agenda, or for those most interested in cozying up to his celebrity.

In 2017, he agreed to do an interview and photo shoot for an *ESPN The Magazine* cover story that was billed as a search for the real Aaron Rodgers. "Unmasked and Unfiltered" was the cover headline. The quarterback wanted to do the interview at the Los Angeles home of the assigned writer, Mina Kimes, rather than at the traditional settings of such sit-downs—the subject's home court or a neutral site. Rodgers also taped the interview (another rarity for a celeb) so, he said, he could not be quoted out of context. Kimes wrote that the quarterback was unusually cautious and choosing his words "like a surgeon plucking instruments from a table."

Rodgers did open up on his decision to pull away from organized religion, the very foundation of his upbringing, and to forge a friendship with an author named Rob Bell. He was the son of a Reagan-appointed federal judge and a pastor who embraced progressive thoughts debunking old-school Christian concepts such as Hell as an eternal punishment ground for sinners who deserved their fiery fate.

Bell believed things, or at least strongly suggested things, that ran contrary to what Rodgers had been taught growing up, and the quarterback connected with those thoughts. He decided organized religion had a "mind-debilitating effect" on people, and at age twenty-five or twenty-six he chose to break from its inflexible articles of faith.

Rodgers told Kimes that decreased privacy and the stress put on friendships and romantic relationships represented the downsides of his celebrity. He said he did not publicly discuss the divide in his family because "a lot of people have family issues. I'm not the only one that does." He said the estrangement, as a topic of conversation, "needs to be handled the right way."

If Rodgers was happy with the interview, he had an entirely different experience at the ESPN photo shoot. Known to be very particular about photos used by outlets he had cooperated with, Rodgers hated the pictures from the first go-around, thinking they did not at all fit the tenor of the sit-down. Those shots were described as "whimsical" and "cutesy" by multiple people with knowledge of them. His reps asked for a second shoot to be conducted by a photographer whom the quarterback had worked with before, Randall Slavin.

On the subject of Team Rodgers' requests for the second shoot, which cost ESPN a pretty penny, Slavin said, "I think they wanted something simple and masculine and direct. I think that was the vibe, and why that cover was a close-up of his face."

Slavin worked with Rodgers on three separate shoots in all and came away liking him and his dry humor. "He's the definition of still waters running deep," Slavin said. "You can see there's a lot of stuff going on, but he's pretty quiet and calm and cool and fairly unruffled.

"I think he's relatively impenetrable. . . . Especially in the Green Bay spotlight, where people hold their football heroes in such godlike [standing], maybe he had to be really protective of himself. He's a very interior person who certainly does not wear his heart on his sleeve."

His rented sleeve. ESPN had paid good money to rent a dark leather jacket for Rodgers to use for the second shoot, and sure enough, he absentmindedly walked off the set wearing the jacket and never sent it back. One person at the second shoot occasionally saw Rodgers wearing it on TV.

Hey, he was always just as elusive as the glowing unidentified flying object he spotted with his college buddy and teammate Steve Levy before the 2005 draft, at Levy's Cornwall, New York, home, before the UFO took off with apparent fighter jets in pursuit. The incident compelled Rodgers to conduct research about UFOs.

He was always conducting research about something because he was always fascinated by the "why" of everything. Why do people believe this? Why do people believe that? Why does Big Pharma push this agenda? Why does the mainstream media push that agenda? Why aren't the critical thinkers who challenge conventional thought given a fair hearing?

Why? Why? Why?

Rodgers started challenging his family's religious beliefs, which led to him challenging just about everything. A believer in magic and miracles and a devoted fan of science fiction, Rodgers was never afraid to dive headfirst into a rabbit hole. His fascination with conspiracies started in his sophomore year of high school when he studied the life and death of President John F. Kennedy for a project. Rodgers thought the conclusion that Lee Harvey Oswald acted alone in the 1963 assassination was, in his words, "fucking bullshit."

He read numerous books about JFK and discussed with friends their shared theories about the murder. "As long as I've known him," said one old friend, "we're both alike as in, you don't really count anything out. We believe in miracles, and when you believe in that, you have to believe in anything.

"JFK was a big one always. We both agree there was someone on the grassy knoll. The fatal shot, where JFK's head went back and to the left, it only makes sense. Lee Harvey Oswald was the fall guy. And the mob was in on it. We have always questioned everything."

Questioning the JFK killing inspired Rodgers to question an unending list of historical truths. If it was ever possible to read too much, Rodgers read too much, or at least too much about conspiracies that fueled his nihilistic approach.

He researched a 1962 plan from senior United States military leaders known as "Operation Northwoods," which proposed committing acts of terrorism against American military and civilian targets that could be falsely blamed on Cuba as justification to start a war. Though President Kennedy rejected that evil plot, Rodgers had cited the case as one of the sources of his distrust of official government narratives. He was apparently seeing different versions of "Operation Northwoods" brewing behind other national and global crises.

Rodgers's backup in 2018, DeShone Kizer, told podcaster Adam Breneman the story of how his first meeting with Rodgers started behind closed doors with the starter asking him this question: "Do you believe in 9/11?" When Kizer assured his new teammate that he had no reason not to believe in the facts of the 9/11 terrorist attacks that claimed nearly three thousand lives, Rodgers said, "You should read up on that."

Kizer explained it was a thought experiment designed to examine 9/11 conspiracy theories that led to conversations about other conspiracy theories, including those involving Inner Earth, the moon landing, and reptile people. Kizer said he bonded with Rodgers over these talks, then advised skeptics to "go do your research."

Rodgers ultimately did it for them, with podcaster extraordinaire Joe Rogan and politician and anti-vaxxer Robert F. Kennedy Jr. among his sources of inspiration. Rodgers would come to adore RFK Jr.'s 2021 book, *The Real Anthony Fauci*, which assailed the director of the National Institute of Allergy and Infectious Diseases, and he would come to believe Fauci advocated only for HIV/AIDS and COVID treatments that he had a stake in.

"The blueprint, the game plan, was made in the eighties," Rodgers said in a later podcast hosted by Eddie Bravo, a martial arts instructor who said he believed COVID-19 was not an actual virus. "Create a pandemic with a virus that's going wild, right?" Rodgers continued. "Fauci was given like over $350 million to research this, to come up with drugs, new or repurposed, to handle the AIDS pandemic, and all they came up with was AZT. . . . Create an environment where only one thing works. Back then, AZT. Now? Remdesivir until we get a vaccine." (Fauci declined an interview request for this book.)

Rodgers actually came to believe that the COVID vaccine was, in his words, "experimental gene therapy that changes your DNA." He had rarely met a conspiracy theory that he would not at least entertain. Rodgers questioned the circumstances surrounding John F. Kennedy Jr.'s fatal plane crash in 1999. He seemingly embraced xenophobic views of immigration at the southern border as a potential threat to national security. On a less serious front, he was fascinated by the obscure Tartarian Empire conspiracy that revolved around holdover architecture from a supposed lost civilization that had gone unacknowledged by historians.

And yet when Rodgers talked about mainstream historical narratives, there was no shortage of people who listened. Future teammate Thomas Morstead, longtime NFL punter, said the quarterback influenced his worldview in conversations about major events.

"I won't single out any specific event," Morstead told me, "but certain events in history as we've learned them, he'd be like, 'Aaaah, that's the old version they taught you in school. But go look up this. Go read this. Go see this. This is how this thing was covered up.' Some people call them conspiracy theories, but when I've gone back and read some of these things . . . the thing that's amazing to me is his recall. He can digest and comprehend and remember amazingly, so he can argue points."

The evidence said Rodgers was not just a contrarian who loved to explore forbidden worlds, or a provocative independent thinker with his own book club, or a relentless attention seeker who was hyperaware of everything said and written about him, and who needed to create news cycles to avoid the one thing he feared most—irrelevance.

He was also a legitimate card-carrying conspiracy theorist, and one who believed that many recent conspiracies had been proven to be true.

Rodgers always appeared to be searching for something out there to make himself more whole. He spoke of a day on the beach with friends using magic mushrooms—and feeling as if he were merging with the ocean—as one of the best days of his life. Before the pandemic hit, Rodgers took a trip to Peru with his then-girlfriend Danica Patrick to experience ayahuasca, a plant-based psychedelic, that he called a life- and career-altering experience.

Rodgers was first informed about the ancient psychoactive brew by his close friend Jordan Russell, who made a 2019 trip to an Amazonian retreat known as the Temple of the Way of Light in Iquitos, Peru. The shamans there performed what they believed to be tantamount to psycho-emotional surgery on their guests. In layperson's terms, Russell described the ayahuasca experience as a lucid dream with embedded messages. He sat with ayahuasca on five nights, and during his fourth ceremony Rodgers (who was not present) emerged as what his friend called "the star of the entire show."

This was how Russell described his hallucinogenic vision for this book: "I saw into who Aaron is, and I saw the reason that his potential was not being met, because his potential is not who he is on the football field. That is what has given him the platform and profile to give his gift, is the way I see it.

"In the ceremony that night . . . I saw him for exactly who he is and it brought me to tears. I stand in awe of him as a man, and in so many ways he's trapped inside of his own archetype, trapped inside this shell, this ego of a famous football player, when really what he is, is a warrior of a man who has an absolutely gigantic heart and who just wants to love and be loved."

A few months later Russell had a golf date with Rodgers and told him about his experience. That conversation inspired Rodgers's trip to Peru with Patrick and a couple of subsequent retreats with Russell in Costa Rica.

Rodgers sat with Russell for six ceremonies, including one dedicated to healing the trauma caused in their relationship when the quarterback sent him to the Island for years.

"What I saw that night was, he is on a mission, and I'm here in service of his mission," Russell said. "This isn't about me. This is about me serving as a friend and brother. He was destined for the stars from the very beginning."

Rodgers had to cut short his first ayahuasca journey as he raced to leave Peru before the encroaching COVID virus caused the closure of its borders. But he said the two nights on his first trip "gave me a deep and meaningful appreciation for life." He said that the medicine allowed him to feel pure love like never before, and that he could transfer to others the unconditional love he found for himself. Rodgers said ayahuasca allowed him to relate better to the people he cared about.

"I really feel like that experience paved the way for me to have the best season of my career," Rodgers said of 2020.

He followed that season up in 2021 with his third consecutive 13-3 season, his fourth league MVP award (putting him second all-time, behind Peyton Manning's five), and his second straight MVP award since his team drafted his replacement. Rodgers was doing to the Jordan Love plan in Green Bay what Tom Brady had done to the Jimmy Garoppolo plan in New England.

He had become a different player and leader in his relatively old age, at least according to his former offensive coordinator, Joe Philbin, who used to sit in the Lambeau press box in awe of Rodgers's accuracy and textbook mechanics and footwork, while also wincing a bit after the quarterback showed up receivers who made mistakes.

Philbin never wanted to take away Rodgers's competitiveness or chippiness, the edge that made him great. "But now and again I'd grab him and we'd talk and I'd say, 'Look, we want urgency out of the players, but showing frustration in the wrong way at the wrong time isn't helping the situation,'" Philbin told me. "Whether that was having his palms up in front of seventy-five thousand people, he was so competitive early in his career that it just came up.

"It wasn't that he wanted to make Jordy Nelson or James Jones feel bad by showing them up on *Monday Night Football*.... That was the one thing we visited on as much as anything else. The quarterback in the Green Bay offensive system was a huge position, with a lot of autonomy, and with each passing year we gave him more because he could handle it, and then some. And with that is an obligation to set a great example for his teammates."

Did Rodgers get better at that part of his job as he got older?

"Yes, he did," Philbin said.

Allen Lazard, with the Packers since 2018, had a different look at it. Undrafted out of Iowa State, Lazard was forever indebted to Rodgers for noticing his talent during OTAs, approaching him in the lunch line, and making him feel like a few million bucks by telling him he should be practicing with the first-stringers.

After earning the quarterback's trust, Lazard found himself on the wrong end of some harsh rebukes. The 2019 Packers were trailing the Chargers on the road the first time Rodgers yelled at Lazard, after the receiver missed a signal that Rodgers had made up on the fly that week, confusing it with a signal already in the system. Lazard ran a route when he was supposed to block, wrecking a play and compromising the comeback attempt, and then braced for impact.

"I already felt guilty and then I turned around and he's just staring at me," Lazard recalled. "It was just, 'Motherfucker, you've got to do this.' He was just cussing me out and everything. It's all from a good place with him.... He just holds himself to such a high standard that he doesn't lower for anybody, no matter who you are, a rookie or a twenty-year vet."

As his relationship with the front office fell apart, Rodgers maintained a strong rapport with the people who mattered most. He had a solid relationship with Matt LaFleur—though he could've lived without the pre-snap motion LaFleur favored in his Kyle Shanahan–inspired West Coast offense—and great ones with offensive coordinator Nathaniel Hackett and position coach Luke Getsy. Better yet, his teammates held him in high regard.

Tim Boyle, undrafted backup quarterback, said Rodgers made him feel at home from their very first meeting together, asking about his family in a fully engaged way. During the preseason of his rookie year, Boyle went out to dinner with family members (including aunts, uncles, and cousins) at Chives, Rodgers's favorite restaurant. The starter picked up the entire tab without Boyle knowing in advance; the two became close friends.

David Bakhtiari spoke of how kind Rodgers had been to his parents and brothers, and of how gracious the quarterback was in taking a test to become an ordained minister so he could officiate his left tackle's wedding. "He's got a bigger heart than he even knows," Bakhtiari said.

Another good friend, Randall Cobb, made Rodgers a groomsman in his wedding and the godfather to his son Cade and called him "one of the most special individuals that I've been around." Cobb was touched when Rodgers flew to Nashville to celebrate Cade's birthday.

"He came all the way from California to be there for a three-year-old's birthday in the backyard with a bunch of kids," Cobb said. Rodgers also attended the receiver's 2016 commencement ceremony at the University of Kentucky, which meant everything to Cobb as the first member of his immediate family to graduate from college.

The best man at Cobb's 2017 wedding, former Kentucky teammate Ed Berry, met Rodgers at Cobb's bachelor party and became his marketing agent at Creative Artists Agency as well as one of his close friends. Berry asked Rodgers to be his son's godfather.

"I had my own preconceived notions of him before I met him," the agent told me, "what I thought he was in the media. . . . I thought he was a distant, standoffish guy, but when I hung out with him he was just like us. He was a regular dude."

Berry's job at CAA was to make Rodgers as marketable as possible, and the quarterback did not always aid that cause. The agent wanted people to know how generous his client was, and Rodgers often preferred to keep his donations of time and money private. They fought about it all the time.

"If people knew a tenth of the things he did for . . . all the different organizations he partnered with, they'd be shocked," Berry said. "I genuinely respect the way he goes about it. He's not a guy who goes to the hospital and posts a selfie that says, 'Hey, look at me in the hospital.'"

Berry explained to Rodgers that publicity for his charitable deeds would help organizations raise money from other sources. "But he's really, really passionate about keeping it low-key," the agent said. "Almost all of his donations he does anonymously. And I can share countless stories of cars he bought for individuals, and I've never seen that reported. He refuses to put his name behind it. . . . He's one of the most generous humans I've ever met, and he asks for nothing in return."

Rodgers once rigged a white elephant gift exchange at Christmastime so that tackle Luke Tenuta, a Packers practice-squad player making a relatively modest wage, ended up getting his gift—a new Ford Bronco. "I would have loved to have done media around it," Berry said, "but mum's the word. He doesn't say anything."

The agent said that some years ago in Green Bay, Rodgers paid for the Christmas needs of numerous local food banks and sought no publicity on it. Berry himself was on the receiving end of his client's generosity after he moved from New York City to Atlanta.

Rodgers had recalled that at a 2017 State Farm photo shoot, with people passing time by talking about the Porsches and Lamborghinis they would kill for, Berry, a country boy, cited a Ford Raptor as his dream car. About three years later, Rodgers secretly flew Berry's wife out to Green Bay so she could be there when he gave her stunned husband a new Ford Raptor with a red bow on it. The quarterback had jotted down a note to himself in 2017 to buy his friend the car whenever Berry moved out of the big city.

"I couldn't believe he was thoughtful enough to remember that," Berry said. "I broke down. It's a microcosm of who he is."

Rodgers had long made it a point to listen to people talk and to pull tidbits from conversations that might lead to bridge-building gestures down the road. He kept lists of these tidbits in his Notes app on his phone.

"It could be something as simple as their favorite wine, their favorite cigar, or their favorite place to vacation," Rodgers said. "Something funny, an anecdote, a story, their kids' names."

As much as his friends and colleagues appreciated Rodgers's thoughtfulness, he was not adored in every corner of the pro football universe. One prominent NFL figure who was in regular contact with the Packers called Rodgers "a third-rail personality" who reminded him of a professional wrestling heel. In fact, this person had no use for Rodgers and his stance on the COVID-19 vaccine, describing him as "the stupidest smart person I ever heard talk."

This figure knew hundreds of players, including past and present members of every team in the league. And as much as he wished Rodgers would just go away, or at least quit talking about the pandemic for keeps, this person said, "I have to admit, I have yet to meet an NFL player who doesn't like him."

This person had never met Greg Jennings and Jermichael Finley, former Packers who had repeatedly assailed Rodgers for what they believed to be his inadequacies as a leader. The quarterback complained that criticism of his approach kept coming from the same two players who hadn't been in the organization for years, and pointed out that he had spent a couple of hours with Finley in the hospital the night he suffered a serious neck injury.

Years later, Finley recalled that grim night and how much it meant to him that Rodgers was among the first to arrive at the hospital. He already knew the quarterback cared about him from their weekly Saturday night talks, and he wanted it pointed out that he thought of Rodgers as a genius, and that his son Kaydon, a big-time college recruit, was one of A-Rod's biggest fans.

"I knew every freakin' catch from that guy was special," Finley told me. "He was better than [Tom] Brady all day. He can walk away from the game as the best player that ever played . . . But I never had closure talking to 12 about all the things that were said. There's a cutoff with him. If you talk crap about him, you're not his guy. You've got to be on 12's team. You've got to be his guy and do it his way, or you're nothing."

Finley had not been in contact with Rodgers for obvious reasons. One playmaker from those years who did stay in touch, Ryan Grant, said he understood where Finley and Jennings were coming from even though he said he dearly loved Rodgers and did not think he could have been a better team leader.

"All of us would say that hands down we had the best quarterback in the league," Grant said for this book. "But in the same breath we also knew we made him better. We also understood he was able to be Aaron Rodgers because we were actually really good at what we did. . . . I think that was the message they were trying to get across.

"Me and [Finley] always talked about how crazy A-Rod was as a quarterback. He was bananas. . . . Brady is the GOAT, the greatest of all time, but the best quarterback is Aaron Rodgers. Get the fuck out of here with Brady. But we all wanted that acknowledgment that yeah, we were badasses too."

• • •

ON THE NIGHT of January 8, 2023, the Lambeau Field clock reported that there were still five minutes and forty-nine seconds left for the Green Bay Packers to make the playoffs. And yet it was already clear that Aaron Rodgers had played one season too many for the team that had drafted him. He was about to lose his final game as a Packer, to a Detroit Lions team that was on the rise.

This was no indictment of Rodgers or the GM who had signed him to a three-year, $150 million deal in March, a couple of months after the Packers lost yet another playoff game to the 49ers. Rodgers had won the last two league MVP awards and had been the face of the franchise for so long, and his relationship with Brian Gutekunst had improved. The quarterback felt his opinion was valued by the front office, at last, and he was motivated to finally get the Packers that second Super Bowl before he retired.

How do you just move on from that?

But Rodgers had turned thirty-eight years old, and after advancing to the NFC Championship Game the previous two years, he flamed out against San Francisco in the divisional round to end the 2021 season, failing to throw a touchdown pass in a 13–10 defeat that dropped him to 0-4 in playoff games against the 49ers—the last team he wanted beating him in sudden-death situations.

Rodgers did have the Super Bowl ring that the 49ers had not won since he entered the league, and he did have a 6-3 regular-season record against them. That included a remarkable victory in September 2021 that saw him need only 34 of the remaining 37 seconds—without any time-outs—to lead Green Bay from its own 25 into position for the winning field goal, and to exit the field with a Tiger Woods fist pump.

It was a memorable regular season in 2021, as per norm. Rodgers beat the Bears on the road with two touchdown passes and a scoring run in the fourth quarter that he punctuated with his championship-belt celebration and a taunt of the crowd, shouting, "I own you. All my fucking life, I own you." On that day, Rodgers improved his career record against the Bears to 21-5.

Those sights and sounds were forgotten on that cold and snowy postseason night at Lambeau, when Green Bay's dreadful special teams unit came undone again, allowing a blocked field-goal attempt near the end of the first half and a blocked punt-turned-touchdown-return late in the fourth quarter. Special teams players were not the lone fall guys, as Rodgers could not generate a damn thing. He went three-and-out on his last possession after throwing a failed third-down deep ball to Davante Adams, who was double covered, while Allen Lazard was uncovered for a potential huge gain.

The Packers' defense was brilliant against Kyle Shanahan's offense (San Francisco's first lead came on the game's final play, a Robbie Gould field goal), compelling Rodgers to say, "I definitely take my fair share of blame tonight."

As tough as it would have been to trade a first-ballot Hall of Famer who had won thirty-nine regular-season games over the previous three years, and the last two MVPs, that was exactly what Gutekunst should have done.

Rodgers still had value, though his one-and-done playoff performance just indicated that value was about to decline. He had gone eleven straight years without leading the Packers back to the Super Bowl, raising questions about his ability to seize those postseason moments of truth and play like he did during the regular season.

Was Rodgers a mere victim of unexceptional coaching and supporting casts that were too heavy to carry from January into February? Or had he lost that killer postseason mentality that once inspired him to grab a Super Bowl run by the throat with fearless passes, leaving him too concerned about throwing interceptions that could hurt his team and his legacy?

Rodgers's performances in the fourth quarters of recent elimination games had been particularly troubling. The evidence suggesting that he could no longer lead the Packers to the big game was beyond circumstantial.

Rodgers would have benefited from a fresh start with a new team, but in 2022 he no longer felt the way he'd felt about Packers decision-makers the previous offseason. He no longer wanted Gutekunst fired. Rodgers decided he should stay in Green Bay, and the Packers decided they should give him the three-year, $150 million deal to do just that. They also decided to trade away Adams, the All-Pro who had combined for 238 receptions, nearly 3,000 receiving yards, and 29 touchdown catches the previous two seasons.

The result in 2022 was predictable. Rodgers watched rookie receiver Christian Watson, a second-round pick, drop a walk-in 75-yard touchdown in the season-opening loss to Minnesota, setting an ominous tone. The quarterback lost seven of eight starts in the middle of the season to fall to 4-8, in part because he was playing with a fractured right thumb suffered against the Giants in London.

It was a freak injury, suffered on a final-play heave, but that's what happens to older players who slow down. They suffer freak injuries on final-play heaves.

The Packers rallied to win four games to put themselves in position to qualify for the postseason with a Week 18 victory over the Lions. Rodgers's thumb was throbbing on a Lambeau night when the wind chill was in the teens. On the first series, facing a third-and-goal from the 4-yard line, Rodgers had a chance to run to the right corner of the end zone, much like he did on third-and-goal against Tampa Bay two years earlier in the NFC Championship Game.

Once again, he chose to throw a ball that was not caught. That's what old, banged-up quarterbacks do.

Down 20–16 with 5:49 left, Rodgers had the ball at his own 21 with a chance to save the season. He completed two short passes for a first down, an encouraging start. But then he overthrew Lazard on the left sideline, missing an open Christian Watson in the seam, before he fired low and wide of AJ Dillon on the right sideline with Detroit's six-foot-five, 285-pound John Cominsky about to nail Rodgers into the ground.

The quarterback got up slowly, his jersey pulled beneath his right shoulder pad by his crash landing. It was third-and-10 at his own 33 with 3:37 to go. Rodgers called the play and then clapped with his teammates as they broke the huddle and took their positions. He took a few steps toward the line of scrimmage with his hands stuffed in his jersey pouch, called for the snap, and then dropped back to pass for the last time as a member of the Green Bay Packers.

The Lions called a blitz that produced almost immediate pressure up the middle, and Rodgers stood firm and heaved a long ball to the right side while getting hit and hit hard. The ball floated long enough for Detroit rookie safety Kerby Joseph to settle under it as if fielding a punt. Rodgers's final throw as a Packer was much like Brett Favre's final throw as a Packer—an interception, a damaging one. Only this time around, Green Bay was not losing in overtime of the NFC Championship Game. Green Bay was being denied a berth in the playoffs.

His jersey now pulled beneath his left shoulder pad, Rodgers yelled at the sideline as he walked off the field. Detroit kept possession until Jared Goff took a knee and the clock showed zeroes. Rodgers shared long, meaningful embraces with a procession of younger Lions who grew up watching him. Rookie receiver Jameson Williams, the first-round pick from Alabama, asked the opposing quarterback for his jersey.

"I gotta hold on to this one," Rodgers told him.

No. 12 started looking around Lambeau, the temperature making small clouds of his breath. Rodgers took his time leaving the field with Randall Cobb at his side. They put their arms around each other and cut through a tangle of photographers. Rodgers waved at the cheering fans before he hit the tunnel, then told a camera operator to give him space. He again wrapped his right arm around Cobb as the two disappeared down the ramp.

Rodgers was not confirming anything afterward, other than the fact that he would not wait long to tell the Packers that he was retiring, requesting a trade, or requesting one more year at 1265 Lombardi Avenue. "I'm not going to hold them hostage," he said.

But it was already clear how this story needed to end. Rodgers used his final press conference to take a Mike McCarthy–esque shot at Matt LaFleur. "Those last three calls definitely sting a little bit," he said. "But still got to execute." Rodgers had screamed at his head coach over his play calling near the end of a November victory over Dallas in overtime.

After losing to Detroit in the finale, Rodgers was asked why the offense never got untracked during the season. The quarterback borrowed a page from his own passive-aggressive playbook.

"There's a lot of things I can say," he replied, "but I don't feel like saying them right here, right now."

The last question he fielded was conditional: if this was indeed the end, what would Rodgers miss?

He paused and grabbed a bottle of water for a quick sip to clear his throat. Rodgers named a half dozen reporters and cited their individual approaches to the job, having a little fun with it but, in his way, telling those people he appreciated their work. He then said, "I'll miss the guys. I'll miss the fans. Thank you."

And then he walked out. It was over, everyone could see. Rodgers finished 2022 with his career-worst quarterback rating (91.1) and his career-worst yards-per-game average (217.4). He threw 22 fewer touchdown passes than he threw in 2020, and his 12 interceptions were his most since his first year as a starter.

The Packers and Rodgers needed a divorce now as much as the Packers and Favre needed a divorce then. Jordan Love needed to start in his fourth season, just like Rodgers once did, and a trade to make that happen was not a question of if, but of when, and how, and where.

Green Bay was done with the drama. Aaron Rodgers had to find a new cause, and it would come in the form of a faraway franchise that was more desperate to win the big one than he could ever be.

13

HEARTBREAK

As he stood and waited for the snap on the MetLife Stadium field, a surreal sight in New York Jets colors, Aaron Rodgers had everything right in front of him. A new home. A new career. A new ending to write for one of the most improbable football stories ever told.

More people were watching at home on September 11 than had ever viewed an ESPN *Monday Night Football* game—22.64 million in all, surpassing the record 21.8 million viewers for the 2009 clash between the Packers and Vikings. In other words, Rodgers vs. the world now commanded even more attention than Rodgers vs. Brett Favre then.

It was the twenty-second anniversary of the 9/11 attacks, and the Jets' No. 8 was making his grand debut against the Buffalo Bills just across the river from the World Trade Center site and the memorial beams of light ascending to the heavens on what had been a stormy evening.

Wearing the team captain's gold *C* on the upper-right chest of his white jersey, Rodgers stepped out of his pregame routine to say hello to a couple of good friends on the sidelines, Justin Timberlake and Brian Baumgartner. How many people could count the Prince of Pop and Kevin from *The Office* as confidants and golf buds?

Baumgartner had attended his share of Packers games at Lambeau, but this was different. He said that when Method Man called Rodgers out of the tunnel, and his friend came charging out with an outsized American flag, the crowd sounded louder and more energized than any he had ever heard at a Super Bowl, World Series, NBA Finals, or Olympic event.

"That was probably the craziest introduction I've ever been a part of," agreed Rodgers's father, Ed, who was in the stands with his wife, Darla.

Just about everyone inside MetLife said and felt the same thing. This was a Jets crowd unlike any other. This was an opening-night crowd unlike any before it. Bob Wischusen, radio voice of the Jets, was on the field when Rodgers first ran out for warmups with the stadium half-filled. Wischusen had been part of the radio crew since 1997 and, he told me, "I've never experienced that. I've never been down on the field for warmups when you heard a roar rise up in the building like that."

Even lifelong Jets fans who were not in the building felt the electricity in their living rooms. Restaurant owner Frank Garritano, born right after Super Bowl III, had not allowed himself to buy into the Rodgers hype because his beloved team had burned him far too many times.

"But when he ran onto the field with the American flag, that's when I got all in," Garritano said. "He was like Captain America running out there. I felt, finally, this is really happening. It's like when you want to date that beautiful girl and it takes forever to build up the nerve to ask her out, and when you finally do, she says yes. That's how I felt that night."

Former Jets quarterback and current CBS analyst Boomer Esiason was watching in bed—he rises at 4 a.m. every day for the top-rated New York morning radio show he hosts with Gregg Giannotti—and thinking about his personal losses suffered on 9/11 when he saw Rodgers run out with the flag.

Esiason lost a friend and board member of his foundation to fight cystic fibrosis, Timothy O'Brien of Cantor Fitzgerald, in the terrorist attacks that also destroyed the foundation's offices in the North Tower of the World Trade Center.

"The whole thing was amazing," Esiason said for this book. "For someone directly affected by 9/11, it just gave me chills. I felt the Jets just did it right. The right tact. The right reverence for a terrible day. To see him coming out with the American flag, I was envious. I was like, 'I wish I could do that.'"

Once upon a time, Esiason was brought home by the Jets to do what he had done for the Bengals—lead them to the Super Bowl. It did not work out, because things almost never did for the Jets. They had not been to the Super Bowl since man first stepped on the moon. Rodgers and his slingshot arm were hired to change all that. He was hired to do what Favre failed to do in his one-and-done season with the Jets in 2008.

After he ran out with the flag through rows of teammates, low-fiving them with his free left hand, Rodgers and star cornerback Sauce Gardner came together for their personal handshake and greeting—making like they were smoking marijuana—before the quarterback knocked helmets with the mountainous offensive tackle, Mekhi Becton, whom Rodgers had taken on as a project. The introductions were accompanied by billowing, machine-generated smoke, pulsating music, and flashing waves of green LED lights. "The building looked like a giant nightclub," wrote ESPN's Rich Cimini.

Studio 54 meets Season 55—It had been fifty-five years since Broadway Joe Namath and the Jets beat the heavily favored Baltimore Colts in Super Bowl III, changing pro football forever. In his introductory press conference in April, Rodgers threw his first touchdown pass as a Jet when he said he noticed during his morning tour of the team's practice facility "that the Super Bowl III trophy is looking a little lonely."

Standing beside his former Packers teammate Randall Cobb, Rodgers had his eyes closed and his hands behind his back for part of the national anthem sung from the stands by New York City police officer Brianna Fernandez, whose father was a detective working the Ground Zero site who later died of 9/11-related cancer. Rodgers put on his NYPD cap and wrapped Cobb in a bear hug when Fernandez was done, and then it was time to play ball against a quarterback, Josh Allen, who grew up wanting to be just like Green Bay's No. 12.

Buffalo took the ball first, managed only one first down, and punted to the Jets. Rodgers jogged onto the field to thunderous applause. His first snap came from under center, and his first play was simple: hand the ball to Breece Hall, the explosive second-year back coming off a torn ACL, and watch him run left for 26 yards.

The Jets started working off Hall's rust, and it was time to do the same for their thirty-nine-year-old quarterback, who played two series the entire preseason, using one to throw a dazzling touchdown pass to Garrett Wilson against the Giants. Rodgers was asked to throw on the next two plays, and on the first he barely kicked out of a sack before scrambling to his right and throwing it away. On the second, he got hit on a short incomplete pass that was negated by a defensive holding penalty.

HEARTBREAK

It was first-and-10 at the Jets' 43-yard line three minutes and twenty seconds into the opening quarter. Out of the shotgun, with a tight end and two outside receivers to his right and Wilson split to his left, Rodgers leaned forward, barked out the signals, and took the snap as Dalvin Cook exited the backfield for the left flat.

Rodgers took a three-step drop and planted at the 36 as Wilson ran a quick route toward the middle of the field. The brilliant young receiver was open. Aaron Rodgers just had to do what he had done 8,435 times in his regular-season and postseason NFL career.

Throw the damn ball.

• • •

GREEN BAY'S DECISION-MAKERS wanted to trade Aaron Rodgers, make no mistake about that. Adam Schefter reported their preference in January, citing league sources, and after longtime sportscaster Trey Wingo tweeted in March that Rodgers-to-the-Jets was definitely happening, Schefter sent a text to the quarterback looking for confirmation.

"Lose my number," Rodgers texted back. "Good try tho."

Later that month at the owners' meetings in Phoenix, Packers GM Brian Gutekunst told people, "At least Adam got a response from him." Rodgers had not been returning Gutekunst's calls and texts. He also was not returning messages from his head coach, Matt LaFleur, who was said to be angered by the quarterback's criticism of his play calling near the end of the Detroit loss that cost Green Bay a playoff berth.

Gutekunst had said as far back as February, at the draft combine, that the team needed to talk to Rodgers to determine its proper course of action. A scheduled meeting between the two never came off. At the owners' meetings in late March, after Rodgers announced on *The Pat McAfee Show* that he intended to play for the Jets, Gutekunst said he was still coming up empty trying to reach his franchise player despite many attempts.

"I was really looking forward to those conversations with Aaron to see how he fit into that," the GM said. "Those never transpired. So there came a time where we had to make some decisions. We went through his representatives to try to talk to him [about] where we were going with our team. At that point, they informed us that he would like to be traded to the Jets."

Just as the old Packers front office was fed up with Brett Favre's never-ending drama and eager to find out about Rodgers, the current Packers front office was done with Rodgers's drama and anxious to see what it had in Jordan Love.

Green Bay coaches were also fatigued by Rodgers's choice to elect himself the de facto offensive coordinator. The actual offensive coordinator, Adam Stenavich, later admitted that "half the time when you get done with a drive . . . you'd just be trying to figure out what play was called." Stenavich added that when Rodgers made checks at the line, the coaching staff "didn't know exactly what was happening at the time."

In the wake of the Davante Adams trade in the spring of 2022, Rodgers ultimately helped make Green Bay's decision by not showing up for OTA sessions that would have helped him develop chemistry with the three receivers the team had just drafted. Kansas City's Patrick Mahomes, meanwhile, responded to the loss of Tyreek Hill (in a trade to Miami) by attending OTAs after working out with his receivers in Texas and explaining that the extra relationship-building time in the offseason is "what made us so great over these last few years."

Mahomes won his second Super Bowl title and his second league MVP award while Rodgers went 8-9 and, with the season at stake in the Detroit finale, produced next to nothing against the defense that had surrendered the most yards in the league. He failed to throw for 300 yards in any of his seventeen starts.

Rodgers later dismissed any connection between missed OTAs and his declining production, telling Matt Schneidman of *The Athletic*, "I won MVP without doing offseason workouts." Yes, that 2021 season was the second half of what Rodgers liked to call his "back-to-back COVID MVPs." And yet the notion that his absence did not hurt the new receivers defied common sense.

So did his later dog-ate-my-homework claim that poor cell service in his Malibu home was behind his failure to return Gutekunst's messages. "You have to FaceTime me," Rodgers said with a straight face.

He had a problem with the Packers' timing, too. "My point was, if there was a change that wanted to be made, why wasn't that told to me earlier in the offseason?" Rodgers said. If this was an open window on his high-maintenance act in Green Bay, nobody in the Jets' orbit was terribly interested in looking through it. For the time being, anyway.

One former front-office executive who spent eleven years in New York, helping the Giants and a drama-free quarterback (Eli Manning) win two

Super Bowls, said the FaceTime story should have been one of several neon warning signs for the Jets. "Come on, really, who does that?" Marc Ross, former Giants VP of player evaluation and director of college scouting and current NFL Network analyst, said for this book.

"You want a quarterback who is the most low-maintenance person in the building, a real leader. When you have to deal with that high-maintenance stuff every day, you can't win like that. If he brings that here to New York, it's going to be really bad."

Before the Jets could start worrying about how bad it might get, they had to get Rodgers on their roster. They took a decisive step in that direction in late January, when they hired an A-Rod favorite, Nathaniel Hackett, as their offensive coordinator despite his disastrous fifteen-game run as Broncos head coach. Rodgers did not follow Hackett to Denver, though it had been one of his preferred 2021 destinations (his fiancée at the time, Shailene Woodley, had a home in Boulder). The Jets were hoping he might follow Hackett to New York anyway.

First Rodgers needed to decide if he wanted to play a nineteenth season anywhere in the NFL. "I wanted to go into my darkness retreat and sit with it and contemplate," he said. A darkness retreat?

Only Aaron Rodgers could audible to one of those to determine if he should keep slinging footballs for a living. He later told Pat McAfee that he was "ninety percent retiring" on his way into Sky Cave in the wilderness of southern Oregon, near Klamath Falls. He spent four nights there in total darkness, housed in a soundproof, three-hundred-square-foot Hobbit hole equipped with an organic latex mattress, a sink, bath, toilet, and a meditation mat. Guests in the darkness could not see a hand in front of their faces, though they were free to light a candle, turn on a light, or go outside for a walk.

"It's not like an endurance test," Scott Berman, founder of Sky Cave Retreats, told me. "There's no prize for finishing it and not turning on the light. There's no benefit in somebody finishing it, like, zero. The benefit really comes from people intimately connecting with themselves, in their body, and resting and settling with that.

"The first upside is you see what you haven't been able to see, and you feel what you haven't been able to feel. . . . You go into the darkness and your subconscious opens pretty quickly and you begin to see all of these different things that have motivated and informed your behaviors and actions.... As you see that you also feel it in your body, and it's uncomfortable for everybody, no matter how prepared someone thinks they are."

Rodgers stayed in one of the three overnight caves at the retreat. He was served three organic meals, which were delivered through a double door around sunset. Once a day, Berman contacted his guests from the other side of their cave doors. Otherwise, Rodgers was undisturbed in the dark, left all alone with his thoughts.

"There were moments of serenity for sure," he said. "And moments of, 'What the hell am I doing here?' I think I just contemplated life as a retired player and life as an active player, and it gave me a peace about both decisions."

He was leaning toward playing, and he knew that playing for Green Bay was likely off the board. Fans held rallies for Favre in 2008; nobody was rallying for a Rodgers return in 2023.

"Aaron will always be beloved, and he will sell out the banquet when they put him in the Packers' Hall of Fame, and fans will show up in Canton when he's inducted into the Hall of Fame," said Green Bay superfan Kyle Cousineau. "But we went through it for so many years with Favre that we were just sick of the bullshit with Rodgers. As soon as the season was done and he didn't have an answer by the time the Super Bowl was played, everyone was like, 'OK, you're going on a darkness retreat to figure it out? See you later.'"

After suffering through two wildly disappointing seasons with their No. 2 overall pick in 2021, Zach Wilson, the Jets requested and received permission from the Packers to talk to Rodgers, who agreed to meet them in his Malibu villa. Three planes taking off from New Jersey, Florida, and Colorado transported a Jets delegation that included seventy-five-year-old owner Woody Johnson, his brother and vice chairman Christopher, general manager Joe Douglas, head coach Robert Saleh, team president Hymie Elhai, and the human icebreaker, Hackett. Rodgers's agent, David Dunn, also attended the meeting.

Christopher Johnson arrived at Rodgers's place first, and despite later reports that the Douglas-Saleh-Elhai-Hackett plane out of New Jersey was delayed by headwinds, a prominent NFL figure with ties to the Johnsons and the Jets found it interesting that Christopher arrived at Rodgers's place a half hour ahead of everyone else, including his brother. "Everybody will tell you that Chris is a better people person than Woody," the figure said.

The Jets said that there was no such plan of staggered arrivals in place, and that Chris got there early by happenstance. But if the Jets' game plan all along was to get Chris there first?

"It's genius if it was their grand plan," said Rodgers, who had returned from a workout to find Woody's brother waiting for him at his house.

"We had twenty minutes, just him and I," Rodgers said. "I love Chris, I really do. I feel like I'll have a lifetime friendship with him regardless of what happens."

Either way, the prominent league figure said the team had reason to be concerned about Woody spending a five-hour recruiting visit in the company of a sensitive superstar known to analyze every syllable out of everyone's mouth. And a sensitive superstar who had never worked for an actual team owner to boot.

As it turned out, by keeping it light and not throwing hard-sell fastballs at their target, the Jets nearly pitched a perfect game inside Rodgers's $28 million home. Woody got off to a strong start when he gave his host a gift from his time as U.S. ambassador to the United Kingdom: honey from Queen Elizabeth's garden.

"He didn't say a whole lot," the quarterback said of the owner. Rodgers recalled that he spent much of the time talking to Saleh inside while the rest of the group mingled on the outside deck that overlooked the Pacific Ocean.

"There wasn't a whole lot of 'The Woody Show,'" Rodgers told me. "But once we talked, he said all the right things. He wanted to win. He was willing to spend the money and get the right guys, and I enjoyed him. I like Woody."

When I asked him if he joked with Woody, the Johnson & Johnson heir, about his refusal to take the pharmaceutical company's vaccine, Rodgers said, "No. Me and Chris have joked around about it."

During the visit, the Jets' contingent tried and failed to not appear starstruck. Douglas was sitting there asking himself, *Is this really happening? Am I really sitting here talking to Aaron Rodgers about coming and playing for a team that I work with? Is this real?*

It was as real as the whitecaps on the Pacific out back.

"I didn't want to leave," Douglas said.

When Jets officials finally did depart, photographers were waiting for them. Rodgers pointed out that they would not have attracted paparazzi had they not parked their cars on the street in front of his home. He did not commit to the Jets in the meeting. He needed to attack his workouts to see if his body and spirit responded and told him to play on. But everyone in Rodgers's home that day felt good about where this was headed.

In the small hours of March 13, Douglas got the call from Dunn that his client wanted to be a New York Jet. The GM ran around his house "muffling his screams so that he would not wake up his family," wrote Brian Costello of the *New York Post*. Douglas sent texts to his fellow recruiters so they could rise in the morning to the incredible news.

The Jets were about to land the biggest sports star that any New York franchise had chased since the Knicks swung and missed (badly) on LeBron James in 2010. (N.B.: Kevin Durant had been named league MVP once, not four times, before Brooklyn signed him.)

The Packers were pushing for more compensation than the Jets wanted to give, and Rodgers's disclosure, heading into the darkness, that he was 90 percent done, had Woody Johnson worried. None of that mattered. The moment Rodgers entered his desire into the public record with Pat McAfee and A. J. Hawk, the deal had to be made.

The Jets and Packers danced the dance for weeks before concluding that the trade had to be completed by the April 27 start of the draft. They finally agreed on Monday, April 24, that in exchange for Rodgers, the Packers' 2023 first-rounder (No. 15), and their 2023 fifth-rounder, the Jets should send to Green Bay their 2023 first-round pick (No. 13), a 2023 second-round pick, and a 2024 second-round pick that upgraded to a first-rounder if Rodgers played at least 65 percent of the snaps.

"We had a really nice meeting," Aaron Rodgers said of the Malibu sitdown, "and at that point I felt like [New York] is where I was supposed to be. I really try and listen to the signs and synchronicities that the universe puts in our face every day, and this was basically the direction that everything was pointing."

In Green Bay, the *Press-Gazette* ran a poll asking fans if they thought the Packers made the right decision by trading Rodgers, and 88 percent of the respondents answered "Yes." In New York, Jets fans were even closer to 100 percent in their support of the deal.

Rodgers touched down in New Jersey late Tuesday night, unpacked at the hotel, and tried and failed to persuade his West Coast body clock to fall into a deep East Coast sleep. He stayed awake thinking about how special this new opportunity could be.

The Jets scheduled Rodgers's introductory press conference for the following day at 2 p.m. Reporters were asked to show up at least an hour early.

That morning Rodgers rolled up in a dark Chevy Tahoe sporting a stylish new haircut and a neat salt-and-pepper beard, looking nothing like that hollow and haggard figure last seen leaving Lambeau Field with Randall Cobb. As an office address, 1 Jets Drive wasn't exactly 1265 Lombardi Avenue, but it would serve its purpose.

"He's here," the Jets posted on Twitter along with a slow-motion video of Rodgers arriving at the office.

He removed his shades after entering Atlantic Health Jets Training Center and walked into a handshake and half bro-hug from Woody. Meanwhile, someone in the background screeched like a teen who had just spotted Harry Styles at the mall.

Rodgers was greeted by the same men who had visited him in Malibu. The quarterback exchanged hugs and back pats with all. After embracing Douglas, Rodgers stepped back, stuffed his hands in his hoodie pockets, and smiled as he took in a room graced by large photos of Joe Namath and the Jets toppling the Baltimore Colts in Super Bowl III.

"All right," Rodgers said. He was reborn at age thirty-nine.

Unlike Brett Favre, who really wanted no part of the New York market fifteen years earlier, Rodgers saw the big city as a big chance to enhance his legacy and to perform corrective surgery on his brand.

The original A-Rod who identified this opportunity, Alex Rodriguez, got himself traded to the Yankees on Valentine's Day, 2004, and found little love waiting for him. Derek Jeter did not want his former friend on the team, and it seemed half the fan base agreed with the captain. The Yankees had advanced to six World Series in the previous eight years and had won four of them. They did not need Rodriguez and his me-centric ways.

The A-Rod to follow nearly two decades later, Rodgers, faced no such resistance. The Jets did not have a Jeter and had not suited one up since Namath. Every other metropolitan New York team in the four major men's sports had won a championship since the Jets honored Namath's guarantee on January 12, 1969. The Giants had won four, the Yankees had won seven, the Mets had won two, the Knicks had won two, the Nets had won two (ABA), the Rangers had won one, the Islanders had won four, and the Devils had won three.

Rodgers knew that winning a title for a New York franchise that had not won it all in more than half a century would take his historical standing to an entirely different place. He didn't need to ask Rangers icon Mark Messier about that.

"If Aaron Rodgers won the Super Bowl with the Jets," said one of the team's most recognizable fans, longtime New York radio host Joe Benigno, "he would be Messier on steroids."

Or, as longtime *New York Post* columnist and former Jets beat writer Steve Serby put it, "He would be a Messier and a Messiah."

But first things first: Rodgers wanted to win the introductory press conference. As the media waited for him in the auditorium, a large video board served up a loop of Rodgers highlights while the sounds of Charlie Puth's "One Call Away" filled the room. Like the song said, "I'll be there to save the day."

This felt even bigger than the Favre deal, which felt momentous when it was slapped together in the middle of training camp, after the Packers legend had unretired. Favre appeared as a Jet for the first time in a packed interview room in the bowels of Cleveland Browns Stadium, of all places, and admitted before the Jets-Browns preseason game that he would have preferred to stay in the NFC North and play for Minnesota. Green Bay included a poison-pill provision in the trade that would have forced the Jets to surrender three first-round picks if they dared to ship Favre to any club in its division.

NFLShop.com reported that it sold more than 6,500 Favre jerseys in his first full day with the Jets, a one-day record. Mayor Michael Bloomberg welcomed Favre at City Hall, and 10,500 fans greeted him the following day at practice, another one-day record for the team's four decades at Hofstra University.

Johnson compared the Favre phenomenon to an Elvis sighting. But after Favre's arm injury wrecked a promising 8-3 start and cost his team a playoff spot, Elvis left the building. He retired again and ultimately persuaded general manager Mike Tannenbaum and Johnson to grant him an unconditional release so he could sign with the Vikings, with no first-rounders heading to Green Bay.

On arrival, Aaron Rodgers had no such escape from New York highlighted in his playbook. Just as Brady had picked the perfect post-Patriots team in the Tampa Bay Bucs, to prove something to Bill Belichick and everyone else, Rodgers had seemingly found an ideal partner in his second NFL marriage. The Jets had a Loserville history—Belichick had famously walked out on them twenty-three years earlier after twenty-four hours as head coach—and yet they had a roster loaded with talent.

Absurd as it sounds, the Rodgers presser didn't quite match the Tim Tebow presser of 2012, when the presence of more than two hundred reporters forced the Jets to move the circus into their field house. More scribes, broadcasters, and cameras showed up for perhaps the least talented thrower of the football ever than would show up, eleven years later, for perhaps the most talented thrower of the football ever.

It was a memorable occasion all the same. Older generations of reporters and fans knew the full roster of past Jets calamities by way of shorthand. The Mud Bowl. Gastineau's late hit. Marino's fake spike. Testaverde's Achilles. Belichick quitting as HC of the NYJ. The Butt Fumble. And on and on.

Losing impacts everyone and everything in and around an organization, and that's why Rodgers got an ovation from Jets employees in the back of the room when he entered with Saleh and Douglas, the three of them wearing team golf shirts. This wasn't your garden-variety Q&A with the media. This was a pep rally, too, for an organization sick and tired of wearing a "Kick Me" sign on its back.

The men took their seats behind an onstage table, with Rodgers flanked by the GM and coach, before Jets communications chief Eric Gelfand called Woody Johnson to the podium. The owner of the team that had not reached the playoffs since the 2010 season and had not won the AFC East in two decades said the Jets couldn't be happier to employ Rodgers and asked for another round of applause for the guest of honor. Woody's employees obliged.

"Welcome to New York, Aaron," Johnson said. "We're glad to have you."

Rodgers took it from there.

He thanked all the requisite parties, including the Packers for "an incredible run," and called this Wednesday "a surreal day for me." He declared himself ready for a new adventure before saying, "I'll open it up to questions now."

Aaron Rodgers was already running the show.

Fans were closely watching their phones, laptops, and TVs for any sign that the small-town Northern California guy from the smallest NFL market might flinch in the bright lights. He did not. During the formal portion of the give-and-take, Rodgers was asked if he ever thought the trade might not happen.

"Not really. I believed it was going to happen the entire time," he said. "It was just a matter of waiting each other out. My intention coming out of the darkness was to pursue this opportunity."

Out of the darkness. Rodgers admitted that the presence on the staff of his friend Hackett played a significant role in his decision, as did the ballers assembled by Douglas on both sides of the line. "I'm an old guy," he said, "so I want to be part of a team that can win it all. I believe that this is a place we can get that done."

Rodgers scored more points with the downtrodden fans by name-checking the most familiar cheerleader among them, Fireman Ed, and by stating that he was respectfully declining Namath's invitation to wear his retired No. 12—he was planning to wear his No. 8 from Cal—because, in fact, "12 is Broadway Joe and I didn't want to even go down that path." Rodgers went so far as to call the Jets an "iconic" franchise. When was the last time somebody did that?

After he was done answering the first dozen questions he faced as a Jet, Rodgers was escorted around the auditorium for one-on-ones with the local TV stations before he was brought back to the stage for a less formal exchange with beat writers and columnists.

He told them the Jets were among eight to twelve teams with the talent to be Super Bowl champs, and that he felt part of his job was to restore the confidence of a broken player, Zach Wilson. Rodgers confirmed that he would restructure his contract so his new employers would not be on the books for the ungodly sum of $107.55 million he was due in 2024, and that he would almost certainly play at least a second season with the Jets.

The broken thumb that had compromised his final year in Green Bay had healed up, and Rodgers was feeling a lot younger than his birth certificate suggested he should. He compared this adventure to the first time he left his Chico, California, home and headed off to Berkeley to spend a summer preparing for major-college ball.

"There was like this deep sigh that you take where all is right in the world," he said, "and this is exciting and the adventure and the journey is so unknown and mysterious, and that's the beauty in life because you don't know what's going to happen in the future."

The Jets had soundly beaten Rodgers and the Packers at Lambeau en route to a 7-4 start in 2022, but they had come undone with six straight losses to close out the year. Yes, this had long been a Charlie Brown franchise. Only now it seemed that Lucy was finally holding the ball in place.

In Rodgers's first two days as a Jet, Fanatics reported selling Rodgers gear and merchandise alone, in part because more fans watched his presser on social media (750,000 views) than any other live programming in franchise history. Season-ticket sales shot up 250 percent compared to 2022 after the quarterback's initial announcement on McAfee's show.

And then Rodgers had himself a spring and summer for the ages by diving headfirst into everything that greater Gotham had to offer, taking teammates along for the ride. He attended Knicks and Rangers playoff games, drawing huge ovations at Madison Square Garden. He showed up at the Tony Awards and took in *Chicago* and *Wicked* on Broadway. He went to Taylor Swift and Ed Sheeran concerts at the Jets' stadium, MetLife, and shopped and dined in Manhattan.

He attended OTAs too. The Packers loved seeing that.

Rodgers cherished the luxury of occasionally blending into the background of a city with about eight and a half million residents. He attended Game 6 of the Rangers-Devils playoff series with teammates Breece Hall, Allen Lazard, Connor McGovern, and Tim Boyle, and savored the relatively anonymous stroll for a bite to eat. "We got pizza, and I was talking to him," Hall said. "He said it was cool for him to just walk around like a normal person because he wasn't able to do that for the past million years."

Rodgers still got recognized, a lot. Lazard recalled the quarterback getting out of their car in Manhattan just as a man carrying an umbrella stopped and shrieked, "Oh shit, that's Aaron Rodgers." The quarterback played it cool, said hello, and walked into a store to do some shopping.

"We weren't going out in Green Bay and strolling down Packerland Drive," Lazard said. "We're in the Lower East Side, we're in Manhattan, we're all over the place. So just seeing him interact with people and just embracing the city and the fans and all that, it's something special. And I think that's just a rejuvenation of this place and the energy that the city brings, that can restore a whole new career.

"I know he's really enjoying it. He's stopping, taking pictures with the fans, signing autographs. Those are things that in the past he probably would've just kept pushing and gone about his day just because it would've caused a twenty-minute delay in what he was trying to do. People here . . . whatever they're doing, they care about way more than stopping and following Aaron Rodgers around for twenty minutes."

Rodgers could not possibly live in Manhattan—the commute across the Hudson River to Florham Park would be too taxing—so in late June he settled for a stunning hilltop view of the city skyline via an eight-bedroom, 9.5-bathroom mansion on the Montclair–Cedar Grove border in Jersey that cost him $9.5 million (down from the $11 million asking price in May). Locals found it interesting that Rodgers's home sat between a liberal stronghold (Montclair) and a town that projected a more Trumpian vibe (Cedar Grove). A fitting place for an enigma to live.

A month after the purchase, as a show of great faith to his new neighbors, the quarterback handed back $35 million to the Jets in a contract restructuring designed to help the club sign the likes of Dalvin Cook and improve their championship odds.

Back at the office, starstruck players and coaches were raving about Rodgers's leadership in the huddle, in the locker room, and in the cafeteria. The quarterback made sure he regularly shared meals with distinct groups of teammates and asked other Jets to do the same. He bounced from meeting room to meeting room and, when Hackett was present, did not hesitate to interrupt him to make or enhance a point.

"I've been around a lot of superstars in this league that are very standoffish, that are very isolated, do their own thing, and he's as inclusive as I've ever been around, especially for a player of that caliber," said defensive coordinator Jeff Ulbrich, who had played and coached in the NFL for two decades.

Rodgers was patient with some guys and short with others. Though he hugged offensive tackle Mekhi Becton every day because he thought the mountain man needed that love, Rodgers was never afraid to jump on guys as if he were a coach instead of a teammate.

This was noticed by Marty Lyons, a former Jets defensive lineman who was in his twenty-second year as the team's radio analyst. Lyons saw Rodgers talking to defensive lineman Quinnen Williams one minute, before the entire defensive line gathered around to listen the next. He saw Rodgers talking to cornerback Sauce Gardner one minute, before the entire secondary gathered around to listen the next.

Lyons also heard the quarterback talking shit to Gardner, the all-everything second-year man, during seven-on-seven drills. "So, after practice I introduced myself to Rodgers and said, 'You know what, you really talk a lot of smack out there, don't you?'" Lyons told me. "And he came right out and said, 'I came here to fucking win. And these guys have got to understand that to win on Sunday, you've got to win Monday through Friday.'

"And that's the first time I've ever heard a quarterback with the Jets say that."

The fans embraced Rodgers's approach and turned the team's open practices into block parties. If the Jets became the Boys of Summer, it was because of their leader. Rodgers was nurturing teammates and protecting coaches. He tutored Wilson and ripped Broncos coach Sean Payton for ripping his predecessor, Hackett. He inspired thousands of fans at training camp to chant his name before and after he fired spirals through the tightest of windows to everyone from Garrett Wilson to Corey Davis, including throws of the no-look variety. Several Jets said it seemed at times that Rodgers was just playing *Madden NFL* from the pocket.

"He is a little kid in an old man's body," Saleh had said. "He's having a blast." HBO's *Hard Knocks* crew members were there to capture the joyful mood in training camp. From the moment Green Bay dealt Rodgers to the Jets for a package of draft picks, it was clear Florham Park was the only place for *Hard Knocks* to go.

"I don't care what nobody says about [number] Eight. Eight is a special dude," thirteen-year defensive tackle Al Woods said on the show. "And he's cool as fuck."

Then Woods grabbed a boom mic above his head, pulled it toward his mouth, and added: "Whatever they said about Aaron Rodgers on TV is a lie."

So many things had been said about Aaron Rodgers, it was hard to separate fact from fiction. Was he a diva who showed his true colors in the middle of the 2022 season, when he called for Packers coaches to bench the players who were making mistakes? Did he believe there was one set of rules for his fifty-two teammates, and another for him?

Or was there merely a perception carryover to the field from a

COVID-19 vaccination stance that saw him plummet in Morning Consult's annual survey of American adults rating the likability of NFL players? State Farm had ended its twelve-year partnership with Rodgers, a parting that was inevitable after the vaccination debacle. Controversy-free Patrick Mahomes had become the insurance giant's leading man.

Almost to a player and coach, the Jets were surprised by how eager Rodgers was to build relationships on every level of the building, from the business offices to the equipment room.

"I don't know if I would have thought he was that way prior to him coming here," Ulbrich said. "Some of the things that we all have heard and seen—but he is a fantastic teammate."

Physically, Rodgers hit only one speed bump all preseason. Right out of the gate during OTAs in May, he tweaked his right calf in conditioning drills that saw him hopping around with a medicine ball and dragging a weighted sled that was tethered to his waist—odd things to ask an aging franchise player to do. Asked about it afterward, Rodgers seemed less than thrilled with the drills and responded in a passive-aggressive way that was familiar to the Packers' faithful.

"I haven't done it before," he said. "I haven't done it in eighteen years, but obviously there's some science behind it."

Politically, he committed only one unforced error all preseason. While attending the U.S. Open in early September, Rodgers supported Novak Djokovic's unvaccinated status in an Instagram post that included the hashtag "novaxdjokovic" and a red line obscuring a Moderna ad on a side wall. It was as if Rodgers was testing New York's love for him. It was if he was poking the liberal, pro-vaccine bear. By and large, the fans and the local news media gave him a pass on it.

As much as Rodgers did not initially want HBO cameras documenting his first Jets camp, *Hard Knocks* turned out to be an invaluable infomercial for him. Scores of Jets fans and viewers nationwide came away from that series saying the same thing:

I had no idea he was that good of a guy.

The optimism generated by Rodgers's interviews and *Hard Knocks* appearances, and by the way he looked in practice, made for a strange bedfellow with the indomitable force that was Jet-fan fatalism. Ira Lieberfarb, known in the talk-radio world as "Ira from Staten Island," was representative of a generation of Jets diehards who watched Super Bowl III as kids on small black-and-white TVs in places like Sheepshead Bay. Lieberfarb initially remained skeptical that Rodgers would be the one to duplicate what Namath did back then.

"I thought he was a prima donna," he said, "and everything I thought was wrong. Once I heard him talk, I changed. I never dreamt Rodgers would be like this. There's always been this dark cloud that takes over the organization at the wrong moments, but I think we're finally out of that."

Joe Benigno, local radio legend, watched Super Bowl III at his grandmother's house in Paramus, New Jersey, and collected about $150 in bets from high school classmates who were sure Baltimore was going to win. (One friend paid off the $10 bet with a bag full of one thousand pennies.) "It's basically been fifty-five years of pain ever since," Benigno said.

The talk-show host was about to turn seventy, and he did not want to wait any longer for that second title. "The average Jet fan hasn't been beaten up for close to sixty years like I have," he said. "I haven't had a drink in over ten years because of a hiatal hernia and gout, but if Rodgers and the Jets win the Super Bowl, I will have a double Beefeater Martini."

• • •

AARON RODGERS'S FATHER was sitting in my passenger seat, and Aaron Rodgers's mother was sitting in my back seat. It was late afternoon on September 11, 2023, and we were heading east on Route 3 in New Jersey to attend perhaps the most anticipated regular-season opener in the 104-year history of the National Football League.

All because Aaron Rodgers was playing quarterback for the New York Jets.

Ed Rodgers was wearing a dark Jets cap, a green long-sleeved Jets shirt, and camouflage pants. Darla Rodgers was wearing her own green long-sleeved Jets shirt and rolled-up jeans. Appearing no less fit and athletic than most people half their age, husband and wife were pulled from the pages of a catalogue featuring sixtysomething bliss.

They looked very much like the parents of a star quarterback.

When I pulled up in a Lexus SUV best identified by its dusty shade of autumn shimmer and a "Life's Better with a Beagle" sticker, the statuesque, six-foot-three Ed and the statuesque, five-foot-ten Darla were standing side by side near the tall hedges outside their Airbnb home in Montclair, New Jersey, three and a half miles from their son's $9.5 million mansion.

At Ed's request, I had emailed him transportation options to MetLife Stadium, including possible game-day Uber prices and the New Jersey transit train schedule running through Secaucus Junction. As a backup option, in case they were stuck, I also offered a ride going or returning—free of charge, of course.

They took me up on it, both ways, because (I'm guessing) they were 2,840 driving miles from their relatively quiet, smaller-town existence in Chico, California, and it was best to have a somewhat familiar face and hardened veteran of the Jersey highways navigate the road to and from MetLife.

I had flown across the country in July to visit Chico and to meet Ed for a lengthy interview at a coffee shop; Darla later agreed to a lengthy interview by Aaron's preferred method of communication, FaceTime. Ed and Darla had continued attending Packers home openers and other games here and there even after Aaron had stopped communicating with them, and they felt they needed to be present for the first act of his second professional life. They showed up, even under the most adverse circumstances. It's what mothers and fathers do.

They had bought their tickets through the Jets, and Aaron knew that his parents would be among the 83,345 fans in the house. Ed and Darla were beyond excited to see their own flesh and blood take center stage eight miles from the Broadway shows that Aaron had seen over the summer.

On the ride in, I cautioned Ed and Darla that MetLife Stadium was not exactly Lambeau Field, the shrine that was the Packers' home and the NFL's answer to Wrigley Field and Fenway Park. Completed in 2010 at a cost of $1.6 billion, sold and advertised as a necessary upgrade on old Giants Stadium, MetLife's sweeping grayness placed it among the least aesthetically pleasing ballparks in America.

But as we arrived in the Meadowlands, Darla mentioned that she thought, in fact, the building's exterior was easy on the eye. After we parked in a distant lot, Darla strained to see Aaron's image on two billboards near the stadium's Pepsi Gate, promoting Zenith watches. "Is that him?" she asked her husband. It was all a little hard to believe.

Even the Jets' third-year head coach, Robert Saleh, an optimist hell-bent on avoiding the on-field disasters that had long defined the franchise, had struggled to accept the fact that his new quarterback was a four-time league MVP, a Super Bowl champ, and a certain first-ballot Hall of Famer.

"If anyone would've asked if Aaron Rodgers can be your quarterback two years ago," he said at the introductory press conference in April, "I would have laughed in your face."

Saleh said that Rodgers was more like a coach than a player, and that he was already comfortable enough in his Jets skin on that first day in April to walk around barefoot in a meeting. That detail made its way into accounts that were printed and posted all over social media. Rodgers was no longer the best quarterback on the planet—that distinction belonged to Kansas City's Patrick Mahomes—but he had a strong claim to being the most interesting man in sports.

Opening night at MetLife came complete with apocalyptic-looking clouds and air-to-ground lightning strikes and jarring cell-phone warnings for fans to shelter in place. I joked with Aaron's parents that I had been nervous about the possibility of a flat tire or some other breakdown preventing me from delivering them to their son's big game, and they responded that they knew the feeling from those bygone carpooling days of their son's childhood.

We bounced easily from small-talk topic to small-talk topic as the weather imprisoned us in my SUV. The storms finally subsided, and a majestic double rainbow appeared in the sky, a perfect 9/11 visual. Before we left the car, I made sure the radio was tuned to the Jets' home station, ESPN New York, 98.7 FM, so the quarterback's parents could sit and listen to their son's postgame press conference while I was busy attending it. I had no reason to believe that Aaron Rodgers would not hold a postgame press conference.

I asked Ed and Darla a bit about their son's first year of playing football, as an eighth grader with the Chico Jaguars. I asked them if they still got nervous in the hours leading up to a game.

Ed said he sometimes has difficulty getting a good night's sleep on the eve of a big one. Darla said she still worried all the time about her boy getting hurt.

"I get nervous over the fact that the whole defense is after Aaron," his mother said. "He's got a target on him."

We got out of the car and walked toward the stadium entrances. I was curious to see if anyone recognized Aaron's mother and father—there were Green Bay loyalists wearing old No. 12 jerseys tailgating in the lots—but nobody appeared to.

I headed toward media check-in, and Ed and Darla veered right toward fan admission. They were striding side by side, anonymously, into a crowd of long-suffering but hopeful and downright giddy people wearing Jets jerseys graced by their surname.

Nothing is scripted in sports, so nobody on-site had any idea what he or she was walking into, including the all-time great quarterback and the man and woman who raised him.

• • •

BUFFALO BILLS LINEBACKER Leonard Floyd was closing hard from Aaron Rodgers's left side, and that was not a good thing. Floyd was a tall, rangy athlete who ran a 4.6 forty-yard dash and posted nearly a forty-inch vertical leap at the draft combine before the Chicago Bears made him the ninth overall pick in the 2016 draft.

Floyd had thirty-three regular-season and postseason sacks the previous three years for the Los Angeles Rams, including one in a Super Bowl victory over Cincinnati. He also had an established history of sacking Rodgers entering the 2023 season opener—he had gotten him down nine times, and once stripped him of the ball and recovered the fumble for a touchdown.

On this first-and-10 at the Jets' 43, the fourth snap of the night for the home team, the play called for left tackle Duane Brown to cut block Floyd. Brown and right tackle Mekhi Becton had used the same technique on Rodgers's only other official pass, and the quarterback nearly got sacked before throwing it away.

The cut block requires the offensive lineman to lunge at the defensive player's legs to clear air space for the quarterback's quick throw. "But if you cut him, you'd better get him down," said one Super Bowl–winning offensive line coach. "We never really cut block, especially nowadays. As athletic as these guys are, they just jump over the cut. [Nathaniel] Hackett knows Aaron, and he has the authority to tell a lineman or coach not to do it. You can't afford to lose your franchise guy that way.

"I've got a lot of respect for Duane Brown, but Leonard Floyd is not a guy I would cut block. He's too good of an athlete. He will just jump over you."

Floyd did not hurdle Brown. As the offensive tackle lunged for his legs, the linebacker used his hands to shove him to the side and made his beeline for Rodgers, who was supposed to take his three-step drop, plant, and fire. Robert Saleh said that the play "extended further than the timing of the play" and that Brown was not at fault for what was to come. The head coach confirmed that it was a scripted quick pass that went off-schedule. (The Jets never again used the cut block technique in the 2023 season.)

The Jets had asked a thirty-eight-year-old tackle coming off shoulder surgery to throw this block against a younger, more agile opponent. But Rodgers had to get rid of the ball, and there was an open window to get it to Garrett Wilson, moving from the quarterback's left to right. Rodgers never threw it.

Was he trying to hit one of the two receivers who had drifted into the middle of the field from his right to left, C. J. Uzomah or Allen Lazard, with Uzomah running a seam and Lazard running underneath? Did he simply miss Wilson? Did a receiver run the wrong route?

"I felt like presnap that the safety was going to come down, so I think I played it all a little bit too quick," Rodgers said for this book. "And I was thinking about getting it backside to the under. So, I probably should have just thrown it right to Garrett.

"Garrett really flattened off his route, and I thought if he goes vertical at all . . . because I thought [Micah Hyde] was going to crash down on that. So, I kinda looked left, and I was going to come back and throw the under to the right. I almost threw it to [Lazard]."

Almost. But Floyd had a clear shot from the blind side because Brown did not execute his cut block. When asked later if he was generally opposed to that technique, Rodgers cited his left tackle in Green Bay. "I didn't like David Bakhtiari doing cut blocks," he told me, "because he was terrible at it."

When I asked him if it was a good idea for Hackett and offensive line coach Keith Carter to have Brown try to cut block a defender with a history of getting to Rodgers, the quarterback said:

"I should have thrown it to Garrett. That's how I look at it."

Earlier in his career, Rodgers was criticized at times for holding the ball too long, making life difficult for his offensive linemen. "But that's also what made him amazing," Bakhtiari said for this book. "You get mad at him for holding the ball too long, then he flicks his wrist and throws a 65-yard absolute dime off his back foot rolling to his left. How can you get mad at that?"

No absolute dime was about to be delivered on this play. As Floyd closed in, he said to himself, "Aaron, please still hold the ball." Aaron held the ball.

Some of Rodgers's most spectacular plays from his Packers prime came on spin moves that sent pass rushers flying by while he drifted left and made an absurd throw. Those moves were easier to execute at age twenty-nine than they were at thirty-nine, and when Rodgers tried it on this night, Floyd wrapped him up and put him right down.

The linebacker skipped off to celebrate. Down on his back, Rodgers bounced the ball off of Buffalo's DaQuan Jones. Laken Tomlinson helped pull Rodgers up from the MetLife turf, and then the man of the hour started hopping with his left leg elevated.

He lowered his left foot to the field, put his hands on his hips, and stared at the sideline. Rodgers was virtually certain that he had just torn his Achilles tendon, the thickest and strongest tendon in the human body. He shook his head.

Rodgers sat down, threw himself back to the field, and with his hands behind his legs lifted his knees toward his face mask before sitting up again. Brown stood next to him, doubled over as he realized that the defender he was responsible for had just hurt his quarterback.

"As we were trying to lift [Rodgers] up or talk to him about getting up, he was just like, 'No, I'm not getting up,'" said guard Alijah Vera-Tucker. "Any time a player says that you know it's probably not good."

The Jets' medical team raced out to Rodgers, followed by Saleh, who leaned forward, his hands digging into his knees, wearing a look of dread on his face. A crowd of 83,345 that had pumped so much energy into this must-see event had suddenly gone still and silent. Nobody could believe it was real. Garrett Wilson was off to the side, alone, taking a knee and lowering his head.

Watching from home, Boomer Esiason told himself that Rodgers had no business holding on to the ball and taking the sack. "I know it's not on the offensive line that he got hurt," Esiason said.

Rodgers wrapped each arm around a trainer and was helped to the sideline, where he removed his helmet and dropped it. He did not even make it through four official minutes of game time before entering the team's blue medical tent.

Four snaps with the Jets. One for every MVP he won with the Packers.

Zach Wilson entered the game, but it seemed everyone was focused instead on that blue tent, hoping against hope that No. 8 would reappear for a quick tape job and a return to action. Rodgers's parents, Ed and Darla, were sitting in the lower bowl near the 25-yard line, up about thirty rows from the Jets' sideline. They just wanted so badly for their son to come out of that tent with a bad ankle sprain.

"It was shocking, honestly, so bizarre," Ed Rodgers recalled. "It took the wind out of the whole stadium. The people around us didn't know who we were, but nobody said anything negative like, 'This is what happens with an older quarterback.' It was, 'Oh no. Oh no. Tell me it's not true.' . . . It literally happened right across from us."

Sitting in Woody Johnson's private box, Vinny Testaverde told me he did not try to talk to the owner as the scene unfolded. "I saw the look on Woody's face when it happened," said the former Jets quarterback.

How did Johnson really feel with his franchise player in that tent? "What does it feel like to have your arm chopped off?" he said.

Testaverde had walked out for the pregame coin toss as the Jets' honorary captain, and now he was reliving a nightmare. After his 1998 Jets lost a second-half lead to John Elway's Broncos in the AFC Championship Game, the '99 Jets entered the season as Super Bowl favorites. They were loaded on offense and defense, and they had Bill Parcells (head coach) and Bill Belichick (defensive coordinator) leading them. This was going to be the year the Jets won their first championship in three decades.

And then Testaverde blew out his Achilles in the season opener against New England when he tried to go after a Curtis Martin fumble in the second quarter. He heard a popping sound, and turned around thinking someone was behind him, only to go down himself in a heap. Testaverde grabbed his left leg and writhed in pain. He punched the turf with his fists and was carted away flat on his back.

"It was like a piece of every one of us was being carted off the field with him," Martin said.

Nearly a quarter century later, with Rodgers in the tent, Testaverde sat there thinking, *This is eerie. Here I am at this game, and the same thing happens. The Super Bowl expectations. The quarterback goes down right away. The same thing. I feel bad for Aaron, for the team, for the fans, and for Woody.*

Testaverde felt worse when he saw the closeup replay of Rodgers's left leg as Floyd was sacking him. The quarterback planted his left foot with the linebacker wrapped around him, and the visible detonation up and down the lower leg reminded many of the closeup of Kevin Durant's injury in the 2019 NBA Finals. "You could see the pop of Aaron's Achilles when it snaps," Testaverde said. "Yeah, I knew."

Ira Lieberfarb—"Ira from Staten Island"—kept staring at the blue tent directly beneath him, missing play after play in the game. A member of the inaugural class of the Jets Fan Hall of Fame, Lieberfarb confirmed that this had been the most electric crowd he had ever been a part of. And now that crowd had no discernible pulse.

"I saw some Jets personnel go into that tent that I had never seen go in there," Lieberfarb said. He had been worried about a Rodgers injury after seeing him stumble and fall on a preseason throwaway against the Giants, thinking that the quarterback looked old on that play and that he could never make seventeen starts.

But Lieberfarb never expected a catastrophic event in the opener. Fans around him were scrolling on their phones and seeing reports of a likely Achilles injury. "I hate to use the term 'Same Old Jets,'" Lieberfarb said, "but they are just jinxed. There were a lot of longtime season-ticket holders around me, and they all had that blank stare in their eyes, looking at each other like we can't believe what we just saw."

Across the field, Brian Baumgartner—Kevin from *The Office*—had a glimmer of hope when he thought he saw his good friend tossing a ball in the air. He told Dan Patrick that he asked the man he was with, "Is that [number] 8? Is that 8?" The guy with better eyesight responded, "No, that's 5. The punter. It's not 8."

Eventually a white cart pulled up behind the medical tent. "That's when I knew this was really not good," Ed Rodgers said. His son was wearing an FDNY cap when he was loaded onto the back of the cart and driven a short distance to the tunnel. Aaron Rodgers was helped off and escorted down the runway as he hobbled, badly, to the X-ray room. While sitting on a table, Rodgers was already thinking about the late, great Kobe Bryant, who had torn his Achilles in 2013.

How could anyone possibly believe that the Jets were not cursed after this?

Rodgers was transported through the bowels of MetLife while wearing a boot on his left foot and holding his phone in his right hand. In the locker room, he feared that his career was likely over. Rodgers thought to himself, *This is it. You don't come back from this injury.* He contacted Dr. Neal ElAttrache, team physician for the Los Angeles Dodgers and Rams who had worked on Rodgers's broken collarbone in 2017. ElAttrache was an orthopedic surgeon to sports stars the likes of Tom Brady and Shohei Ohtani, and he had surgically repaired Bryant's Achilles. Rodgers wanted to know if the good doctor could fix his too.

Saleh was informed during the first half of the preliminary diagnosis. When he heard the news on the sideline, the Jets coach thought of the look of devastation on Rodgers's face before he went down for good.

At halftime, Zach Wilson said, "the whole team went up to [Rodgers]." The backup told the injured starter, "I love you, man." Other Jets, including Brown, told him the same. Saleh gave Rodgers a hug and assured him that his story was not over. Garrett Wilson gave him a hug and expressed his love for the quarterback who was going to bring out the best in him.

"Sorry, kid," Rodgers replied.

Emotionally drained, the Jets held it together on the field, erasing a 13–3 halftime deficit to force overtime and winning the game on a 65-yard punt return from an undrafted rookie, Xavier Gipson, that compelled Saleh to do a full sprint into the end zone as the crowd exploded. After everything that Jets fans had endured, they at least deserved a happy drive home.

In the locker room afterward, with Rodgers already gone, players such as Laken Tomlinson were wiping tears from their eyes. Brown was emotional about his quarterback, saying, "I hate to not see him out there." One of Rodgers's best friends, Randall Cobb, called it a sad day and reminded reporters of the game's occupational hazards. "Every moment we walk through that tunnel onto the field," Cobb said, "we're taking a risk."

He then asked the credentialed media around him to let him do what he needed to do for Rodgers. "I'm really just trying to get out of here so I can go call him and talk to him and check in on him," Cobb said, "and be the best friend I can be for him."

Rodgers had been driven to his Montclair, New Jersey, home by friend and podcaster Aubrey Marcus. The quarterback's phone rang around half past midnight—punter Thomas Morstead was calling. A fifteen-year NFL veteran, Morstead had not been a big Aaron Rodgers fan from a distance. He did not like the way his personality came across in the media and, as a member of the Players Association executive committee, he did not agree with Rodgers's opposition to the 2020 collective bargaining agreement.

But the more Morstead got to know Rodgers, the teammate, the more he liked him. He liked how Rodgers had gotten to know the name of every janitor in the building and how he built relationships with staffers in all departments.

The punter was going to shoot Rodgers a text before thinking his teammate was likely getting hundreds of texts and might prefer an actual conversation with someone who had been in the league almost as long as he had.

"He picked up on the first ring," Morstead recalled for this book.

They talked for a while, and they cried, and the punter told the quarterback to please let him know if anyone on the team could do anything to help him through this. Morstead sent Rodgers an old Kobe Bryant post that went viral right after the Lakers superstar got hurt. Bryant said he wrote it at 3:30 a.m., with his foot feeling like dead weight and his head spinning from the pain meds.

"This is such BS!" he opened. "All the training and sacrifice just flew out the window with one step that I've done millions of times! The frustration is unbearable. The anger is rage. Why the hell did this happen?!? Makes no damn sense. Now I'm supposed to come back from this and be the same player Or better at 35?!? How in the world am I supposed to do that?? . . .

"Maybe I should break out the rocking chair and reminisce on the career that was. Maybe this is how my book ends. Maybe Father Time has defeated me . . . Then again maybe not!"

Rodgers felt that he had let down so many people. He was planning to be the same dominant force he was in 2020 and 2021, and that vision was stolen from him in a flash.

"People think he's got everything. He's got all the money, he's had a great career, all these different things," Morstead said. "But he loves playing ball. It's pure, you know what I mean? He's not thinking about lost marketing opportunities. He was excited to play with this team and try to do something special this year, and now it's not going to happen for him."

Rodgers spent most of that Tuesday crying and feeling sorry for himself, at least until he realized that he could control his attitude, if nothing else. "I can either attack this rehab and turn it into a positive," he said, "or I can go into another dark cave for six months."

He chose to attack his rehab and attempt to pull off one of the most stunning comebacks in sports history. He flew out west so Dr. ElAttrache could start the process. Players everywhere were blaming the MetLife turf and criticizing the league for refusing to install grass fields in all NFL stadiums, but ElAttrache said he did not think the playing surface had a role in the Achilles injury suffered by Rodgers "because of the way you saw the direct compression of [his] foot onto the turf."

The doctor was confident he could fix his patient. Rodgers had surgery on Wednesday, September 13, the same day he posted an Instagram thank-you message to the countless people across the nation who had reached out to him.

"I'm completely heartbroken and moving through all of the emotions," he wrote, "but deeply touched and humbled by the support and love. Please keep me in your thoughts and prayers as I begin the healing process today.

"The night is darkest before the dawn. And I shall rise yet again."

Two days later Rodgers was back on *The Pat McAfee Show*, now an ESPN production, warning the skeptics that their pessimism would only fuel his desire to return faster than just about anyone ever had. An Achilles rehab was forever seen as a yearlong proposition, but Rodgers did not rule out the unthinkable—returning late in the 2023 season.

He quoted Kevin Garnett's line, "Anything is possible." He asked the skeptics to go ahead and give him that one extra percent of inspiration.

"That's all I need," Rodgers said. "So, give me your timetables. Give me your doubts. Give me your prognostications.

"And then watch what I do."

14

THE COMEBACK

ROBERT SALEH WAS at the front of the ballroom in his team's New Jersey hotel, running the standard Saturday night meeting, when he noticed a guest enter through the back doors. The coach announced that he was turning it over to a surprise motivational speaker who had a few things to say before the Jets faced the Kansas City Chiefs the following night.

Aaron Rodgers was on crutches, and when his teammates saw him, they let out a collective *holy shit*. Maybe the quarterback had given a quiet heads-up to one of his boys, a Randall Cobb or a Tim Boyle, that he had gotten medical clearance to fly in from California, but essentially the entire team was stunned to see him.

"He came into the team room like Batman, honestly," said Allen Lazard. "And it was just kind of a Hollywood-esque moment of just like Aaron Rodgers appearing, walking. I thought he was about to fly."

The Jets had lost to Bill Belichick's New England Patriots the previous Sunday for the fifteenth consecutive time, scoring a lousy 10 points and falling to 1-2. Of equal consequence, the sideline scenes of running back Michael Carter shouting angrily at position coach Taylor Embree and of an exasperated Garrett Wilson pointing at Nathaniel Hackett's iPad while addressing Zach Wilson suggested the team was on the verge of imploding.

On the mend from surgery, Rodgers had used his weekly Tuesday appearance on *The Pat McAfee Show* to express his frustration with present and past Jets, including the most famous among them, Joe Namath, who had blasted Zach Wilson on ESPN New York radio's *The Michael Kay*

Show, describing his play as "disgusting" and calling on the team to get rid of him. Rodgers did not cite Namath by name, but he did lump in "our former players" with panicking fans and chided, "You're not helping the cause."

In five months, Rodgers had gone from respectfully declining Namath's invitation to wear his No. 12 because he did not believe he was worthy to telling the franchise icon to shut up on national TV.

No. 8 did not care about Namath as much as he cared about what he was seeing on the field. "I really think we need to hold our poise a little bit better, really just offensively," he said. "We need to not have some of those things happen on the sideline . . .

"There's been, I think, too many little side conversations and we need to grow up a little bit on offense, and lock in and do our jobs, everybody, and not point fingers at each other. And that's everybody. We don't point fingers at the coaching staff, don't point fingers at each other, just get back to work and get the job done."

Rodgers told McAfee how difficult it was being away from the team, and how much he wished he could fill the leadership void. "I feel like if I was there," he said, "some of these things wouldn't be happening. . . . It's more the side stuff that I don't like, and that I want to see us stick together through the tough times."

Four nights later, Rodgers repeated the message in person in that Saturday meeting. He spoke for six or seven minutes in an otherwise silent room. Rodgers used his powerful presence and command voice to tell the younger Jets that the blame game needed to die a sudden death. No more finger pointing, he told them. And that was an order.

Truth was, Rodgers wanted to reconnect more than he wanted to rebuke. He was more self-effacing than usual while sharing his thoughts and experiences since his devastating injury.

"I rearranged my goals," he told his teammates. "We all need to rearrange our goals. And we can do that by sticking together."

Rodgers reminded his teammates that they were only three games deep into the season, that they still had everything they wanted to accomplish in front of them. He also reminded his teammates how important they were to him. "I chose to be a Jet," he said. "I didn't have to come here."

He did not shed tears in his speech, but there was a moment when it appeared he got emotional and paused to take a breath. After Rodgers was done, his audience gave him a rousing ovation. The Jets formed a wedding line so each player could give him a high five and a hug.

Funny, but along with the wet-ball practice drill used to simulate playing in the rain, Rodgers despised few NFL traditions more than the hotel stayover for the home team the night before a game. (Why not take full advantage of playing at home by allowing guys to sleep in their own beds?) And yet here he was doing his best work of the year in that very setting.

Saleh said this reunion was one of the coolest football things he had ever seen. As it turned out, Rodgers's visit and speech made an impact on the team's performance too. The following night in MetLife Stadium, with Travis Kelce's new girlfriend, Taylor Swift, in the house, the Jets pushed the defending Super Bowl champs to the brink of defeat.

Rodgers was there on crutches, marking the first time he was in the same building with Swift since he had attended her MetLife concert in May and, with confetti falling around him, had shouted, "The Jets won the Super Bowl."

These Jets were not about to win a championship, even though they more or less contained Patrick Mahomes and erased a 17–0 deficit to tie the game in the third quarter before losing, 23–20. Wilson had already proven he was incapable of leading a contending team. Unless he showed dramatic improvement, sooner rather than later, the Jets would finish with a losing record.

But before the game that night, while working the sidelines, a camera caught Rodgers calling for a football, pulling aside his right crutch, and throwing the ball to an unseen receiver. Oh, and he also made official for a national audience what he was telling people once he got done crying on September 12, the night after his injury. Rodgers told NBC's Melissa Stark that his goal was to play again in the 2023 season.

The Jets won their next three games—avenging Sean Payton's verbal takedown of Nathaniel Hackett in Denver, beating an Eagles team that had just won a conference title, and somehow beating the Giants in overtime after some astounding and un-Jets-like clock management at the end of regulation. Out of left field, Rodgers's appearance and his expressed optimism about a return for a playoff run had pumped new life into his team. The Jets were nearly 4-0 since his speech, and nearly 2-0 against the teams that had played in the most recent Super Bowl.

Rodgers just needed the Jets to stay competitive long enough for him to attempt the unthinkable. Another Neal ElAttrache patient, running back Cam Akers, had returned to the Rams five and a half months after rupturing his right Achilles tendon in 2021, though he ruptured his left Achilles the following season. Rodgers would have to beat that recovery timetable to achieve his goal of playing for the Jets in December and/or January. As always, he was motivated to challenge the constraints of conventional science.

ElAttrache performed the Arthrex Minimally Invasive Achilles Midsubstance SpeedBridge repair on his ruptured tendon. According to Arthrex, a global medical device company based in Naples, Florida, the procedure requires high-strength SutureTape to repair the tendon, which is "reinforced and protected by securing the SutureTape with two SwiveLock anchors in the heel bone. The repair is performed through very small incisions (about two to three centimeters) and is knotless, creating a strong construct and removing knots that could cause irritation. Allowing for early mobilization and minimizing the risk of knot slippage can help accelerate recovery and restoration of normal function."

Arthrex also said that ElAttrache "chose to put JumpStart antimicrobial wound dressing" over Rodgers's repair, and that embedded in the dressing were "microcell batteries of silver and zinc, which generates an electrical current and kills a broad spectrum of harmful bacteria to help reduce the risk of infection."

In a race against time, Rodgers's rehab involved stem-cell treatment, hyperbaric chambers, AlterG antigravity treadmills, blood-flow restriction training, and red-light therapy. The quarterback worked with a thirty-six-year-old body specialist and movement coach, Aaron Alexander, author of *The Align Method*, a manual on aligning physical and psychological health. Alexander met Rodgers through Aubrey Marcus, the founder of Onnit, a holistic health and fitness company, and had helped him cut body fat and sharpen his rotational movements before the start of Jets camp.

After the Achilles surgery, Alexander worked with Rodgers every day and moved into his homes in Malibu and New Jersey. In the early hours of rehab, Alexander said they were focused on lymphatic drainage and improving the circulation in his injured leg. "At the PT clinic they were flabbergasted," Alexander said. "They said, 'This is the fastest we've ever seen someone recover, period.'"

To help prevent infection and keep the site of the surgery sterile, Alexander put a bag around Rodgers's left foot and filled it with ozone, which also helped repair the tissue. The quarterback was using cold laser therapy, e-stim treatment for muscle recovery, a muscle stimulation training suit, radiofrequency treatment, and pulsed electromagnetic frequency, or PEMF, up and down his leg, which helped decongest the injured area and maintain proper cell function.

Rodgers was injected with mesenchymal stem cells to expedite the tissue regeneration, Alexander said, weeks into his rehab. He said those stem cells were "like live cells coming from an umbilical cord." According to the National Library of Medicine, mesenchymal stem cells "have the ability to self-renew and also exhibit multilineage differentiation. MSCs can be isolated from a variety of tissues, such as umbilical cord, endometrial polyps, menses blood, bone marrow, adipose tissue, etc." The Mayo Clinic reported that MSCs "can differentiate into a variety of cell types, including bone cells, cartilage cells, muscle cells, and fat cells."

Rodgers had one hyperbaric chamber delivered to his Malibu home, another delivered to his Montclair, New Jersey, home, and he would use them for sixty to ninety minutes a pop. Alexander also wrapped the quarterback's leg as often as possible for red-light therapy treatments, which help provide adenosine triphosphate, or ATP, that fuels cellular function. The quarterback and the body specialist worked for hours and hours in Rodgers's home, and the physical therapist kept telling them that the injured area was "the most well-circulated Achilles we've seen post-surgery." This was the result of a commitment Rodgers made to recovery the night before his September 13 surgery.

It was a brutal process and, from the outside looking in, it might have seemed that Rodgers was not going to make it to the other side. He had told Alexander and other friends that he needed their help and support on the days he stopped believing that he could pull off this comeback.

"He went through an incredibly dark period after that [injury]," Alexander said for this book. "There were questions like, 'Will they want me back? What does my life look like now? I let everyone down.' . . . I was with him through all of that. I'd be working with him at ten o'clock at night, working on his foot, and he was in a place of processing the weight of the experience."

Alexander tried to lighten Rodgers's burden with a joke or two, when appropriate. They played cards and trivia games. Alexander tried to normalize a situation that was a million country miles from normal.

"If you are on the couch and you have to use crutches to hobble yourself over to take a shit, and you're used to being a superhero," Alexander said, "that's going to be really challenging."

Rodgers threw everything he had at those demons and told Alexander from the start that he had every intention of playing again in 2023. The body man loved his attitude but was not as enthusiastic about a return in December or January unless the Jets had a realistic chance of advancing to the Super Bowl.

Alexander had never been so emotionally invested in a client in his two decades in the trade. "I cared for his recovery like I would have cared for a child's," he told me. "It was like, 'I will kill for this recovery.' If anything fucked this up, it would've been devastating for me."

He worried that if Rodgers rushed back and tore his Achilles a second time, the quarterback might not find the motivation to go through the grueling rehab all over again. He thought it made more sense to heal up, return in 2024 at full capacity, and then make a Super Bowl run. Alexander expressed his opinion to his client.

Rodgers shot it down. "It wasn't a conversation," Alexander said. "He was like, 'I'm doing this.'"

During his rehab Rodgers also consulted with Brigham Buhler, the founder of Ways2Well, a health and wellness company. Buhler said Rodgers was recovering at an accelerated pace "because Aaron thought outside the box and Aaron is doing all of these extra things that most traditional medicine is ignoring, and Aaron was open-minded enough to do that."

Rodgers had strangers sending him treatment suggestions from all over creation, including growth hormone, that he rejected because they were outlawed by the NFL. He had done his own research, of course, and heard from others who had suffered Achilles tears. Rodgers chose to use what he called "a lot of great modalities that are legal that are amazing that I think have been helping me." He was rehabbing practically from sunup to sundown, getting out of bed, and doing it all over again.

Rodgers studied Kobe Bryant's rehab. He also found that his diet was critical to recovery and consumed high levels of collagen and curcumin, drinking bone broth daily and staying clear of inflammatory foods.

The quarterback was back on his feet much quicker than most. Jesse

Morse, a sports medicine physician and regenerative medicine specialist in Miami who had treated more than a hundred NFL players, described a timeline of six months from the date of injury to a return to competition as ultra-aggressive, even with stem-cell treatments.

"The fact that [Rodgers] is trying for three, four months out is insane, regardless of age," said Morse, who did not treat the quarterback.

But Rodgers did not want to wait until the fall of 2024. His 2023 cause was aided by the shape he was in entering the season. Rodgers had trained for years at Ryan Capretta's Proactive Sports Performance facility, and his lower-than-usual body-fat levels gave him a leaner and meaner look before the injury; his physique was sculpted, in part, by Aaron Alexander's workouts. One video Alexander posted showed the trainer, Rodgers, and surfing legend Laird Hamilton taking dumbbells into the deep end of a pool for underwater lifting sessions.

In mid-October, five weeks after tearing his Achilles, Rodgers flew across the country for the Jets-Eagles game and, without any crutches in sight, threw to a team staffer and to Sauce Gardner for five minutes during pregame warmups, stepping into his passes. Rodgers kept making these trips and kept showing up before games, working on his dropbacks and throwing with more velocity, looking, at times, as if nothing had ever happened to him.

Jay Glazer of Fox reported in November that the quarterback sent the Jets video of his workouts that "blew their minds" and planned to start practicing with the team around his fortieth birthday, December 2, and to play in games shortly thereafter. The Christmas Eve home game against the Washington Commanders was later penciled in as the probable date of a Rodgers comeback, with one caveat: the Jets had to remain in playoff contention for the quarterback to pull this off.

The biggest obstacle separating Rodgers from a most unlikely return was the most likely development of all—the Jets being the Jets. Rodgers was holding up his end of the bargain, and of course his team was not.

In fact, the Jets scored a grand total of 45 points over five consecutive defeats. At a time when NFL rules made it next to impossible for defenders to actually play defense and encouraged offenses to adopt a high-flying NBA fast-break approach, the Jets' field seemed 150 yards long. They could not move the ball. They actually went 12 quarters and 40 consecutive possessions without scoring a touchdown.

Wilson got benched for Tim Boyle, and Tim Boyle got benched for Trevor Siemian. While he was wearing a headset, Aaron Rodgers's body language kept getting worse and worse. His arms were often folded in front of his midsection with a look of dismay and/or disgust on his face, and sometimes he just shook his head as if he were a disappointed dad watching a comedy of Little League errors. During the fifth straight defeat, a 13–8 loss to Atlanta, Rodgers and Wilson looked at each other on the sideline as if they could not believe what they were seeing.

Rodgers had a date that night at Zero Bond, a private club in New York's trendy NoHo neighborhood, for a fortieth birthday party that was attended by an eclectic group of past and present teammates, celebrity pals, and longtime friends who flew in from out west, including Joey Kaempf, his childhood teammate in Oregon, and Nate Raabe, his partner in a consumer growth equity firm known as RX3. Late in the event some guests gave emotional speeches about what the man of the hour meant to them.

The next day, *The Athletic* reported that Wilson would be reluctant to take back his starter's job, if asked, and that Rodgers tried to talk him off that position. The day after that, the Jets released Rodgers's good friend Boyle after two starts gone south. Rodgers used his *McAfee* appearance to attack the Wilson report, deliver a journalism lecture or two, and call on the organization to finally plug the leaks that undermine it. The day after that, Robert Saleh offered that starter's job back to Wilson and, wouldn't you know it, the kid accepted.

Four days in the life of the New York Jets.

Before that extended drama played out, Rodgers had actually returned to practice on November 29, and posted on Instagram a photo of himself wearing his red No. 8 jersey over a hoodie along with this message: "Been a long 77 days. Good to be back on the field with the guys."

Seventy-seven days. No matter how people felt about Aaron Rodgers, nobody could deny that was a superhuman feat.

"Wow!!! Simply INCREDIBLE!!" LeBron James posted on X, above a slow-motion video of Rodgers throwing a beautiful spiral. "Back where he belong!"

Rodgers sat down with the team's beat writers in the same conference room in the team's Florham Park, New Jersey, facility where they had talked at the end of August, when the new quarterback said the Jets had a legitimate chance to win the whole thing. The mood was entirely different three months later.

The Jets were on the verge of becoming a 4-8 team with five games to play. Many people in Rodgers's life were telling him to surrender to the obvious, back off, and get ready for the 2024 season. The quarterback countered that there was no downside to pushing his body to the max, figuring that if he tore his Achilles again, he would still have time to return by the start of training camp.

In one breath, Rodgers left open the possibility that he could play for the Jets at Miami on December 17, a week earlier than his projected return date. In another breath, Rodgers said that it would not make sense to play again if the Jets were out of the playoff hunt, and that his body could only cooperate so much during the recovery process. "I'm not anywhere near ready to play," he conceded.

Nobody on his medical team told him that he could *not* do this. At the same time, nobody on his medical team told him that he could do this either. Who wanted to stake his or her reputation on that one-in-a-zillion call?

"I was more into not having to risk going back to the bottom of the abyss," Alexander said. "Not for myself. I didn't want to re-experience it for him."

And yet Rodgers was willing to take that monumental gamble. "If [the Jets] win the game against the Dolphins," he told Alexander, "I'm playing."

Just as impressive as his attempted comeback was the amount of news and conversation he generated. Aaron Rodgers was on the field for four snaps all year, and he was still the most talked-about player in the NFL.

The *McAfee* show was a big part of it, making Tuesdays what his Sundays used to be—game days. Rodgers could create a news cycle rolling out of bed, and now that he was an injured star in New York, looking less likely to return in 2023 to a losing team, that talent was the only one at his disposal. And before he could get out of Gotham and get back to his offseason sanctuary in Malibu, that talent would get Rodgers in trouble once again.

• • •

ON THE OTHER side of midnight, after 9/11 had become 9/12, Ed and Darla Rodgers had been quiet on our ride from MetLife Stadium to their

Montclair Airbnb. They had stayed for the wild ending of the Jets' overtime victory over the Bills, while their son, the starting quarterback for the home team, was watching on TV in his own Montclair home.

What odds could anyone have gotten on that at the start of the night?

Hosts and analysts were talking on ESPN New York radio about Aaron's injury, over and over, and replaying Bob Wischusen's call of Xavier Gipson's walk-off punt return in overtime, punctuated by the line, "This game is over!" Wischusen later said that he leaned into that call because he was thinking, with Rodgers out, that he might not get many more chances to shout with excitement on the air.

Ed and Darla told me they were actually able to enjoy the ending despite what had happened in the first quarter; they stood and cheered right along with all those Jets fans who were so gutted when Aaron got carted off to the runway. "It took us to the third quarter to realize, 'OK, we're Jets fans now,'" Darla said. "We were really feeling it and . . . no one knew who in the heck we were."

In the MetLife parking lot before the game, Darla had said she got nervous watching her middle child play because "the whole defense is after Aaron. He's got a target on him." A mother's intuition.

That Buffalo defense hit the target early, and on the ride back to Montclair, before the official diagnosis was clear, Rodgers's parents were talking about Aaron as a quick healer. His mother recalled the time in high school when her son suffered a knee injury, and the orthopedist told him he should give up football. Aaron just strengthened his leg and played with a brace.

Ed and Darla arrived at their Airbnb place around the same time their heartbroken son was trying to sleep off the worst night of his career three and a half miles away. Aaron's parents traveled to their Chico, California, home the following day, the house their middle son had built for them. Three months later, with Aaron still out of contact, they remained hopeful for an end to the estrangement that had lasted longer than nine years.

Rodgers spoke of that possibility with Aubrey Marcus in a 2022 podcast. Marcus said that he knew Rodgers was praying every night to rebuild the bridges back to his family, and that he saw in his friend's heart an intention to heal the fracture in that relationship.

Rodgers told Marcus that he had gratitude for the way he was raised and for the morals he was taught, that many people have family issues, and that he always tried to deal with his privately.

"That hasn't always been the case or hasn't been good enough for a lot of people who want to write about it, or pick it apart, or talk about it, or even some things that my family has said or done over the years that's been public," Rodgers said.

He spoke of his appreciation for his father's decision to "take a chance and go through the poverty that we experienced to make a better life for his kids by going back to school as a middle-aged man." Rodgers said that he did believe in healing, and that he had no bitterness or resentment in his heart for his parents.

Rodgers made a point that was emphasized by his close friend Jordan Russell about the environment that Ed and Darla had raised him in. "If I hadn't been raised that way," Rodgers said, "all the good and all the frustrating, there's no way I'd be sitting here today."

Ed and Darla wanted a couple of things made clear in this book, about where they stood on their middle son, beyond the obvious fact that they dearly loved him. For one, they wanted it understood that they were perfectly willing to resume a relationship with Aaron without any resolution of the issues that had divided them.

"Yes, we're all about forgiving and forgetting," Darla told me. "We would be so happy to move on. . . . Maybe we don't see him all the time. We're OK with however it's framed. The new relationship needs to start and it just feels weird that we can't communicate even big-life things with him."

Ed added: "And we have unconditional love for him. No matter what happened, we would just like the relationship."

Aaron was raised in a family that, according to his mother, turned just about every decision into a prayer project. Outside of sports, Aaron's parents wanted his childhood to revolve around the Neighborhood Church of Chico, part of the Christian and Missionary Alliance, and Young Life, a Christian ministry group.

But Aaron had told *ESPN The Magazine* that organized religion "can have a mind-debilitating effect." He told his then-girlfriend Danica Patrick in a 2019 podcast that he no longer connected with religion, and that he had started questioning his commitment to it in high school. Over time, Rodgers had come to reject the binary tenets of religion. "It's us and them," he said. "It's saved and unsaved. It's heaven and hell. It's enlightened and heathen. It's holy and righteous and sinner and filthy.

"I don't know how you can believe in a God who wants to condemn most of the planet to a fiery hell. What type of loving, sensitive, omnipresent, omnipotent being wants to condemn most of his beautiful creation to a fiery hell at the end of all this?"

No longer religious, Rodgers described himself as spiritual. Though his parents were not overjoyed to hear about his critique of church teachings, or about his allegiance to progressive pastor Rob Bell, they said they would fully accept their son regardless of his stance on religion.

"I think we're tolerant people," Ed Rodgers said for this book. "We'd be totally accepting for whatever he's got going. I would love to turn that narrative the other way. We're not rigid. We're not hard-line, or whatever people have said in the news. We're just people trying to follow God. We're not divisive.

"The stuff that's out there that I've read, it's just not true. Our view on all that, on God, religion, was not part of the divisiveness that happened. It was not a part at all, and people think it was. It's not."

Even though they could not talk with Aaron—they did not have his cell number—Ed and Darla tried to show support. In numerous Twitter posts, while blasting liberal and Democrat policies and philosophies on many fronts, Ed had backed his son's position on the COVID-19 vaccine, challenging its efficacy and touting natural immunity. He was among the 2,800 Twitter users who retweeted a 2021 Hodge Twins post asking users to retweet if they "think Aaron Rodgers vaccination status is his business, and his alone."

Ed also tweeted a 2022 column from zonecoverage.com that was headlined, "Tom Brady Highlights the Aaron Rodgers Double Standard," and that claimed Brady got a pass for missing eleven days of training camp for personal reasons, while Rodgers would have been roughed up by the media for the same sabbatical and placed "on the FBI's 10 Most Wanted list."

Ed and Darla were trying to stay in their son's life in some small way. That was why they occasionally attended Aaron's games after he stopped communicating with them.

Few parents of accomplished professional athletes could fathom what they were going through, outside of Bill and Jeannette Reed, estranged for years from their son Patrick, who won the Masters in 2018 while his unwelcome family watched in their Augusta, Georgia, home, a ten-minute drive away. The Reeds still attended whatever tournaments they could while keeping a low profile.

"It's difficult not to be able to share in your children's success," said Bill Reed, who was aware of the Rodgers family divide. "In those moments that maybe you're feeling down or sad about it, you try to go back to the source of what the objective is as a parent. You give him or her the opportunities to be successful . . . and you do it without expecting anything in return.

"We still go to tournaments to let Patrick know we still support our son and . . . we feel if we go to a tournament, that could be the one time something breaks and a conversation will start. If you never go, that opportunity will never present itself."

As Ed and Darla Rodgers waited for that opportunity, some people in Aaron's life had impressed upon him the importance of reconciliation with his family. Multiple sources said Aaron's first coach in Green Bay, Mike McCarthy, had encouraged him in conversations to reestablish a relationship with his family, or to at least reestablish one with his mother, though the quarterback had a slightly different view of those talks.

"[It was] not in a way where it's like, 'Hey, I'm going to big-brother you and you should do this,'" Rodgers told me. "But of course, we talked about everything. But it wasn't like sitting down and, 'Hey listen, you need to do this and this and this.'"

Jordan Russell had also spoken to Rodgers about the estrangement and described a family reconciliation as a necessity for his longtime friend.

"There's no greater purpose I can have as a friend than to help him reconnect with his family," Russell said. "It's a very contentious and sticky issue. . . . My personal opinion is it's absolutely essential. I have absolutely no agency over that happening.

"I have stated my case. He knows very clearly where I stand on that. I believe it's important for him in the story of life, as it relates to love and family, for him to do the best that he can to make amends. . . . It's absolutely the most delicate thing he and I can talk about."

Russell stood as the embodiment of full-circle possibilities. He lost his friendship with Rodgers over a loan dispute, reunited with him after years of no contact, and now was running a natural beverage company (Ra) with the quarterback as a financial backer.

Russell described his friend's internal battle over whether to attempt to reconcile with his family as "a civil war of his heart against his head. His heart wants to make amends, but his head has all the reasons why that shouldn't happen." Russell had seen in Rodgers "a softening of his heart" after the ayahuasca retreats, a sign, he hoped, of a man starting to transition to the next phase of his life, post-football, defined by family, love, and perhaps children of his own.

Rodgers said he wants to be a father because he wants to "care for somebody who relies solely on you for so many things—food, protection, housing, life." Fatherhood can be a monumental challenge—Ed Rodgers could tell Aaron a thing or two about that. Months after he shared a warm and long-overdue embrace with his middle child on a Lake Tahoe golf course, Ed was holding out more hope than ever that a reconciliation would happen.

"It's definitely possible," Aaron said.

How could the possibility become a reality?

"It's just timing, just timing," Aaron told me. "Every time I think it's getting closer, some weird things happen. But I would like a relationship with my dad for sure."

• • •

IT WAS TUESDAY, January 2, 2024, the last game day of the year for Aaron Rodgers. The Jets had activated him off injured reserve on December 20, three weeks after opening his twenty-one-day practice window, but not for the purpose of playing in the final three games. They had added him to the fifty-three-man roster simply to practice and to elevate his teammates with his presence.

So, Rodgers suited up for Tuesdays with Pat McAfee, at a salary of more than a million bucks a year. The former Pro Bowl punter for the Colts had singlehandedly built a media empire with his football expertise, broculture humor, pro-wrestling persona, and ability to attract the highest-profile guests. He sold his services to ESPN for $85 million, and figured it made sense to reward a man who helped him grow the brand, Rodgers, with a nice payday on the side.

As McAfee was an entertainer and talk-show host, not a journalist, the deal with the quarterback was a no-harm, no-foul proposition. Numerous outlets paid active coaches and star players to make weekly appearances. It was part of the biz, and McAfee understood how valuable Rodgers was as a guest. In fact, when asked if the host had done more for the quarterback or vice versa in their partnership, the industry's preeminent sports media analyst, Andrew Marchand, voted in favor of the quarterback.

"Rodgers helped McAfee more," he said. "Rodgers became appointment listening because the whole sports world was listening to hear what he said . . . and he was saying it all on McAfee's show."

In a season with no games, Rodgers found his competition on McAfee's show, where he called Chiefs star and Taylor Swift boyfriend Travis Kelce "Mr. Pfizer" for filming a commercial promoting Pfizer's COVID vaccine, and where he proposed a vaccine debate between Kelce and former White House chief medical advisor Dr. Anthony Fauci (whom the quarterback called a "pharmacrat") and Rodgers and anti-vaxxer presidential candidate Robert F. Kennedy Jr.

The football star was a human headline even when he was not being a football star. On cue, the Jets could not win enough games to get their franchise player on the field.

Though the Jets' defense would finish the year ranked third in the league in yards allowed, their offense was a disaster, finishing thirty-first in yards gained. The line was an injury-riddled mess. Nathaniel Hackett, offensive coordinator, was completely lost without Rodgers. Robert Saleh wore a sideline expression that suggested the game was moving too quickly for him, at least when his Jets had the ball.

Joe Douglas, general manager, had to absorb the biggest hit of all for drafting Zach Wilson out of Brigham Young with the second pick of the 2021 draft, and then for doubling down by installing him as Rodgers's backup and (strangely enough) heir apparent. Douglas was aware of the relatively weak BYU competition that Wilson faced in 2020 and the impact that might have had on the explosive jump in production from 2019 and picked him anyway. That decision ultimately left Douglas's boss, Woody Johnson, furious with the GM and Saleh near the end of 2023.

A month after that season ended, with Wilson still on the roster, Johnson conceded that his team needed a backup quarterback. "We didn't have one last year," the owner said.

It was a fireable offense by Douglas, especially when the Jets had a surplus of intel on their recent employee Joe Flacco, the free agent who would lead the Cleveland Browns to the playoffs. But nobody who had a role in landing Aaron Rodgers was getting fired until No. 8 played a season in Jets green.

It didn't matter that Green Bay would make the playoffs and score a huge first-round upset over Dallas, or that, despite Matt LaFleur's private misgivings about pairing a new starting quarterback with the league's youngest team, Jordan Love would make the Packers the undisputed winners of the Rodgers trade by showing off his franchise-player potential.

The Packers were in another conference and in another world. For the Jets, it was all about Aaron in 2024.

And in his first appearance of 2024, on *McAfee*, Rodgers committed his first turnover of the year, a doozy. The January 2 show started off innocently enough with Rodgers speaking from the wine room in his home, talking about the sleep he had caught up on, and the football games he had watched, and the message he had posted on Instagram Stories about meeting his happiest and saddest self in 2023.

Rodgers spoke about ayahuasca, and Fireman Ed, and bad officiating, before the conversation turned to the conspiracy theory that the NFL season was, in fact, scripted. Forever willing to run with such theories, Rodgers brought up the colors of recent Super Bowl emblems and how they matched up with the teams that played in those games.

"This have something to do with the Epstein list that came out?" blurted *McAfee* co-host A. J. Hawk, the former Packers linebacker and current Rodgers confidant.

The "list" referring to released court documents that named people connected to financier Jeffrey Epstein, the convicted sex offender who was arrested on federal charges of sex trafficking of minors before he died by suicide in jail. The grand jury indictment said Epstein "sexually exploited and abused dozens of minor girls at his homes." One of those homes was infamously known as "Epstein's Island," in the U.S. Virgin Islands, near Saint Thomas.

Nobody wanted to be near any list associated with a man accused of being a monster. But after Hawk asked his strange question, Rodgers did not meet it with dead air. Instead, he laughed and replied, "That's supposed to be coming out soon. That's supposed to be coming out soon."

"There's a lot of people, including Jimmy Kimmel, who are really hoping that doesn't come out."

McAfee immediately sensed the danger zone that Rodgers had entered and jumped in with an emergency dose of context. Kimmel, the late-night ABC giant, had mocked Rodgers in March for suggesting that the government was attempting to shift the public's focus away from a pending Epstein list drop and toward UFOs.

"Hey, I tell you what," Rodgers said, "if that list comes out, I definitely will be popping some sort of bottle."

Only nobody at ESPN or ABC or their parent company, Disney, was in the mood for champagne. This was a DEFCON 1, get-me-Bob-Iger-right-now crisis. This was Disney-on-Disney crime.

Rodgers might not have thought he had just suggested that Kimmel was a pedophile, but he got roasted from coast to coast for doing just that. The late-night host turned to X with this response:

> Dear Aasshole: for the record, I've not met, flown with, visited, or had any contact whatsoever with Epstein, nor will you find my name on any "list" other than the clearly-phony nonsense that soft-brained whackos like yourself can't seem to distinguish from reality. Your reckless words put my family in danger. Keep it up and we will debate the facts further in court. @AaronRodgers12

McAfee apologized the following day "for being a part of it." Two days later, ESPN executive Mike Foss said Rodgers had made "a dumb and factually inaccurate joke" about Kimmel that "should never have happened." Meanwhile, the quarterback who was allergic to the words "I'm sorry" practiced on with the 6-10 Jets, who were preparing to end their season (mercifully) in New England, where six-time champ Bill Belichick would be coaching the Patriots for the final time.

By all accounts, Jets players and officials were not overly concerned about the raging Kimmel controversy. They felt that on-field success with Rodgers would be the ultimate deodorant, if the Jets could ever get around to, you know, winning games. Theirs was a philosophy shared by the most successful sports executive in town, Brian Cashman, who had seen it all in more than a quarter century as general manager of the Yankees.

"You can be anything and everything you want to be in New York as long as you perform," Cashman said. "You can be understated and perform and be loved, or you can be controversial and boisterous and perform and be loved. Everything gets written around the performance."

Many saw the Kimmel case as the price of doing business with Rodgers, the outspoken superstar who was going to lead them into contention in 2024. In fact, on the same day that an ESPN suit ripped him for his comments, Rodgers was named by his teammates as the Jets' most inspirational player of 2023.

And nothing captured the essence of Rodgers better than that. Vilified by a nation on Tuesday. Honored by a locker room on Friday.

Rodgers got emotional as he walked from his seat to pick up the award named for Dennis Byrd, the former defensive lineman who was paralyzed in a 1992 game and who died in a 2016 car crash. The quarterback did his best not to cry in front of his team. "Thankful for my guys looking at me that way," he said.

The dichotomy of Rodgers was a living, breathing thing. Some of his close friends were frustrated by the damage his self-generated controversies did to his public image, and wished strangers knew the quarterback the way they knew him.

They talked often about Rodgers's generosity, his outsized heart, and the money he had donated in the wake of the great wildfire and the great pandemic. Rodgers had given more than $160,000 to Salvation Army Christmas programs in his final Green Bay years. Nate Raabe, his longtime friend and business partner, talked about the big things Rodgers would do—helping raise $1.6 million for an RX3 charity event—and the smaller things—taping a heartfelt video message for Raabe's third-grader son Grayson to play for his class, telling the students to listen to their teachers and to ignore those who didn't believe in their dreams.

At a June practice, Rodgers had spent twenty one-on-one minutes with a thirteen-year-old Jets fan, Braylon Hodgson, who was dying of a rare cancer found in the brain stem known as DIPG. Braylon's father, Ryan, arrived at the practice unsure of what to expect from the quarterback, or if he should expect anything at all. "I heard he wasn't a good guy through the news media," Hodgson said. "So, you're like, 'Is he going to be a good dude? Is he going to say hello?' And he could not have been more cool.

"I was shocked to see how friendly he was and how generous he was with his time. It wasn't just, 'I gotta say hello and move on.' He definitely cared about Braylon."

Rodgers gave a signed red practice jersey to the boy who was named after former Jets receiver Braylon Edwards. On the night of September 11, with the TV tuned to the Jets-Bills game, Braylon Hodgson had that No. 8 jersey with him while under hospice care. He died the following day.

The time that Rodgers had spent with his son, Ryan Hodgson said, "made Braylon smile and feel good about himself, and just made a huge difference. It felt like Aaron understood that, and we are incredibly thankful."

The Packers saw Rodgers do these things, a lot. The Jets were just learning about that side of him. But the unforced Kimmel error hurt Rodgers outside the team facility, around the country, about as much as his 2021 COVID deception did.

Winning cures everything, they say. It was going to take a long winning streak to cure this.

In the final few practices of the season, Rodgers dazzled teammates by slicing up the first-string defense like he did before his injury. And then it was on to New England, where Rodgers spent some warmup time with Belichick before the Jets beat the Patriots for the first time in sixteen games, closing out a nightmare season with a 17–3 victory.

On Monday, Rodgers met with the media that regularly covered the team and said that if the Jets wanted to be a successful organization "the bullshit that has nothing to do with winning needs to get out of the building."

Longtime league observers were struck by the audacity of that statement, believing that nobody on the Jets created more distractions than Rodgers did, through his paid TV gig. In New York, Eli Manning had set the standard for maintenance-free stardom, following the lead of Derek Jeter. Manning had kept his personality sealed away somewhere until he retired and started his second career.

Rodgers had no interest in doing that. As a fearless and unapologetic disseminator of opinions on the topics of the day, he had missed his calling as a columnist or talking TV head.

"I thought that would be a disaster here, and it was," NFL Network analyst Marc Ross, an executive who helped the Giants win two Super Bowls, said for this book. "Eli [Manning] was always about the Giants. It was never about him. Aaron always seemed to be about him and not the Jets."

In his press conference the day after the Jets sent out Belichick with a loss, Rodgers effectively told reporters to butter their popcorn for his *McAfee* segment the next day. "Tune in," he said.

Before Rodgers could get there, Kimmel delivered a scathing seven-minute monologue on his ABC show that was much like a typical Jets pass—missing its intended target—when it ridiculed Rodgers's intelligence, and then spot on when it rebuked the quarterback for linking him to pedophilia.

Kimmel said he'd be ready to move on if Rodgers apologized, "which is what a decent person would do. But I bet he won't."

Kimmel won his bet.

Up front with McAfee, Rodgers mentioned "the woke establishment," signaling no intention to turn this appearance into an act of contrition. He cited the jokes Kimmel told at his expense during "COVID times," and the criticisms the comedian leveled against unvaccinated people and those (including Rodgers) who used Ivermectin. He said Kimmel was wrong for believing the vaccines were safe and effective.

On the Epstein front, Rodgers did not say what he could have said—that he had no intention of discussing Epstein, or Kimmel, until his friend Hawk brought up "the list" out of nowhere, and that he was sorry for making a hurtful and irresponsible remark in an attempt to be funny on the fly. Rodgers was not going to put this on his friend.

Instead, he explained that he was never suggesting that Kimmel was on "the list," but merely responding to the comedian's past ridicule. "I'm not stupid enough . . . to accuse you of [pedophilia] with absolutely zero evidence," Rodgers said.

Before he was done, Rodgers took a shot at ESPN's Mike Foss for misspeaking on his behalf, and railed against the pandemic lockdowns that shuttered businesses, exacerbated mental-health issues, and widened the wealth gap between the haves and have-nots.

Rodgers was in the middle of a fully guaranteed, two-year, $75 million deal when he delivered that take. He was a full-blown *have* who was always worth the money he made, which always made him worth the trouble he caused.

But by mid-March, it was apparent that Rodgers had caused the Jets far more trouble than they had bargained for. The news that independent presidential candidate Robert F. Kennedy Jr. considered the quarterback a potential running mate—leaked while Rodgers was in Costa Rica on another ayahuasca retreat—was one thing: Rodgers had already committed to playing two or three more seasons, and the leak always smelled like an RFK Jr. publicity stunt, nothing more. (The candidate named attorney and entrepreneur Nicole Shanahan his running mate on March 26.)

The follow-up report by CNN about Rodgers's alleged heinous comments about the 2012 Sandy Hook Elementary School shooting in separate private conversations with a CNN reporter and an unnamed source could not be dismissed. Though Rodgers rarely rushed to defend himself in public, he posted a carefully worded denial on X the following day without directly refuting the reported conversation with CNN's Pamela Brown at a 2013 Kentucky Derby party or the second conversation with the unnamed source years later. He did remind readers that he had already been on record calling the Sandy Hook murders "an absolute tragedy" and that he hoped "we learn from this and other tragedies to identify the signs that will allow us to prevent unnecessary loss of life."

Rodgers did not need the Jets to tell him that he could not let these disturbing claims go unchallenged. He had a conversation with his CAA marketing agent, Ed Berry, who thought this was an easy fire for his client to extinguish, given his recorded comments on the tragedy in a 2012 ESPN Milwaukee interview. Rodgers also wrote on X, "My thoughts and prayers continue to remain with the families affected along with the entire Sandy Hook community," and posted a heart emoji. Rodgers later said on the *I Can Fly* podcast, "I got mentioned as a finalist to be vice president on a ticket, and they fuckin' attacked me with some bizarre story from years ago that was a third-hand account or something. They're terrified. They're terrified of people who think for themselves who aren't controlled. I'm not beholden to anybody. . . . I have very few sponsors now. . . . Nobody controls my messaging. Nobody controls my social media. Nobody controls me."

Meanwhile, the Jets had to manage yet another loud Rodgers controversy, this one having nothing to do with McAfee's show. The team was getting all of the diva's downside as a personality, and none of his upside as a quarterback, and you know what everyone around New York had to say about that.

Same. Old. Jets.

· · ·

AARON RODGERS OPENED his offseason by taking his offensive linemen to Las Vegas to start building them back up. They were beaten down, primary culprits in the 7-10 season, and Rodgers showed them some love.

Oh, and he also found time during the getaway to make a hole-in-one in his first golf round since his surgery.

At the end of January, a report in *The Athletic* on the Jets' culture by Dianna Russini, who had done some intensive reporting on the team, painted a picture of behind-the-scenes chaos. The report quoted one coach calling for change and saying, "It's such a fucking mess," and quoted one AFC general manager saying, "Aaron Rodgers isn't the assistant GM. Joe Douglas is the assistant GM."

For all intents and purposes, Rodgers was running the organization. He protected Douglas, Robert Saleh, and Nathaniel Hackett against a possible firing—Douglas was 27-56 as the Jets' GM, and Saleh was 18-33 as their head coach. Rodgers was the reason Woody Johnson was willing to run it back with the same crew despite being as angry with his chief decision-makers as he had ever been and hitting them with a win-or-else mandate.

But if the quarterback was indeed the Jets' GM, he did not receive any votes for Executive of the Year. The people he recruited and/or recommended and/or wanted in place before he arrived included:

Hackett. Allen Lazard. Randall Cobb. Tim Boyle. Billy Turner. Adrian Amos. Dalvin Cook.

Not one of them worked out.

Maybe they all would have worked out, had Rodgers stayed healthy. Maybe the Jets would have gone 11-6 and won a playoff game or two, had Rodgers thrown the ball when he was supposed to on first-and-10 from his own 43 on the night of 9/11.

Maybe the Jets would not have watched a receiver they had no use for, Mecole Hardman, catch the winning Super Bowl touchdown pass in overtime for his old team, the Kansas City Chiefs, or listened to him trash their culture. Maybe Rodgers would not have watched Patrick Mahomes officially hurdle him on those unofficial GOAT rankings, even if A-Rod entered the 2024 season as the NFL's all-time leader in passer rating, edging the Chiefs' three-time champ by a 103.6–103.5 margin.

But it was not meant to be. In those last practices in January, when Rodgers was the training-camp Rodgers and the Jets felt like the Boys of Summer all over again, sans the chanting fans, the quarterback was blitzed by some bittersweet thoughts.

"There was excitement and also the 'what if' kind of hits you in the face pretty hard," Rodgers said, "because, obviously, if you saw what we were able to do, there's a lot of 'what could have been.'"

In the end, Rodgers was hired by the Jets to get rid of that "what could have been." Instead, he became the face of a collapse that was shocking even by Jets standards.

So, Douglas, Saleh, and Hackett would be fired if the Jets do not win, and win big, in 2024. Rodgers would likely get run out of town too.

Or . . . Rodgers would stay healthy and write the happiest possible ending to his Hall of Fame career. Either way, the pen was in his hand. He was the one who could make that Super Bowl III trophy in the Jets' facility feel a lot less lonely and take his own legacy to a different place.

The son of small-town Chico, the legend from small-town Green Bay, still had a shot to make it big in the big city. It was going to be all or nothing for the quarterback in his twentieth NFL season, a year that shaped up as a beautiful mystery with only one certainty:

The league was a far more interesting place with Aaron Charles Rodgers in it.

AFTERWORD

It was such a magical night that Aaron Rodgers did not want it to end. He was hoping his defense could get one last stop against New England so he could return to the MetLife Stadium field and soak it all in.

One year and eight days after he ruptured his Achilles and collapsed on this same turf, Rodgers wanted to take the final snap in the final seconds and drop to a knee. A full house of more than eighty thousand fans had chanted his name throughout the second half of the New York Jets' 24–3 victory, and who could blame him for wanting to hear it one last time?

Aa-ron Rod-gers . . . Aa-ron Rod-gers . . . Aa-ron Rod-gers.

These were the same fans who had watched in horror when No. 8 went down for all of 2023 after four snaps into his Jets career, the same fans who had suffered through thirteen straight nonplayoff seasons. Some were old enough to remember what it felt like when Joe Namath was in his prime, leading the franchise to its one and only title in Super Bowl III.

That was what it felt like inside MetLife, even though Rodgers was forty years old, coming off a brutal rehab from a brutal injury, and playing on short rest on a Thursday night. He was young and athletic again, scrambling outside the pocket and throwing lasers on the run as if he had cut some Faustian deal the day before the game. At one point the Amazon Prime analyst in the booth, Kirk Herbstreit, said he didn't want to waste any time talking because he preferred to sit there and just appreciate what he was witnessing.

"Beautiful," Herbstreit called the ballet in front of him.

"Man, he looks good tonight," the announcer said later.

"As good as ever," added his legendary partner, Al Michaels.

• • •

WHEN IT WAS over, nobody cared that Patriots rookie Drake Maye took the final snap while his childhood idol watched from the Jets' sideline.

I was in the building that night, September 19, 2024, when it was hard to believe that Rodgers & Co. would end up being anything other than what they were advertised to be—a playoff team, at least. The Patriots were a lousy opponent, but still, this was the same franchise that had tormented the Jets for more than two decades. Beating them meant something profound even if Bill Belichick and Tom Brady were off doing other things.

How strong were the Jets? Four months earlier, NFL analyst and fantasy football expert Mike Clay wrote an ESPN.com piece headlined "Why the Jets, Aaron Rodgers Will Win the Super Bowl," which claimed, "You'd be hard-pressed to compare this roster with those of the other 31 NFL teams and not come away thinking this is a legitimate title contender."

Clay surveyed the Jets' elite defense, improved supporting cast on offense, Rodgers's return to health, the diminished state of the AFC East, and a relatively easy schedule and came away with a logical conclusion: These bums were finally going to win the whole damn thing.

And that would have been the best story in sports. Maybe that was why Rodgers's comeback game in the home opener felt so big. The quarterback had looked rusty in a losing season opener at San Francisco, as expected, and made the throws he needed to make to beat the Titans on the road. A lot of smart football people thought that if the Jets could start 2-1, their schedule would set them up for an 11-6 type of year.

Just like I had the previous September for the grand debut gone awry, I drove Rodgers's parents to the game. This book had already been out for a month and, predictably enough, much of the coverage of it revolved around the quarterback's decade-long estrangement from his family—and related on-the-record quotes from Rodgers, his parents, and other relatives. I didn't know exactly what Ed and Darla thought of my unauthorized biography of their son, and of how I covered the estrangement. I mean, who really wants their family issues written about in a book?

But the fact that they agreed to reenact our 2023 drive—in hopes of a much better MetLife outcome—suggested that they were largely OK with it. And that turned out to be the case when I picked them up at their New Jersey Airbnb, with Darla decked out in her son's No. 8 Jets jersey.

They were surprised by a couple of statements in the book, like Aaron's claim that former girlfriend Olivia Munn had no meaningful role in causing the family divide. "Did he really say that?" Darla asked as we drove toward the stadium. And they challenged my reporting on the approximately $15,000 in cash gifts that their son had given them—information furnished by Aaron himself. But by and large, they said they thought the book was honest and fair.

On the estrangement front, there actually had been a couple of recent emails exchanged between Aaron and his parents that were optimistic in tone. As a human being, not a journalist, I had always hoped that this book would somehow help the healing process. It was a long shot, but I thought the published scene of Ed Rodgers and his son embracing at Lake Tahoe might be a difference maker. Ed and Darla were staying a few extra days in New Jersey in case Aaron was willing to meet after the game. He knew his parents would be in the crowd—the Jets had left tickets for them—just like he knew they were there when he got hurt in 2023.

We all agreed on the way into the stadium that win, lose, or draw, we just wanted Aaron to get through the game healthy. None of us wanted any part of another postgame drive like the one we had experienced twelve months earlier.

It was a warm and dry night, ideal conditions for the oldest active player in the NFL. Given his superstitions, Rodgers was glad he was not asked again to run out of the tunnel carrying an outsize American flag. The crowd greeted him with a deafening roar, and on the second play from scrimmage, he announced that this year was not going to be anything like the previous year. He ran left for five yards and a first down before dropping into a baseball slide. The fan base exhaled and then cheered.

The rest of the night was a dazzling display from inside and outside the pocket. Rodgers escaped New England's pressure with ease, just like he had for so many years in Green Bay. His rollout throws to the outside shoulders of his receivers were absurdly accurate. His two-yard touchdown pass to Garrett Wilson was an all-timer because the coverage by New England's gifted young cornerback, Christian Gonzalez, left open a six-inch window for Rodgers to make the completion. If the quarterback let loose a good pass, not an extraordinary one, Gonzalez would have intercepted the ball and raced untouched for a pick-six.

"That's an unbelievable throw by Aaron," the cornerback said. "That's why he is who he is."

On what he called "a special night," Rodgers completed 27 of 35 passes for 281 yards and two touchdowns. He arrived at his postgame press conference dressed in black and looking fresher than any man who had played three NFL games in eleven days had a right to look.

"I felt like I was myself, quite a few years ago," he said.

Rodgers took some hits from Patriots defenders, but he played without fear. He had left his Week 1 anxiety behind in San Francisco, and now it was time to let it all go. The Jets should expect to win, Rodgers said. "The next step is expecting and dominating."

He called the chanting of his name "really meaningful," and soon enough he was back in the locker room gathering his things and rushing somewhere to enjoy the extra time off given all Thursday night combatants. Rodgers did not set up a sit-down with his parents. Whenever football season was underway, he was always incredibly hard to pin down. He was a superstar athlete, after all, and a ton was on the line for the franchise and the franchise quarterback.

The Jets were off to a strong start with a home debut that was almost perfect. Almost. After taking a 14–0 lead over the Patriots, Rodgers approached head coach Robert Saleh on the sideline, accepted his congratulatory handshake, then planted two hands on his chest and pushed the head coach as he attempted to hug the quarterback. Rodgers glared at Saleh as he walked away, and the video caught fire on social media.

"He's not a big hugger usually, so I didn't know he was going for the hug," Rodgers explained. "He likes to do the two-hand chest push as well. He talks a lot about two-score leads. So, I kind of gave him a push and said, 'Two-score lead.'"

Both men dismissed the awkward scene with humor, and everyone got home safely. But that clip kept coming back to life throughout the season, if only because it reminded everyone that there was always something fundamentally wrong with the makeup of these Jets. Even on the good nights, something was clearly off.

When was the last time a prominent quarterback shoved his head coach in front of millions of witnesses, stared him down, and then called it an inside joke?

As it turned out, as always, the joke was on the New York Jets.

• • •

ON JANUARY 5, 2025, Aaron Rodgers took the field for what many believed to be the final time as an NFL player, or at least as a member of the Jets.

It was a lot colder than it was during his home-opening triumph over New England, but Rodgers looked just as good against Miami on a four-touchdown day that included the five hundredth of his career. He stepped up in the pocket in the second quarter and threw short to tight end Tyler Conklin in the end zone to hit a milestone reached only by Tom Brady, Drew Brees, Peyton Manning, and Brett Favre.

Rodgers kept the ball for No. 500 and earned the 153rd regular-season victory of his career, this one by a score of 32–20.

If you had just watched those two MetLife games against the Patriots and the Dolphins—played three and a half months apart—you would have thought Rodgers would have been preparing for the playoffs and, perhaps, weighing his chances to tie Peyton Manning with a record fifth league MVP award.

But if you watched every snap of the Jets' 2024 season, you would have known precisely why they finished with a ghastly 5-12 record and, when measured against expectations, why they were considered among the most disappointing New York sports teams ever.

Oh, and why a lot of football fans thought Aaron Rodgers's twentieth season in the league should also be his last.

The plunge started against Denver in Week 4, when the rain was just as annoying as the fourteen hits the Broncos put on the home team's quarterback. "The weather sucked, but so did some of my throws," said Rodgers, who was left hobbling with another left leg injury during this 10–9 defeat.

While this was a dispiriting turn of events, even the most fatalistic Jets fan couldn't have fathomed that the Denver loss would trigger a complete collapse that saw these alleged contenders lose eight of their next nine games to fall to 3-10. The Jets had devolved into the Kansas City Chiefs of losing. Every week they invented new ways to blow leads and end up with fewer points than the opposition.

What happened?

What didn't happen?

To his surgically repaired Achilles tendon Rodgers added injuries to his knee, hamstring, and ankle. He did not take any time off to heal because he was hell-bent on achieving his goal of playing all seventeen games. The situation begged for a strong coaching or front-office voice to tell Rodgers that the team had paid good money to a pro's pro, backup QB Tyrod Taylor, for a reason, and that Taylor needed to play a game or two to give Rodgers a chance to get healthy.

But the Jets had no strong coaching or front-office voices. Instead, they had middle-aged men who acted more like giddy teenagers around Rodgers, shrinking in his presence, dropping during the season one by one.

Robert Saleh was fired by Woody Johnson after the Week 5 loss to Minnesota in London, where the former ambassador to the UK was embarrassed by a shoddy performance that included three interceptions thrown by Rodgers, most notably a pick-six in the first quarter and an underthrown game killer in the final minute. Rodgers's good friend, offensive coordinator Nathaniel Hackett, was demoted. Six weeks later, with the Jets in a full death spiral, general manager Joe Douglas was fired.

The three football men who were part of the 2023 party dispatched to Malibu to recruit Rodgers had been effectively cannibalized by the three suits who were along for the ride, Woody and Christopher Johnson and team president Hymie Elhai. Not that Rodgers was solely responsible for the meltdown as he tried and failed to perform with injured legs and almost no mobility.

Greg Zuerlein, a reliable veteran kicker who had made 92 percent of his field-goal attempts in 2023, cost the Jets multiple games by making only 60 percent in 2024, the worst rate of his thirteen-year career. The Jets were already 2-4 by the time they traded for Rodgers's dear friend and favorite Green Bay target, Davante Adams, and they were already 2-5 by the time the Pro Bowl pass rusher acquired from Philadelphia, Haason Reddick, ended his absurd contract holdout.

Reddick only added dysfunction to a defensive unit that was equal parts heartless and clueless. Star cornerback Sauce Gardner suddenly struggled to make elementary plays in the passing and running games. Reddick,

AFTERWORD

Micheal Clemons, and Javon Kinlaw were routinely getting destroyed up front, and interim head coach Jeff Ulbrich was routinely covering for them in press conferences with enabling gibberish.

Ulbrich later admitted that he should have surrendered his defensive play-calling duties once he replaced Saleh, to get a better handle on the entire team. That he didn't accept this obvious fact during the season speaks to why he delivered some of the worst coaching longtime New York observers had ever seen in the market.

I grew up in New Jersey as a Dallas Cowboys fan, largely because the Jets and Giants were terrible back then, and because Dallas was forever featured in the one nationally televised Sunday game we'd get in a precable age. So, it wasn't until I wrote this book and hopped on the Jets' tattered bandwagon that I truly understood how maddening and soul-crushing it could be to root for this team.

The monumental failure was a team effort on every level. And yet when people talked about this Jets' season, they talked about one figure above all. Rodgers put that bull's-eye on his back by being an all-time great and by being his polarizing self.

Rodgers got ripped in the preseason for missing a couple of mandatory minicamp practices while in Egypt, and got ripped again in-season for revealing that receiver Mike Williams ran the wrong route on a fatal interception against Buffalo. Rodgers assailed ESPN's talking heads while speaking as an ESPN talking head on *The Pat McAfee Show* and engaged in a nasty back-and-forth with ESPN's Ryan Clark, because of course he did.

Rodgers also hit Woody Johnson with some hard jabs to the nose after a report in *The Athletic* detailed more of Woody's Woody-ness, including the fact that the owner suggested the quarterback should be benched in September—ten days after his stirring performance against New England had the crowd chanting his name—and that Johnson's teenage sons were influencing the team's personnel moves, something Johnson has strongly denied.

On the subject of potentially getting cut by the Jets, Rodgers went out of his way to ridicule Woody, telling McAfee, "I've never been released before, so being released would be a first. Being released by a teenager, that would also be a first. Hey, I'm open to everything, and I find the comedy in all of it. If that happens, hey, it's a great story."

Rodgers had earlier implied to reporters that Johnson was not as supportive of his decision-makers as owners should be. One source close to Rodgers said that while he still felt love for Christopher Johnson ("I feel like I'll have a lifetime friendship with him regardless of what happens," Rodgers had told me for this book), he had little use for Woody, and that he blamed the owner's style of leadership (or lack thereof) on the persistent organizational leaks that embarrassed the team.

In the end, this was a quarterback who questioned everything and challenged everyone.

As the on-field losses mounted and the criticism intensified, Rodgers sent a message to his parents that was far less hopeful about a potential reconciliation with his family than the emails he had sent months earlier. This was just before his Netflix docuseries, *Aaron Rodgers: Enigma*, aired in three parts and included his stated belief that his parents thought he was "soft growing up" and that they didn't often express their pride in his early achievements, forcing him to "be my own parent in those moments and say, 'Hey, fuck being perfect. I'm proud of who you are and what you've accomplished on and off the field.'"

Ed Rodgers said he and Darla did not watch the docuseries, had no desire to watch it, and had no comment on what their son said. They were still hoping that a reunion with Aaron could happen. On the football front, Ed said he would love to see his son play one more season in New York in the hope that the new coaching staff would maximize the considerable talent on the roster.

First, Aaron had to determine if he wanted to play in 2025 for anyone. Following his season-ending victory over Miami, he gave an emotional interview to Fox sideline reporter Pam Oliver, who had covered much of his career, that had the feel of goodbye. So did Rodgers's walk off the field with Davante Adams, which mirrored his final walk out of Lambeau with Randall Cobb.

• • •

THE QUARTERBACK HAD tears in his eyes as he sat at his locker with his jersey and shoulder pads already removed, and again as he embraced Conklin. If this was indeed the end, Rodgers could at least feel good about going out on a near masterpiece against Miami a week after getting blown

AFTERWORD

out in Buffalo in the penultimate game. He could retire as the all-time leader in passer rating, with his 102.6 edging Patrick Mahomes's 102.1.

And yet there was a case to be made to the Jets' next head coach and general manager that Rodgers should be brought back. His final numbers—3,897 passing yards, 28 touchdowns, and 11 interceptions—represented one of the best quarterbacking seasons in franchise history. Rodgers was in the top ten in the league in yards and touchdowns, and he managed one eight-game stretch defined by fourteen scoring passes against one interception.

"People said Aaron is washed, but he's not," said his junior college coach and longtime friend, Craig Rigsbee. "If you put his passing statistics next to Mahomes's this year they're almost identical, and they said Mahomes was the greatest thing since sliced bread and Aaron was terrible. And that's with Aaron having a much worse coach, a much worse team, and a much worse program.

"You can't judge Aaron against him in his prime anymore. You've got to judge him against other quarterbacks in the league. The Jets' season went haywire early, when the kicker should've beaten Denver and Buffalo and the owner panicked and fired Saleh and everything went to hell. If the owner had stayed the course I think they would've had a much better season, and Aaron would've been excited to come back, and nobody would be saying a word."

But those opposed to signing up for another year of the Rodgers experience had their case, too. They pointed out that Rodgers had thrown for at least 300 yards only once—in a December loss at Miami—and for the first time in three years. They pointed out that the Jets ranked twenty-fifth in the league in points scored, and that Garrett Wilson seemed unhappy enough with his role and the relentless losing over his three seasons to consider asking for a trade.

Once again, Rodgers was going to be the center of a fascinating offseason debate. "If you look at a lot of teams," Rigsbee said, "Aaron was way better than what they had at quarterback. If he came back to the Jets another year removed from the Achilles, I think they would be pretty damn good. And he'd be a good mentor if they drafted a young quarterback, just like he was a good mentor to Jordan Love.

"If Aaron stays, the Jets get Davante back, and their two receivers, tight end, and running back are as talented a group as any in the league. I think he should go one more year. If you've never run out in a stadium with a hundred thousand people cheering for you, and if you've never had that experience of celebrating a big win with your teammates in the locker room, there's no drug that can get you feeling that good. That's a hard thing to let go of."

Was he ready to give it all up for good? Dressed in black again (including a beanie and pinstriped blazer) for his final postgame presser of the season, Rodgers said he needed time away to recover physically and mentally and to measure his appetite to continue on. He maintained that he wouldn't be offended if the Jets decided to let him go, and he reiterated that his time in the New York market amounted to "the best two years of my life."

Rodgers addressed his teammates in a meeting the night before the Miami game, telling them that his perspective had changed after his Achilles injury and that he had no regrets over joining the Jets. The relationships in the sport meant everything to him, and he cherished the bonds he established in the Jets' locker room.

Without his time in New York, Rodgers said in his presser, "I would have had a big hole inside me that only these two years could have filled."

Rodgers made it clear he believed that he could still play at a high level, and that he proved he could as his legs healed later in the season. For those looking for the most conspicuous clue about his intentions—beyond his stated willingness to take another pay cut—it was found in his comparison to his Green Bay exit after the 2022 season. Rodgers said he was 90 percent retired heading into his darkness retreat that winter. He said he had lost his love for the game and was trying to recover it.

Everything felt different this time around. After beating the Dolphins with those four touchdown passes, Rodgers said, "I have tremendous love for the game now."

Would that love conquer all in the decisions to come?

• • •

THE JETS' NEW head coach and former star cornerback, Aaron Glenn, and new general manager, Darren Mougey, informed Aaron Rodgers in a pre–Super Bowl meeting in New Jersey that they would be starting a different quarterback in 2025. Jay Glazer of Fox broke the news on February 9.

AFTERWORD

Even with a 5-12 record, Rodgers was trending on Super Bowl Sunday... because of course he was. People all over the league were talking about him before and after the Philadelphia Eagles shredded the Kansas City Chiefs and their three-peat aims.

Rodgers's dream of finishing his career with a most improbable New York championship was now dead. Glenn and Mougey concluded that they could not establish a fresh identity, their own identity, as long as Rodgers was in the building. The future Hall of Famer won five games for the Jets in two years, not counting the official victory he earned on that September 11 night that wrecked everything.

Many of his teammates were dismayed by the news. Defensive lineman Quinnen Williams, a three-time Pro Bowler and the Jets' best player, posted a thumbs-down and eye-roll emojis and the words "another rebuild for me I guess" before deactivating his X account. It didn't matter. The Jets were moving on.

It didn't take long for other teams to make a move on one of the most high-profile free agents in league history. In fact, two of the NFL's most storied franchises offered Rodgers their starting quarterback jobs. The Pittsburgh Steelers and New York Giants, owners of a combined ten Super Bowl titles, looked past his age (41) and some unflattering 2024 metrics (a league ranking of 25th in QBR and 28th in yards gained per pass attempt) and saw on tape a man who could still sling the football better than most.

Though the Giants offered Rodgers a chance to remain in his New Jersey home, they represented another big gamble the quarterback could not afford to take. The Giants had lost twenty-five of their thirty-four games over the previous two seasons and employed a coach and general manager who would surely be let go if the team didn't show considerable improvement in 2025.

Could Rodgers really risk ending his career by going 5-12 for both New York teams before getting released?

He was not ready to answer that question by the time the Giants decided in March that they could no longer wait, signing Russell Wilson and Jameis Winston to be their starter and backup, respectively. The Giants also realized that their roster was not as attractive to Rodgers as Pittsburgh's.

Not that the Steelers amounted to the only remaining alternative to retirement.

Rodgers actually wanted to suit up for Minnesota, even if that choice would duplicate Brett Favre's circle of life as an NFL starter—Packers to Jets to Vikings. Minnesota coach Kevin O'Connell had some degree of interest (O'Connell is a longtime friend of Aaron's) but preferred to replace the departed Sam Darnold with 2024 first-round pick J.J. McCarthy, who was coming off a knee injury that required two surgeries.

Though the 14-3 Vikings gave him the best shot at the Super Bowl, Rodgers knew he couldn't wait around for O'Connell to reconsider in the event McCarthy looked raw and rusty in the summer. That wouldn't be fair to anyone, especially the Steelers, who were being mocked for keeping their offer to Rodgers on the table for what felt like an eternity.

Pittsburgh is a proud working-class city, and the majority of locals seemed to no longer care that Rodgers had once beaten the Steelers in the Super Bowl, and that he had a long-standing bromance with Mike Tomlin, the vanquished head coach in that game. Fans were urging Tomlin, general manager Omar Khan, and owner Art Rooney II to find a different quarterback to end their streak of eight straight years without a playoff victory, even though Rodgers was communicating with the coach and sending back-channel signals that things would ultimately work out. Many seemed to be asking, *Have we really been reduced to beggars at the feet of a declining drama queen who had just been cut by the hapless Jets?*

Still unsigned on April 17, Rodgers ended his extended public silence by appearing on *McAfee* and committing to absolutely nothing, other than the fact he felt disrespected in his Jets exit meeting by Aaron Glenn. Rodgers complained that he flew across the country "on my own dime" expecting a lengthy conversation about whether they had a future together, only to be released before he could get settled into his seat.

Rodgers was clearly wounded by the terms of a divorce dictated by the other party and motivated to settle a couple of scores. But the Jets had already signed Justin Fields to replace him, and the world had moved on, and all any listener cared about now was whether he'd sign with Pittsburgh or retire.

The quarterback said he was still "open to anything and attached to nothing," and maintained that he had been up front with the teams that had pursued him. Rodgers told McAfee he was willing to play for $10 million, a huge pay cut. He revealed that personal issues were responsible for the delay in his decision.

AFTERWORD

"Right now, my focus has been and will continue to be on my personal life," Rodgers said. "That's what I've told the coaches. . . . The conversation about where I was at in my personal life, the stuff that I am dealing with off the field—in my inner circle—that has to take my attention right now. I wasn't stringing anybody along. I wasn't holding anybody hostage."

The Steelers had met with Rodgers in Pittsburgh, coming away more determined to sign him. They were pleased when a social media video surfaced showing their potential new quarterback throwing with their new star receiver, DK Metcalf, at UCLA. The Steelers were willing to wait for Rodgers, but they didn't want to wait forever.

They proved at the draft that they were optimistic Rodgers would indeed sign. Despite their deficiencies at quarterback, the Steelers passed on Colorado star Shedeur Sanders, Deion's son, and every other passing prospect with their three picks in the first four rounds and waited until the sixth round to take QB Will Howard of Ohio State.

Of Rodgers, Rooney told *Steelers Nation Radio*, "He does want to come here, so I do think we may get word soon."

That word still had not arrived by the start of May. Pittsburgh was hoping Rodgers would hop aboard by May 27, the start of organized team activities, or OTAs. The vast majority of league executives, coaches, and players believed that Rodgers would in fact play for the Steelers in 2025.

But if the quarterback had demonstrated anything over his twenty-year career, it was this: The only thing predictable about him was his unpredictability.

Oh, and this: Aaron Rodgers was going to be the biggest story in the NFL no matter what he did.

ACKNOWLEDGMENTS

Aaron Rodgers granted a sit-down interview for this unauthorized biography when he was under no obligation to do so, and that was greatly appreciated. It should also be noted that Rodgers did not prevent some of his closest friends from talking to me for this book.

I would like to thank Aaron's parents, Ed and Darla Rodgers, for their time, patience, and trust in telling their story. While I was visiting Aaron's hometown of Chico, California, his junior college coach, Craig Rigsbee, could not have been a more gracious host. His Pleasant Valley High School coaches, Sterling Jackson and John Shepherd, also made me feel welcomed.

The detailed narrative of Edward Rodgers's heroism as a combat pilot in World War II would not have been possible without the relentless work of Dan Matthews, a longtime military records expert who was inspired by the service of his father and uncle during the war. Dan's passion and institutional knowledge made this a much better book, and I cannot thank him enough for that. I would also like to acknowledge Tom Faulkner, who somehow flew a B-24 in combat as a teenager, and who, at age ninety-eight, gave me a firsthand account of what Edward Rodgers faced in fighting the Hitler war machine as a fellow pilot with the 737th Bomb Squadron.

The New York Jets credentialed me for practices and games—not a professional courtesy all teams and leagues extend to authors—and I remain appreciative of that. A special thanks to senior VP Eric Gelfand for arranging the Rodgers interview, among other things, and to rising PR star Ryan Stefanacci (for putting up with my many requests), Jared Winley, Meghan Gilmore, and Danielle Bonnett.

ACKNOWLEDGMENTS

Rodgers's teammates and coaches from Pleasant Valley, Butte, Cal, the Green Bay Packers, and the New York Jets were overly generous with their time for a stranger who called out of left field looking for help. This book would not have been possible without them. Thanks to Mike McCarthy for taking my call too.

My reporting and writing were informed by accomplished journalists who covered Rodgers's career on a daily basis. The staff of the *Chico Enterprise-Record* did a terrific job documenting his developmental years at PV and Butte, including Greg Ball, Dave Davies, Darren J. Gendron, Gary Kelley, Michael Lowman, and Luke Reid. Bay Area writers whose pieces on Rodgers and the Cal Golden Bears were helpful included Bruce Adams, Daniel Brown, Neil Hayes, Jay Heater, Tim Kawakami, Ron Kroichick, Kevin Lynch, Jerry McDonald, Dave Newhouse, and Ray Ratto. Writers whose work covering the Green Bay Packers made for a thorough education included Rob Demovsky, Pete Dougherty, Bill Huber, Michael Hunt, Chris Jenkins, Bob McGinn, Aaron Nagler, Lori Nickel, Rob Reischel, Matt Schneidman, Tom Silverstein, Dylan Tomlinson, and Jason Wilde, whose weekly ESPN Milwaukee radio shows with Rodgers were enlightening and entertaining. Radio legends Mike Clemens, Wayne Larrivee, and Bill Michaels were kind enough to lend their insights. The iconic Packers patriarch, Bob Harlan, was a treasure.

In New York, the great Rich Cimini and Brian Costello provided a valuable daily roadmap with their coverage of the Jets, as did Mark Cannizzaro, Jeane Coakley, Ryan Dunleavy, Connor Hughes, Al Iannazzone, Dan Leberfeld, Zack Rosenblatt, Antwan Staley, Andy Vasquez, and Dennis Waszak Jr. Star columnists Steve Politi, Steve Serby, and Mike Vaccaro were always thought-provoking and on point.

Nationally, the heavyweight reporting and commentary of Greg Bishop, Albert Breer, Tyler Dunne, Sam Farmer, Mike Florio, Kalyn Kahler, Tim Keown, Mina Kimes, Peter King, Tim Layden, Jeff Pearlman, Tom Pelissero, Ian Rapoport, Charles Robinson, Dianna Russini, Adam Schefter, Peter Schrager, and Mike Silver were most informative. Andrew Marchand, Gary Myers, Kevin Van Valkenburg, Seth Wickersham, Trey Wingo, and Gene Wojciechowski were among the distinguished journalists and voices who offered a helping hand. Pearlman's 2017 bestselling biography of Brett Favre, *Gunslinger*, was a tremendous resource, as was Reischel's 2011 book,

ACKNOWLEDGMENTS

Aaron Rodgers: Leader of the Pack. Michele Soulli, genealogist, did excellent work in piecing together the Rodgers family tree.

Others who made notable contributions included Aaron Alexander of *The Align Podcast*, Jim Bates, Ed Berry, Tad Carper, Kyle Cousineau, Jack Curry, Robert DiTonno, Micala Drews Martin, Mark Duffner, Ryan Glasspiegel, Bob Gregory, Joey Kaempf, Kyle Lewis, Mike MacNaughton, Ryan MacNaughton, Reed Mauser, Roger Mauser, Mike Mayock, Terrence Murphy, Keola Pang, Tanya Quackenbush, Nate Raabe, Kyle Rice, Dennis Roberts, Jordan Russell, Emiliano Salazar, Jiri Sasek, Michele Shover, Chris Simms, David L. Snead, Mike Sullivan, Joe Thatcher, Barrett Tillman, and Adam Woullard.

A special nod to the late, great Chris Mortensen, for teaching me how to be a reporter back when I didn't have a clue. And thank you to Murray Bauer, who was a dear and loyal friend to the end.

My literary agent, David Black, solidified his standing as the GOAT of his profession. His support and guidance through six books together has meant a ton. At Mariner, Peter Hubbard did exceptional work in cutting and sharpening the first draft and was always a sensible voice when needed. Mark Steven Long showed a seasoned scout's eye as a copy editor, and Evan Hulka and David Palmer were great stewards of the manuscript. Jessica Vestuto was of immense help on just about everything.

Finally, for the sixth straight time, my wife, Tracey, and son, Kyle, formed the world's best support system for an author, husband, and dad. No way this gets done without them. No. Way.

SOURCES

This book was built on the author's exclusive interviews, including those conducted with Aaron Rodgers, his parents, his longtime friends, some relatives, and scores of teammates, coaches, opponents, and teachers from childhood through his twenty-year career with the Green Bay Packers and New York Jets. Some quotations were pulled from news conferences and other general media availabilities. The following is a chapter-by-chapter summary of other sources that made important contributions to the narrative.

CHAPTER 1. AMERICAN HERO

Edward W. Rodgers, interview with war-crimes investigators, Judge Advocate General's Department—War Department. Conducted on June 27, 1945, by William N. Markham Jr., Agent, Security Intelligence Corps, Eighth Service Command.

Edward W. Rodgers, Draft Card, Austin, TX, Local Board No. 3 Court House, October 16, 1940.

Austin American-Statesman, "Rodgers-Odell Wedding in Hillsboro Takes Place Today," October 20, 1940.

Declassified First Combat Mission Summation, Headquarters 454th Bombardment Group, February 8, 1944.

Barrett Tillman, *Forgotten Fifteenth: The Daring Airmen Who Crippled Hitler's War Machine* (Washington, DC: Regnery Publishing, 2014).

Tom Faulkner with David L. Snead, *Flying with the Fifteenth Air Force* (Denton, TX: University of North Texas Press, 2018).

Consolidated B-24D Liberator, National Museum of the United States Air Force.

Joseph Chalker and John S. Barker Jr., *The Flight of the Liberators: The Story of the Four Hundred and Fifty-Fourth Bombardment Group* (Rochester, NY: The Du Bois Press, 1946).

Erik Goldstein and Stephen Calker, "Aircraft and Airmen of 454th Bombardment Group in Italy During World War II," 454thbombgroup.it.

United Press, "Sassy Lassy Lands on Wing and Prayer to St. Patrick," *Evansville* [IN] *Courier and Press*, March 19, 1944.

United Press, "Irish Luck, Prayer, Aid Anniston Sergeant in Miraculous Escape," *Anniston* [AL] *Star*, March 19, 1944.

Mission Summary, Headquarters 304th Bomb Wing, Operations for July 7, 1944.

Summary of Operations, Headquarters Mediterranean Allied Strategic Air Force Office of Assistant Chief of Staff, for July 7, 1944.

Casualty Questionnaires of Robert Christie, Walter Mauser, John Baran, and Karl Renz, and Witness Statements of Charles Stanley and Jack Graham, Headquarters 737th Bombardment Squadron, 454th Bombardment Group, July 9, 1944.

Associated Press, "110,000 Free at Moosburg," *New York Times*, May 1, 1945.

Jim Lankford, "The 14th Armored Division and the Liberation of Stalag VIIA," The Army Historical Foundation.

Bill Livingstone, "Stalag VIIA: Oral History," Moosburg.org.

"Pittsburgh, Twin Cities Vie for Title," *Sacramento Bee*, November 7, 1981.

"Cougars Gain Title with 61–7 Triumph," *Sacramento Bee*, November 9, 1981.

California Football History, "Twin Cities Cougars," funwhileitlasted.net.

"Darla Leigh Pittman Betrothed to Edward Wesley Rodgers Jr.," *Ukiah* [CA] *Daily Journal*, October 12, 1979.

CHAPTER 2. THE PRODIGY

"Free Throws Are His Forte," *Ukiah* [CA] *Daily Journal*, January 3, 1993.

Aaron Rodgers, *Tuesdays with Aaron*, with Jason Wilde, ESPN Milwaukee, 540 WAUK-AM, radio program, November 20, 2012, and December 10, 2013.

Big Cat and PFT Commenter, *Pardon My Take*, with Aaron Rodgers, Barstool Sports, podcast, August 8, 2022.

CHAPTER 3. PLEASANT VALLEY

Ben Sherman, "Pleasant Valley Frosh Defense Shuts Down Chico High 6–0," *Enterprise-Record*, October 23, 1998.

Brett Hughett, "Junior Vikes Pull It Out in Fourth Quarter," *Enterprise-Record*, October 23, 1999.

Jeff Chesemore, "Cheering on Aaron: Tales of Friendship Between an Area Director and a Field General," *Relationships* magazine, Spring 2013.

David Fleming, "Dear Me: Aaron Rodgers," *ESPN The Magazine*, June 27, 2013.

Bob McGinn, "Tough Enough," *Milwaukee Journal Sentinel*, September 21, 2008.

Luke Reid, "Vikings Signal Return from the Depths in Win," *Enterprise-Record*, September 2, 2000.

Gary Kelley, "Rodgers Passes PV Past LP," *Enterprise-Record*, September 30, 2000.
Michael Lowman, "Historic Roasting in Almond Bowl," *Enterprise-Record*, November 4, 2000.
Greg Ball, "Vikings Air Show Makes Most of Limited Flights," *Enterprise-Record*, November 4, 2000.
Michael Lowman, "Vikings Stung by Hornets in Sectional Semifinals," *Enterprise-Record*, November 18, 2000.
Tim Keown, "Above It All," *ESPN The Magazine*, July 26, 2010.
Pete Holmes, *You Made It Weird*, podcast, March 23, 2016.
Darren J. Gendron, "Vikings Get Revenge," *Enterprise-Record*, November 10, 2001.
Joseph Shufelberger, "Enterprise Ousts PV, Will Travel to Take On Top-Seeded Lassen," *Record Searchlight* (Redding, CA), November 17, 2001.
Darren J. Gendron, "Hornets End PV's Season in Semifinals," *Enterprise-Record*, November 17, 2001.

CHAPTER 4. RIGSBEE

Big Cat and PFT Commenter, *Pardon My Take*, with Aaron Rodgers, Barstool Sports, podcast, August 8, 2022.
Dave Davies, "Butte Downs West Hills," *Enterprise-Record*, September 15, 2002.
Lindsay Brauner, "From the Desert to the Moon: The Journey of a Rugby Player to Afghanistan and Back," *SBNation*, April 15, 2015.
Graham Bensinger, *In Depth with Graham Bensinger*, with Aaron Rodgers, YouTube, video, December 21, 2016.
Dave Davies, "Butte Roars Back to Win," *Enterprise-Record*, December 8, 2002.

CHAPTER 5. BERKELEY

Jay Heater, "Full House at Quarterback; Bears Draw a Crowd at Quarterback," *Contra Costa* [CA] *Times*, August 11, 2003.
Dave Newhouse, "Robertson Takes QB Reins, for Now at Least," *Alameda* [CA] *Times-Star*, August 19, 2003.
Ron Franklin and Mike Gottfried, ESPN broadcast of California vs. Kansas State, Black Coaches Association Classic, August 23, 2003.
Bruce Adams, "Bears Upbeat Despite Defeat," *San Francisco Chronicle*, August 24, 2003.
Lee Corso, Kirk Herbstreit, and Mike Tirico, ESPN broadcast of California vs. Utah, September 11, 2003.
Mike Golic and Mark Malone, ESPN broadcast of California vs. Virginia Tech, Insight Bowl, December 26, 2003.
Keith Jackson and Dan Fouts, ABC broadcast of California vs. UCLA, October 18, 2003.

Paul Coro, "Thrilling Insight Win Signals Cal's Arrival on National Scene," *Arizona Republic*, December 27, 2003.

Keith Jackson and Dan Fouts, ABC broadcast of California vs. USC, October 9, 2004.

Joe Rogan, *The Joe Rogan Experience*, with Aaron Rodgers, podcast, August 27, 2022.

Petros Papadakis and Barry Tompkins, FSN Comcast SportsNet broadcast of California vs. Stanford, November 20, 2004.

Jay Heater, "Bears Run by Cardinal in Big Game," *Contra Costa Times*, November 21, 2004.

Ray Ratto, "BCS Takes Cal on Holiday," *San Francisco Chronicle*, December 6, 2004.

Neil Hayes, "This Is No Way for Rodgers to End His Career at Cal," *Contra Costa Times*, December 31, 2004.

CHAPTER 6. THE PLUNGE

Matthew Barrows, "49ers Coveting Rodgers, Smith," *Sacramento Bee*, February 27, 2005.

Michael Marot, "Smith vs. Rodgers at NFL Combine," Associated Press, *Deseret [UT] Morning News*, February 26, 2005.

Kevin Lynch, "Smith's Throws Wow Pros; QB's Workout Is Applauded," *San Francisco Chronicle*, March 17, 2005.

Kevin Lynch, "Rodgers Matches Smith's Workout," *San Francisco Chronicle*, March 18, 2005.

Bob McGinn, "Quarterbacks Reasonable Doubt; Former Pupils of Rodgers' Tutor Have Struggled," *Milwaukee Journal Sentinel*, April 19, 2005.

Daniel Brown, "Rodgers Is Hoping His Style Fits 49ers," *San Jose Mercury News*, April 14, 2005.

Jerry McDonald, "Raiders' Gruden Looking at Quarterbacks Because That's His Job," *East Bay [CA] Times*, April 3, 2019.

Jerry McDonald, "Rodgers Performs for Gruden," *East Bay Times*, April 10, 2005.

Gil Brandt, "The Inside Story Behind Aaron Rodgers' Freefall at the 2005 NFL Draft," NFL.com, January 21, 2021.

Rob Demovsky, "Green-Room Nightmare: Inside Aaron Rodgers' Draft-Day Fall," ESPN.com, April 25, 2017.

Chris Berman, Chris Mortensen, Mel Kiper Jr., Torry Holt, and Suzy Kolber, ESPN broadcast of 2005 NFL Draft.

Peter King, "One Extreme to the Other," *Sports Illustrated*, May 2, 2005.

Jeff Pearlman, *Gunslinger: The Remarkable, Improbable, Iconic Life of Brett Favre* (New York: Mariner Books, 2016).

Aaron Rodgers interview with KPIX-TV, CBS, San Francisco, April 23, 2005.

Aaron Rodgers interview, *Dan Patrick Show*, ESPN Radio, radio program, April 26, 2005.

CHAPTER 7. BRETT

Jerry Glanville interview with Thom Abraham, WNSR Radio, Nashville, TN, March 2010.

Peter King, "Thank You, Thank You, Thank You: Peter King Says Farewell to SI's Monday Morning QB," SI.com, May 21, 2018.

Lori Nickel and Tom Silverstein, "Packers Notes; Rodgers Makes Good First Impression," *Milwaukee Journal Sentinel*, April 30, 2005.

Dylan Tomlinson, "Rodgers Resonates; Rookie QB Impresses at First Packers Minicamp," *Capital Times* (Madison, WI), April 30, 2005.

Sam Farmer, "Rodgers Knows a Thing or Two About Rejection," *Los Angeles Times*, August 5, 2005.

"Rodgers Shows Potential During First Training Camp Practice," Packers.com, July 30, 2005.

Pat McAfee and A. J. Hawk interview with Aaron Rodgers, *The Pat McAfee Show*, YouTube, video, November 24, 2020.

Aaron Nagler, "'I Get It Now': Brett Favre Says Aaron Rodgers Understands Famous 'Contract' Quote," Packersnews.com, June 19, 2018.

Michael Hunt, "Ted Thompson Takes Huge Risk with New Hire," *Milwaukee Journal Sentinel*, January 13, 2006.

Tim Kawakami, "Aaron Rodgers, Mike McCarthy and That 2005 Decision by the 49ers, Still Relevant 14 Years Later," *The Athletic*, April 5, 2019.

Bob McGinn, "Packers Pick McCarthy: Open Mike," *Milwaukee Journal Sentinel*, January 12, 2006.

Mark Chmura interview, *Miller Lite Football Show*, Fox Sports Radio, WTLX-FM, 100.5, radio program, Madison, WI.

Chris Roth and Mark Tauscher interview with Aaron Rodgers, WBAY-TV, January 8, 2009.

Jim Corbett, "Rodgers Plays the Waiting Game," *USA Today*, August 11, 2006.

Jason Wilde, "Defending Woodson; The Cornerback Attributes Monday's Failures to a Long Week of Practice," *Wisconsin State Journal*, August 31, 2006.

Greg Gumbel and Dan Dierdorf, CBS broadcast of New England Patriots vs. Green Bay Packers, November 19, 2006.

Ernie Johnson interview with Aaron Rodgers, Josh Allen, Tom Brady, and Patrick Mahomes, for *The Match*, TNT, June 1, 2022.

Lori Nickel, "Rodgers Does His Best to Be Ready," *Milwaukee Journal Sentinel*, January 5, 2007.

Pete Dougherty, "Confident in Rodgers," *Green Bay Press-Gazette*, July 23, 2007.

Bryant Gumbel and Cris Collinsworth, NFL Network broadcast of Green Bay Packers vs. Dallas Cowboys, November 29, 2007.

CHAPTER 8. A STAR IS BORN

Kevin Seifert, "The Packers, Brett Favre and the Limitations of Loyalty," ESPN.com, July 17, 2015.

Chris Jenkins, "GM, Coach: Packers Don't Plan to Release Favre," Associated Press, July 12, 2008.

Carrie Antlfinger, "Packer Fans Rally, Want Favre as QB," Associated Press, July 14, 2008.

Tony Walter, "Fans Ignore Storm to Welcome Favre," *Green Bay Press-Gazette*, August 3, 2008.

John Kuhn interview with Nick Collins, *Nine 2 Noon*, 97.3 The Game, radio program, Milwaukee, January 27, 2023.

Tyler Dunne interview with Brett Favre, *Go Long*, podcast, September 8, 2023.

Chris Ballard, "Welcome to the Club," *Sports Illustrated*, July 7, 2008.

Mike Tirico, Ron Jaworski, Tony Kornheiser, and Michele Tafoya, ESPN broadcast of Minnesota Vikings vs. Green Bay Packers, September 8, 2008.

Mike Vandermause, "Rodgers Learns Soldiers' Mindset," *Green Bay Press-Gazette*, May 25, 2008.

Cyd Zeigler, "Favre Won't Speak to Aaron Rodgers," Outsports.com, January 29, 2009.

Joe Buck, Troy Aikman, and Pam Oliver, Fox broadcast of Green Bay Packers vs. Atlanta Falcons divisional playoff game, January 15, 2011.

Joe Buck, Troy Aikman, and Pam Oliver, Fox broadcast of Green Bay Packers vs. Chicago Bears conference championship game, January 23, 2011.

Greg Jennings, "Ask Me Anything," Reddit, February 15, 2023.

Karen Crouse, "Made in Chico," *New York Times*, January 31, 2011.

Joe Buck, Troy Aikman, and Pam Oliver, Fox broadcast of Green Bay Packers vs. Pittsburgh Steelers, Super Bowl XLV, February 6, 2011.

Rob Reischel, *Aaron Rodgers: Leader of the Pack* (Chicago: Triumph Books, 2011).

Kyle Nagel, "Hawk Looking Forward Following 'Unique Year,'" *Dayton* [OH] *Daily News*, May 20, 2011.

Greg Garber, "Aaron Rodgers Makes Real Difference," ESPN.com, January 1, 2014.

CHAPTER 9. PAIN

Joe Buck, Troy Aikman, and Pam Oliver, Fox broadcast of New York Giants vs. Green Bay Packers divisional playoff game, January 15, 2012.

Aaron Rodgers, *Tuesdays with Aaron*, with Jason Wilde, ESPN Milwaukee, 540 WAUK-AM, radio program, December 31, 2013, and September 23, 2014.

Aaron Rodgers and David Gruber, with Annie Bartosz, "Gold in September" initiative, ItsAaron.com, March 12, 2015.

Bob McGinn, "Drive to Survive: Clutch Plays Lift Green Bay Into Playoffs," *Milwaukee Journal Sentinel*, December 30, 2013.

Dan Wiederer, "Burn Notice," *Star Tribune* (Minneapolis, MN), July 25, 2013.

Scott Venci, "Donald Driver on Rodgers, Jennings: 'I Love Them Both,'" *Green Bay Press-Gazette*, August 16, 2013.

Joe Buck, Troy Aikman, and Pam Oliver, Fox broadcast of Green Bay Packers vs. Seattle Seahawks conference championship game, January 18, 2015.

CHAPTER 10. THE ISLAND

Michele Soulli, genealogist, Aaron Rodgers family tree.

Ronald Marcus, "Elizabeth Clawson . . . Thou Deseruest To Dye," Stamford Historical Society, Inc., 1976.

Judith Wellman, "We Took to Ourselves Liberty," the Organization of American Historians and the National Park Service, January 2022.

Aaron Rodgers, *Tuesdays with Aaron*, with Jason Wilde, ESPN Milwaukee, 540 WAUK-AM, radio program, February 5, 2015.

Andy Cohen interview with Olivia Munn, *Andy Cohen Live*, SiriusXM, radio program, May 23, 2018.

Brent Holland Studios, Facebook post, May 25, 2015.

Grover Films, "Francis and Randi's Thomas Fogarty Winery Wedding," groverfilms.com, September 21, 2015.

Troy Kirby interview with Luke Rodgers, *The Tao of Sports*, podcast, April 17, 2015.

Tom Pelissero, "How Aaron Rodgers Defined Pack's Year with 'R-E-L-A-X,'" *USA Today*, January 7, 2015.

Elise Menaker interview with Luke Rodgers, WTMJ-TV, Milwaukee, March 2, 2017.

Joelle "JoJo" Fletcher and Jordan Rodgers, *The Bachelorette*, season 12, ABC-TV, May 23–August 1, 2016.

Nick Wilson, "Aaron Rodgers Named Chico Sportsperson of the Year," *Enterprise-Record*, May 11, 2011.

Tyler Dunne, "Can Aaron Rodgers Be the Type of Leader the Packers Need?" *Bleacher Report*, November 18, 2016.

Karen Crouse, "Aaron Rodgers Connects with His Hometown, but the Family Huddle Is Broken," *New York Times*, January 15, 2017.

Jim Nantz, Phil Simms, and Tracy Wolfson, CBS/NFL Network broadcast of Green Bay Packers vs. Detroit Lions, December 3, 2015.

Al Michaels, Cris Collinsworth, and Michele Tafoya, NBC broadcast of Green Bay Packers vs. Arizona Cardinals divisional playoff game, January 16, 2016.

Ian O'Connor, "Aaron Rodgers Made Sure GOAT Isn't Out of Reach," ESPN.com, January 15, 2017.

CHAPTER 11. NO LOVE LOST

Ian O'Connor, "A Rodgers-Belichick 'Limitless' Combo? Imagining Ultimate 'What If,'" ESPN.com, October 31, 2018.

Kirk Minihane and Gerry Callahan interview with Tom Brady, *Kirk & Callahan*, WEEI, radio program, Boston, October 30, 2018.
Tom Brady, Larry Fitzgerald, and Jim Gray, *Let's Go!* SiriusXM, podcast, January 16, 2024.
Tyler Dunne, "What Happened in Green Bay," *Bleacher Report*, April 4, 2019.
Marcedes Lewis interview, *Mostly Football*, Yahoo! Sports, January 3, 2019.
Kalyn Kahler, "How It All Went Wrong in Packerland," *Sports Illustrated*, November 29, 2018.
Greg Jennings with Skip Bayless, Shannon Sharpe, and Joy Taylor, *Undisputed*, Fox Sports, July 12, 2017.
Rob Demovsky, "Inside Mike McCarthy's Split with Packers and What's Next for Him," ESPN.com, April 3, 2019.
Joe Buck, Troy Aikman, and Erin Andrews, Fox broadcast of Tampa Bay Buccaneers vs. Green Bay Packers conference championship game, January 24, 2021.
Kyle Brandt interview with Aaron Rodgers, *10 Questions with Kyle Brandt*, The Ringer Podcast Network, July 28, 2020.
Rich Eisen interview with Brett Favre, *The Rich Eisen Show*, NBC Sports Network and SiriusXM, radio program, April 29, 2020.

CHAPTER 12. DIVORCE

Ian O'Connor, "The Bucs Built It, Tom Brady Came. Now What? Inside the GOAT's Ultimate Gamble," ESPN.com, April 5, 2020.
Adam Schefter, "Aaron Rodgers Doesn't Want to Return to Green Bay Packers, Sources Say," ESPN.com, April 29, 2021.
Charles Robinson, "If Packers Remain Dug In Against Trading Aaron Rodgers, a Holdout or Retirement Is Possible," Yahoo! Sports, May 1, 2021.
Bob McGinn, "The Packers' Rift with Aaron Rodgers Is Real, but the Draft Class Might Be Legit Too," *The Athletic*, May 5, 2021.
Pat McAfee and A.J. Hawk interviews with Aaron Rodgers, *The Pat McAfee Show*, YouTube, videos, November 5, 2021, and November 9, 2021.
Mina Kimes, "The Search for Aaron Rodgers," *ESPN The Magazine*, August 30, 2017.
Adam Breneman interview with DeShone Kizer, *The Breneman Show*, podcast, November 29, 2022.
Eddie Bravo interview with Aaron Rodgers, *Look Into It*, podcast, February 23, 2024.
Jeg Coughlin III and Morgan Hoffmann interview with Aaron Rodgers, *I Can Fly*, podcast, April 9, 2024.
Aubrey Marcus interview with Aaron Rodgers, *Aubrey Marcus Podcast*, YouTube, video, August 3, 2022.
Mike Tirico, Cris Collinsworth, and Melissa Stark, NBC broadcast of Detroit Lions vs. Green Bay Packers, January 8, 2023.

SOURCES

CHAPTER 13. HEARTBREAK

Joe Buck, Troy Aikman, and Lisa Salters, ESPN broadcast of Buffalo Bills vs. New York Jets, September 11, 2023.

Dan Patrick interview with Brian Baumgartner, *The Dan Patrick Show*, Peacock and Fox Sports Radio, radio program, September 13, 2023.

Rich Cimini, "Reaction from Jets, Bills to Play That Ended Aaron Rodgers' Season," ESPN.com, September 12, 2023.

Matt Schneidman, "Aaron Rodgers, the Packers and the Long Succession: 'Just Tell the Truth, You Wanted to Move On,'" *The Athletic*, May 31, 2023.

Chris Long interview with Joe Douglas, *Green Light*, podcast, September 1, 2023.

Brian Costello, "The Inside Story Behind the Twists and Turns That Brought Aaron Rodgers to the Jets," *New York Post*, May 8, 2023.

Albert Breer, "Late-Night Texts, Discreet Meetings and the Brett Favre Precedent: Inside the Aaron Rodgers Trade Negotiation," *Sports Illustrated*, May 8, 2023.

Franchise access: *Hard Knocks: Training Camp with the New York Jets*, HBO, August 8–September 5, 2023.

Ian O'Connor, "Severed Tendon, Broken Heart," Gannett Newspapers, September 13, 1999.

Jeg Coughlin III and Morgan Hoffmann interview with Aaron Rodgers, *I Can Fly* podcast, April 9, 2024.

Alan Hahn and Bart Scott interview with Garrett Wilson, *Bart & Hahn Show*, ESPN New York Radio, September 12, 2023.

Vince Ferragamo and Jackie Slater interview with Dr. Neal ElAttrache, *OnPoint Live*, YouTube, video, September 17, 2023.

Pat McAfee and A. J. Hawk interview with Aaron Rodgers, *The Pat McAfee Show*, ESPN, September 15, 2023.

CHAPTER 14. THE COMEBACK

Michael Kay and Don La Greca interview with Joe Namath, *The Michael Kay Show*, ESPN New York Radio 98.7 FM, radio program, September 25, 2023.

Pat McAfee and A. J. Hawk interviews with Aaron Rodgers, *The Pat McAfee Show*, ESPN, September 26, 2023, January 2, 2024, and January 9, 2024.

Mike Tirico, Cris Collinsworth, and Melissa Stark, NBC broadcast of Kansas City Chiefs vs. New York Jets, October 1, 2023.

Aaron Rodgers surgery detail: "Arthrex Innovation Helping Professional Football Players," newsroom.arthrex.com, October 10, 2023.

Dah-Ching Ding, Woei-Cherng Shyu, and Shinn-Zong Lin, "Mesenchymal Stem Cells," National Library of Medicine, pubmed.ncbi.nlm.nih.gov.

Joe Rogan interview with Brigham Buhler, *The Joe Rogan Experience*, podcast, December 27, 2023.

Aaron Alexander workout: *The Ultimate Pool Circuit*, with Laird Hamilton and Aaron Rodgers, YouTube, video, September 4, 2023.

SOURCES

Zack Rosenblatt, Dianna Russini, and Jeff Howe, "Zach Wilson Reluctant to Step Back into Starting Role as Jets Mull QB Change: Sources," *The Athletic*, December 4, 2023.

Aubrey Marcus interview with Aaron Rodgers, *Aubrey Marcus Podcast*, YouTube, video, August 3, 2022.

Mina Kimes, "The Search for Aaron Rodgers," *ESPN The Magazine*, August 30, 2017.

Danica Patrick interview with Aaron Rodgers, *Pretty Intense Podcast*, YouTube, video, December 26, 2019.

Spencer Nelson, "The Aaron Rodgers–Tom Brady Double Standard Is Once Again on Full Display," zonecoverage.com, September 26, 2022.

Pamela Brown and Jake Tapper, "RFK Jr.'s VP Prospect Aaron Rodgers Has Shared False Sandy Hook Conspiracy Theories in Private Conversations," CNN.com, March 13, 2024.

Zack Rosenblatt and Dianna Russini, "Aaron Rodgers, Robert Saleh and How the Jets' Season Fell Apart: 'Something Has to Change,'" *The Athletic*, January 31, 2024.

INDEX

NOTE: The abbreviation AR indicates references to Aaron Rodgers.

"14 H Corner" play, 60
"44 Drop Pass" play, 71
"86 Y Shake" play, 70
"98 Strike" play, 140

Abraham, John, 165
Adams, Andrew, 247
Adams, Davante
  2016 season, 226
  2018 season, 228, 237
  2020 season, 244, 246–247
  2021 season, 272
  traded to Raiders, 273
Aikman, Troy, 172, 187–188
Akers, Cam, 307
Alexander, Aaron, 307–310
Alexander, Jaire, 246
Alexander, Lorenzo, 99
The Align Method (Alexander), 307
Allen, Bruce, 108–109, 112–113
Allen, Jared, 179
Allen, Josh, 278
Allen, Larry, 55
Almond Bowl XXX, 46
Aloi, Joseph, 156
Archibald, Garth, 48–49
Arians, Bruce, 241, 245

Arizona Cardinals, 115, 164, 223–225, 238
Arrington, J. J., 76, 84, 88, 94
Arth, Tom, 138
Arthrex, 307
Associated Press polls, 96, 188
Athletes First, 153
Athletes in Action, 73
The Athletic, 280, 311, 325
Atlanta Falcons, 163, 165, 226
Atogwe, Oshiomogho, 93

The Bachelorette (TV show), 212–213
Bakhtiari, David
  on AR–McCarthy relations, 233
  on AR's kindness, 268
  on AR's talent, 224, 254, 297
  on AR's west coast life, 1
  contract extensions, 252
  cut blocks, 297
Baldwin, Doug, 198–199
Ball, Greg, 46
Ball, Russ, 238
Baltimore Ravens, 99, 101, 131–132
Banta-Cain, Tully, 142
Baran, John, 10
Barnett, Nick, 134

INDEX

Barr, Anthony, 227
Barrett, Jim, 44
Barry, Rick, 66
Barstool Sports relief fund, 259
Barton, Greg, 54
Bartosz, Annie, 191
Bartosz, Jack, 191
Baumgartner, Brian, 276, 300
Bears. *See* Chicago Bears
Becton, Mekhi, 278, 290, 296
Beemer, Frank, 85
Belichick, Bill, 142, 229–230, 232, 244
Bell, Rob, 262, 315
Benigno, Joe, 293
Benson, Cedric, 113, 114
Berman, Chris, 114–115
Berman, Scott, 281–282
Bernal, Bobby, 63, 70
Berry, Ed, 269–270, 324
Berwanger, Jay, 116
Bethea, James, 84
Bevell, Darrell, 134
Bills. *See* Buffalo Bills
Bischofberger, Brett, 67
Blackburn, Chase, 187
Black Coaches Association Classic, 75
Blair, Arba, 204
Blakeman, Clete, 225
Blay-Miezah, Francis, 92, 208–209
Bloomberg, Michael, 286
Bodden, Leigh, 162
Bodiford, Shaun, 61
Boerigter, Marc, 140
Boley, Michael, 187
Boller, Kyle, 64–65, 74, 98–100
Bootman, Scott, 58
Bostick, Brandon, 196–197, 199
Botts, Bryan, 58–59, 61, 70
Bowl Championship Series (BCS), 95–97
Boyle, Tim, 268, 311
Bradshaw, Ahmad, 186
Bradshaw, Terry, 173
Brady, Tom, 229–232, 240–241, 244–248, 252
Brandt, Andrew, 119–120, 122, 126–127, 148, 151

Brandt, Gil, 110–113
Brate, Cameron, 244
Bravo, Eddie, 265
Breneman, Adam, 264
Brodie, John, 19
Broncos (Denver), 197
Brown, Antonio, 252
Brown, Duane, 296–298
Brown, Larry, 66
Brown, Mack, 95–97
Brown, Pamela, 324
Brown, Ronnie, 113, 114
Browns. *See* Cleveland Browns
Bruschi, Tedy, 142
Bryant, Dez, 193
Bryant, Kobe, 302
Buccaneers. *See* Tampa Bay Buccaneers
Buck, Joe, 173, 198–199
Buffalo Bills, 227, 276–278, 296–297, 313
Buhler, Brigham, 309
Burnett, Morgan, 197
Bush, Reggie, 85
Bushard, Tim, 51, 175
Butler, LeRoy, 158
Butte College (Chico, California), 53–71
  AR playing football at, 52–53, 56–62, 66–71
  AR's academics and social life, 66, 68–69
  AR's knee injury, 53
  leaving for UC Berkeley, 62–66
  Northern California title game, 66–71
  recruitment of AR, 53–56
Byrd, Dennis, 321

California State University, Chico (California), 17, 27–28
Cameron, Andrew, 74, 78, 87–88, 90–91
Campbell, Calais, 224
Capretta, Ryan, 310
Cardinals. *See* Arizona Cardinals
Carolina Panthers, 161
Carr, David, 108
Carroll, Pete, 88, 89–90
Carter, Keith, 297
Cashman, Brian, 320

Casselman, Austin, 210
Catrett, Taylor, 54
Caviglia, Tony, 62
Celebrity Jeopardy! (TV show), 200, 253
Champion Christian school (Chico, California), 30–31
Check, Joshua, 69
Chicago Bears, 114, 167, 191–192, 227, 272
Chico Enterprise-Record (California), 44, 46, 67
Chico High School (California), 35–36, 45–46
Chmura, Mark, 139–140
Christian and Missionary Alliance, 314
Christie, Rob, 58, 67
Cignetti, Frank, 239
Cimini, Rich, 278
Clark, Ryan, 170
Clason, Elizabeth (ancestor), 203
Clements, Mike, 175, 235
Clements, Tom, 138, 142
Cleveland Browns, 108, 111–112, 114
Clinton-Dix, Ha Ha, 197
Cobb, Randall
  2013 season, 192
  2014 season, 198
  2022 season, 274–275
  on AR's injury, 301
  on AR's kindness, 268–269
  on AR's talent, 255
  injury, 239
Cohen, Andy, 207
Coleman, Charles, 46–47, 57–58
Colledge, Daryn, 171
Collins, Doug, 153
Collins, Kerry, 118
Collins, Nick, 150, 170
Collinsworth, Cris, 145–146, 224
Colwes, Curtis, 39
Cominsky, John, 274
conspiracy theories, 263–265, 319–320
Cook, Bus, 126, 149
Cook, Dalvin, 279, 290
Cook, Jared, 226
Coppage, Randi, 209

Corrente, Tony, 198
Corso, Lee, 78–79
Cortez, George, 74, 86–87, 91
Costello, Brian, 284
Coughlin, Tom, 184
Cousineau, Kyle, 161, 217–218, 282
Cousins, Kirk, 256
COVID-19 pandemic
  AR's vaccination status and controversy over, 252, 255–260, 264–265, 292, 315, 323
  lockdowns resulting from, 323
  restrictions during 2020 season, 240–241
  Ed Rodgers on vaccinations, 315
Cowboys (Dallas), 145–147
Crabtree, Tom, 218
Creative Artists Agency, 269
Critchfield, Russ, 66
Crosby, Mason, 186, 198, 224, 226, 237, 247
Cross, Garrett, 61, 63, 68, 73
Crouse, Karen, 217
Cumbie, Sonny, 96

Dallas Cowboys, 145–147
Dansby, Karlos, 164
Davies, Dave, 67
Davis, Al, 118
Demovsky, Rob, 144, 150, 229
Denver Broncos, 197
Detroit Lions
  2008 season, 158, 162
  2011 season, 191
  2015 season, 222–223
  2018 season, 239
  2022 season, 271, 273–275
Dierdorf, Dan, 142–143
Dilfer, Trent, 101, 108, 153
Dillon, AJ, 274
Djokovic, Novak, 292
Dorsey, John, 112
Dougherty, Pete, 145
Dougherty, Scott, 26
Douglas, Joe, 2, 282–283, 285, 318
Drews, Micala, 40, 47–48, 51, 157

INDEX

Driver, Donald
  2006 season, 142
  2008 season, 162
  2011 season, 187
  AR hitting with football, 127
  criticism of AR, 194–195
  Super Bowl XLV, 171
  treatment of AR, 135
Dunn, David, 108, 153, 282, 284
Dunn, Grover, 11, 13–14
Dunne, Tyler, 217, 232

Echauri, Joaquin, 57, 58, 69
Echemandu, Adimchinobe, 83
Eckley, Gary, 17
Edwards, Braylon, 113, 114
Edwards, Mike, 247
Eisen, Rich, 249
ElAttrache, Neal, 301–303, 307
Elhai, Hymie, 2, 282
Epstein, Jeffrey, 319–320, 323
Erro, Clay, 50–51
Erro, Ryan, 51
Esiason, Boomer, 277, 298
ESPN (TV network)
  Gruden's QB Camp, 109
  NFL Draft of 2005, 116
ESPN (radio network), *Tuesdays with Aaron* on 540 WAUK-AM, 189–192, 317–320, 322–323
ESPN The Magazine, 262–263, 314
Excel Sports Management, 205

Falcons. *See* Atlanta Falcons
Fauci, Anthony, 264–265, 318
Faulkner, Tom, 8–9
Favre, Brett, 123–148
  2005 season, 131–135
  2006 season, 137, 139–140, 142–143
  2007 season, 143–147
  2008 season, attempt to return for, 149–153
  AR and, 122, 126–130, 133–135, 141, 144, 152, 163–164, 195
  on AR's career, 249–250
  AR wearing No. 4 at Butte College, 60
  family life, 128
  Gunslinger (Pearlman), 129, 189
  injuries, 142–143, 145, 147, 162
  marketing deal from Green Bay Packers, 149–150
  Minnesota Vikings, playing for, 163
  New York Jets, playing for, 286
  NFL awards show, copresenting with AR, 195
  popularity of, 124, 125, 132, 139–140, 143, 145, 150–153
  retirements, 118, 132, 139, 148, 149, 164, 170
  substance abuse and treatment, 124
  Super Bowl wins, 124
  talent and dedication of, 124–125, 131
  Tampa Bay Buccaneers, playing for, 153, 162
  Wonderlic test score, 130
Ferguson, Robert, 141
Fernandez, Brianna, 278
Fewell, Perry, 182–188
Finkelstein, Eric, 117
Finley, Jermichael, 187, 194–195, 270–271
Fitzgerald, Larry, 225
Flacco, Joe, 318
Fleischer, Ari, 152
Fletcher, JoJo, 212, 217
"Flood Tip" play, 186
Floyd, Leonard, 296–298
Foo Fighters, 218
Foss, Mike, 320, 323
Foster, Bob, 63–64
Fournette, Leonard, 245, 252
Fouts, Dan, 82
Fox, Keyaron, 173
Franklin, Ron, 75–76
Fredrickson, Tyler, 73, 75, 81–82, 84–85
Frerotte, Gus, 108
Fritch, Jeff, 85, 91–92

Gardner, Sauce, 278, 291
Garnett, Kevin, 303
Garoppolo, Jimmy, 232, 244
Garrett, Jason, 226

INDEX

Garritano, Frank, 277
Gay, William, 170
Gee, John, 123, 125–126, 155
Gelfand, Eric, 287
Getsy, Luke, 242
Giannotti, Gregg, 277
Giants. *See* New York Giants
Gilliam, Garry, 196
Gipson, Xavier, 301, 313
Gladstone, Steve, 86
Glanville, Jerry, 124
Glasspiegel, Ryan, 161
Glazer, Jay, 310
Goff, Jared, 274
Golden Bears. *See* University of California, Berkeley
Gold in September (G9) foundation, 191
Goodell, Roger, 151
Gottfried, Mike, 76
Graham, Jack L., 12
Grant, Deon, 188
Grant, Ryan, 157, 185, 187, 271
Grap, Peter, 35
Gray, Kenzie, 18
Green Bay Packers. *See also* Favre, Brett; NFC Championship games
  2004 season, 128
  2005 season, 131–135
  2006 season, 137, 139–143
  2007 season, 143–146, 149
  2008 season, 149–159, 161–164
  2009 season, 165–166
  2010 season, 164–165
  2011 season, 163–166, 183–188, 191–192
  2012 season, 192–193
  2013 season, 192–193
  2014 season, 193, 196–200, 235
  2015 season, 222–225
  2016 season, 225–226
  2017 season, 233
  2018 season, 227–228, 233, 236–239
  2020 season, 240–244, 267
  2021 season, 253–255, 267, 272
  2022 season, 271–272, 273–275
  2023 season, 318–319
  annual Friday Night scrimmage, 140–141
  AR at training camp for, 125, 127–130
  AR–McCarthy relations, 137–141
  AR's contract and contract extensions with, 124, 125, 159, 192, 227, 254–255, 273
  AR's interviews and public relations, 155, 160–161, 163–164, 251–252, 262–263
  AR's involvement in talent acquisitions, 252–253
  AR's last game with, 274–275
  AR's workouts and physical training for, 179–181
  AR traded to New York Jets, 2, 279–284
  community outreach, 123–126
  Family Night 2008, 149–153
  fans' reception of AR as quarterback, 155–162
  Favre, marketing deal, 149–150
  Favre traded to Tampa Bay Buccaneers, 153
  Lambeau Field, 155–157
  McCarthy fired, 228–239
  NFL Draft of 2005, 112, 118–122, 202
  NFL Draft of 2020, 242–244
  stockholder ownership of, 123
  Super Bowl XXXI, 124
  Super Bowl XLV, 166–176, 183–184
  Super Bowl XLV, post-game strategy, 183–184
  talent acquisitions, AR's involvement in, 252–253
  Tedford curse and, 104, 120
Green Bay Press Gazette, 144, 145, 150, 229, 252, 284
Grohl, Dave, 218
Gronkowski, Rob, 252
Gruber, David, 190–191
Gruden, Jon, 108–110, 112
Gruden's QB Camp (ESPN), 109
Guillon, Marc, 33–34
Gulbrandsen, Ryan, 38
Gumbel, Bryant, 146–147
Gumbel, Greg, 142

Gunslinger (Pearlman), 129, 189
Gutekunst, Brian, 231, 238, 241, 252–254, 272–273, 279–280
Gutierrez, Ryan, 90

Hackett, Nathaniel
  2023 season, 297, 318
  AR traded to New York Jets, 2
  coaching AR, 242
  New York Jets, offensive coordinator for, 281, 288
  recruiting AR to New York Jets, 282
Hackett, Paul, 108–109
Hail Mary touchdown passes, 222–225
Hall, Brandon, 84
Hall, Breece, 278
Hall, DeAngelo, 81
Hall, Korey, 157–158
Hanks, Merton, 121
Hard Knocks (TV show), 291–292
Hardman, Mecole, 325
Harlan, Bob, 118–119, 150, 163, 233
Harper, Shaun, 79
Harris, Al, 134
Hauschka, Stephen, 196
Hawk, A. J., 148, 169–170, 196, 319
Hawk, Ryan, 173, 176
Hawkins, Taylor, 218
Hayes, Neil, 97
Heath, Jeff, 225
Hejny, Jesse, 56
Helmick, Casey, 38, 46, 175
Henderson, Steve, 48
Herbstreit, Kirk, 78–79
Hetherington, Mark, 62
Hock, Matt, 40
Hodgson, Braylon, 321–322
Hodgson, Ryan, 321–322
Holder, Curtis, 18, 31–32
Holiday Bowl (2004), 95–96
Holmgren, Mike, 132
Holmoe, Tom, 74, 75
Hostler, Jim, 104–105, 136
Huyck, Michael, 35, 37
Hyde, Micah, 297

Insight Bowl (2003), 81, 83–85
Irving, Kyrie, 259
"It's Aaron" YouTube videos, 191

Jackson, David, 35
Jackson, Keith, 82, 88, 89, 95
Jackson, Sterling, 43–45, 49–50, 80
Jagodzinski, Jeff, 138, 140–141
James, LeBron, 311
Janis, Jeff, 223
Jennings, Greg
  2006 season, 142
  2007 season, 146
  2008 season, 157, 164
  2011 season, 186–187
  criticism of AR, 194–195
  on McCarthy's coaching, 238
  on playing of AR, 163
  Super Bowl XLV, 170, 172
  on unity of team, 168
Jeopardy! (TV show), 253
Jeter, Andrew, 178, 205
Jeter, Derek, 322
Johnson, Christopher, 2, 282–283
Johnson, Woody, 2–3, 282–285, 287, 299
Jones, Aaron, 245
Jones, DaQuan, 298
Jones, James, 165, 171–172, 267
Jordan, Jeff, 63, 68
Joseph, Kerby, 274
Judge, Aaron, 56
Judge, Wayne, 56

Kaempf, Joe, 26, 175
Kaempf, Joey, 26–27, 139, 175, 196, 199
Kaepernick, Colin, 192
Kahler, Kalyn, 235
Karges, Murphy, 177
Kawakami, Tim, 136
Kearse, Jermaine, 199
Kebric, Bruce, 117–118
Kelce, Travis, 318
Kellar, Bill, 154
Kelley, Bernie, 19–20
Kelly, Mark, 200
Kennedy, John F., Jr., 265

INDEX

Kennedy, John F., Sr., 263–264
Kennedy, Robert F., Jr., 5–6, 264, 318, 323
Kid Rock (singer), 175
Kiesau, Eric, 87
Kiley, Irvin, 163–164
Kiley, Kevin, 163–164
Kimes, Mina, 262
Kimmel, Jimmy, 319, 322–323
King, Kevin, 245, 248
King, Martin Luther, Jr., 257–258
King, Peter, 114
Kiper, Mel, Jr., 113, 115
Kizer, DeShone, 264
Koal, H., 202
Kolber, Suzy, 115–116
Kramer, Jerry, 261
Kuhn, John, 165–166, 169, 171–172, 176, 186
Kumerow, Jake, 252

Lacy, Eddie, 198
LaFleur, Matt, 241–242, 245–249, 253–254, 279
Lambeau Field, Green Bay, 155–157
Lambeau Leap, 158, 162, 186
Lanflisi, Kevin, 188
Larrivee, Wayne, 121–122, 170, 233
Late Show with David Letterman (TV show), 176
Lawler, Bette, 21–22
Lawrence, Derek, 49, 51, 56
Lazard, Allen
  2020 season, 246
  2021 season, 272
  2022 season, 274
  2023 season, 297
  on AR in New York, 289
  on AR's injury, 304
  AR's leadership and, 267–268
  COVID-19 pandemic and, 260
Leach, Vonta, 131
Lee, Donald, 143, 157
Lee, Scott, 67, 68–69
Leinart, Matt, 85, 90, 94
Leonard, Linda (AR's aunt), 24
Leonard, Nelson (AR's uncle), 24

Levy, Steve, 263
Lewis, Kyle, 33
Lewis, Marcedes, 235
Licht, Jason, 252
Lieberfarb, Ira, 292–293, 300
Linsley, Corey, 224
Lions. *See* Detroit Lions
Lions Northern California All-Star football game (2002), 53
Lions Northern California All-Star game, 53
Lombardi, Vince, 123, 124, 156
Longwell, Ryan, 130
Los Angeles Rams, 244
Love, Jordan, 242–244, 251, 275, 319
Lucas, Chad, 134
Lyman, Chase, 84, 89
Lynch, John, 254
Lynch, Kevin, 106
Lynch, Marshawn, 88, 92–94, 109, 141, 193, 197
Lyons, Marty, 290–291

Madison, Anthony, 172
Mahomes, Patrick, 230, 280, 295, 306, 325
the Make (band), 177
Makonnen, Jonathan, 89
Manderino, Chris, 87, 90, 95
Mandt, Maura, 235
Manning, Archie, 156, 197
Manning, Eli, 184–188, 322
Manning, Peyton, 188, 197
Manningham, Mario, 187
Marathe, Paraag, 107
Marchand, Andrew, 317–318
Marcus, Aubrey, 301, 307, 313
Marino, Dan, 115
Martin, Ingle, 143, 145
Martin, Ruvell, 142
Martin, Tee, 87
Matthews, Chris, 197
Mauser, Walter C., 11
Mayer, Mary, 27
McAfee, Pat, 304–305, 312, 317–320, 323. *See also The Pat McAfee Show*

INDEX

McArthur, Geoff
  on AR's leadership skills, 91
  on physical appearance of AR, 74
  playing for UC Berkeley, 76, 79, 82–84, 88–89
  on playing of AR, 94
McCarthy, Mike
  2011 season, 186–188
  2012 season, 192
  2014 season, 197–199, 235
  2015 season, 224–225
  2016 season, 226
  2018 season, 236–239
  on AR playing at the annual Friday Night scrimmage, 141
  AR's family relations and, 316
  on AR's foot injury, 143
  on AR's leadership skills, 195
  AR's workout clinics and interviews for NFL Draft, 104–105
  childhood, 135–136
  coaching AR, 137–141
  Favre's attempt to return for 2008 season, 153
  fired, 238–239
  firing of, 228–239
  getting Favre to return for 2006 season, 137
  NFL Draft of 2005 and, 111, 136–137
  Super Bowl XLV and, 168–169, 171
McCleskey, Donnie, 96
McCloughan, Scot, 104–105, 111
McDaniels, Josh, 229
McDonald, Jerry, 109–110
McDonough, Terry, 225
McGinn, Bob, 104, 192, 253–254
McNabb, Wilma, 117
Mehan, Dan, 35
Melton, Tom, 37
MetLife Stadium, 294, 303
Miami Dolphins, 108, 114, 193
The Michael Irvin Show (TV show), 163–164
The Michael Kay Show (radio show), 304–305
Michaels, Al, 224
Michaels, Bill, 121, 128, 139
Michalczik, Jim, 64
Midwest Athletes Against Childhood Cancer (MACC), 190–191
Miller, Heath, 173
Miller, Scott, 245
Milwaukee Journal Sentinel, 104, 192
Minneapolis Star Tribune, 194
Minnesota Vikings, 153, 157–158, 163, 170, 273
Moe, Doug, 66
Morse, Jesse, 309–310
Morstead, Thomas, 265, 301–302
Moss, Randy, 147
Mostert, Raheem, 242
Munn, Olivia, 192, 204–208, 220
Murphy, Chris, 84
Murphy, Mark
  on AR, 261
  on AR's input on choosing head coach, 240
  on AR's playing, 225
  Favre's retirement and, 149
  firing Mike McCarthy, 238
  hiring Matt LaFleur as head coach, 241
Murphy, Terrence, 134–135
Mygrant, Michael, 178

Nall, Craig, 129, 133
Namath, Joe, 304–305
Nantz, Jim, 223
Neighborhood Church (Chico, California), 29, 314
Nelson, Jordy, 170–172, 196, 198, 239, 267
New England Patriots
  2006 season, 142–143
  2014 season, 200
  2016 season, 226
  2023 season, 304, 322
  Packers compared to, 229–232
  Super Bowl wins, 241
Newhouse, Dave, 91
New Orleans Saints, 131
Newton, Cam, 256
Newton, Destiny, 177, 205

INDEX

New York Giants, 147, 149, 170, 183–188, 225–226
New York Jets
  2022 season, 289
  2023 season, 276–279, 293–301, 304–306, 310, 312–313, 317–318, 320, 322
  2024 season hopes, 325–326
  AR's Achilles tendon injury and rehab, 299–303, 307–312
  AR's contract and contract extensions with, 288, 290, 323
  AR's controversial comments and, 317–320, 323–324
  AR's speech to team following injury, 304–305
  AR starting with, 285–289
  culture of, 325
  Favre playing for, 286
  public perception of AR, 289–293
  signing AR, 2, 279–284
New York Post, 284
NFC (National Football Conference) Championship games
  2007 Packers vs. Giants, 149
  2010 Packers vs. Bears, 167
  2014 Packers vs. Seahawks, 196–200, 235
  2017 Packers vs. Falcons, 226
  2019 Packers vs. San Francisco 49ers, 241–242
  2020 Packers vs. Buccaneers, 240–242, 244–249
NFL (National Football League). *See also* Rodgers, Aaron, NFL training and preparation of; *individual teams*
  AR as best passer in, 2, 325
  AR's MVP awards, 2, 174–175, 188, 267, 271
  conspiracy theory on, 319
  COVID-19 pandemic and, 258–260
  NFL Draft of 2005, 101–105, 110–122, 137, 202
  NFL Draft of 2020, 242–244
Nicholas, Stephen, 165
Nicks, Hakeem, 186

Nike, 154
9/11 terrorist attacks (2001), 77–78, 276–278
Nolan, Mike, 103–107, 118, 136–137, 159, 234

Oakland Raiders, 117–118, 147
Obama, Barack, 257
O'Brien, Timothy, 277
O'Dell, Dan, 80
O'Dell, Ron, 49, 80
Olberg, Ben, 44
O'Leary, Kevin, 200
Oliver, Pam, 167
Onibokun, Mark, 63, 70
Ortiz, Travis, 39

Pabst, Jason, 6
Palmer, Carson, 225
Pang, Keola, 45, 49, 51, 178, 205–206
Panthers (Carolina), 161
Parrish, Mark, 57, 65–66, 68–69
The Pat McAfee Show (podcast), 257, 279, 303, 304, 311–312, 319, 322–323
Patrick, Danica, 1, 243, 254, 266, 314
Patriots. *See* New England Patriots
Pawlawski, Mike, 92
Pearlman, Jeff, 129, 189
Pepper, Julius, 167
Peprah, Charlie, 186
Performance Enhancement for Professional Athletes, 98
Peterson, Patrick, 224
Pettine, Mike, 229, 245
Philbin, Joe, 154–156, 184–185, 193, 228, 236–239, 267
Philip, Marvin, 92, 94
Pierre-Paul, Jason, 247
Pitsker, Ric, 34–35
Pittman, Barbara (AR's grandmother), 19, 28, 169, 174–175, 203–204, 217
Pittman, Cheryl (AR's aunt), 117, 219, 221
Pittman, Chuck (AR's grandfather), 19, 28, 169, 174, 217
Pittman, Chuck (AR's uncle), 220
Pittman, Valerie (AR's aunt), 219–221

INDEX

Pittsburgh Steelers, 164, 168, 170–172
plays
   "14 H Corner" play, 60
   "44 Drop Pass" play, 71
   "86 Y Shake" play, 70
   "98 Strike" play, 140
   "Flood Tip" play, 186
   "Right Tom R Spin 437 Stretch Boot R Slide" play, 83
   "Strong Left, Trips 27 Tampa" play, 172
   "Utah" play, 61
Pleasant Valley High School (Chico, California), 33–51
   AR playing baseball at, 53, 55
   AR playing basketball at, 36
   AR playing football at, 33–39, 41, 43–51
   AR's college recruitment, 48–50, 53
   AR's knee injury, 41
   AR's social life and grades at, 36–37, 40–43
   Lions Northern California All-Star football game and, 53
   parents' preference for, 46
Polamalu, Troy, 170, 172
Poli, Angelo, 179–182
Poli, Gino, 181–182
Poppinga, Brady, 133–134, 140–141, 146, 148, 152
Prescott, Dak, 226
Prevea Health, 260
Prichard, Heath, 56, 58, 68, 70, 83
Proactive Sports Performance, 310
Pro Merch (apparel company), 191, 210

Quarless, Andrew, 171

Raabe, Nate, 321
radio and podcast interviews of AR
   The Michael Kay Show (radio show), 304–305
   The Pat McAfee Show (podcast), 257, 279, 303, 304, 311–312, 319, 322–323
   Tuesdays with Aaron on 540 WAUK-AM, 189–192, 317–320, 322–323
Raiders. *See* Oakland Raiders
Rams (Los Angeles), 244
Randle El, Antwaan, 171
Ravens. *See* Baltimore Ravens
Ray, Matt, 58
Redmond, Will, 244
Reed, Bill and Jeannette, 315–316
Reed, Patrick, 315–316
Reese, Floyd, 113
Reese, Jerry, 185
Reid, Luke, 44
Renz, Karl, Jr., 10
Rice, Jerry, 109–110
Riehlman, Pete, 17–18
"Right Tom R Spin 437 Stretch Boot R Slide" play, 83
Rigsbee, Craig
   AR and NFL Draft of 2005, 127
   on AR playing for UC Berkeley, 77, 80
   on AR's fame, 214–215
   AR's family rift and, 213–215
   AR's recruitment to UC Berkeley and, 63–66
   childhood and home life, 59–60
   as coach at Butte College, 54–62, 68, 70–71
   on Favre's treatment of AR, 135
   on Jordan Love, 243
   recruitment of AR to Butte College, 54–56
Rigsbee, Glen, 59–60
Rigsbee, Jordan, 213
Roadrunners. *See* Butte College (Chico, California)
Roberson, Ell, 75, 77
Robertson, Reggie, 72–75, 78, 81
Robinson, Charles, 253
Rodgers, Aaron
   ayahuasca use, 265–267, 323
   best NFL passer, 2, 325
   celebrity golf tournament, 3–5
   childhood, 21–28, 30–31, 33–51, 53, 219. *See also* Pleasant Valley High School (Chico, California)
   college football for Butte College, 52–71. *See also* Butte College (Chico, California)

INDEX

college football for UC Berkeley, 72–97.
  See also University of California,
  Berkeley
community advocacy and charity work
  of, 190–191, 215–216, 259, 269–270,
  321–322
conspiracy theories, interest in,
  263–265, 319–320
COVID-19 pandemic and vaccination
  status, 252, 255–260, 264–265, 292,
  315, 323
family history and genealogy, 7–16,
  203–204
family relations, 4–5, 203–221, 313–317
Favre and, 122, 126–130, 133–135,
  141, 144, 152, 195
with Green Bay Packers. *See* Green Bay
  Packers
Hail Mary touchdown passes, 222–225
homes of, 1, 177–179, 290
with New York Jets. *See* New York Jets
NFL awards show, copresenting with
  Favre, 195
nicknames, 37, 141
party culture, rejecting, 47–48, 68–69,
  85, 90, 176
physical appearance of, 33, 48, 56, 59,
  74, 80, 100, 141–142, 179–182
radio and podcast interviews, 189–192,
  257, 279, 303, 304–305, 311–312,
  317–320, 322–323
record-setting consecutive passes, 87, 239
religious beliefs, 29, 39–40, 73, 121,
  220, 262, 314–315
romantic relationships, 177, 192,
  204–208, 220, 243, 254
sexuality, 189–190
sponsorships of, 154, 178, 200, 216, 292
Super Bowl XLV win, 166–176
Suspended Sunrise Recordings record
  label, 177, 200
throwing style and talent, 34, 45, 50,
  72–73, 77, 78–79, 83–84, 104–105,
  109, 229–230
TV appearances of, 163–164, 176, 191,
  195, 200, 253, 291–292

Rodgers, Aaron, awards
  Associated Press Male Athlete of the
    Year, 182
  Chico Sportsperson of the Year, 214
  Dennis Byrd Most Inspirational Player,
    321
  MVP awards, 2, 174–175, 188, 267,
    271
  Super Bowl MVP, 174–175
Rodgers, Aaron, character traits
  confidence, 30, 42–43, 67–68, 90–91,
    106–107, 114, 139, 145, 155
  criticisms from teammates, 194–195,
    270–271
  defiance, 41, 134, 140–141
  grudges and cutting people out,
    202–221
  leadership skills, 47, 66–68, 73, 85–86,
    91–92, 159–160, 195, 267–271,
    290–292, 305
  as loner, 261
  sense of humor, 41, 84, 99, 127, 129,
    263
Rodgers, Aaron, injuries of
  Achilles tendon, 299–303, 307–312
  broken collarbone, 192
  broken foot, 143–144
  calf injury, 193, 198
  concussions, 164, 167
  fractured thumb, 273–274
  hamstring injury, 147
  tibial plateau fracture, 227–228
  torn ACL, 41, 53
  at USC, 81–82
Rodgers, Aaron, NFL training and
  preparation of, 98–122
  NFL Draft of 2005 and, 110–122,
    202
  representation and contract
    negotiation, 107–108
  Tampa Bay Buccaneers interview,
    108–110
  training techniques, 98–101
  Wonderlic test score, 101, 130
  workout clinics and interviews,
    101–109, 111

INDEX

Rodgers, Darla Pittman (mother)
  on AR playing for Green Bay Packers, 159
  AR's childhood and, 21–24, 30–31, 47–48
  AR's college education and, 54
  at AR's first New York Jets game, 293–296, 312–313
  AR's recruitment to UC Berkeley, 65
  career, 23–24
  childhood, 19
  Christian faith of, 29–30, 206, 314
  house gifted from AR, 207
  marriage to Ed Rodgers, 20
  at NFL Draft of AR, 115
  on repairing relationship with AR, 314–317
  rift with AR, 204–209, 212–213
  at Super Bowl XLV, 174
Rodgers, Edward, Jr. (father)
  on AR playing for UC Berkeley, 77
  AR playing with Green Bay Packers, 133
  AR's childhood and, 24–26
  AR's college education and, 54
  at AR's first New York Jets game, 293–296, 299–300, 312–313
  AR's high school football playing and, 39, 47, 50
  on AR's love of football as a child, 21
  birth and childhood, 15–16
  career, 22–24, 30, 179
  Christian faith of, 29–30, 117, 314
  COVID-19 vaccinations and, 315
  on Edward Rodgers Sr.'s WWII service, 28–29
  as football player, 16–19
  house gifted from AR, 207
  marriage to Darla Pittman, 20
  at NFL Draft of AR, 115, 117
  on repairing relationship with AR, 4–5, 314–317
  rift with AR, 204–209, 212–213, 217
  at Super Bowl XLV, 174
Rodgers, Edward Wesley, Sr. (grandfather)
  death, 28–29
  family and career, 15–16
  WWII and, 3, 7–15, 28–29
Rodgers, Jack Jordan (nephew), 217
Rodgers, Jordan (brother)
  AR's generosity with, 208
  in AR's shadow, 212
  on *The Bachelorette*, 212–213
  childhood, 24–25
  marriage to JoJo Fletcher, 217
  playing football for BC Lions, 211
  as quarterback at Vanderbilt, 179
  rift with AR, 211, 216
Rodgers, Kathryn Odell (grandmother), 8, 16
Rodgers, Luke (brother)
  childhood, 21, 25
  children of, 217
  marriage to Aimee Wathen, 217
  moving to Green Bay to live with AR, 129
  moving to San Diego to live with AR, 178, 208
  Pro Merch (apparel company), 191, 210
  rift with AR, 207–213, 216
Rodgers, Richard, 223
Rodgers Chiropractic (Chico, California), 179
Roethlisberger, Ben, 164, 169, 170–173
Rogan, Joe, 264
Rogers, Carlos, 194
Rolfing technique, 100
Rolfson, Adam, 151–153
Rolfson, Erick, 151–153
Rolle, Antrel, 113, 115, 184
Rose Bowl, 94–97
Rosemann, Nick, 49, 175
Ross, Marc, 281, 322
Rossley, Tom, 120, 128, 131
Ruby, Larry and Diane, 29
Rush, George, 70
Russell, Jordan
  AR's family relations and, 5, 316–317
  on AR's generosity, 208
  ayahuasca use, 266–267
  friendship and rift with AR, 201–202, 206, 221–222
  NFL Draft of AR and, 113
Russini, Dianna, 325

INDEX

Ryan, Jon, 196
Ryan, Matt, 165, 183

Saban, Nick, 103, 111, 113
Saints (New Orleans), 131
Saleh, Robert
  2023 season, 297–298
  on AR's character, 291
  AR's injury and, 301
  AR's speech following injury, 304–305
  on AR's talent, 294–295
  AR traded to New York Jets, 2
  coaching New York Jets, 318
  recruiting AR to New York Jets, 282–283
Sandy Hook Elementary School shooting (2013), 6, 324
San Francisco 49ers
  2005 season, 137
  2008 season, 164
  2012 season, 192
  2018 season, 237
  2021 season, 272
  AR's campus workout clinic and interview with, 103–107, 111
  NFC Championship Game 2019, 241–242
  NFL Draft of 2005, 101–103, 111, 114, 122, 136–137
  Alex Smith's contract with, 124
  Tedford curse and, 105
San Francisco Chronicle, 106
Savage, Phil, 103
Savoy, Steve, 103
Schefter, Adam, 253, 279
Schneider, John, 148
Schneider, Tom, 90
Schneidman, Matt, 280
Schwartz, Richard, 72–75, 81
Scott, Hillary, 177
Seattle Seahawks, 132, 193, 196–200, 235
September 11, 2001 terrorist attacks, 77–78, 276–278
Shanahan, Kyle, 254, 272
Shelton, Matt, 45
Shepherd, John, 36

Sherman, Mike, 118, 128, 132, 133, 135
Sherman, Richard, 197, 199
Shoulders, William, 57, 67, 71
Shull, Andrew, 76
Siemian, Trevor, 311
Simmons, John, 13
Simms, Chris, 230–231
Simms, Phil, 223, 230
Sinclair, Melissa, 41–42
Sitton, Josh, 224
60 Minutes (TV show), 195
Sky Cave Retreats, Oregon, 281–282
Slavin, Randall, 262–263
Slocum, Shawn, 199
Smith, Alex
  2008 season, 159
  2012 season, 192
  college football with UC Berkeley, 78, 80
  college football with Utah Utes, 78
  contract with San Francisco 49ers, 124
  NFL Draft of 2005 to San Francisco 49ers, 111, 113–114, 136–137
  NFL training and preparation, 101–103, 106–107
  traded to Kansas City, 193
Smith, Noah, 88
Smith, Stephen A., 254
Souza, Ron, 33–34, 38–39, 43, 45, 53
Sports Illustrated, 155, 236
Sproles, Darren, 75
Spytek, John, 252
St. Brown, Equanimeous, 237, 239, 245–246
Stallings, JJ, 52–53, 67, 71
Stallings, Roderick, 52, 57
Stanley, Charles, 13
Stark, Melissa, 306
Starr, Bart, 156
Starr, Cherry, 156, 254
State Farm Insurance, 178, 200, 216, 292
Steel, Zack, 33, 35
Steelers. *See* Pittsburgh Steelers
Steinberg, Mark, 205
Steliga, Jan, 22–23
Stenavich, Adam, 280
Stoops, Bob, 96

Strang, Vinny, 74, 79, 83–84, 90, 145
"Strong Left, Trips 27 Tampa" play, 172
Suh, Ndamukong, 246–247
Sullivan, Mike
   advocating for AR in Green Bay
      Packers, 148
   on AR's Super Bowl win, 176, 222
   fired by AR, 153–154
   negotiations for AR's NFL contract,
      107–108
   NFL Draft of 2005 and, 110–114,
      120–121
Super Bowl XXXI (1997), 124
Super Bowl XLII (2008), 183
Super Bowl XLIII (2009), 173
Super Bowl XLV (2011), 166–176
   AR as Super Bowl MVP, 174
   AR's dinner before, 166–169
   AR's family and, 169, 174–175
   championship party, 175–176
   home viewership, 171
   McCarthy on, 168
   Packers winning, 173–174
   score and plays throughout, 170–173
   stadium fans, 172
Super Bowl XLIX (2015), 200
Suspended Sunrise Recordings, 177, 200
Sverchek, Tom, 75
Szohr, Jessica, 177

Tafoya, Michele, 158
Tagliabue, Paul, 110, 113, 121
Tallerico, Tony, 33, 37
Tampa Bay Buccaneers, 108–115, 153,
   164, 240, 244–245, 252
Tatum, Mike, 17
Taylor, Ike, 172
Tedford, Jeff
   childhood, 86
   choosing AR as 2nd quarterback,
      74–75
   as coach of BC Lions, 211
   as coach of Golden Bears UC Berkeley,
      72, 74–82, 85–90, 95–96
   on NFL Draft of 2005, 116
   recruiting AR to UC Berkeley, 62–65, 72

Tedford curse, 104–105, 120
Temple of the Way of Light, Iquitos, Peru,
   266
Tennessee Titans, 113, 115
Tenuta, Luke, 269
Testaverde, Vinny, 299–300
Tetuan, Jesse, 76
Thatcher, Joe, 166–168, 178–179
Thomas, Adalius, 132
Thompson, Ted
   on Mike McCarthy, 135
   NFL Draft of 2005 and, 118–122, 126
   roster building of, 231
   on trading AR, 147
   on unretirement of Favre, 152
Timberlake, Justin, 276
Tirico, Mike, 78
Toler, Burl, 79, 82–83
Tomlinson, Dylan, 130–131
Tomlinson, Laken, 298
Tonyan, Robert, 246
Topete-Tallerico, Janet, 37
Trimmer, Dick, 18
Tuesdays with Aaron on ESPN 540
   WAUK-AM (radio show), 189–192,
   317–320, 322–323
Turner, Ron, 49, 80, 81
TV appearances of AR
   Celebrity Jeopardy!, 200, 253
   Hard Knocks, 291–292
   "It's Aaron" YouTube videos, 191
   Jeopardy!, 253
   Late Show with David Letterman, 176
   The Michael Irvin Show (TV show),
      163–164
   60 Minutes, 195
Tynes, Lawrence, 147

Ulbrich, Jeff, 290, 292
Umenyiora, Osi, 187
Ungerer, Dave, 63
University of California, Berkeley,
   72–97
   academic reputation of, 73, 93
   AR playing football at, 72–90, 93–97
   AR's recruitment to, 62–66, 72

AR's social life and academics at, 90–93
Insight Bowl (2003), 81, 83–85
Rose Bowl and, 94–97
Urlacher, Brian, 167
USA Today/ESPN poll, 96
"Utah" play, 61
Uzomah, C. J., 297

Valdes-Scantling, Marquez, 239, 246, 251–252
Van Pelt, Alex, 239
Vera-Tucker, Alijah, 298
Vick, Michael, 108, 165
Vikings. *See* Minnesota Vikings; Pleasant Valley High School (Chico, California)
Visinoni, Dino, 18
Vought, Mike, 41–43

Walker, Javon, 135, 139
Wallace, Mike, 164, 171, 173
Walter, Tony, 150
Warfield, Brandon, 80
Warner, Kurt, 164
Warren, Paris, 103
Washington, Fabian, 118
Wathen, Aimee, 217
Watson, Christian, 273, 274
Weatherspoon, Thomas, 74, 98–100, 102–103, 127
Webster, Corey, 147
Weir, Nate, 167
West, Ryan, 6, 178
Whelan, Thomas, 10
White, Devin, 245
White, Resolved (ancestor), 203
White, Susanna and William, 203
Whitticker, Will, 131
Whole Body Fitness (Chico, California), 179–182, 207
Wilde, Jason, 189–192, 206, 256
William, Cadillac, 114–115
Williams, Jamaal, 246
Williams, Jameson, 274
Williams, Quinnen, 290–291
Williams, Tramon, 173, 199
Willson, Luke, 197
Wilson, C. J., 168
Wilson, Garrett, 278–279, 297–298, 301
Wilson, Russel, 193, 196–200, 216
Wilson, Thomas, 30–31, 36, 50, 83
Wilson, Zach, 288, 298–299, 301, 304–306, 311, 318
Wingo, Trey, 279
Wischusen, Bob, 277, 313
Wolf, Ron, 124, 156
Wood, Glen, 34
Wood, Ryan, 252
Woodley, Shailene, 254, 281
Woods, Al, 291
Woodson, Charles, 139, 171
World War II, 7–15, 28–29
Woullard, Adam, 152, 155, 160
Wright, Eric, 89
Wright, Manuel, 88

Yiskis, Louis, 37, 44–45
Young, Steve, 155
Young Life (Christian ministry group), 40, 314

Zachary, Ryan, 177

ABOUT
MARINER BOOKS

Mariner Books traces its beginnings to 1832 when William Ticknor cofounded the Old Corner Bookstore in Boston, from which he would run the legendary firm Ticknor and Fields, publisher of Ralph Waldo Emerson, Harriet Beecher Stowe, Nathaniel Hawthorne, and Henry David Thoreau. Following Ticknor's death, Henry Oscar Houghton acquired Ticknor and Fields and, in 1880, formed Houghton Mifflin, which later merged with venerable Harcourt Publishing to form Houghton Mifflin Harcourt. HarperCollins purchased HMH's trade publishing business in 2021 and reestablished their storied lists and editorial team under the name Mariner Books.

Uniting the legacies of Houghton Mifflin, Harcourt Brace, and Ticknor and Fields, Mariner Books continues one of the great traditions in American bookselling. Our imprints have introduced an incomparable roster of enduring classics, including Hawthorne's *The Scarlet Letter,* Thoreau's *Walden,* Willa Cather's *O Pioneers!,* Virginia Woolf's *To the Lighthouse,* W.E.B. Du Bois's *Black Reconstruction,* J.R.R. Tolkien's *The Lord of the Rings,* Carson McCullers's *The Heart Is a Lonely Hunter,* Ann Petry's *The Narrows,* George Orwell's *Animal Farm* and *Nineteen Eighty-Four,* Rachel Carson's *Silent Spring,* Margaret Walker's *Jubilee,* Italo Calvino's *Invisible Cities,* Alice Walker's *The Color Purple,* Margaret Atwood's *The Handmaid's Tale,* Tim O'Brien's *The Things They Carried,* Philip Roth's *The Plot Against America,* Jhumpa Lahiri's *Interpreter of Maladies,* and many others. Today Mariner Books remains proudly committed to the craft of fine publishing established nearly two centuries ago at the Old Corner Bookstore.